RECOGNITION, SOVEREIGNTY STRUGGLES, & INDIGENOUS RIGHTS IN THE UNITED STATES

A SOURCEBOOK

Edited by Amy. E. Den Ouden & Jean M. O'Brien

THE UNIVERSITY OF NORTH CAROLINA PRESS   CHAPEL HILL

This book was published with the assistance of the
THORNTON H. BROOKS FUND *of the University of North Carolina Press.*

Library of Congress Cataloging-in-Publication Data
Recognition, sovereignty struggles, and indigenous rights in the United States :
a sourcebook / edited by Amy E. Den Ouden and Jean M. O'Brien.
    pages cm
  Includes bibliographical references and index.
  ISBN 978-1-4696-0215-8 (cloth : alk. paper)
  ISBN 978-1-4696-0216-5 (pbk. : alk. paper)
1. Indians of North America—Civil rights.   2. Indigenous peoples—
Legal status, laws, etc.—United States   3. Indians of North America—
Legal status, laws, etc.   4. Indians of North America—Government
relations.   5. United States—Race relations.   6. States' rights
(American politics)   I. Den Ouden, Amy E.
  KF8210.C5R43 2013
  342.7308'72—dc23   2012044360

"State Recognition and 'Termination' in Nineteenth-Century New England"
by Jean M. O'Brien is drawn in part from the author's *Firsting and Lasting:
Writing Indians Out of Existence in New England* (Minneapolis: University
of Minnesota Press, 2010). Copyright 2010 by the Regents of the University
of Minnesota. Used by permission.

For **VINE DELORIA JR.**, who inspired so many of us

Contents

Recognition, Sovereignty Struggles, & Indigenous Rights in the United States

Introduction

AMY E. DEN OUDEN & JEAN M. O'BRIEN

Why "Recognition" Matters

Few issues are as fractious in contemporary indigenous affairs in the United States as the official recognition of the separate political status of tribal peoples by external governments. Haunted today by such divisive issues as Indian gaming, disputes over the "authenticity" and racial identity of native peoples, and charges made by non-Indians that "special rights" should not be extended to Native Americans, debates over federal recognition—the formal or legal acknowledgment of the sovereign political status of tribal nations—have been a major preoccupation in Indian Country into the twenty-first century.[1] When the Red Power movement emerged in the 1960s and 1970s, indigenous activists and organizations pressed for an end to the overtly destructive if not genocidal federal policy of "termination" that had been launched midcentury.[2] Against this effort to legislatively dismantle indigenous sovereignty and treaty rights, native leaders and activists asserted the enduring history of indigenous self-determination—a lived experience that was in no sense a "gift" from the U.S. federal government. Formal public statements by indigenous organizations made that point clear. The 1961 Declaration of Indian Purpose—composed at the American Indian Chicago Conference during which more than 450 native participants came together to address their nations' social, political, and economic concerns—proclaimed it in the clearest terms: American Indian peoples had exercised "the inherent right to live their own lives for thousands of years before the white man came."[3] Yet as Vine Deloria Jr. argues in his classic study, *Behind the Trail of Broken Treaties: An Indian Declaration of Independence* (1974), while American Indian leaders and activists persisted in "raising their claims of national independence on the world scene," even "the most sympathetic non-Indians" did not at the time grasp the deep history and political significance of indigenous activism: "Few people were able to look backward to the four-hundred-year struggle for freedom that the Indians had waged and recognize that if the United States and its inhabitants had regarded the Indians as another domestic minority group, the Indians did not see themselves as such."[4] Deloria's words are a fitting point of departure for this volume. As the essays here demonstrate, indigenous struggles for recognition in the twentieth and early twenty-first centuries are deeply rooted in history. They have entailed complex confrontations and engagements with U.S. federal and state laws and policies, and they are struggles that remind us of the destructive power of the racial stereotypes and popular myths about Indians that persist today and that have obscured not only how native nations and communities see themselves but also what they have surmounted to sustain themselves as peoples.[5]

The Connecticut Effect

In New England, for example, the myth of Indian disappearance that was generated in the colonial period was reinvigorated in the late twentieth century as tribal nations seeking acknowledgment from the U.S. federal government garnered unprecedented media attention, as did several newly recognized tribal nations that launched hugely successful gaming operations after their federal recognition was secured. Then, as now, the native peoples of New England have faced the charge that they are not "real Indians" and are thus undeserving of recognition by the U.S. government.[6] As explained by Renée Ann Cramer, a leading scholar on federal acknowledgment and racialized reactions to it, the Mashantucket Pequot tribal nation's federal recognition by an act of Congress in 1983 and their creation of what is now the largest casino complex in the world, Foxwoods Resort Casino, elicited "intense scrutiny and controversy." Not only has their casino "been a political hot potato" since the mid-1990s, but their identity as Indian people has been subjected to relentless assaults as well.[7] Fomenting in public reactions to the Mashantuckets' casino and in the context of rancorous debates that erupted over other tribal acknowledgment cases in Connecticut at the time, the racist stereotype of the "casino Indian" took hold in the region and has had an increasingly negative impact on public attitudes toward federal recognition.[8] As Cramer argues in a recent essay, a new anti-Indian racism that is "fueled by casino success" has transformed "Pequot" into "a trope for everything a 'real' Indian is not," and the backlash against the Mashantuckets' economic success—and against Indian gaming more generally—"has turned into a backlash against tribal recognition."[9]

Thus, the "Connecticut effect" offers an important introductory example of the complexity and contentiousness of recognition and of the way in which it is enmeshed with wider U.S. economic and sociopolitical concerns. Racism and its impact on the rights and futures of indigenous peoples is certainly one of those wider concerns. In the Mashantucket Pequot case, we are compelled to consider how racial assumptions about Indian identity have shaped public assessments of the right to federal recognition.[10] Likewise, we must question how the anti-Indian racism Cramer describes has hampered possibilities for expanding public knowledge of the specific histories of the native peoples in Connecticut, deflecting questions about the historical foundation of late twentieth- and early twenty-first-century federal acknowledgment efforts and the long history of tribal-state relationships.[11] In spite of what Mark Edwin Miller aptly terms the "deluge of press coverage" that has rendered the Mashantucket Pequots "the dominant face of recently acknowledged Indian tribes in the United States," what does the public know about the Mashantuckets' pre-twentieth-century history as a state-recognized tribal nation?[12] Or about the state recognition of other tribal nations in Connecticut? A recent *Connecticut Post* editorial, "As Wealth Looms, Recognition Fades," makes a point rarely addressed in the local media: Despite all the public attention to the issue of tribal gaming in the state and the uproar over the federal recognition efforts of the Eastern Pequot, Schaghticoke, and Golden Hill Paugussett tribal nations, Connecticut's long relationship with the indigenous peoples within its borders—evidenced in its own statutes and laws dating back to the colonial period—appears to be ignored. "You could look it up," the editorial chides.[13]

More than just tribal nations' historical relationships with the state have been obscured in the anti-Indian/anticasino discourse that has flourished in the region since the opening of the Mashantucket Pequot casino. Also overlooked is a central question that would help a public audience better understand what is at stake for tribal nations and communities that seek recognition: What choices are available for native peoples in the United States today as they contend with problems of unemployment and lack of adequate access to health care, housing, and education? As Algonquin scholar Paula Sherman has phrased it in a recent analysis of the Mashantuckets' struggle for sovereignty and the political and social costs of gaming, "What is required to make sustainable Native communities in the twenty-first century?" Casinos, Sherman contends, have become "the most important tool Native people have today for national renewal": Mashantucket Pequot "dreams of community revitalization only happened through the adoption of gaming."[14] Nonetheless, Sherman emphasizes that native people have serious concerns and disagreements about whether gaming is an economically sustainable and culturally appropriate means of indigenous nation building.[15] And as anthropologist Jessica R. Cattelino has argued, a persisting colonial mentality in the United States expects "real Indians" to be poor and casts the economic successes of tribal nations that operate casinos as historical anomalies proving that they have "lost" their "genuine" Indian culture.[16]

Just as federally acknowledged tribal nations seeking to develop viable economies through gaming have been pummeled by racial notions and myths to which they are expected to adhere, so too are they subjected to federal and state legal controls. Federal regulations imposed on Indian gaming in 1988 compel tribal nations to enter into financial agreements with states to operate casinos with slot machines. Gaming thus has created a new way for states to appropriate tribal nations' resources and potentially to undermine their sovereignty. After their federal acknowledgment, Mashantucket Pequot tribal leaders agreed to a compact with the State of Connecticut that allowed for the establishment of their casino. The compact requires that the Mashantuckets pay the state 25 percent of their gross annual revenues from casino slot machines. The Mohegan tribe's government did likewise after it became federally acknowledged by the Bureau of Indian Affairs in 1994, and it also pays the state 25 percent of slot revenues each year. As of 2011, the Mashantucket Pequot and Mohegan tribal nations have paid the state a combined total of more than 5 billion dollars since the signing of their compacts with the state in 1991 and 1994, respectively.[17] The enormity of the state's financial gain as a result of tribal gaming must not be overlooked. As the former dean of the University of Connecticut School of Law, Nell Jessup Newton, remarked during a public forum on federal acknowledgment held in Hartford in 2005, Connecticut "could not balance its budget" without the payments it receives from these two tribal nations.[18] Yet today the Mashantucket Pequots' tribal government faces a major financial crisis, "struggling under a mountain of 2.3 billion in debt," as a Connecticut newspaper reports, while dealing internally with concerns about tribal leadership on matters of fiscal policy.[19] As Sherman points out, whether gaming can be a viable means of asserting and defending tribal sovereignty in the long term remains under debate. What does seem clear, however, is that Mashantucket Pequots' recognition by the federal government produced new political, cultural, and economic dilemmas as well as important new possibilities for revitalizing and sustaining the tribal nation.

Recognition as Contested Terrain

This is but a small excerpt from one of many indigenous sovereignty struggles that are ongoing in the United States. It is also a key example of a compelling reality that informs this volume: Recognition does not settle sovereignty struggles. In fact, it can initiate new struggles and perpetuate or reignite old ones—among the oldest in the United States being the struggles that inure in relations between competing sovereigns (tribal nations, the federal government, and individual states). A central aim of this volume is to bring together new scholarly analyses of the historical, cultural, and politico-legal facets of these ongoing struggles to shed much-needed light on what they mean to the tribal nations and communities involved. Native peoples in New England, for example, have shown that petitioning for federal recognition of tribal sovereignty through the U.S. Bureau of Indian Affairs (BIA), part of the Department of the Interior, entails a struggle to narrate their own histories from their local perspectives while responding to externally imposed definitions of Indianness and tribal existence enforced by the government officials who evaluate and decide whether to grant federal recognition. Tribal nations' knowledge of their own histories, vital to struggles for sovereignty, can be articulated in federal acknowledgment petitions, but the process subjects tribal nations' knowledge to bureaucratic interpretations that are based on concepts and practices that objectify, trivialize, and discredit Native Americans' cultures, identities, and histories. Tribal nations' struggles for recognition through the BIA process can persist for decades, and the outcome can be devastating. In a 1992 analysis of the BIA's "inconsistent," "often injudicious," and "contradictory if not arbitrary" findings in a number of cases, anthropologist William Starna contends that official denials of federal acknowledgment based on such findings are tantamount to "administrative genocide."[20]

As the essays in this volume demonstrate, understanding why recognition matters requires a basic understanding of the federal and state laws and policies that affect tribal nations as they assert and defend their sovereignty. Studies by native and nonnative legal scholars have shown that what is generally referred to in the United States as "Indian law" embodies a central paradox: While it has sought to justify and facilitate the domination and even the destruction of indigenous peoples—"conquest masquerading as law," in Vine Deloria Jr.'s phrasing[21]—it has also long acknowledged American Indian peoples' existence as distinct polities and nations possessing their own legal traditions.[22] In fact, Robert Clinton argues that "the effort to protect the autonomy of the Indian tribal community" has been "a central theme in Indian law" since the Mohegan land claim case in eighteenth-century Connecticut, in which the colony's claim of jurisdiction over the Mohegan people was rejected by a Crown-appointed commission, whose decision in support of the Mohegans' land rights described them as "a separate and distinct people" who "have a polity of their own."[23] Euro-American legal practices and governmental narratives acknowledging the inherent rights and the autonomous sociopolitical existence of indigenous peoples are thus as old as the colonial period; similarly, the concept of recognition and tribal nations' contemporary engagement with laws and policies that validate it are inextricably embedded in an ongoing history of colonialism and its grossly unequal power relations.[24]

To be recognized, then, is purportedly to be incorporated into and subsumed by the dominating legal system. As Mohawk scholar Audra Simpson has explained, because indigenous nations in North America are "enframed by settler states," "much of the struggle within Indian country (broadly defined) is about native peoples regaining authority and institutional power to define and recognize themselves as well as the need for institutions of recognition and resolution that are free from state power."[25] The essays in this volume indicate that some tribal nations' decisions to petition for federal recognition or to negotiate with the governments of individual states are indeed a part of that broader struggle, and such a strategy of political engagement with the legal system of a nation-state cannot readily be equated with acquiescence to state power. On this point, we draw from the foundational analysis of legal scholar S. James Anaya, who explains that in defending their communities, their lands, and their political and legal traditions against the legal systems of nation-states, indigenous peoples "have employed a number of strategies, including those that enlist the law and legal process of the world beyond their communities."[26] As several of the essays here demonstrate, tribal nations seeking recognition in the late twentieth and early twenty-first centuries have also challenged the legitimacy of laws and policies imposed by the federal and state governments and in so doing have incited debates that foreground indigenous sovereignty as a political, cultural, and legal issue with wide significance. In that sense, the struggles for recognition addressed in this volume are important examples of what Lenape scholar Joanne Barker has referred to as the "rearticulations" of sovereignty that emerge in particular contexts in which "it is evoked and given meaning" by indigenous people. These rearticulations urge us to understand "the historical and cultural embeddedness of indigenous peoples' multiple and contradictory political agendas for empowerment, decolonization, and social justice."[27]

Following the seminal contributions of Deloria and Anaya, we are especially attuned to the ways in which colonial and Euro-American law and policy have enacted, masked, and justified what have been and are genocidal processes and to how native peoples have defended their sovereignty by asserting inherent rights and engaging with the law and legal processes of the nation-state. These historical and politico-legal processes are ongoing here in the United States and in the international arena, and recent scholarship on the creation and implementation of the UN Declaration on the Rights of Indigenous Peoples illuminates both the dilemmas and possibilities for genuine transformation that characterize the current moment in the long history of relations between indigenous peoples and nation-state governments. As Kenneth Deer puts it in a recent essay on the significance of the Declaration and strategies for its implementation, "No state will 'give' rights to Indigenous peoples, and no state will 'offer' them."[28] The actual agents of politico-legal and historical transformation, Deer emphasizes, are indigenous peoples asserting and exercising inherent rights against enduring patterns of colonial oppression and the destructive policies and practices of states. This essential principle of indigenous agency and this understanding of the intractability of state-based logics of domination are central to our theorizing and are in conversation with the work of other scholars whose analyses of relations between indigenous peoples and states point to possibilities for transformation and even disruption of the assumed legitimacy of nation-state sovereign power and, more specifically, of the United States as a creator and arbiter of the rights of indigenous peoples. In particular, Mark Rifkin's analysis of the precariousness of U.S. claims to sovereignty and jurisdiction over a national or "domestic" territory as they are articulated through and dependent on the discourse of Indian policy is immensely important. Rifkin explains that the United States must continuously "cope with the presence of preexisting polities on what it seeks to portray as domestic space" and has thus produced a self-legitimizing legal discourse that "translates autochthonous, self-governing Native polities . . . as either collections of bodies in need of restraint/protection or [exceptional] cultural aggregations." In effect, Indian policy exposes the "fundamentally circular and self-validating, as well as anxious and fraught, performance" of the nation-state's sovereignty. Via laws and bureaucratic practices of "management" of native peoples as "residents—as a kind of racialized, endangered, or enculturated body," the "self-evident" politico-legal and territorial domain of the United States is created and enforced. Rifkin's argument identifies this as a peculiar and tenuous authority, a claim to sovereignty whose content is essentially empty. Thus, "the problem of legitimacy . . . returns insistently to trouble U.S. legal discourses." Following Rifkin's lead, we suggest that careful analysis of recognition struggles—particularly cases and strategies of governmental opposition to federal and state recognition of tribal nations—enlarges our understanding of what Rifkin refers to as the "persistent anxiety about the validity of U.S. rule" and allows us to track "the processes by which the United States legitimizes its management of indigenous peoples" as well as the specificity of the local challenges to those tactics of rule and the discourses on which their legitimacy depends.[29]

In an important sense, then, we distinguish our approach from those that foreground the settler state's "logic of elimination," as defined by Patrick Wolfe as the primary analytic framing or the definitive element of the historical and politico-legal context in which contemporary recognition cases are rooted. In a comparative study of settler colonialism, Wolfe argues that the logic of elimination "is premised on the securing—the obtaining and the maintaining—of territory," and that its genocidal strategies include what he terms "repressive authenticity," by which settler colonialism works to eliminate "large numbers of empirical natives from official reckonings." Such practices of imposing and regulating the authenticity of colonized peoples might constitute an "even more effective mode of elimination than conventional forms of killing, since it does not involve such a disruptive affront to the rule of law that is ideologically central to the cohesion of settler society."[30]

Wolfe's argument offers a far-reaching theorization of the connection between genocidal processes and their ideological underpinnings in a global context. But recognition struggles raise questions about the efficacy of a purportedly inexorable logic of elimination, and bring attention to the instabilities of settler colonialism and its claims of mastery over the lives, and fates, of indigenous people, particularly in contemporary contexts. The idea of "the rule of law" is itself the most precarious assertion of colonial legitimacy, and the continuous ideological reaffirmations and violent assertions of power that have been required to defend it as the essence of nation-state authority over tribal nations betray the tenuousness of its own "legal" standing. Posing multiple challenges to the logic of elimination, struggles for recognition in the United States are perhaps among the most unpredictable outcomes of settler colonialism. In a fundamental way, then, this volume rejects settler colonialism's foundational claims of inevitability and legitimacy. We seek to illuminate not only the complexities of recognition struggles but also their disruptive or "unsettling" capabilities as they unfold within and work against the normative legal codes and entrenched regulatory institutions of a nation-state system. Proceeding analytically from the ground up, as we see it, the essays in this volume highlight and explore moments of indigenous communities' engagement with and resistance to nation-state–legislated modes of existence and external standards of authentication. Rather than simply affirming the existence of the nation-state's compulsion to obliterate indigeneity within its claimed territory and its specific politico-legal techniques of eradication, we contend that indigenous struggles for recognition mark significant moments of refusal of the logic of elimination and potential disruption of the governmental discourses and strategies deployed to legitimize the nation-state's claim to power over indigenous peoples and their identities, lands, and histories. In fact, the arguments about cultural and racial authenticity that figure so prominently in sovereignty struggles in the United States reflect not only the impact of genocidal logics imposed by colonially established bureaucracies (for example, federal regulations on acknowledgment) but also the political significance of indigenous critiques and strategies and the persistence of indigenous knowledge in the face of forms of power that are intended to wholly consume or obliterate them. Each of the chapters in this volume is more closely attuned to the real-world impact of indigenous strategies of resistance and of history making (and, indeed, federal acknowledgment struggles constitute a form of indigenous history making).

We consider one of the most significant and timely aspects of this volume to be its featuring of scholars who focus on the historical and contemporary struggles of "unrecognized tribes." Many of the authors have extensive experience working with and for—and are members of—tribal nations that have been engaged in federal recognition efforts. These essays represent new and original multidisciplinary research that grapples with the state-centric discourses and demands of recognition. Their arguments are attuned to the ways in which the imposed legal regulations and external scrutiny to which unrecognized tribal nations are subjected work to preserve colonial patterns of domination and to establish new strategies of state control. This volume does not argue that a tribal nation's recognition by federal or state governments is an ultimate good. Indeed, as J. Kēhaulani Kauanui elaborates, indigenous peoples in the United States have articulated powerful antirecognition arguments, illuminating the ways in which federal recognition can undermine indigenous struggles for self-determination. Mindful of cases in which recognition is rejected altogether, these essays also reflect the contributors' pragmatic sensibilities and activist commitments, and their analyses are informed by the immediate concerns of tribal nations whose struggles for recognition are part of their efforts to preserve community life, protect their lands, and shape their own futures.

Finally, this volume is intended to respond to the pressing question of how scholarship on the historically and politically enmeshed issues of recognition and tribal sovereignty can educate the wider public about ongoing indigenous struggles for rights and justice. A main concern of this volume is to provide to multiple audiences—in particular, undergraduate and graduate students—a thorough overview of what recognition struggles reveal about how tribal sovereignty is envisioned, asserted, defended, and attacked in the United States. Osage/Cherokee legal scholar Rennard Strickland puts it quite plainly: "Understanding sovereignty is crucial for all students of Native American studies"; yet, he notes, Native American studies curriculums in U.S. universities have not paid adequate attention to the topic of indigenous sovereignty or have simply overlooked it entirely.[31] This volume is intended to encourage discussions of indigenous sovereignty in the classroom and to help students in various disciplines understand that tribal recognition is not an obscure issue on the periphery of U.S. society but rather is directly relevant to major public policy issues, including debates about cultural diversity and multiculturalism and how or whether genuine pluralism can be realized within the geopolitical boundaries of the United States. Here again, we are mindful of the critiques of indigenous political theorists such as Jeff Corntassel who argue that indigenous sovereignty is inevitably undermined when indigenous people seek recognition from nation-state governments. In Corntassel's view, this process results essentially in a "paper right" that fosters an "illusion of inclusion" without dismantling the state-imposed system of domination and its definitions of indigenous peoples' rights. Yet as Anaya has argued, the indigenous rights movement has engaged with international law effectively to challenge state-centrism and Eurocentrism, bringing indigenous principles of justice and freedom into global human rights discourse. Indeed, according to Anaya, the struggles waged by indigenous peoples in the global arena from the mid-twentieth century on demonstrate that indigenous peoples "have ceased to be mere objects of the discussion of their rights and have become real participants in an extensive multilateral dialogue" with states and with other nonstate actors and organizations. This volume builds on Anaya's point that in the context of such dialogue, indigenous peoples have "articulated a vision of themselves different from that previously advanced and acted upon by dominant sectors." In the tribal recognition struggles addressed here, we see meaningful challenges to state-centered policies and practices articulated by tribal nations, and we contend that the ultimate outcome of these struggles and the extent to which they may work to transform relations of domination remain to be seen.[32]

Given what is at stake for unrecognized tribal nations, we consider tribal recognition to be a human rights issue connected to the expanding global recognition of the human rights of indigenous peoples expressed in the UN Declaration on the Rights of Indigenous Peoples, which was adopted by the UN General Assembly on September 13, 2007. A central goal of the Declaration is to ensure that nation-states implement measures that acknowledge and defend indigenous peoples' rights to preserve their lands, resources, cultural identities, and cultural knowledge, and their collective existence as distinct peoples.[33] In her analysis of the history of the Declaration and the arguments made by the nation-state governments (including that of the United States) that originally voted against its adoption, legal scholar Aliza Gail Organick explains that "the U.S. opposed the Declaration from its early stages," and the country's intransigence with regard to "the issue of collective rights, coupled with the right to self-determination," were made explicit during negotiations on the draft of the Declaration.[34] In November 2006, an *Indian Country Today* editorial argued that U.S. resistance to the Declaration implies a fear that recognition of tribal self-determination "gives indigenous peoples too much power." But on December 16, 2010, the United States finally announced that it would endorse the Declaration. Jefferson Keel, president of the National Congress of American Indians, remarked that it is "amazing that the United States is finally getting on board with the Declaration. The United States has avoided it for so long, but finally we're seeing some results."[35] The executive director of the Indian Law Resource Center, Robert Tim Coulter, commented that "our work to ensure justice for Indian nations in this country begins in earnest with the United States' endorsement of the U.N. Declaration," which now provides a means "to support and advocate for positive legislation and positive government action relating to Indian peoples" as well as "a basis for making demands that the federal government fulfill its responsibilities to tribes and carry out its obligations to promote and respect the human rights of Indian nations and tribes."[36] But Steven Newcomb, cofounder and codirector of the Indigenous Law Institute, contests this view in "Has U.S. Changed Position on Declaration? Not Really," urging that "Indian Country . . . spend considerable time carefully analyzing and discussing" the federal government's current statement of "support" for the Declaration, which does not imply fundamental change in "law and policy constructed by the United States for the reduction, control and containment of originally free and independent nations." "It remains to be seen," Newcomb concludes, "to what extent the Declaration will enable Indian nations and peoples to create true and positive reform of a racist and domineering system of federal Indian law and policy instituted by the United States during the past 200-plus years."[37]

The positions of both Coulter and Newcomb compel native and nonnative educators, students, and activists as well as U.S. citizens more broadly to examine what the U.S. endorsement of the Declaration may and should mean for the rights of native peoples now and in the future. Their commentaries remind us of the necessity of elaborating the specificity and the scope of the human rights issues with which indigenous nations in the United States contend and of the need for vigilance in responding to and countering persistent misrepresentations and denials of the rights and the existence of indigenous peoples as *peoples* inherently possessed of the right to self-determination. As a FoxNews.com report on the endorsement of the Declaration reveals, the myth endures that acknowledgment of the rights of native peoples constitutes a "threat" and dredges up a remote past: "President Obama's decision . . . to reverse U.S. policy and back a U.N. declaration on the rights of 'indigenous peoples' has touched off a debate on whether the move could boost American Indian legal claims over the ills they suffered dating back to the colonial period."[38] Such a depiction trivializes the Declaration, implying that "the ills" of the past are relevant only insofar as they present potential "legal claims" and suggesting that the rights of American Indians become a matter of interest or "debate" only if they raise legal issues inconvenient for nonnatives. Such commentaries reveal the importance of making thoughtful analyses of current indigenous rights issues in the United States available to a broad audience and in so doing directing attention to the contemporary struggles of Native American peoples who must confront and engage laws, policies, practices, and discourses that threaten or deny their existence as peoples. If the U.S. endorsement of the Declaration signals possibilities for the establishment of new, just relations between tribal nations and the federal government founded on essential, globally recognized human rights principles, we believe that it is time that recognition struggles be considered in light of the transformations in nation-states' human rights policies and practices called for by the Declaration. Indeed, we hope the essays here will contribute to the expansion of human rights education in the United States, bringing greater attention to recognition struggles not as efforts to take power from states or to imitate state-based legal systems but as contexts in which unrecognized tribal nations and communities envision, define, and defend their human rights.

Key Concepts and Definitions

Given the complexity of the issues surrounding state and federal recognition, some accessible definitions are in order. "Sovereignty struggles," as we term them here, include the political, cultural and legal strategies, along with the conflicts, debates, and transformations, that unfold as tribal nations and communities engage with federal and state governments to assert the right to govern themselves and to determine their futures. Sovereignty— which may be viewed simultaneously as a political status in relation to other sociopolitical entities, an inherent right to self-governance and self-determination, and the core of the collective existence of a people—is the subject of a now vast interdisciplinary scholarly literature in Native American and indigenous studies. To provide definitions essential for our readers of diverse backgrounds and varying disciplinary perspectives, we draw on *American Indian Politics and the American Political System* by David E. Wilkins and Heidi Kiiwetinepinesiik Stark. "Sovereignty," a Western concept, stems from the notion of the state as "the ultimate arbiter of its own fate in relation to the outside world," a separate "sovereign" in international society. The realities of international interdependence and globalization, they point out, have undermined the notion or possibility of absolute sovereignty; instead, in its contemporary manifestation, it refers to "legal competence" in the protection and limitations of personal freedoms through institutions.[39] Wilkins and Stark define "tribal sovereignty" as "the spiritual, moral, and dynamic cultural force within a given tribal community empowering the group toward political, economic, and most important, cultural integrity, and toward maturity in the group's relationships with its own members, with other peoples and their governments, and with the environment."[40] Pointing out that there is no universally accepted definition, they define an "Indian nation" as a group sharing an ideology, institutions, customs, common ancestry and "sense of homogeneity" within an area controlled as a homeland. An Indian nation considers itself vitally unique and may or may not be within, beyond, or coterminous with the boundaries of a state. We would add to this definition that many of the nations under consideration in this volume do not control land in the strictly legal sense, but they all regard their homelands as central in defining their separateness in the most fundamental way.[41]

"Federally recognized tribes" are those tribal nations whose status is recognized (or acknowledged) by the United States as standing in a government-to-government relationship established "by treaty or agreement, congressional legislation, executive order action, judicial ruling, or the secretary of the interior's decision." Recognition renders tribal nations eligible for services and programs earmarked specifically for them and administered through agencies such as the BIA and the Indian Health Service and through the federal trust doctrine and plenary power.[42] Recognized status qualifies them for the rights and responsibilities of tribal nationhood, including the honoring and protection of treaty rights and treaty substitutes. Federally recognized tribes are also referred to as "domestic dependent nations," following the 1831 U.S. Supreme Court decision *Cherokee Nation v. Georgia*; Chief Justice John Marshall coined that term to describe tribal nations as neither nations nor states.[43] Marshall's opinion described the relationship as instead "resembl[ing] that of a ward to a guardian," thereby providing the "legally specious, and now largely defunct" concept of guardianship/wardship. "State-recognized tribes" include some tribes that have been recognized as separate entities since the earliest colonial encounters; particularly for the purposes of this volume, this status differs entirely from federal recognition. State-recognized tribes are by definition in this sense not federally recognized and thus are not extended the rights entailed in that status.[44] States vary widely in their relationships with tribal nations, and an overview of these arrangements and their implications is the focus of K. Alexa Koenig and Jonathan Stein's chapter in this volume. Other tribes are non-recognized and/or unacknowledged by the United States as separate political entities even though they retain a strong sense of their own separateness as Indian peoples. Some of these tribes never engaged in military conflict with the United States; others never attracted the attention of the United States because of their geographic isolation; and many have never "participated in a treaty or benefited from the trust relationship that forms the basis of most contemporary recognized tribes' status."[45] "Termination policy" refers to the federal policy in place from 1953 through the 1960s that aimed to "terminate" the government-to-government relationship between tribes and the federal government, to discontinue federal obligations to the tribes, to dismantle reservation land bases, to decentralize the administration of Indian affairs, and to relocate Indian peoples to urban areas. Ushered in by House Concurrent Resolution No. 108, termination was officially repealed in 1988.[46] "Trust doctrine," or the "trust relationship," obligates the federal government legally and morally "to assist Indian tribes in the protection of their lands, resources, and cultural heritage." Even though not explicitly a constitutional dictate, the trust doctrine holds the federal government "to the highest standards of good faith and honesty in its dealings with Indian peoples and their rights and resources."[47]

"The extension of federal recognition by the United States to a tribal nation is," in the words of Wilkins and Stark, "the formal diplomatic acknowledgment by the federal government of a tribe's legal status as a sovereign."[48] Although for most tribal nations, such recognition is rooted in a history of treaty relations that evidenced a diplomatic relationship between nations, several other means constitute explicit acknowledgment of this status, including congressional statutes, presidential and administrative orders, and judicial rulings. By the 1870s, notions about federal recognition began to crystallize in a "formal jurisdictional sense" to describe the political relationship of affirming tribal sovereignty and acknowledging a trust relationship of the federal government to tribal nations as defined in the legal and judicial system.[49] "Questions around whether a tribe is federally recognized, state-recognized, non-recognized, or terminated have direct bearing on the internal and external political dynamics of tribes, and directly affect intergovernmental relations, since only recognized tribes may engage in gaming operations that are not directly subject to state law, may exercise criminal jurisdiction over their members and a measure of civil jurisdiction over nonmembers, and are exempt from a variety of state and federal taxes."[50]

The precise parameters of tribal sovereignty have been vexed in many ways by U.S. law and policy, which has sought to limit tribal sovereignty even as the federal government has proclaimed support for tribal self-determination. The federal-tribal relationship has been dynamically negotiated and frequently ambiguous, as tribal sovereignty has been curtailed through federal legislation and policy and in court decisions.[51] This state of affairs has persuaded some tribes that federal recognition is not necessarily worth becoming entangled in what can seem an impossibly bureaucratic relationship that simultaneously fetters and acknowledges tribal sovereignty. Furthermore, as Brian Klopotek has argued in a splendid recent study of recognition in Louisiana,

Recognition does not shield tribes from racism, colonialism, or other social forces, just as federal nonrecognition does not prevent tribes from participating in revitalization movements or developing their political and economic infrastructure. Moreover, recognition consistently undermines certain aspects of traditional tribal cultures, especially in the areas of government and the regulation of community boundaries, suggesting the need for careful attention to the negative aspects of federal recognition as well.[52]

As Klopotek's broad outline of resistance to recognition by tribal nations suggests, not all native peoples agree that recognition represents the best path to actualizing indigenous sovereignty in the colonial context. He also points out that without recognition, tribes are hamstrung in their efforts to protect their culture, values, and sovereignty on the same legal and political terrain as recognized tribes. In addition, they lack access to resources to protect their social, economic, and physical well-being, and they struggle to defend their lands.[53] While there is a well-articulated position that rejects federal recognition as any sort of panacea for tribal nations, this volume overwhelmingly (with the exception of Kauanui's chapter on Kanaka Maoli) represents the position that more is to be gained through federal recognition than through rejecting it as a hopelessly fraught colonial relationship that true sovereigns need not pursue.

The Federal Acknowledgment Project

As the example of the Mashantucket Pequot tribal nation demonstrates, tribes potentially realize tremendous gains through federal recognition: legal acknowledgment and protection of homelands, the extension of a formal diplomatic relationship with other governmental entities, and the possibility of political, social, cultural, and economic revitalization. The Mashantucket Pequot case is particularly dramatic given the long colonial relationship the tribe has endured, including what is acknowledged as the first act of genocide perpetrated against indigenous people by colonists in Anglo-America—the English massacre of Pequots at Mystic, Connecticut, in 1637, which was followed by a colonial effort legislatively to eradicate the identity and the land rights of Pequot survivors. The Pequots have engaged with, resisted, and accommodated the non-Indian peoples who came to surround them. In part, the complexity of these processes of cultural change as well as the dominant society's obfuscation of the destructive and enduring impacts of colonialism has made it so difficult for outsiders to recognize tribal nations in New England, for example, as Indian communities. Carrying stereotypical as well as racist ideas of "Indian phenotype" and "authentic" culture (including the denial of culture change as normative for Indians), non-Indians do not lend credence to many Indian peoples who have sought and/or secured recognition.[54] Changes that accompanied Mashantucket Pequot and other tribal peoples' survival include histories of intermarriage, and this fact is important to take into account in studies of recognition. As Wilkins and Stark note, Indian nations are political units, not minorities. At the same time, as Klopotek clearly demonstrates, racial politics are not irrelevant to the processes at work, and in recognition situations, racial thinking cannot be ignored.[55]

Efforts by previously unrecognized tribes to secure recognition have a long history, but the movement crystallized in the post-termination and -relocation era, which spurred Indians' activism in defense of their sovereignty. The cause of recognition found expression at the American Indian Chicago Conference in 1961, which included non–federally recognized participants, supported the cause of recognition, and provided a catalyst for creating a network of advocates to strategize. In *Passamaquoddy v. Morton* (1975), the U.S. Court of Appeals ruled that the seizure of Passamaquoddy land in 1794 by the state of Maine (then the northern part of Massachusetts) violated the Indian Trade and Intercourse Acts.[56] The decision established that the federal government's failure to recognize tribes did not free it from its obligations to them. The problem of federal recognition was taken up in earnest by the American Indian Policy Review Commission in the 1970s.[57] In 1978, the United States established a formal acknowledgment process to address the situation of unrecognized tribes under the auspices of the BIA's Branch of Acknowledgment and Research. Officials outlined a set of guidelines for extending recognition to tribal groups that for various reasons had never previously stood in this relationship to the United States. The Federal Acknowledgment Project (FAP, later renamed the Office of Federal Acknowledgment [OFA]) spelled out seven criteria for recognition, including providing evidence for the tribe's continual identification as a people from historic times to the present and providing evidence of a tribal land base. The criteria hewed closely to stereotypical notions of what constituted "Indianness" in the mythic past and posed steep barriers for many tribes, especially those in the East whose long histories of interaction with non-Indians had produced radically different peoples in the contemporary world. The recognition guidelines have been rewritten several times in response to critiques that their rigidity made them nearly impossible to meet; they nevertheless remain a formidable obstacle.

The OFA's seven current criteria are officially titled *Procedures for Establishing That an American Indian Group Exists as an Indian Tribe*, and they require that:

83.7(a) The petitioner has been identified as an American Indian entity on a substantially continuous basis since 1900.

83.7(b) A predominant portion of the petitioning group comprises a distinct community and has existed as a community from historical times until the present.

83.7(c) The petitioner has maintained political influence or authority over its members as an autonomous entity from historical times until the present.

83.7(d) The petition includes a copy of the group's present governing document, including its membership criteria. In the absence of a written document, the petitioner must provide a statement describing in full its membership criteria and current governing procedures.

83.7(e) The petitioner's membership consists of individuals who descend from a historical Indian tribe or from historical Indian tribes that combined and functioned as a single autonomous political entity.

83.7(f) The membership of the petitioning group is composed principally of persons who are not members of any acknowledged North American Indian tribe.

83.7(g) Neither the petitioner nor its members are the subject of congressional legislation that has expressly terminated or forbidden the federal relationship.[58]

Petitioners must meet all seven criteria to receive federal acknowledgment through the OFA. The petitioning process is an enormous and expensive undertaking, entailing exhaustive research and the preparation of a document that sometimes numbers hundreds of pages and consumes years. Petitioning tribes employ experts—historical and legal advisers who assist in the preparation process and provide testimony in support of recognition efforts. The process is highly contested by local and state officials and at times by other tribal nations.

Once the group has submitted its petition for consideration, it enters a process of preliminary review, and the group is extended an opportunity to address perceived deficiencies. After supplemental material is presented to address such shortcomings, the petition enters "active consideration" by OFA staff. The assistant secretary for Indian affairs typically issues a "proposed finding" within a year after the completed petition is filed. At this stage of the process, a comment period of 180 to 360 days is opened, during which the group as well as any third parties are allowed to respond to the initial finding. Once this stage is completed, all of the documentation is reviewed by the assistant secretary for Indian affairs, who then issues a final determination either acknowledging the petitioning group as an Indian tribe or denying the petition. At this point, the decision can be appealed to the Interior Board of Indian Appeals—yet another process of contestation over acknowledgment.

In more than three decades of its operation, the OFA has received regular criticism on numerous grounds. The process has been characterized as capricious, inconsistent, and incompetent. Critics have argued that the standards for proof have been ratcheted up, the evaluators of petitions have been biased, and criteria have been excessively stringent. Staff have been excoriated as unqualified, secretive, and overly powerful. The process has been viewed as flawed for relying unduly on outside observers for evidence regarding Indian authenticity, for featuring an official unwillingness to consider oral history as evidence, and for having biases against petitioners with African ancestry. And almost no one would argue against the charge that the process has been agonizingly slow.[59]

As Klopotek observes,

> Federal recognition contains a constellation of rewards, tensions, and contradictions. . . . [F]ederally non-recognized tribes do not have access to the political status of tribes recognized under federal law and are therefore exposed to serious threats to their self-governance, but they also do not face the same regulatory intrusions and risks that federally recognized tribes do; casino development can have an enormous economic impact and can enable tribal members to move back to the home community, but it can also exacerbate class stratification and tilt the focus of tribal members toward materialism and the kind of economic system that kept them impoverished in the past; recognition procedures and tribal decisions to pursue recognition have

provided surprising benefits to federally recognized tribes, while at the same time weighing heavily on community resources; and the nearly powerless but unregulated "self-determination" of tribal existence outside the federal domain can only be exchanged for the vagaries of exercising "self-determination" within the "domestic dependent nations" formulation of sovereignty in the federal-state relationship.[60]

Tribes must weigh these potential gains and losses as well as the time, money, and contention that the process entails when deciding whether to move forward.

Time has told us that tribes have overwhelmingly decided to risk the costs for the benefits: Since the inception of the FAP, 332 groups not recognized by the U.S. federal government have submitted letters of intent to file for federal acknowledgment. Between 1978 and 2008, completed petitions were submitted by 82 tribal groups, although only 16 received formal recognition, and 30 were denied (including Wisconsin's Brothertown Indian nation, whose story is presented by Kathleen Brown-Perez in this volume).[61] Further, Mark Edwin Miller explains that from the mid-1980s to the mid-1990s, the BIA acknowledged just 2 tribes, and the controversies that ensued over the BIA's findings in favor of acknowledgment in a number of cases resulted in its "literally 'raising the bar' on groups in fear of being sued over gaming and other sundry sovereignty issues."[62] Since the late 1980s, Miller observes, petitioning groups have "increasingly turn[ed] to legislation to circumvent the painfully slow bureaucratic process."[63] Shedding further light on the unpredictability and intensifying politicization of the process of petitioning for federal acknowledgment are the recent decisions concerning two Connecticut tribes with long-standing state recognition, the Eastern Pequot tribal nation and the Schaghticoke tribal nation, which received federal acknowledgment by the BIA in 2002 and 2004, respectively. Those positive final determinations were overturned the following year by the Interior Board of Indian Appeals, which "rejected the BIA's previous use of state recognition as evidence" for meeting several of the federal government's acknowledgment criteria.[64] The political influence exerted by the Connecticut Attorney General's Office in this case has yet to be fully examined, but a celebratory May 2005 press release from Richard Blumenthal, the state's attorney general, offers insight into the intensity of the opposition directed at petitioning groups by state officials. Blumenthal described the decisions to overturn the Eastern Pequots' and Schaghticokes' federal acknowledgment as "huge and historic . . . a knockout punch, a monumental and momentous victory for Connecticut."[65] These and other federal acknowledgment cases are crucial examples of the immensely complex political situation of both recognized and unrecognized native peoples in the United States today.

As of August 2012, the *Federal Register* reports that the federal government acknowledges 566 "tribal entities."[66] Yet being unrecognized as a tribal entity is not an indicator of political insignificance with respect to an indigenous people's relationship with the federal government or individual state governments. A number of Native American tribes have been continuously recognized by state governments, as they had been by prior colonial governments. According to Koenig and Stein, fourteen states have a total of seventy-three state-recognized tribes that are not currently acknowledged by the federal government.[67] The extent to which state and federal recognition are to be construed as unrelated political statuses has become a major point of contestation in recent federal acknowledgment cases, as Koenig and Stein point out in this volume. Also unresolved and highly contentious is the political status of Native Hawaiians (Kanaka Maoli), who are construed by the United States as Native Americans legally for some purposes while they are also in a distinct political situation because of the particular history of their relationship with the United States.[68] Many Kanaka Maoli hold the position that the overthrow of Queen Liliʻuokalani constituted an illegal action and that the United States, as an illegal occupier, should leave Hawaiʻi altogether. Thus, for many Kanaka Maoli, recognition by the United States would represent a diminution of their sovereignty, which ought to be adjudicated under international law rather than within the U.S. political system: the political goal for proponents of Hawaiʻi's sovereignty is instead the complete restoration of their autonomy.[69]

Further complicating the situation is the racial desire that has prompted some to assert illegitimate claims to Indian nationhood. Circe Sturm has recently written insightfully about the problem of "race shifting" in accounting for the phenomenal increase in those claiming native descent between 1960 and 2000—a 349 percent increase that demographers say cannot be explained by a surplus of native births over deaths. When those who claim native descent along with other racial categories are included, that rate balloons to 647 percent. Sturm's main concern is the massive increase in Cherokee descent claims, and she points out the emergence of dubious descent or heritage groups that have problematically sought to gain state recognition.[70] The problem of false recognition claims must be taken seriously, and the complex social and racial alchemy analyzed so ably by Sturm is part of the terrain on which sovereignty struggles occur.

The U.S. government's termination policy—intended, as Wilkins and Lomawaima explain, "to void the federally recognized political existence of tribes"—has also created distinct and problematic political situations.[71] More than one hundred tribal groups were terminated under this policy, which was opposed by native activists, who pressed for "relief from the hovering spectre of termination."[72] Although some terminated tribes have been reestablished as federally acknowledged native nations, that "hovering spectre" nonetheless endures. Indeed, as Wilkins and Stark argue, threats to tribal self-determination loom in the U.S. government's claims to power over tribal nations, claims that presume "the inherent right to disenfranchise, disempower, and dispossess indigenous peoples."[73]

Local opposition to and debate over recognition struggles have highlighted the extent to which indigenous peoples' assertions of a right to self-determination have been misconstrued and misrepresented by state and federal officials and others who reject the historical and legal reality of an inherent Native American sovereignty that predates the formation of colonial governments and the U.S. federal and state governments. Indeed, in the 1990s, as the federal recognition petitions of both the Eastern Pequot and Golden Hill Paugussett tribal nations came under intensifying scrutiny by the popular media and the Attorney General's Office in Connecticut, the Connecticut state historian proclaimed that Native American sovereignty is a "legal fiction." Thus, the argument would follow that recognition struggles are irrelevant, since there is no "real" Native American sovereignty for the U.S. government to acknowledge.

The extension of federal recognition to previously unrecognized tribes has also been opposed by leaders of some long-recognized tribes on several grounds, and such opposition composed one factor in the founding of the National Tribal Chairmen's Association in 1971 by leaders of recognized tribes who expressed concern about diluting definitions of Indianness. Recognition policies have been debated by the National Congress of American Indians, and in numerous regions, the leaders of particular tribes have opposed the recognition of others.[74] In 2009, the Cherokee Nation of Oklahoma produced a video, *Cherokee Nation: What Is a Real Indian Nation? What Is a Fake Tribe?*, that denounced more than two hundred "descent groups" for their claims to Cherokee nationhood and adamantly pointed out that there are three federally recognized Cherokee tribes: the Cherokee Nation of Oklahoma, the United Keetowah Band, and the Eastern Band of the Cherokee Nation, lending additional evidence to the issue of racial claims that are the subject of Sturm's book.[75] Klopotek summarizes these objections: concern about the diversion of federal funds to those who are "'not very' Indian, if they are Indian at all" (falling prey to colonial racial logic); claims that other petitioners are predominantly some other "race" than Indian; belief that petitioners have "lost" their cultures and languages and thus are no longer Indian; and fear that the extension of recognition to "groups not perceived as racially and culturally Indian at first glance to most people will diminish the strength of arguments for tribal sovereignty in the public eye."[76]

Such opposition has taken a tremendous toll on the unrecognized and those who have overcome the struggle to attain recognition. In a memorable statement prior to the acknowledgment of the Mashantucket Pequots, their leader, Skip Hayward, indignantly declared, "I resent the implication that I am a second-class Indian." In this atmosphere of suspicion surrounding Indian identity, individual and cultural well-being are at risk. In pursuing recognition, tribal nations seek to secure "indigenous survival and well-being" and are "engaging in an inherently anticolonial and antiracist act." They hope to secure economic development, access to better education, healthy lives, tribal cohesiveness as a resource for members, and a land base; to "end speculation about their tribal legitimacy"; and ultimately to "help the people survive as a tribe."[77] As Klopotek has pointed out, unrecognized tribes can still attain these goals, and recognition does not automatically or rapidly translate into their achievement.[78] The efficacy of recognition, like the many colonial legacies that accompany it, remains contested, but this volume pursues stories of on-the-ground struggles to secure recognition as the best means of protecting tribal sovereignty.

Thematic Overview
Part 1: Race, Identity, and Recognition

The four chapters in this section address race, identity, and authenticity as they come to bear on recognition as a problem. Analyzing the racialization of native peoples historically and in contemporary struggles surrounding recognition, these chapters set up the problem of recognition and lay out central issues that recur across the chapters that follow and that haunt the process of recognition more broadly. Angela A. Gonzales (Hopi) and Timothy Q. Evans (Haliwa-Saponi) examine the disconnect between the Ramapough (New Jersey) world of social and ethnic boundaries and the rigid legal definitions of "tribe" demanded by the FAP, which translated into the Ramapoughs' failure to gain federal recognition. Malinda Maynor Lowery (Lumbee) illuminates the science in the construction of race in 1930s North Carolina by analyzing how racial segregation, science, and BIA bureaucracy mutually constituted each other for a tribal nation that has fought (and continues to fight) for recognition. Joanne Barker (Lenape nation of eastern Oklahoma, the Delaware tribe) demonstrates how the discourse of recognition within racialized notions of cultural identity has affected the implementation of the 1990 Native American Graves Protection and Repatriation Act, undermining the possibility of making human rights claims under the act for unrecognized tribes. K. Alexa Koenig and Jonathan Stein offer an essential overview of state recognition of tribal nations in the context of the U.S. federalist system. Their chapter sets a broad context for many of the vexing issues surrounding state recognition from a legal and political perspective.

Part 2: State and Federal Recognition in New England

Perhaps the most visible location of contemporary agitation over recognition because of the enormous profitability of Connecticut's Mashantucket Pequot and Mohegan casinos, New England stands as emblematic of the controversy over contemporary recognition. New England occupies a central place in the struggle over sovereignty historically and in the contemporary recognition process. Beginning with the colony of Connecticut's attempt to legislate the Pequots out of existence in the wake of the brutal Pequot War (1637), New Englanders have continuously tried to make Indians disappear through policy making and narratives of local history that followed up on wars of conquest. Indians, however, have steadfastly resisted effacement, pressing their claims in Congress and the courts and setting crucial precedents for recognition in a process that is still in formation. The four chapters in this section illuminate the larger themes of state and federal recognition by focusing on its historical context in this region. Collectively, these chapters probe the tensions embedded in state and federal recognition, the termination of state recognition, links and parallels between state and federal policy, and the problem of citizenship in a long history of colonialism in New England. Jean M. O'Brien (White Earth Ojibwe) demonstrates that recognition struggles in New England date to the nineteenth century, when the governments of Connecticut, Massachusetts, and Rhode Island took steps to terminate their official recognition of tribes based on the state's racialized notions about Indians. Amy E. Den Ouden examines recognition struggles and the narratives of Indian policy in late twentieth- and early twenty-first-century Connecticut, arguing that the region's popular antirecognition discourse is anchored in the colonial theme of Indians as threat and Indian policy as benevolent. Casting tribal recognition as a danger to the nonnative citizenry and validating racialized notions of tribal legitimacy, the generators and narrators of the state's Indian policy obscure questions about native rights, the core issue of recent recognition cases. Ruth Garby Torres (Schaghticoke tribal nation), takes up the Schaghticoke recognition case. The tribe received federal recognition in 2004, only to fall prey to privately funded anti-Indian groups, who cooperated with state officials to have recognition overturned. Torres argues that this reversal solidified a new public policy of termination for the Schaghticokes and other Connecticut tribes. Rae Gould (Nipmuc) reconstructs the Nipmucs' nearly three-decade-long but unsuccessful battle for recognition, contending that the federal acknowledgment process participates in the use and misuse of historical documentation. Moreover, she argues, new stereotypes about Indians from the twentieth and twenty-first centuries affect perceptions about New England Indians in the present.

Part 3: Contemporary Recognition Controversies

Given the agonizingly slow pace of the recognition process as well as the ongoing battles over its justice in practice, these struggles promise to embroil native peoples and the federal government into the distant future. The four chapters in this section are case studies of contemporary recognition cases. The first three are FAP cases that have been denied but continue to be contested in the Northeast, Midwest, and Pacific Northwest; the fourth illuminates the complexities of sovereignty politics through the lens of native Hawai'i. Kathleen A. Brown-Perez (Brothertown Indian nation) plots the long acknowledgment struggle of the Brothertown nation in Wisconsin, which fought for its sovereignty beginning in the nineteenth century through the novel means of seeking U.S. citizenship while retaining their political relationship as sovereigns until the United States discontinued this relationship in the 1970s. Brown-Perez examines the Brothertowns' continuing quest for reacknowledgment. John R. Robinson takes up the unacknowledgment of the Chinook in the Pacific Northwest. Though they are ever-present in the iconography of the region, they must continue their struggle for recognition—most recently through legislative channels—following the denial of their petition in 2002. Les W. Field, Alan Leventhal, and Rosemary Cambra focus on the termination and ongoing denial of federal acknowledgment in the case of the Muwekma Ohlone tribe of the San Francisco Bay area, illuminating the ways in which the convoluted and illogical exigencies of the federal acknowledgment process have been informed and bolstered by the discourses of cultural anthropology and archaeology. Field's analysis adds crucial insights to continuing calls for the decolonization of these disciplines in the name of social justice for indigenous peoples. J. Kēhaulani Kauanui (Kanaka Maoli) analyzes the politics surrounding the current battle over the Akaka Bill, which seeks to impose federal recognition on Native Hawaiians, a situation that illuminates the complexities of sovereignty politics across the similar yet very different political and legal situations for indigenous peoples in Indian Country, Native Alaska, and the Pacific.

———

The contributors to this volume hope that it will serve as a provocative contribution to the burgeoning scholarship on the vital and volatile issue of recognition in the broader context of sovereignty struggles. We also hope that the vocabulary and set of analytic tools offered by these essays will be useful to all readers who wish to gain a better understanding of the shifting and complex political, legal, and cultural terrain of indigenous rights in the United States.

Notes

1. Brian Klopotek, *Recognition Odysseys: Indigeneity, Race, and Federal Tribal Recognition Policy in Three Louisiana Indian Communities* (Durham: Duke University Press, 2011), 23.

2. For an overview of the forms of genocide to which indigenous peoples have been subjected, see Samuel Totten, William S. Parsons, and Robert Hitchcock, "Confronting Genocide and Ethnocide of Indigenous Peoples: An Interdisciplinary Approach to Definition, Intervention, Prevention, and Advocacy," in *Annihilating Difference: The Anthropology of Genocide*, ed. Alexander Laban Hilton (Berkeley: University of California Press, 2002). The authors explain, "The genocide of indigenous peoples is a widespread phenomenon, occurring on every continent and in a variety of social, political, economic, and environmental contexts" (66). Colonial and U.S. laws and policies that denied the existence and the rights of tribal nations, such as the termination policy imposed in the mid-twentieth century, must be

analyzed in terms of their genocidal implications. A 1959 resolution of the National Congress of American Indians described termination as a policy that "can only lead to tremendous suffering by the Indian people" ("Reaffirmed NCAI Policy Resolution for Indian Program, 1959," in *Of Utmost Good Faith*, ed. Vine Deloria Jr. [New York: Bantam, 1971], 336). In 1969, Vine Deloria Jr. wrote, "In practice, termination is used as a weapon against the Indian people in a modern war of conquest" ("The Disastrous Policy of Termination," in *Custer Died for Your Sins: An Indian Manifesto* [Norman: University of Oklahoma Press, 1988], 76).

3. *Declaration of Indian Purpose: The Voice of the American Indian* (Whitefish, Mont.: Kessinger, 2006), 5.

4. Vine Deloria Jr., *Behind the Trail of Broken Treaties: An Indian Declaration of Independence* (Austin: University of Texas Press, 1985), 3–4.

5. Of note are three recent volumes. Renée Ann Cramer's *Cash, Color, and Colonialism: The Politics of Tribal Acknowledgment* (Norman: University of Oklahoma Press, 2005) is an essential starting point for framing federal acknowledgment issues. Cramer's book is a comparative study of the relevance of ideas about race and contests over resources in federal acknowledgment cases in New England and in the Deep South. Likewise, Sara-Larus Tolley's *Quest for Tribal Acknowledgment: California's Honey Lake Maidus* (Berkeley: University of California Press, 2006) and Mark Edwin Miller's *Forgotten Tribes: Unrecognized Indians and the Federal Acknowledgment Process* (Lincoln: University of Nebraska Press, 2004) offer crucial analyses of the problem of acknowledgment for tribes in the West, which are often overlooked in discussions about recognition. All three of these volumes document the centrality of the gaming issue to recognition battles. Bruce Granville Miller contributes important material about unrecognized indigenous peoples in a global comparative context in *Invisible Indigenes: The Politics of Nonrecognition* (Lincoln: University of Nebraska Press, 2003), and Elizabeth A. Povinelli's *The Cunning of Recognition: Indigenous Alterities and the Making of Australian Multiculturalism* (Durham: Duke University Press, 2002) is an important touchstone for theoretical considerations about recognition globally.

6. See, e.g., Cramer, "Cash, Color, and Colonialism in Connecticut," in *Cash, Color, and Colonialism*, 137–62; Amy E. Den Ouden, "'Race' and the Denial of Local Histories," in *Beyond Conquest: Native Peoples and the Struggle for History in New England* (Lincoln: University of Nebraska Press, 2005), 181–208; Jean M. O'Brien, *Firsting and Lasting: Writing Indians Out of Existence in New England* (Minneapolis: University of Minnesota Press, 2010); Laurence M. Hauptman, "There Are No Indians East of the Mississippi," in *Tribes and Tribulations: Misconception about American Indians and Their Histories* (Albuquerque: University of New Mexico Press, 1995), 93–108.

7. Cramer, *Cash, Color, and Colonialism*, 137.

8. Seneca legal scholar Robert Porter has argued that the emergence of the rich casino Indian stereotype may elicit "more openly predatory" attitudes toward native peoples from nonnatives in the United States, intensifying what he describes as the "new termination era" of federal Indian policy. The Indian Gaming Regulatory Act, he contends, is a cornerstone of the U.S. government's late twentieth-century efforts to undermine tribal sovereignty by giving excessive powers to individual states to appropriate native wealth, with the new justification being that all Indians may now be labeled as rich casino Indians. See Robert Odawi Porter, "American Indians and the New Termination Era," *Cornell Journal of Law and Public Policy* 16 (2007): 474–75.

9. Renée Ann Cramer, "The Common Sense of Anti-Indian Racism: Reactions to Mashantucket Pequot Success in Gaming and Acknowledgment," *Law and Social Inquiry* 31 (2006): 325–26.

10. The stigma associated with the Euro-American racial category "black Indian" and its application as a term intended to denigrate the Indian identity of particular native communities has had a significant impact on the way in which the public assesses (or is instructed to assess) the history and rights of tribal nations in Connecticut whose membership includes individuals of both Native American and African American ancestry. Golden Hill Paugussetts, for example, were subjected to viciously racist ridicule in a 1993 editorial cartoon in a major Connecticut newspaper, the *Hartford Courant*, which depicted Paugussetts as frauds and swindlers whose supposed devious character was conveyed as "obvious" in their "black" appearance (see Den Ouden, *Beyond Conquest*, 201–7). That the long and complex history of relations between Native and African American peoples in the United States remains largely misunderstood or disparaged as wholly destructive of "authentic" Indian identity is a matter taken up in Gabrielle Tayac, ed. *IndiVisible: African–Native American Lives in the Americas* (Washington, D.C.: Smithsonian Institution Press, 2009), which documents the impact of entrenched notions of racial purity and the racist practices and governmental policies that have denied the legitimacy of kinship and shared histories of struggle among Native and African American peoples. As Angela A. Gonzales explains, for example, racial categories imposed and normalized by the U.S. Census in the nineteenth and twentieth centuries "pigeonholed [Native Americans and African Americans] into official governmental divisions" that maintained white supremacy and facilitated control of people whose complex and interwoven histories defied the established racial hierarchy in the United States ("Racial Legibility: The Federal Census and the (Trans)Formation of 'Black' and 'Indian' Identity, 1790–1920," in *IndiVisible*, ed. Tayac, 67).

11. State recognition of the Mashantucket Pequot, Mohegan, Eastern or Pau-catuck Pequot, Schaghticoke, and Golden Hill Paugussett tribal nations has been described as the "unique legal status" of "five indigenous tribes" whose direct rela-tionships with Connecticut began in the colonial period (Stephen L. Pevar, *The Rights of Indians and Tribes* [Carbondale: Southern Illinois University Press, 2002], 292). However, as Koenig and Stein discuss in detail in this volume, state recogni-tion is also a political and legal status that has emerged in more recent negotiations between tribal nations and individual states. Legal scholar Matthew L. M. Fletcher argues that "a new and dynamic relationship between states and Indian tribes is growing": "Many states now recognize Indian tribes as *de facto* political sover-eigns, often in the form of a statement of policy whereby the state agrees to engage Indian tribes in a government-to-government relationship mirroring federal pol-icy" ("Retiring the 'Deadliest Enemies' Model of Tribal-State Relations," *Tulsa Law Review* 43 [2007]: 75). There is also concern that agreements between tribal nations and individual states may undermine indigenous sovereignty and subor-dinate it to the sovereignty claimed by states. See, e.g., Jeff Armstrong, "Deadly Embrace: From State Sovereignty to Cooperative Agreements in a Public Law-280 State," *Indigenous Policy Journal* 19 (2008), http://indigenouspolicy.org/Articles /VolXIXNo2/DeadlyEmbrace/tabid/154/Default.aspx.

12. Mark Edwin Miller, *Forgotten Tribes*, 2.

13. "As Wealth Looms, Recognition Fades," *Connecticut Post*, October 15, 2011.

14. Paula Sherman, "Gaming and IGRA: A Tool for Self-Determination or Elim-ination?" *Journal of Aboriginal Economic Development* 2 (2002): 80–83.

15. See, e.g., Robert B. Porter, who argues that gaming constitutes "auto-coloniz-ing behavior": "The gaming phenomenon demonstrates just how deeply the Immi-grant nation's economic values have been assimilated by Indigenous peoples. This aggressive pursuit of excess wealth reflects an incorporation of the values underly-ing the colonizing nation's economic system" ("Pursuing the Path of Indigeniza-tion in the Era of Emergent International Law Governing the Rights of Indigenous Peoples," *Yale Human Rights and Development Journal* 5 [2002]: 149).

16. Jessica R. Cattelino, "The Double Bind of American Indian Need-Based Sov-ereignty," *Cultural Anthropology* 25 (2010): 248.

17. This current total amount of revenues accrued from the Foxwoods and Mohegan Sun casinos by the state of Connecticut is reported by the New England Gaming Summit (www.newenglandsummit.com). The gaming compacts, along with details regarding casino revenues paid to the state, may be viewed at the web-site of the Connecticut Department of Consumer Protection, Gaming Division (www.ct.gov/dcp/cwp/view.asp?a=4107&q=480854). A January 2010 report of the Senate Republican Office, "Where Does All the Casino Money Go?," lends

insight into state legislators' sense of entitlement to the enormous sums extracted from the Mashantuckets and Mohegans since their compacts were signed. Republicans and Democrats squabble over control and allocation of "casino money," which seems not to be enough to satisfy the state: In 2009 alone, "the state received nearly $378 million in revenue from the casinos. While this is indeed a lot of money it is down considerably from the over $430 million the state received in 2007, certainly a sign of these troubled economic times" (www.senaterepublicans.ct.gov /press/witkos/2010/012010.html).

18. "Federal Recognition or Flawed System: Pride, Politics, and Connecticut's Native American Tribes," public forum hosted by the Connecticut Historical Society and WNPR/Connecticut Public Radio, March 15, 2005. The forum featured presentations by Nell Jessup Newton and three other speakers: Connecticut's attorney general, Richard Blumenthal; Chief Richard Velky of the Schaghticoke Tribal Nation of Kent, Connecticut; and Nicholas Bellantoni, Connecticut state archaeologist. The forum attracted a large audience and took place at the height of public controversy over the federal acknowledgment of the Eastern Pequot and Schaghticoke tribal nations in 2002 and 2004, respectively. For further discussion of the Eastern Pequot and Schaghticoke federal acknowledgment cases, see the essays in this volume by Torres and Den Ouden (both of whom attended the March 2005 forum).

19. "Poor Choice for Mashantucket," *New London Day*, October 6, 2011. The editorial also notes that both the Mashantuckets' and Mohegans' casinos "have suffered losses and been forced to lay off workers in recent years in large part because of a global economic downturn."

20. William A. Starna, "'Public Ethnohistory' and Native American Communities: History or Administrative Genocide?," *Radical History Review* 53 (1992): 133–35.

21. Vine Deloria Jr., "Conquest Masquerading as Law," in *Unlearning the Language of Conquest: Scholars Expose Anti-Indianism in America*, ed. Wahinkpe Topa (Four Arrows) (Austin: University of Texas Press, 2006), 94–107. Deloria summarizes the major contradiction inherent in the legality of U.S. Indian law: A "survey of the history of federal Indian law reveals that it is possible to be legally condemned and lynched at the same time. Although guaranteed justice in the federal courts, Indians have discovered that far too often legal doctrines purported to ensure their political and treaty rights are used to confiscate their property, deny their civil rights, and deprive them of the benefits that accrue with United States citizenship" (95). And the central Euro-American fictions about Indians—that their lands were "discovered" by "superior" societies and that they were destined

to be conquered and made "wards" of the United States—became "the mythical pillars on which federal Indian law has been built" (100).

22. As legal scholars Robert Yazzie and James W. Zion point out, "The concept that distinct peoples should be governed by their own law is ancient and fundamental to Western thought" ("Indigenous Law in North America in the Wake of Conquest," *Boston College International and Comparative Law Review* 20 [1997]: 58). Similarly emphasizing that neither indigenous sovereignty nor external governments' recognition of it is a new phenomenon in the global political arena, David E. Wilkins and Keith Richotte explain that "the original peoples of North America . . . constituted the *de facto* governments of the continent and wielded variable proprietary control over the lands they inhabited. As European colonization ensued, beginning in the late fifteenth century, *de jure* indigenous sovereignty was recognized by various European military and political authorities via treaties, agreements, and other diplomatic protocols that acknowledged the national status, land titles, and other rights of aboriginal groups" ("The Rehnquist Court and Indigenous Rights: The Expedited Diminution of Native Powers of Governance," *Publius: The Journal of Federalism* 33 [2003]: 84). See also S. James Anaya, "Indian Givers: What Indigenous Peoples Have Contributed to International Law," *Washington Journal of Law and Policy* 22 (2006): 107–20.

23. Robert Clinton, "State Power over Indian Reservations: A Critical Comment on Burger Court Doctrine," *South Dakota Law Review* 26 (1981): 434–35. For a detailed analysis of the Mohegan nation's defense of its political autonomy during this land suit against the colony of Connecticut, see Den Ouden, *Beyond Conquest*.

24. For important overviews of the imposition of colonial power relations in native North America and the justification of colonial domination in European and Euro-American law, see Frank Pommersheim, "The Colonized Context: Federal Indian Law and Tribal Aspiration," in *Braid of Feathers: American Indian Law and Contemporary Tribal Life* (Berkeley: University of California Press, 1995), 37–56; S. James Anaya, *Indigenous Peoples in International Law* (Oxford: Oxford University Press, 2004), 3–34; David E. Wilkins and K. Tsianina Lomawaima, *Uneven Ground: American Indian Sovereignty and Federal Law* (Norman: University of Oklahoma Press, 2001); Bradley Reed Howard, *Indigenous Peoples and the State: The Struggle for Native Rights* (DeKalb: Northern Illinois University Press, 2003), 34–66.

25. Audra Simpson, "On the Logic of Discernment," *American Quarterly* 59 (2007): 490.

26. S. James Anaya, "Indigenous Law and Its Contribution to Global Pluralism," *Indigenous Law Journal* 6 (2007): 4.

27. Joanne Barker, "For Whom Sovereignty Matters," in *Sovereignty Matters: Locations of Contestation and Possibilities for Self-Determination*, ed. Joanne Barker (Lincoln: University of Nebraska Press, 2005), 17–21.

28. Kenneth Deer, "Reflections on the Development, Adoption, and Implementation of the UN Declaration on the Rights of Indigenous Peoples," in *Realizing the UN Declaration on the Rights of Indigenous Peoples: Triumph, Hope and Action*, ed. Jackie Hartley, Paul Joffe, and Jennifer Preston (Saskatoon: Purich Publishing, 2010), 28.

29. Mark Rifkin, "Indigenizing Agamben: Rethinking Sovereignty in Light of the 'Peculiar' Status of Native Peoples," *Cultural Critique* 73 (2009): 99, 92, 99, 96, 114, 105, 106.

30. Patrick Wolfe, "Settler Colonialism and the Elimination of the Native," *Journal of Genocide Research* 8 (2006): 387, 402.

31. Rennard Strickland, "The Eagle's Empire: Sovereignty, Survival, and Self-Governance in Native American Law and Constitutionalism," in *Studying Native America: Problems and Prospects*, ed. Russell Thornton (Madison: University of Wisconsin Press, 1998), 267, 247–48.

32. Jeff Corntassel, "Toward Sustainable Self-Determination: Rethinking the Contemporary Indigenous Rights Discourse," *Alternatives* 33 (2008):105–32. See also Glen S. Coulthard, "Subjects of Empire: Indigenous Peoples and the 'Politics of Recognition' in Canada," *Contemporary Political Theory* 6 (2007): 437–60; S. James Anaya, *Indigenous Peoples in International Law*, 2nd ed. (Oxford: Oxford University Press, 2004), 56; S. James Anaya, "International Human Rights and Indigenous Peoples: The Move toward the Multicultural State," *Arizona Journal of International Law* 21 (2004): 13–61.

33. For important introductory overviews of the creation and significance of the Declaration, see, e.g., Kenneth Deer, "Reflections on the Development, Adoption, and Implementation of the UN Declaration on the Rights of Indigenous Peoples," in *Realizing the UN Declaration on the Rights of Indigenous Peoples: Triumph, Hope, and Action*, ed. Jackie Hartley, Paul Joffe, and Jennifer Preston (Saskatoon: Purich Publishing, 2010), 18–28; Les Malezar, "Dreamtime Discovery: New Reality and Hope," in *Realizing the UN Declaration*, ed. Hartley, Joffe, and Preston, 29–46; Claire Charters and Rodolfo Stavenhagen, "The UN Declaration on the Rights of Indigenous Peoples: How It Came to Be and What It Heralds," in *Making the Declaration Work: The United Nations Declaration on the Rights of Indigenous Peoples*, ed. Claire Charters and Rodolfo Stavenhagen (Copenhagen: International Work Group on Indigenous Affairs, 2009), 10–15.

34. Aliza Gail Organick, "Listening to Indigenous Voices: What the UN Declaration on the Rights of Indigenous Peoples Means for U.S. Tribes," *U.C. Davis*

Journal of International Law and Policy 16 (2009): 173–210. For a comprehensive and detailed overview of the history of the UN Declaration on the Rights of Indigenous Peoples and a thorough analysis of opposition by "no-vote" states, see Charters and Stavenhagen, *Making the Declaration Work*.

35. "Victory!: U.S. Endorses U.N. Declaration on the Rights of Indigenous Peoples," *Cultural Survival*, December 16, 2010 (www.culturalsurvival.org).

36. Robert Tim Coulter in "U.N. Declaration Sets New Agenda for U.S.-Indian Relations," *Indian Country Today*, December 30, 2010.

37. Steven Newcomb, "Has U.S. Changed Its Position on Declaration? Not Really," *Indian Country Today*, December 31, 2010.

38. Judson Berger, "Obama's Reversal on 'Indigenous Peoples' Rights Stirs Concern over Legal Claims," FoxNews.com, December 25, 2010.

39. David E. Wilkins and Heidi Kiiwetinepinesiik Stark, *American Indian Politics and the American Political System*, 3rd ed. (New York: Rowman and Littlefield, 2011), 312.

40. Ibid., 312–13.

41. Ibid., 3, 310–11.

42. Ibid., 308.

43. Ibid.; *Cherokee Nation v. Georgia*, 30 U.S. 1 (1831).

44. Wilkins and Stark, *American Indian Politics*, 11.

45. Ibid., 8.

46. Ibid., 312, xxii.

47. Ibid., 313.

48. Ibid., 4.

49. Ibid., 4–5.

50. Ibid., 17.

51. Klopotek, *Recognition Odysseys*, 21–22.

52. Ibid., 5.

53. Ibid., 22–23.

54. O'Brien, *Firsting and Lasting*.

55. Klopotek, *Recognition Odysseys*, esp. 7.

56. *Passamaquoddy v. Morton*, 528 F. 2d 370 (1975).

57. Klopotek, *Recognition Odysseys*, 23–30.

58. Ibid., appendix, 273.

59. Ibid., 4.

60. Ibid., 239.

61. Wilkins and Stark, *American Indian Politics*, 8.

62. Mark Edwin Miller, *Forgotten Tribes*, 53–54.

63. Ibid., 52–53.

64. K. Alexa Koenig and Jonathan Stein, "Federalism and the State Recognition of Native American Tribes: A Survey of State-Recognized Tribes and State Recognition Processes across the United States," 36, http://ssrn.com/abstract=968495.

65. State of Connecticut Attorney General's Office, "BIA Overturns Schaghticoke, Eastern Pequot Recognitions, Attorney General Announces," Press Release, May 13, 2005, http://www.ct.gov/ag/cwp/view.asp?A=1949&Q=293554.

66. U.S. Department of the Interior, Bureau of Indian Affairs website, http://www.bia.gov/cs/groups/mywcsp/documents/text/idc-020733.pdf.

67. Koenig and Stein, "Federalism and the State Recognition," 7.

68. Wilkins and Stark, *American Indian Politics*, 1–3.

69. See J. Kēhaulani Kauanui, *Hawaiian Blood: Colonialism and the Politics of Sovereignty and Indigeneity* (Durham: Duke University Press, 2008), 189–96.

70. Circe Sturm, *Becoming Indian: The Struggle over Cherokee Identity in the Twenty-First Century* (Santa Fe, N.M.: School for Advanced Research Press, 2011), 5.

71. Wilkins and Lomawaima, *Uneven Ground*, 132.

72. Cramer, *Cash, Color and Colonialism*, 20–21; Kevin Bruyneel, *The Third Space of Sovereignty: The Postcolonial Politics of U.S.-Indigenous Relations* (Minneapolis: University of Minnesota Press, 2007), 156. See also George Pierre Castile, *Taking Charge: Native American Self-Determination and Federal Indian Policy, 1975–1993* (Tucson: University of Arizona Press, 2006), 11–12.

73. Wilkins and Stark, *American Indian Politics*, 232.

74. Klopotek, *Recognition Odysseys*, 31–36.

75. http://www.youtube.com/watch?v=gp7Z4eiEuaw.

76. Klopotek, *Recognition Odysseys*, 35–36.

77. Ibid., 39.

78. Ibid., 40.

Part I
Race, Identity, and Recognition

The Imposition of Law

The Federal Acknowledgment Process
and the Legal De/Construction of Tribal Identity

ANGELA A. GONZALES & TIMOTHY Q. EVANS

> The European is to the other races of mankind what man himself is to the lower animals; he makes them subservient to his use and when he cannot subdue he destroys them.
>
> —ALEXIS DE TOCQUEVILLE, *Democracy in America* (1835)

> Society must be remade before it can be the object of quantification. Categories of people and things must be defined, measures must be interchangeable; land and commodities must be conceived as represented by an equivalent in money. There is much of what Weber called rationalization in this, and also a good deal of centralization.
>
> —THEODORE PORTER, *Objectivity as Standardization* (1994)

This chapter considers how American Indian identity is ensconced in federal law through the Federal Acknowledgment Process (FAP). As the primary way by which groups can become legally recognized as a tribe, the FAP relies on evidence of "Indianness" and "tribalness" that is rendered legible through legal and social scientific analyses. Through an examination of the Ramapough Mountain Indians' petition for federal acknowledgment—a petition ultimately denied by the Secretary of the Interior—we consider some important questions: What are the effects of requiring groups to provide evidence of their social, cultural, and political organization as an Indian tribe, historically and continuously, to prove their "authenticity" in a legal arena? To what extent do the dicta of federal regulations in the acknowledgment process allow for or accommodate conflicting perspectives of native self-understanding, identity, and group life? And how can the adjudication of such matters be deemed unbiased when the evidence itself is the product of historical policies and practices aimed at the diminution of native existence?

Introduction

A problem calls for a solution. The problem: Beginning in the 1970s, an increasing number of Indian groups not formally recognized by the federal government sought legal recognition as tribes. Requests from groups seeking federal recognition previously had been handled on an ad hoc basis, based mostly on or through treaties, legislative and executive agency action, or judicial decree. In 1977, the American Indian Policy Review Commission reported that hundreds of Indian tribes had been left out of the federal trust relationship because of the lack of a single, formal acknowledgment process and the sometimes arbitrary actions and omissions of the federal bureaucracy.[1] The solution, according to the secretary of the interior: Delegate authority to the assistant secretary of Indian affairs to establish a formal process by which the U.S. government acknowledges an Indian tribe. Such authority, intended to provide the assistant secretary with an informed and well-researched basis for making any decision to acknowledge an Indian tribe, culminated in the establishment of the FAP in 1978.[2]

In the United States, with ultimate power and authority residing at the federal level, officials created and codified into law a standardized and synoptic view of what the federal government believes to constitute an Indian tribe. In so doing, the FAP has supplanted the diverse tribal histories, cultures, and customs of Indian groups seeking legal recognition with a simplified and standardized process and criteria to make these groups legible as Indian tribes.[3] Through its authoritarian power and practical logic and form necessary for the categorization of Indian groups, the FAP encodes and enforces an understanding of tribal identity both homogeneous and absolute. Such categories, writes James C. Scott, "begun as the artificial inventions of [federal officials,] end by becoming categories that organize people's daily experiences precisely because they are embedded in state-created institutions that structure that experience."[4] Charted historically, the categorization of Indian groups as "federally recognized" or "non–federally recognized" acquires its force from the fact that these categories reflect federal officials' perception of what they believe (or believed) to be the characteristics and qualities constituting Indian tribes. Given the centrality and importance of the federal government in the lives of American Indians, the FAP has had the power not only to transform American Indian self-understanding and identity but also to reinforce boundaries of difference between Indians and non-Indians and among tribal groups.[5]

For the 566 federally acknowledged Indian tribes and Alaska Native villages, the term "federal acknowledgment" (used interchangeably with "federal recognition") signifies a trust relationship by the federal government toward an Indian tribe that is legally acknowledged, or recognized, by both parties.[6] A foundational concept necessary for understanding this relationship is that American Indian tribes have historically been governmental entities with inherent group political authority over their lands and people.[7] Culturally unique and territorially distinct, each Indian nation exercised its sovereign political authority relatively freely, limited only internally by the amount of authority conferred on the group by individual tribal members and externally by the boundaries set by other Indian nations.

After contact with European nations, the external limitations on and the nature of tribal sovereignty changed. These outside European powers assumed the roles of proscribing and supplanting tribal political authority. Europeans rooted their assertions of absolute authority and sovereignty over the indigenous peoples of the Americas in a theological-political viewpoint built on a "divine right" to take and colonize the lands of non-Christian peoples. This imposition of paramount external authority conflicted with the history and practice of Indian nations governing themselves. Soon after contact, conflict between native nations and European powers began to grow, and Europeans sought a way to manage the situation. They often did so through treaties, wherein natives conceded land and resources in exchange for rights in other reserved lands, weapons, commodities, and other promises by European nations. However, the physical and economic power of the European nations in the New World eventually left little doubt as to their ability to impose their political and legal will over the Indian tribal nations. Vestiges of tribal self-rule continued, but as a later U.S. Supreme Court ruling rationalized, "The rights of the original inhabitants were, in no instance, entirely disregarded; but were, necessarily, to a considerable extent, impaired. They were admitted to be the rightful occupants of the soil . . . but their rights to complete sovereignty, as independent nations, were necessarily diminished, and their power to dispose of the soil, at their own will, to whomsoever they pleased, was denied by the original fundamental principle, that discovery gave exclusive title to those who made it."[8]

Still, the survival of tribal nations and their treaties with European powers necessarily required each side to acknowledge both the existence and the continuing political authority of the other, whatever its extent. Over time, this recognition of tribal nations by outside powers would be handed from the European powers to their colonies in the New World and eventually to the U.S. federal government. In theory, the federal government and tribes today recognize each other as mutual sovereigns; in practice, however, the plenary power granted by the U.S. Constitution to Congress over Indian affairs and confirmed by the Supreme Court enables the federal government to limit tribal sovereignty and circumscribe the meaning of tribal identity. One of the foundational tools for circumscribing tribal identity is federal acknowledgment—the ability of the federal government to deem as an American Indian tribe a particular group to whom it will extend an official political and legal relationship.

Historically, federal recognition has had two distinct meanings and uses, the intrinsic and the jurisdictional.[9] Prior to 1870, federal officials and the general public used and understood "recognition" as an intrinsic and self-evident quality and characteristic of Indian tribes that required no additional explanation. Marked by territorial boundaries and differences in physiognomy, language, culture, and lifestyle, Indian tribes existed as identifiable and distinct entities. But by the early 1800s, federal policy became increasingly concerned with delimitating boundaries between natives and nonnatives and more specifically among tribal groups.

Beginning in the 1870s, "recognition" began to be used in a more formal, jurisdictional sense and found its legal underpinnings in a series of three Supreme Court opinions—*Johnson v. M'Intosh* (1823), *Cherokee Nation v. Georgia* (1831), and *Worcester v. Georgia* (1832)—originally written by Chief Justice John Marshall a half century earlier to clarify the relationship among Indian tribes, states, and the federal government.[10] Most relevant for the concept of recognition, in *Worcester v. Georgia*, Marshall argued that under treaties made with the Cherokee, the United States had "assum[ed] the duty of protection."[11] Using a historical account of tribes as independent entities with special status, Marshall opined, "The Indian nations had always been considered as distinct, independent political communities, retaining their original natural rights as the undisputed possessors of the soil from time immemorial, with the single exception of that imposed by irresistible power [of the European nations]. The very term 'nation,' so generally applied to them, means 'a people distinct from others.'"[12] Known as the Marshall Trilogy, these three cases establish the legal foundation for the special political status of Indian tribes as sovereign albeit "domestic dependent nations" whose relationship to the United States resembles that "of a ward to his guardian."[13]

As a conceptual category, federally recognized tribes were formally decreed in 1934 with the passage of the Indian Reorganization Act (IRA).[14] In defining the term "Indian" as "persons of Indian descent who are members *of any recognized Indian tribe now under Federal jurisdiction*,"[15] the IRA introduced the concept of nonrecognized tribes, to which its provisions and a plethora of subsequent legislation would not apply.[16]

To determine the application of the IRA and subsequent legislation aimed at recognized tribes, it became increasingly necessary to delineate the differences between federally recognized and nonrecognized tribes. This necessity culminated in the establishment of the FAP by executive agency action in 1978 and officially titled *Procedures for Establishing That an American Indian Group Exists as an Indian Tribe.*

In circumscribing the procedures to be used and criteria to be met by groups petitioning for federal acknowledgment, the FAP is a legal process for establishing a political relationship between the group as a tribe and the federal government. It takes into account but is distinct from and not wholly dependent on answers to the related questions of whether the group's individual members are "racially" or ethnically American Indian or whether the group exists as a tribe independent of the federal relationship. To illustrate this distinction, the foremost treatise on American Indian law, Felix Cohen's *Handbook of Federal Indian Law*, notes that the definition of "Indian" under federal law varies based on context, but in the most general terms a person must meet two requirements: (1) have Indian ancestry, and (2) be regarded as an Indian by his or her tribe or community.[17] The U.S. Census Bureau requires even less, relying solely on an individual's self-identification as Indian. Neither means of establishing individual Indianness is determinative of collective tribalness.

Through its authoritarian power and administrative need to identify those groups with whom it has a government-to-government relationship, the FAP distinguishes federally recognized tribes from the two other categories of American Indian tribes in the United States: state-recognized and nonrecognized tribes. State-recognized tribes lack federal acknowledgment but have been recognized pursuant to state law and may have certain rights recognized by the federal government by virtue of such tribal status. Nonrecognized tribes are groups with neither federal nor state recognition but that nonetheless assert a self-ascribed American Indian tribal identity. The importance of these distinctions notwithstanding, the lack of federal recognition does not necessarily mean that a tribe does not exist. For example, federal courts have upheld treaty rights of nonrecognized tribes,[18] and state and federal courts have upheld the defense of sovereign immunity for state-recognized tribes.[19] Finally, even tribes that are not federally recognized may be eligible for certain federal programs reserved exclusively for Indian tribes. For example, the Small Business Administration's 8(a) business development program for tribes will accept state or federal recognition in support of a showing of economic disadvantage.[20]

If state-recognized and non–federally recognized tribes enjoy many of the rights and protections afforded federally recognized tribes, why would groups subject themselves to the authoritarian power of the federal government to rule on their identity as Indian tribes? An initial answer is that federal acknowledgment confers on tribes and their members eligibility for and access to a wider variety of federally funded programs and services, among them health care, housing assistance, and educational and economic development opportunities. Furthermore, federally acknowledged tribes may transfer tribally owned land into federal trust, preventing it from being sold or lost to tax forfeiture. Tribal business operations on such land historically have been exempt from most state regulatory laws and taxes, and such operations may include tribal gaming operations. Finally, for some groups such as the Ramapoughs, federal acknowledgment provides an opportunity for social justice and restitution. After years of social marginalization, racial discrimination, and prejudice, such acknowledgment may affirm an identity as Indian long denied or at least questioned by outsiders.[21]

By examining how American Indian identity is circumscribed by federal law in defining a "tribe," a primary goal of this chapter is to answer the following questions: To what extent do the federal acknowledgment regulations allow for or accommodate competing perspectives of group life, sociopolitical organization, and sense of peoplehood? And how does this legal process, with its imposed criteria and standards of interpretation, reshape our understanding of tribal identity vis-à-vis its power to rule on the validity and authenticity of a people's identity?

As the Ramapough Mountain Indians' petition for federal acknowledgment helps illustrate, the authoritarian power of the federal government to rule on a group's ethnic identity has engendered norms and forms of identification that groups must provide if they are to succeed in petitioning the federal government for acknowledgment as an Indian tribe. Through an examination of the group's failed petition for federal acknowledgment, we can see how legal definitions on the one hand clearly and conveniently define a group as a tribe, delimiting rigid and narrow boundaries of inclusion but on the other hand fail to account for the reality of fluid social, cultural, and political identities.

A Quest for Recognition: The Ramapough Mountain Indians

The Ramapough Mountain Indians are a community of about three thousand members living on the New York/New Jersey border in the towns of Mahwah and Ringwood, New Jersey, and Hillburn, New York. In their petition, they identify as descendants of a group of Algonquin-speaking Indians known as the Munsees and of remnants of the Tuscaroras who traveled through the Ramapo Pass on their way to join the Iroquois in Upstate New York.[22]

The Ramapoughs, like many other Indian tribes along the Eastern Seaboard who experienced early and sustained contact with Europeans, began to disperse from their homelands in the late seventeenth century as Europeans encroached and settled in the area. In 1758, the Munsees, also known as the Lenapes, signed the Treaty of Easton with the governor of New Jersey. By virtue of that treaty, the tribe relinquished claim to 3,044 acres of land in New Jersey in exchange for a cash settlement and continued fishing and hunting rights on the land.[23] At the time of the treaty, many Munsees already lived on the Brotherton Reservation in southern New Jersey, and many who had adopted Christianity remained there after the treaty was signed. Others scattered throughout New Jersey; some moved westward into Pennsylvania, Ohio, Kansas, Oklahoma, and Wisconsin; and still others moved north into New York and Canada.[24] According to the group's petition, many from the Brotherton Reservation eventually moved into the Ramapo Mountains in northern New Jersey and southeastern New York, where in isolation they held onto a small portion of land and continued their cultural traditions. The land had few roads or trails and was too rocky for farming, so white settlers in the area paid little attention to the Indians living in the surrounding mountains. The Ramapoughs survived by hunting and fishing for food and growing crops in small gardens, venturing out of the mountains only to trade or sell their wares.[25]

"Facts" and Findings: The Branch of Acknowledgment and Research Review[26]

The long and arduous journey of the Ramapough Mountain Indians through the FAP began on August 14, 1978, with a single-page letter to the secretary of the interior stating their intent to petition for federal acknowl-edgment.[27] Twelve years later, on April 23, 1990, the group submitted its petition, which consisted of more than one thousand pages of documents, including legal affidavits; photocopied birth, marriage, and death certifi-cates; torn and faded newspaper clippings; and other documents believed by the group to provide evidence of their existence as an Indian tribe from historical times to the present. Three years later, on December 8, 1993, the Branch of Acknowledgment and Research (BAR) published its proposed findings in the *Federal Register*, recommending against federal acknowledg-ment of the group.[28]

Using historical, anthropological, and genealogical research methods, BAR staff reviewed the Ramapoughs' petition and supporting documents and found that the group failed to meet four of the seven mandatory criteria for federal acknowledgment under the 1978 regulations: 83.7(a) continuous identification of the group from historical times until the present as "Ameri-can Indian" or "aboriginal"; 83.7(b) descent from and continuous identifica-tion as a distinct American Indian group inhabiting a specific area; 83.7(c) continuous and autonomous political authority over group members; and 83.7(e) evidence that current group members descended from a tribe known to have historically existed as an autonomous entity.[29] In accordance with the regulations, failure to meet all seven criteria requires a determina-tion by the assistant secretary of Indian affairs that the group does not exist as an Indian tribe.

In 1994, the federal acknowledgment regulations were revised to make more explicit the kinds of evidence that could be used to meet the required criteria and to increase the speed with which petitions were processed.[30] The revised regulations also changed criterion 83.7(a) and no longer required groups to provide proof of having been identified by outside observers as American Indian since colonial contact, but only since 1900. The Rama-poughs were given and accepted the option to have their petitions evalu-ated under the revised regulations.[31] The Ramapoughs were able to satisfy the modified criterion 83.7(a) but still remained unable to satisfy the other three criteria.

On February 6, 1996, assistant secretary of Indian affairs Ada Deer issued a "Notice of Final Determination" in the *Federal Register*, declining to acknowledge that the Ramapoughs exist as an Indian tribe within the meaning of federal law.[32] The Ramapoughs appealed the decision, but on November 11, 1997, nearly twenty years after the group's initial communi-qué expressing its intent to petition for federal acknowledgment as a tribe,

Assistant Secretary Deer issued a "Reconsidered Final Determination Declining to Acknowledge That the Ramapough Mountain Indians Exist as an Indian Tribe."[33]

To understand the difficulty of requiring groups petitioning for federal recognition to provide incontrovertible proof of their Indianness and tribalness from historical times to the present, we examine the three criteria the Ramapoughs failed to meet.

A Community (In)Distinct from Others

83.7(b) Evidence that a substantial portion of the petitioning group inhabits a specific area or lives in a community viewed as American Indian and distinct from other populations in the area, and that its members are descendants of an Indian tribe which historically inhabited a specific area.

In their petition, the Ramapoughs claimed that their ancestors had inhabited the Ramapo Mountain region since the eighteenth century, naming four families—VanDunk, DeGroat, DeFreese, and Mann—as progenitors of the current tribe. In its initial summary of findings, the BAR found that the Ramapoughs failed to provide evidence from "authoritative, knowledgeable external sources" that the group's ancestors had lived as a separate and distinct community in the Ramapo Mountain area before 1850.[34] According to the BAR, individual Ramapough ancestors began moving into the area after 1770, but they did not do so as part of a community, Indian or otherwise. Moreover, these families lived not in the Ramapough Mountains, as the group claimed, but in the valley below. The BAR additionally found an absence of evidence that these families comprised or were identified as a separate community until the 1870s, when outsiders noted the existence of an isolated "colored community" living in the area.[35]

The anthropological report prepared by BAR staff found that although the Ramapoughs had existed as an isolated, distinct community for nearly two hundred years, they did so not as an Indian community but as a "colored community" with some Indian ancestry.[36] According to the BAR, the insularity of the community began very soon after their arrival in the Mahwah area of the Ramapo Mountains around 1800. From that time on, the Ramapoughs struggled to maintain a separate identity from whites and blacks, even while sometimes choosing to participate in white and/or black social and religious organizations. According to the BAR's initial findings, because the group's ancestors lived in close proximity to and participated in the economic and religious activities of the surrounding communities, they were deemed to have assimilated and abandoned their distinctive tribal culture and identity.

The Ramapoughs' petition cited scholarly references to outside observers in the 1900s who described the community as a "tribe" or a "clan"; however, the BAR interpreted these references as synonyms for "a kinship-based, *non-white* community distinct from the surrounding society."[37] According to the initial findings, the Ramapoughs' petition provided no evidence of any significant historical and/or cultural differences between their community and other populations in the area.

The Ramapoughs see it differently. As an underlying principle to their petition that has been argued by scholars more generally, community is a qualitative aspect of social relations among members connected by shared origin, kinship, social obligation, and other ties overtly expressed or tacitly assumed. Similar to the absence of overt markers of Lumbee identity discussed by Karen I. Blu, a century of contact with both whites and African Americans dimmed many visible markers of Ramapough identity. Lacking in large part distinct customs, crafts, language, and arts, the Ramapoughs challenged anthropological and sociological expectations regarding social and cultural distinctiveness.[38]

The absence of overt markers of difference rendered the Ramapoughs invisible to outside observers. An example of this oversight was cited by BAR officials in support of the finding of a lack of community among the three Ramapough settlements: "The only reliable evidence presented by the petitioner that could be used to evaluate whether the petitioner had maintained its community between 1950 and 1992 was the 1992 membership list. The members living in those three settlements only accounted for 44 percent of the individuals on the 1992 membership list. There was only anecdotal evidence regarding social connections between the 56 percent living outside of the three settlements and the 44 percent living in the settlements. This was insufficient evidence to establish the required social connections between those living inside the three settlements and those living outside of them."[39]

Markers of identity meaningful to the Ramapoughs include, among others, behavioral characteristics embedded within kinship relations and enacted through the acknowledgment and fulfillment of social obligations. These markers, although illegible to outsiders, are indelible markers of one's identity and membership in the Ramapough community.

Despite the group's evidence that it had existed as a distinct Indian community and that members are descendants of an Indian tribe known to have inhabited the area, the initial proposed findings stated that at no time prior to the group's incorporation in 1978 had the group or its ancestors been identified in state or federal records as American Indian. Further, the proposed findings prepared by the BAR assert that not until the late 1800s did some of the group's ancestors begin to view themselves as distinct, and not until the 1970s did they view themselves as Indian.[40]

In reviewing the Ramapoughs' petition and in independent research conducted as part of its review, the BAR asserted that no evidence established the existence of any Indian tribes or bands remaining in the area after the Treaty of Easton in 1756.[41] The BAR further alleged that no historical connection existed between the Ramapoughs and any of the tribal groups from which they identified themselves as having descended.

In the summary of proposed findings, the BAR found that the Ramapoughs did not meet the requirements of criterion 83.7(b) between 1850 and the present despite evidence that they constituted a socially cohesive and distinct community during this period: "They were not distinct as Indians, as called for by the criterion."[42] However, under the 1994 revised regulations, the BAR acknowledged that from approximately 1870 until 1950, the group had been viewed as a community distinct from others in the area. But as in its earlier finding, the BAR asserted that the community had not been viewed as American Indian or comprised of the descendants of an Indian tribe that historically inhabited the region. Under the revised regulations, the BAR acknowledged that the group had been recognized as a distinct community from 1870 to 1950.

Political Authority

83.7(c) A statement of facts which establishes that the petitioner has maintained tribal political influence or other authority over its members as an autonomous entity throughout history until the present.

In its summary of proposed findings, the BAR asserted that the Ramapoughs provided insufficient evidence demonstrating political leadership or influence over the group until the 1940s.[43] In their petition, the Ramapoughs identified several prominent individuals as community leaders at various times in the group's history. The group identified several generations of DeGroat family members as tribal leaders prior to 1850. According to the BAR's analysis of the petition, the DeGroat family owned large plots of land; however, the BAR contended that landownership, regardless of the quantity, was insufficient to prove political authority or leadership. Journalistic accounts from the late 1800s and early 1900s reference some individuals as patriarchs or matriarchs, but neither the articles nor the Ramapoughs themselves provided any information regarding these persons' political leadership activities. The Ramapoughs also identified the pastor of the Brook Chapel in Hillburn, New Jersey, as a community leader; however, the BAR asserted that there was no evidence to indicate that his leadership and authority extended beyond his congregation. And although the Ramapough petition mentioned several organizations as precursors to the current tribal organization, the BAR deemed them to be social rather than political organizations whose leadership coalesced around single issues.[44]

The group identified members of several religious, fraternal, and civic organizations as community leaders between 1950 and the group's formal incorporation as the Ramapough Mountain Indians in 1978. Although the BAR acknowledged two individuals named in the petition, Otto Mann Sr. and William "Pooch" Van Dunk, who exercised unambiguous community leadership, their sphere of influence was limited in duration and to specific geographical communities, not the tribal community writ large.[45]

The formal leadership structure identified by the Ramapoughs in their petition consisted of an elected chief and three clan chiefs representing the towns of Ringwood and Mahwah, New Jersey, and Hillburn, New York. Under each clan chief were three subchiefs, all of whom served on the tribal council as elected officials. Auxiliary to the council was a group of tribal matriarchs known as the Clan Mothers, whose role was to advise the council on important community and cultural matters. In the anthropological report prepared by the BAR, historical journal references to "clans" were determined to be more a "generic reference to extended kin living in close proximity and not identification as Indian,"[46] and the modern-day "clans" were found to be more geographically based groups corresponding to the three settlement communities than kinship groups. Thus, the BAR found that the clan divisions were more an artifact of the group's incorporation in 1978 than a cultural or historically based kinship system; the BAR also dismissed early journalistic references to ancestors of the Ramapoughs as "clans" as "generic references to extended kin living in close proximity and not identification as Indian."[47]

Since the Ramapoughs were found not to have existed as a distinct community until the 1850s as described under criterion 83.7(b) of the 1978 regulations, there could be no exercise of political leadership or influence prior to that time. However, under the 1994 revised regulations, the BAR reversed its earlier finding and ruled that the Ramapoughs did not meet the criterion except for the period between 1870 and 1950. However, since the revised regulations did not change the requirement of continuous existence as a political entity, the group still failed to meet this criterion. Thus, the final determination issued by the assistant secretary of Indian affairs ruled that the Ramapoughs failed to demonstrate that they had maintained tribal influence or authority over their members as an autonomous entity throughout history until the present.

Racial (Mis)Labeling

83.7(e) A list of all known current members of the group and a copy of each available former list of members based on the tribe's own defined criteria. The membership must consist of individuals who have established, using evidence acceptable to the Secretary [of the Interior], descendancy from a tribe which existed historically or from historical tribes which combined and functioned as a single autonomous entity.

As evidence of their tribal descent, the Ramapoughs submitted 836 ancestry charts tracing lines of descent for current members back five generations using U.S. Census and other records.[48] The group's main progenitors include four families—the DeFreeses, DeGroats, Manns, and Van Dunks. In addition, the group submitted two documents, "The Jackson Whites: A Study of Racial Degeneracy" (known also as the Vineland Study) and "A Branch of the Ramapough DeGroat Family of Upstate New York, Ontario, Wisconsin, and Minnesota," along with federal and state Census records and vital records from New York and New Jersey.

Census records submitted by the Ramapoughs included the 1870 U.S. Census, the first to include all "Indians out of their tribal relations, and exercising the rights of citizens under State or Territorial laws." At the time, Census enumerators were instructed to write "Ind in the column for Color"; however, many Indian people living along the Eastern Seaboard continued to be identified as "colored" or "mulatto" even though most were members of groups locally known and distinguished from white, black, and colored communities.[49] The Ramapoughs were included among these groups, along with the Lumbees, Schaghticokes, and other groups mentioned in this volume.

By the late 1800s, the Ramapough Mountain Indians became increasingly referred to as "Jackson Whites."[50] Although the precise origin of the term is unknown, outsiders used it to refer to a distinct, "racially mixed" local community of African, white, and American Indian ancestry.[51] In 1950, the U.S. Census Bureau adopted a policy for recording a person's race using local racial designations, including "Turks," "Moors," "Croatans," "Red Bones," "Guineas," "Melungeons," and "Jackson Whites."[52] Using local knowledge of these groups, enumerators ascribed these designations based on external identification and classified many Ramapoughs as "Jackson Whites" in the 1950 Census.[53] But despite categories commonly used to denote persons of mixed African, white, and American Indian ancestry, the BAR found neither such isolated designations nor these broader "racial" categories capable of substantiating the group's existence as a separate and exclusive American Indian, Munsee, or other tribal community.

To the extent that the FAP regulations state that "groups of descendants will not be acknowledged solely on a racial basis," establishing descent often necessitates the use and submission of historical records and other documentary evidence that used racial identifiers such as those found in the federal Census. Requiring groups to provide evidence of their Indian ancestry and identity sometimes forces them to resort to documentary evidence that used pseudoscientific methods for nefarious purposes in their identification and categorization of individuals. One such piece of evidence the Ramapoughs submitted with their petition was an unpublished sociological study, "The Jackson Whites: A Study of Racial Degeneracy," written around 1910 by persons connected to New Jersey's Vineland Training School.

Written during the height of the eugenics movement, the Vineland Study represents one of many such documents in the late nineteenth and early twentieth centuries that targeted mixed-race groups and other "pockets of degeneracy" believed to result from the inheritance of "poor genetic stock." At the time, researchers at the Vineland Training School believed the Jackson Whites offered one of the best possible natural laboratories for testing the influence of genetics on intelligence. Using a standard intelligence test on the group, examiners concluded that racial miscegenation rather than environmental factors negatively influenced intelligence among mixed-ancestry groups and that the best way for the state to care for these racial "degenerates" was to institutionalize and sterilize them before they could reproduce.[54] Despite the study's nefarious motivation and questionable science, because it identified the Ramapoughs as both Jackson Whites and of "mixed Indian-Negro blood," it was submitted as evidence of the group's Indian ancestry.[55]

In the end, none of the evidence submitted by the Ramapoughs satisfied the regulations' need for both adequate and acceptable proof of ancestry from a historic Indian tribe. Despite the preponderance of evidence provided by the Ramapoughs, the issue was a matter not simply of how much proof was needed but of the type of evidence necessary to satisfy the regulations. Unable to provide "acceptable" evidence tracing descent of current group members to progenitors from a historical Indian tribe, the Ramapoughs' quest for federal acknowledgment came to a halt.

The Politics of Identification and Identity

Questions of Indian identity abound in many arenas, from college admissions to the marketing, labeling, and sale of Indian art to employment eligibility. Answers to the question of Indian identity are equally diverse, and standards of proof vary across situation and time. In many instances, evidence of membership in a federally recognized Indian tribe is required, and most institutions, organizations, and individuals regard this as incontrovertible proof.

The clarity that membership in a federally recognized Indian tribe accords the individual belies the complexity of the process that groups must navigate to achieve such recognition. In evaluating whether the evidence provided by the Ramapoughs met the criteria required for federal acknowledgment as an Indian tribe, the BAR staff imposed their own interpretations on evidence that group leaders thought demonstrated the Ramapoughs' existence as an Indian tribe from historical times until the present. In applying the regulations, the BAR could not accommodate or reconcile divergent perspectives and interpretations of historical events, social practices, and cultural traditions. In trying to make legible the materials provided by the Ramapoughs, the staff at the BAR had to evaluate the evidence provided by the group according to the administrative criteria and processes identified in the federal regulations.

Based on the group's petition and supporting documentation, the BAR found what it considered to be insufficient evidence that the present-day Ramapough Mountain Indians were descendants of the Munsees or another historical tribe indigenous to the New York/New Jersey area at the time of European contact. According to the BAR, the group's progenitors included freed African slaves, Dutch settlers, and American Indians, but for the latter no tribal-specific ancestry could be determined. Historical records, including genealogical and U.S. Census data variously identifying the group's progenitors as "mulatto" or "tri-racial," served as evidence for such findings. The latter categories were commonly used to include persons with Indian ancestry, but the existence of unaffiliated Indian ancestry for the Ramapoughs could not satisfy the FAP regulations. Although the group and its members may have identified as American Indian or been identified as having Indian ancestry, the question was a matter not of general Indian identity or ancestry but of specific tribal identity and ancestry. According to the BAR, the mere presence of Indian ancestry in a group as noted by outside observers does not automatically qualify the group for federal acknowledgment.[56]

The FAP and its mandatory criteria are intended to extend federal recognition to those indigenous North American Indian groups able to demonstrate continuous existence as tribal communities with proven political authority or influence over their members since the first sustained contact with Europeans. The difficulty in documenting continuous existence as an Indian tribe—culturally, socially, and politically—is that the FAP regulations require standards of proof that can be fulfilled only with "objective" documentation. Such objectivity, however, is inherently subjective because the only acceptable evidence is that contained in written records created and maintained by outsiders. In the Ramapough case, such records—birth, death, and marriage certificates; property deeds; and court documents— did not reflect the Ramapoughs' understanding or experience of their history, culture, or identity. The definition of "tribe" as set forth in the FAP regulations failed to capture the specifics of what it means or meant to belong to the Ramapough people. Because of this disjunction between the ethnolegal categories and the group's self-understanding and lived experience, the group's petition for acknowledgment never quite signified the idiom of tribalness or the resulting Indianness used in the regulations.

For more than two centuries, the Ramapough Mountain Indian community existed without tacit recognition from the surrounding communities or society at large as American Indian or as a tribe. Since the group historically issued no membership certificates and maintained no tribal roll, the Ramapoughs defied definition in the rigidly formalized sense required for federal acknowledgment. But in assessing the historical existence of the community as American Indian, the FAP regulations rely on evidence in the form of written records—that is, vital statistics, family genealogies, tax and probate records, and similar documents that can be analyzed and evaluated. Such records, however, reflect the racial nomenclature of the period and place (for example, "mulattos," "Melungeons," "Moors," "Jackson Whites"), making it difficult for Indian groups such as the Ramapoughs to provide documentary evidence to the contrary. Although the Ramapoughs provided more than one thousand pages of supporting materials, the BAR found them to be inconclusive in demonstrating that the group had existed socially, culturally, and politically as an American Indian tribe. This privileging of the BAR's interpretation of certain historical documents over the Ramapoughs' interpretation of those same documents reflects the asymmetrical power granted by law that enables one group to impose itself on the telling of another group's history.

James C. Scott and others studying the state's need to ascribe names to local features to render them legible and more widely useful at a removed, macro level is particularly analogous to the BAR's application of the FAP criteria:

> The sum of roads and place names in a small place, in fact, amounts to something of a local geography and history if one knows the stories, features, episodes, and family enterprises encoded within them. For officials who require a radically different form of order, such local knowledge, however quaint, is illegible. It privileges local knowledge over synoptic, standardized knowledge. In the case of colonial rule, when the conquerors speak an entirely different language, the unintelligibility of the vernacular landscape is a nearly insurmountable obstacle to effective rule. Renaming much of the landscape therefore is an essential step of imperial rule. . . . The conflict between vernacular, local meaning in place names and a higher-order grid of synoptic legibility . . . rests ultimately on the divergent purposes for which a semantic order is created.[57]

From the Ramapoughs' perspective, the BAR failed to realize the full implications of their local "stories, features, episodes, and family enterprises" because the FAP criteria and review process lend greater credence to those features as told and understood through the language of outsiders. Moreover, just as Scott and his coauthors discuss the potential cross-purposes between state officials seeking to access local communities and the intermediaries they used to gain such access, there is no guarantee of congruence between the purposes for which such descriptions were initially written and the purposes for which they were later read and understood by BAR staff. For example, Census workers historically have been concerned with ensuring that every enumerated person falls within a delineated group and consequently used such terms as "Jackson Whites." Unlike present BAR staff, however, enumerators were not concerned with a detailed examination of a person's asserted Indianness.[58]

While federal recognition of a group as a tribe does not exclusively determine individual American Indian identity, it does reflect certain attributes taken to signify "authentic" markers of both Indianness and tribalness. The question of whether the Ramapoughs met the definition of a tribe according to the mandatory criteria outlined in 25 C.F.R. Part 83 is contingent on a legal definition based on absolutes. Because the Ramapoughs adopted American material culture and lived very much like their neighbors, outside observers failed to recognize them as American Indian. Likewise, the colonial legal system, in which one was either white or nonwhite, resulted in the "documentary erasure" of Indian identity for groups such as the Ramapoughs.[59] In the absence of clear and absolute markers of Indianness and tribalness, the BAR concluded that the evidence submitted by the Ramapoughs was insufficient to prove they existed as an Indian tribe.

Whether described as "mixed race," "colored," "mulatto" or "tri-racial," the Ramapoughs existed as living "impure products."[60] Clearly neither white nor black, the Ramapoughs were identified and categorized as "mixed," thereby representing the tension and historical preoccupation with racial purity and impurity.[61] For the Ramapoughs, however, tribal identity was a matter not of race but of social relations grounded in history, culture, and consanguinity. The power and pervasiveness of the "one-drop rule" (ascribing as black anyone with any known or perceived African ancestry) led to the erasure of the Ramapoughs' Indianness in official records.[62] Largely invisible to outsiders within the biracial system, the Ramapoughs' ancestors were identified in official documents as "free persons of color," "mulatto," or "Jackson White" or labeled in other racialized ways to signify their mixed white, black, or American Indian ancestry.

Therein lies much of the problem. There is a powerful historical legacy and cultural context within which groups such as the Ramapoughs must operate. For many Indian groups along the Eastern Seaboard, long-standing confrontations and associations with successive waves of European immigrant populations and the accompanying slave trade produced a history that intersects with white and black America at many points.[63] As a result, Ramapoughs' tribal cultures, customs, and practices substantially differ from those of the tribes of the Central Plains and Southwest, where such intersections were less pervasive. In the case of the Ramapoughs, these intersections illustrate how the distinct yet interrelated concepts of race, ethnicity, and culture, when conflated, can have profound and lasting implications on the identity of groups and individuals.

As the primary way by which groups can become legally recognized as a tribe, the FAP relies on constructions of tribalness and Indianness that must be rendered authentic through the convention of legal discourse and social scientific analysis. This writing of social categories into law has the power to render as fixed and immutable the relatively fluid social process through which ethnic groups and their boundaries are continually formed and transformed. To deny the process of syncretism or to turn a blind eye to its inevitability after more than half a millennium of contact only perpetuates the notion of culture and identity as static and absolute. The result privileges one perspective over another and invalidates alternative modes of self-understanding and identity.

For social scientists, the FAP raises profound and lingering questions about ethnicity, identity, assimilation, and American Indian nationhood (to say nothing about the ethics of making groups prove their ethnic identity and ancestry). The Ramapoughs, marked by a history of incorporating European cultural and sociopolitical forms and norms as well as Christian religious values and lifestyles, were unable to make vital and visible their historical and continuous identity as an Indian tribe. This shortcoming rendered them largely invisible to outsiders, including the BAR staff and the assistant secretary of Indian affairs, who eventually denied their petition for federal acknowledgment.

Further Implications

The FAP must be understood as part of the general phenomenon that occurs when two distinct populations confront each other, one of whom has greater power (physical, political, and economic) than the other. Such disparities enable the group with the greater power to impose its values, views, and will on the other. In this context, federal laws and regulations establishing a particular view of what is a tribe and who is an Indian must be understood as reflecting the needs of U.S. polity and society as well as the priorities, assumptions, and biases of the particular historical and social context in which they appear. Because the needs, desires, and views of American society have changed over time, answers to the questions of who is an American Indian and what is an Indian tribe have been far from absolute but have evolved and developed.

There may be no better example of this evolution than the Ramapough Mountain Indians' case. Between the time of the initial proposed findings and final decisions on the Ramapough petition for federal acknowledgment, the applicable FAP regulations changed. During the second review, the changed criteria enabled the Ramapoughs to gain ground in their quest for recognition, although they remained unable to satisfy all of the requirements.[64]

The experience of the Ramapough Mountain Indians attests to the politics and problematics of a legally circumscribed identity. Their case exemplifies how the ability of groups to claim and assert an Indian identity is contingent on a set of legal criteria that speaks neither to the diversity of historical experiences nor to the paradoxical situation where both the rules for tribal acknowledgment and their implementation are in the hands of the same government responsible for dispossessing Native peoples of their land, cultural traditions, and practices. This paradox and the political aspects of recognition are even more evident in two related contexts.

First, the BAR staff, after reviewing and evaluating a group's petition, only makes a recommendation to the assistant secretary of Indian affairs regarding whether the group meets the criteria for federal acknowledgment. The assistant secretary—a political appointee who changes with virtually every new presidential administration, if not more frequently—makes the final decision on whether to extend that acknowledgment. These decisions may contravene the BAR recommendation, as in the decisions by Assistant Secretaries Kevin Gover and Neal McCaleb to override a recommendation against recognition of the Eastern Pequot Tribe (though their decisions, too, were later reversed).

Second, groups seeking recognition may pursue an alternative to the FAP: recognition by means of federal legislation. As with other federal legislation, recognition bills must originate from supportive congressional members as sponsors and gain enough political support in both houses of Congress for passage. Enactment of such bills may have as much or more to do with the country's other priorities as it does with the relevant group's "Indianness." This situation is exemplified by the 1956 federal recognition bill for the Lumbee Tribe of North Carolina, which granted the Lumbees tribal status but denied them all of the rights and privileges extended to other federally recognized tribes.[65] Furthermore, the Lumbees have no means of escape from the legislative track for federal acknowledgment—their recognition statute, in conjunction with the FAP regulations, makes them ineligible for the BAR administrative petition process.[66] Their efforts to gain recognition in the politically charged legislative arena are ongoing.

Contrary to the way most people conceptualize individual and collective identity, the debate over American Indian identity remains more than an academic or personal matter. Federal recognition of tribes determines the existence and extent of tribal group political authority as well as the tribe's resultant civil and criminal jurisdiction, land claims, child custody rights, and myriad other legal and financial matters, including natural resources rights and the right to establish tribal gaming operations. For example, the original federal statutory conception of recognized versus nonrecognized tribes and whether a tribe falls "under Federal jurisdiction" as laid out in the Indian Reorganization Act[67] lie at the heart of the 2009 *Carcieri v. Salazar* case, one of the most far-reaching U.S. Supreme Court opinions in Indian Country today because of its potential effect on Indian land title.[68]

The U.S. Supreme Court's opinion in *Carcieri* centered on the IRA's 1934 definition of "Indian" as "persons of Indian descent who are members *of any recognized Indian tribe now under Federal jurisdiction.*"[69] In its opinion, the Supreme Court focused on the word "now" in the definition of "Indian" and found it to mean June 18, 1934—the date of the IRA's enactment. As a result, the court held that another provision of the IRA that applies to "Indians" does not grant the secretary of the interior authority to take land into trust for tribes not "under federal jurisdiction" in 1934. A key issue raised by *Carcieri* is the distinction between a tribe that is "under federal jurisdiction" and one that is "recognized"—if indeed such a distinction exists. The Court has yet to address the issue. As a result, much uncertainty has arisen as to what it meant to have been "recognized" or "under federal jurisdiction" in 1934 as well as to the status of land taken into trust for tribes after 1934 under the IRA, especially for tribes that were recognized after that date via such processes as the FAP.

With so much at stake in the FAP, allegations of impropriety abound. Supporters of petitioning groups allege that the federal government plays more the role of gatekeeper than of impartial arbiter of tribalness and Indianness. The federal government undoubtedly has an interest in reducing the costs of administering its trust relationship with tribes and tribal members and thus has a correlating interest in controlling the number of groups acknowledged as tribes. Those tribes already recognized may have a similar interest in limiting the total number of federally recognized tribes out of fear of competition for scarce federal resources. These interests have combined with historical circumstances to deny the acknowledgment of many groups with Indian ancestry and thereby deny their members the rights and benefits reserved for federally recognized tribes.

Others question the motivation by groups such as the Ramapough for seeking federal recognition, alleging that such status is being pursued only for the material benefits that may ensue.[70] While the materialistic motives for asserting a tribal identity cannot be completely ignored, the practice of describing these groups as "invented" tribes or their cultural traditions as "artificially constructed" does not give us license to dismiss them as illegitimate. Dismissal only begs the question of how far back in time we have to go to satisfy criteria of givenness.[71]

Conclusion

This examination of the FAP reveals that both the criteria used to determine tribal identity and the process through which evidence is evaluated have been not merely the means to make tribes legible but also the means to provide the "authoritative tune to which most of the [Indian] population must dance."[72] In its objectification and standardization of the seven mandatory criteria required of groups seeking federal recognition as Indian tribes, the FAP imposes its definition of what constitutes an Indian tribe. At the same time that it confers recognition on some groups, the federal government has simultaneously created the residual category of non–federally recognized tribes by treating all such classified groups as nontribal entities and their members as nonnatives. In so doing, the federal government, in its need to make legible those tribes to whom it will confer legal recognition, has provided the means by which it and others can discriminate against and between Indian groups and peoples.

By examining how American Indian collective identity is ensconced in federal law as it defines a tribe, we have argued that the "objective" process and criteria used under federal law to recognize groups as tribes rely on inherently simplified and subjective interpretations of historical documents. As a result, certain conceptions of group identity are reinforced and privileged to the exclusion of other forms of social organization and self-understanding. This process, granted authority and made enforceable through federal law and regulation, has been used to assault the right to be Indian in much the same way that it has been used to assault American

Indian rights to lands and resources. And just as the federal government made legible and therefore controllable lands and resources, so, too, has it exercised its authoritarian power by imposing what constitutes the qualities and characteristics of an Indian tribe.

Notes

1. See American Indian Policy Commission, *Report on Terminated and Non-federally Recognized Indians, Final Report* (Washington, D.C.: U.S. Government Printing Office, 1976). See also Mark Edwin Miller, *Forgotten Tribes: Unrecognized Indians and the Federal Acknowledgment Process* (Lincoln: University of Nebraska Press, 2004).

2. When the FAP was first established, the regulations were designated as Part 54 of Title 25 of the Code of Federal Regulations (May 9, 1978). In 1982, the regulations were officially redesignated as Part 83 of Title 25 of the Code of Federal Regulations. See *Federal Register*, March 30, 1982, 13326–28.

3. We are indebted to James C. Scott's critique of how governments use political methods to make "legible" societies, cultures, and practices through the imposition of authoritarian state power that disregards the values, desires, and objections of its subjects. See James C. Scott, *Seeing Like a State: How Certain Schemes to Improve the Human Condition Have Failed* (New Haven: Yale University Press, 1998).

4. Ibid., 81.

5. See, e.g., N. Bruce Duthu, *American Indians and the Law* (New York: Penguin, 2008).

6. A list of federally recognized tribes is published periodically in the *Federal Register*. The most recent list appeared in Department of the Interior, Bureau of Indian Affairs, "Indian Entities Recognized and Eligible to Receive Services from the Bureau of Indian Affairs," *Federal Register*, August 10, 2012, 47868–73.

7. See, e.g., Frank Pommersheim, *Broken Landscapes: Indians, Indian Tribes, and the Constitution* (New York: Oxford University Press, 2007); John R. Wunder, ed., *Indian Sovereignty* (New York: Taylor and Francis, 2005).

8. *Johnson v. M'Intosh*, 21 U.S. (8 Wheat.) 543, 574 (1823).

9. See, e.g., William Quinn Jr., "Federal Acknowledgement of Indian Tribes: The Historical Development of a Legal Concept," *American Journal of Legal History* 34 (1990): 333.

10. *Johnson v. M'Intosh*; *Cherokee Nation v. Georgia*, 30 U.S. (5 Pet.) 1 (1831); *Worcester v. Georgia*, 31 U.S. (6 Pet.) 515 (1832).

11. *Worcester*, 556.

12. Ibid., 559.

13. See David E. Wilkins, *American Indian Sovereignty and the U.S. Supreme Court: The Masking of Justice* (Austin: University of Texas Press, 1997).

14. 25 U.S.C. 461–79.

15. 25 U.S.C. 479; emphasis added

16. Indian groups relocated to Oklahoma during the early 1800s and the many Native Alaska villages and groups falling outside the purview of the IRA sought inclusion in the act's provisions. In response to this problem, Congress passed the Alaska Reorganization Act of 1936, which recognized groups "having a common bond of occupation, or association, or residence with a well defined neighborhood, common unity, or rural distinct" (May 1, 1936, ch. 254, 49 Stat. 1250), and the Oklahoma Indian Welfare Act of 1936, which similarly extended the provisions to groups outside the IRA's limited definition (June 26, 1936, codified at 25 U.S.C. 501–9).

17. Felix Cohen, *Handbook of Federal Indian Law* (Washington, D.C.: U.S. Government Printing Office, 2005), 171–72.

18. See, e.g., *Greene v. Babbitt*, 64 F. 3d 1266 (9th Cir. 1995); *Timpanogos Tribe v. Conway*, 286 F. 3d 1195 (10th Cir. 2002); *United States v. Washington*, 641 F. 2d 1368 (9th Cir. 1981).

19. See, e.g., *Koke v. Little Shell Tribe of Chippewa Indians of Montana, Inc.*, 315 Mont. 510, 68 P. 3d 814 (2003); *Gristede's Foods, Inc. v. Unkechuage Nation*, 660 F. Supp. 2d 442 (E.D.N.Y. 2009).

20. See 13 C.F.R. 124.109 (b)(3)(ii).

21. For an examination of the competing definitions and ways American Indian identity is contested and negotiated, see Eva Marie Garroutte, *Real Indians: Identity and Survival in Native America* (Berkeley: University of California Press, 2003). See also Brian Klopotek, *Recognition Odysseys: Indigeneity, Race, and Federal Tribal Recognition in Three Louisiana Indian Communities* (Durham: Duke University Press, 2011); Mark Edwin Miller, *Forgotten Tribes*; Joanne Barker, *Native Acts: Law, Recognition, and Cultural Authority* (Durham: Duke University Press, 2011).

22. Petition received by the Assistant Secretary–Indian Affairs from the Ramapough Mountain Indian Tribe seeking Federal Acknowledgment as an Indian Tribe under Part 83 of Title 25 of the *Code of Federal Regulations* (25 C.F.R. 83), 1992, 2.

23. Herbert C. Kraft, *The Lenape: Archaeology, History, and Ethnography* (Newark: New Jersey Historical Society, 1986).

24. Ibid., 232. See also Edward J. Lenik, *Indians in the Ramapos: Survival, Persistence, and Presence* (Ringwood: North New Jersey Highlands Historical Society, 1999).

25. Ramapough Mountain Indian Petition 1992; see also Ramapough Lenape Nation website http://www.ramapoughlenapenation.org/history.

26. Many of the source documents used in this section can be found on the U.S. Department of the Interior, Bureau of Indian Affairs, Office of Federal Acknowledgment website, http://www.bia.gov/WhoWeAre/AS-IA/OFA/index.htm. The primary document used in our analyses was U.S. Department of the Interior, Bureau of Indian Affairs, Office of Federal Acknowledgment, *Summary Under the Criteria and Evidence for Proposed Finding, Ramapough Mountain Indians, Inc.* (1993). This document includes the summary conclusions under each of the seven required criteria and historical, anthropological, and genealogical reports prepared by the BAR staff.

27. Ramapough Mountain Indians, "Receipt of Letter of Intent to Petition for Federal Acknowledgment of Existence as an Indian Tribe," *Federal Register*, September 11, 1979, 52890.

28. "Proposed Findings against Acknowledgment of the Ramapough Mountain Indians, Inc.," *Federal Register*, December 8, 1993, 64662.

29. Ibid.

30. "Procedures for Establishing That an American Indian Group Exists as an Indian Tribe: Final Rule," *Federal Register*, February 25, 1994, 9280–9300.

31. See *U.S. Department of the Interior, Bureau of Indian Affairs, Office of Federal Acknowledgment*, "Summary Under the Criteria and Evidence for Final Determination against Federal Acknowledgment of the Ramapough Mountain Indians, Inc.," 1996, 7.

32. "Notice of Final Determination," *Federal Register*, February 6, 1996, 4476.

33. See "Reconsidered Final Determination against Federal Acknowledgment of the Ramapough Mountain Indians, Inc.," *Federal Register*, January 7, 1998, 888–89.

34. *Summary under the Criteria and Evidence*, 6.

35. Ibid.

36. Ibid.

37. Ibid., 5; emphasis added.

38. Karen I. Blu, *The Lumbee Problem: The Making of an American Indian People* (New York: Cambridge University Press, 1980). See also Malinda Maynor Lowery, *Lumbee Indians in the Jim Crow South: Race, Identity, and the Making of a Nation* (Chapel Hill: University of North Carolina Press, 2011).

39. "Reconsidered Final Determination," 12 n. 9.

40. *Summary under the Criteria and Evidence*, 11.

41. Ibid.

42. Ibid.

43. Ibid., 13.

44. Ibid.

45. Ibid., 14.

46. Ibid.

47. Ibid., 15.

48. Ibid., 188.

49. Angela A. Gonzales, "Racial Legibility: The Federal Census and the (Trans) Formation of 'Black' and 'Indian' Identity, 1790–1950," in *IndiVisible: African–Native American Lives in the Americas,* ed. Gabrielle Tayac (Washington, D.C.: Smithsonian Institution Press, 2009); Angela A. Gonzales, Judy Kertesz, and Gabrielle Tayac, "Eugenics as Indian Removal: Sociohistoric Processes and the De(con)struction of American Indians in the Southeast," *Public Historian* 29 (2007): 53–67.

50. See, e.g., Daniel Collins, "The Racially-Mixed People of the Ramapos: Undoing the Jackson White Legends," *American Anthropologist* 74 (1972): 1276–85.

51. David Miller, *The Forsaken Jackson Whites* (New York: New York Herald Tribune, 1961).

52. Calvin L. Beale, "An Overview of the Phenomenon of Mixed Racial Isolates in the United States," *American Anthropologist* 74 (1972): 539. See also Calvin L. Beale, "American Triracial Isolates: Their Status and Pertinence to Genetic Research," *Eugenics Quarterly* 4 (1957): 187–97.

53. See also Brewton Berry, *Almost White* (New York: Macmillan, 1963); Lenik, *Indians in the Ramapos.*

54. For a history of the eugenics movement and its promotion of involuntary sterilization among "degenerates," see Philip Reilly, *The Surgical Solution: A History of Involuntary Sterilization in the United States* (Baltimore: Johns Hopkins University Press, 1991); Daniel Kevles, *In the Name of Eugenics: Genetics and the Uses of Human Heredity* (New York: Cambridge University Press, 1995); Elof Axel Carlson, *The Unfit: A History of a Bad Idea* (Cold Spring Harbor, N.Y.: Cold Spring Harbor Laboratory Press, 2001); Edwin Black, *War against the Weak: Eugenics and America's Campaign to Create a Master Race* (New York: Basic Books, 2003).

55. A closer consideration of the history of eugenics also illustrates the ways in which universities and state and federal governments found themselves intervening in questions of native identity. In such cases, notions of blood and descent were bound up with perceptions of authenticity and the defective biology that tainted certain individuals and the communities to which they belonged.

56. *Summary under the Criteria and Evidence,* 14.

57. James C. Scott, John Tehranian, and Jeremy Mathias, "The Production of Legal Identities Proper to States: The Case of the Permanent Family Surname," *Comparative Studies in Society and History* 44 (2002): 5–6.

58. Ibid., 8–9.

59. Gonzales, Kertesz, and Tayac, "Eugenics as Indian Removal."

60. James Clifford, *The Predicament of Culture: Twentieth-Century Ethnography, Literature, and Art* (Cambridge: Harvard University Press, 1988), 6.

61. See, e.g., Lenik, *Indians in the Ramapos*; Beale, "American Triracial Isolates"; Beale, "Overview"; Berry, *Almost White*; Eugene B. Greissman, "The American Isolates," *American Anthropologist* 74 (1972): 693–94; David Miller, *Forsaken Jackson Whites*; William S. Pollitzer, "The Physical Anthropology and Genetics of Marginal People of the Southeastern United States," *American Anthropologist* 74 (1972): 719–34.

62. Gonzales, Kertesz, and Tayac, "Eugenics as Indian Removal."

63. See also Susan Greenbaum, "What's in a Label?: Identity Problems of Southern Indian Tribes," *Journal of Ethnic Studies* 19 (1991): 107–26; Anne Merline McCulloch and David E. Wilkins, "Constructing Nations within States: The Quest for Federal Recognition by the Catawba and Lumbee Tribes," *American Indian Quarterly* 19 (1995): 361–415; Gerald Torres and Kathryn Milun, "Translating *Yonnondio* by Precedent and Evidence: The Mashpee Indian Case," *Duke Law Journal* 4 (1990): 625–59.

64. *Federal Register*, February 24, 1994, 9280–9300.

65. P.L. 84-570, Act of June 7, 1956, 70 Stat. 254.

66. See 25 C.F.R. 83.3(e), stating, "Groups which are . . . subject to congressional legislation terminating or forbidding the Federal relationship may not be acknowledged under these regulations."

67. 25 U.S.C. 461–79.

68. *Carcieri v. Salazar*, 129 S. Ct. 1058, 555 U.S., 172 L. Ed. 2d 791 (2009).

69. 25 U.S.C. 479; emphasis added.

70. Quinn, *Federal Acknowledgment*; Leah C. Simms, "Unraveling a Deceptive Oral History: The Indian Ancestry Claims of Philip S. Proctor and His Descendants," http://www.eskimo.com/~lesims/tay.acfraud.html.

71. Edwin N. Wilmsen and Patrick McAllister, *The Politics of Difference: Ethnic Premises in a World of Power* (Chicago: University of Chicago Press, 1996), 3.

72. Scott, *Seeing Like a State*, 83.

Racial Science and Federal Recognition

Lumbee Indians in the Jim Crow South

MALINDA MAYNOR LOWERY

To recognize nonreservation tribes under the 1934 Indian Reorganization Act, the Bureau of Indian Affairs (BIA) struggled to derive fair criteria that would conform to Commissioner John Collier's commitment to using social science as an underpinning for policy. But the bureau's notions of Indianness hardly conformed to Indians' own ideas. The BIA's work in North Carolina among the Lumbee Indians is a quintessential example of this conflict. The relationship between the BIA and the Lumbees prompts questions such as "How did Indians simultaneously resist and adopt outsiders' criteria for Indian identity?" and "What are the consequences of using social science methods and assumptions to measure identity?" This essay goes beyond a commonly asked question, "Are Lumbees Indians?" to ask, "Exactly what is 'Indian' from both the federal and tribal perspectives?"

In 1936, Indians in Robeson County, North Carolina, invited three men from the BIA in Washington, D.C., to visit and enroll them as "Siouan" Indians, the first step to gaining long-sought federal acknowledgment of their identity. One of the men was Carl Seltzer, a Harvard-trained physical anthropologist who specialized in anthropometry, the study of human physical measurements—head shape and size, skin color, hair texture, tooth shape, height, and many other features.

The BIA employed Seltzer to determine whether Robeson County's Indians qualified for acknowledgment under the Indian Reorganization Act (IRA). Congress had passed the act in 1934, launching the major policy reform period known as the Indian New Deal. Among its other provisions, the IRA ended the cultural and land loss brought about by the previous generations of assimilation policies. The act's preamble established its intent: "To conserve and develop Indian lands and resources; to extend to Indians the right to form business and other organizations; to establish a credit system for Indians; to grant certain rights of home rule to Indians; to provide for vocational education for Indians." Congress accomplished these provisions by abolishing future allotment of Indian lands; authorizing the restoration of remaining surplus lands to tribal control; providing funds for the acquisition of more land; granting tribes the right to incorporate or write constitutions and by-laws and to form other organizations; establishing a loan fund for economic development; and expanding the federal civil service requirements to include and give preference to Indians.[1]

The IRA defined an "Indian" in several different ways. The definition relied primarily on the political relationship to the federal government that had been enshrined in judge-made Indian law dating back to the 1830s, which in some cases eschewed blood quantum as a standard. In other cases, however, it embraced blood quantum, an identity marker that was measured by ancestry and appearance. According to the act, an Indian was a member of a recognized tribe, "*whether or not* residing on an Indian reservation and regardless of the degree of blood," or a descendant of a member of a recognized tribe living on a reservation, "regardless of blood." Alternately, an Indian could be "a person of one-half or more Indian blood, whether or not affiliated with a recognized tribe, and whether or not they have ever resided on a reservation."[2] Robeson County Indians were members of this final class of persons—provided they could prove their blood quantum eligibility. To be eligible for acknowledgment under the IRA, individuals had to have at least one full-blood Indian parent, and their phenotypes had to conform to physical anthropologists' assessments of what such individuals might look like. The theory behind this requirement presumed that Indians with more "Indian blood" retained a greater degree of "Indian culture" and thus deserved federal acknowledgment.

New Deal Indian policy did not match Robeson County Indians' social order or the order of most tribes that came under its purview. At that time, the BIA was called the Office of Indian Affairs, or OIA, and officials hoped to develop self-governing Indian communities so that Indians could determine their destinies according to their own cultural traditions, "but only in the sense that communities followed the basic ideological guidelines the [OIA] established," according to authors Vine Deloria Jr. and Clifford Lytle.[3] These ideological guidelines contained certain assumptions about Indian identity, and in Robeson County, the OIA (now the BIA) used the same criteria that white southerners had established: ancestry and appearance.

Confident that they would pass Seltzer's tests, Robeson County Indian leaders selected about two hundred individuals to participate. Seltzer asked each person to stand on an exhibit platform while he inspected the individual with tape measures, rulers, calipers, and other instruments. For example, Seltzer measured the cephalic index (the ratio of head length to head width), which anthropometrists considered the key marker of racial ancestry. He also scratched a participant's skin along the breastbone, looking for the color left behind. A red mark was a sign of predominantly "white blood," while a white mark was a sign of predominantly "Indian blood." According to Indian oral tradition, Seltzer also conducted a "pencil test." He stuck a pencil in the subject's hair; if it fell out, the person had "Indian" hair. If the pencil stayed, the subject had "Negroid" hair. He took scrupulous notes, circling symbols on a chart and scribbling numbers, and then he photographed the subject's face and profile—all in the name of determining the quantity and quality of the person's "Indian blood" and "Indian culture." Officials at the BIA recalled later that the Indian subjects stood around in amazement as they watched Seltzer do his work, but the officials had trouble communicating their criteria to their objects of study. "Our task was made difficult at the outset," they remembered, "by the fact that these people did not have a clear understanding of the term Indian."[4] The examination surely mystified the Indian participants, who had very definite ideas about who they were.

For Indians in Robeson County, their functioning social order revolved around identity markers of kinship and settlement and a decentralized, contested political structure. Indians in Robeson County had lived as Indians in that place for hundreds of years, but non-Indians surrounded them. Native Americans lived within a system of racial segregation that circumscribed their ability to express their identity as Indians. They scraped together a living in the midst of an economic depression that crippled much wealthier communities. These changes in the first part of the twentieth century had encouraged many nonwhites to leave the South in search of a better living. But Indians in Robeson County stayed in their homeland and maintained a sense of themselves as an Indian people. To them, an Indian was not an isolated individual, standing on a platform, whose identity could be measured by scientific instruments. Instead, an Indian was a part of a community of people, and Indians' identity expressed what their community thought was important. Hair, teeth, and skin color did nothing to help maintain their community in a society full of racial stereotypes; rather, the key to their identity was community residence, kin ties, and faithfulness to the tribe's social values and institutions. The government men were just as mystified by Indians' criteria as Indians were amazed by the government's ideas. Seltzer's colleagues wrote that these Indians "considered anybody who lived in their community as one of them," articulating that the Indians' criteria for inclusion involved a sense of belonging.[5] For Indians in Robeson County, identity was their birthright; it could not be measured by instruments designed to sort, label, and categorize. Yet they expected their complex web of kinship, place, and community to make sense to a bureaucratic system of federal recognition driven not by belonging but by exclusivity.

Why would a people who had always known who they were subject themselves to Seltzer's tests? The answers to this question begin a half century earlier and are rooted in three exchanges between Indians and non-Indians: how Indians established their own definitions of identity, how southern white supremacists implemented racial segregation, and how the BIA created a supposedly objective racial identity test to apportion limited government resources to Native American people. Indians agreed to the tests because they thought the BIA would accept their identity markers to rescue them from the dependency to which segregation subjected them. But the BIA decided to use its own definitions.

Modernity, White Supremacy, and the Indian New Deal

Southern segregation had the same roots as anthropometry. Both systems of thought sprang from notions of modernity that enthralled policy makers in the late nineteenth and early twentieth centuries at both the local and federal levels. In many ways, segregation arose from the quest to categorize and order what the industrial economy had made into a rather anonymous, impersonal South. "Modernity" is a sociologist's shorthand for industrial civilization—U.S. historians often use it to talk about the nineteenth and twentieth centuries. The temporal and regional boundaries of the modern United States are vague and subject to debate, but segregation seems in some ways to have marked the visible emergence of a modern South. The systematic rules of segregation arose from the anonymous social interactions typical of urban spaces, where a black person's inferior economic status could not be assumed. Several scholars have shown how such a social structuring enterprise provided evidence of the South's modernity. Modern spaces and states were legible to outsiders; defined strict categories and hierarchies of people, ideas, and things; and valued administrative simplification. Segregation essentialized the South's spectrum of ethnicities and economic statuses and made white supremacy a seemingly natural device to keep society peaceful, prosperous, and "progressive." As people moved into industrialized spaces, those in power found it necessary to make new rules and institute exceptions to old ones. Law and policy reflected those rules, which sought to reinforce white supremacy. Indians were not simply passive victims of these changes, however—they rejected and accommodated modern America as well.[6]

With the exception of historian Philip Deloria's work, little has been done to understand Indians' relationship to modernity. In *Indians in Unexpected Places*, Deloria argues that whites stereotyped Indians as premodern or primitive not because Indians did not participate in modern society but so that whites could better measure their own modernity—whites could be scientific, rational, and wealthy if Indians were superstitious, incompetent, and poor. In other words, the premodern/modern dichotomy did not exist without white privilege.[7]

This dichotomy was part of the foundation of white supremacy in its twentieth-century form—the system's authority lay in its power to include or exclude based on whether a group or individual fit the modern mold. White supremacy's authority lay not in the system's power completely to ban all nonwhites but in its power to control the gateway to the status that accompanied a white identity. Whites—and no one else—controlled who had what kind of access to the privileges of whiteness. Being modern was one of those privileges. The creation of segregation required that white supremacists engage in modernity and see the world in terms of essentially "white" and essentially "black" people; Indians fit neither category but had to be rationalized in some way to be subject to the system's rules.

Indian New Deal policy also stemmed from similar ideas about modernity. The relationship between Jim Crow and federal Indian policy may seem unexpected, but only if one expects that Indians belonged outside the framework of southern race relations or that southern Indians belonged outside the framework of federal Indian policy.[8] The BIA deployed ideas about Indian identity that were the same as those white southerners had established: ancestry and appearance. But rather than relying on local knowledge to determine legitimacy, as white southerners did, the BIA used the "science" of anthropometry. Collier believed that the IRA offered a modern policy solution to problems rooted in Indians' premodern existence, and the assumptions behind those solutions were scientific in nature. White supremacy—a viewpoint that Collier never shared—also capitalized on the dichotomy between the modern and the premodern to sustain its authority. Unwittingly, the IRA supported white supremacist assumptions in Robeson County.

Race and the Roots of Robeson County Indian Identity

Indians in Robeson County forged their identity in a crucible of cultural and political diversity. In the late seventeenth and eighteenth centuries, Indian families from different Iroquoian, Siouan, and Algonkian language groups migrated to Robeson County from distant places. They sought refuge from European diseases, warfare, and slavery. In the nineteenth century, Indians shaped their core identity around kin ties and the specific settlements that extended families constructed. An ethic of reciprocity knit together these social and geographic communities. Tribal names, constitutions, bounded territories, and the other aspects of tribal life we take for granted today had no place in the eighteenth- and nineteenth-century world of Robeson County Indians. Kinship created a sense of belonging in the group. These Indians have claimed different political affiliations since their coalescence, yet all acknowledge that they are part of the same extended kinship group and share a deep attachment to their homeland in Robeson County. Their ability to disagree politically yet preserve their underlying unity, combined with their kinship and place connections, suggests that their sense of themselves as Indians is the product of a kind of layering process. This layering allows for disagreement within the group on some levels while they preserve their common identity and their distinctiveness from their black and white neighbors.

Much of the historical literature on Indian ethnicity has defined an Indian as an individual who is racially different from American immigrant groups; who has a historical, continuous attachment to a particular place; and who belongs to a community that shares a common political organization and set of rituals different from its neighbors. As historian Alexandra Harmon has summarized, "Too often Indians' history is written as if protagonists, authors, and readers have no reason to wonder who is Indian," yet Indian people are burdened with defending their identity more often and more extensively than any other American ethnic group. Historians' criteria seem to stem from organic characteristics of Indian tribes, but sociologists and legal historians have identified how such criteria depend more on non-Indian concerns than on anything "true" or "natural" about Indian communities. Many Indian communities are more accurately characterized by geographic movement (rather than attachment to one specific place) and expansive attitudes about adoption and cultural exchange (resulting in racial mixing and cultural adaptation). Yet their identities as Indians do not dissipate as a result of these changes. In response to these trends, ethnic identity has been described more accurately as a process resulting from one group's attempt to differentiate itself from another group, or, as sociologist Fredrik Barth called it, "boundary maintenance." Identity is a group's process of inclusion and exclusion, a constant renegotiation that can include racial ancestry but is not exclusively linked to it.[9]

Seltzer and the BIA nevertheless believed that understanding racial ancestry was key to understanding Indian identity. Lumbees seem to have a particular reputation for multiracial ancestry. Perhaps our seemingly anomalous position in the South raises the question—whites, the argument goes, must have classed the nonwhite Lumbees socially with African Americans; therefore, many Lumbees must have married African Americans because they could not have married anyone who was white.[10] Such reasoning is a product more of scholars' own impressions of a black/white color line than it is a historical reality of earlier times. At the heart of these arguments are two converging assumptions: (1) that ancestry and cultural identity are consanguineous rather than subject to the changing contexts of human relations, and (2) that white supremacy is a timeless norm rather than a social structure designed to ensure the dominance of a certain group.[11] While it may not have been the norm for whites to marry or have offspring with partners outside of their own communities, it certainly happened with enough frequency to generate a wealth of lawsuits regarding miscegenation.[12] That body of law also indicates that although whites benefited from lumping blacks and Indians together legally as "nonwhite," Indians and blacks did not always see themselves in those terms and actively resisted such homogenization.[13] Throughout the United States, whites, Indians, and blacks certainly interacted, had relationships, conducted business with one another, and shared political aspirations. Some families and individuals choose to identify with their multiracial heritage, and some do not. Such choices had little to do with whether a group articulated a black, white, or Indian identity.[14] Rather, that articulation was based on layers of identity that evolved over hundreds of years.

For example, Lumbees tend to discuss ancestry and kinship as somewhat distinct layers of identity. I was taught that our mixed racial ancestry does not make us any less Indian—outsiders who marry in can stay in because they can live with and even adopt some of the symbols and attitudes that Lumbees have used to maintain our community. The children of such unions are Lumbees because they have Lumbee family and perhaps because they and their descendants stay in the community and contribute to it for generations, upholding the values their non-Indian ancestor initially embraced. This view, I think, generally sums up Lumbee attitudes about our mixed-race ancestry.

Yet much scholarship about the Lumbees has taken ancestry as its central question rather than as one among a number of factors to consider in identity; these authors have reinforced the idea that Lumbees are unique in their multiracial roots. Outsiders typically have overestimated the extent of Indian-white or Indian-black offspring in Robeson County, while Indians themselves have underestimated it. Thanks to the U.S. Census's highly obscure and constantly changing definitions of race and the silence of the nineteenth century's local marriage records on the subject of race, we have little written evidence to back up either assertion. The most openhanded estimates of intermarriage based on the Census, which include households that showed any indication of a possible interracial relationship, demonstrate that the rates were highest in the earliest decades after the American Revolution and steadily declined through 1880. In 1790, 16 percent of Indian households contained members described as different races, while by 1880, that number had shrunk to 2 percent. The vast majority of these households contained people with Indian surnames and people described as white. The marriage records, which are arguably more reliable because they included both spouses' surnames, present a somewhat different picture. Between 1799 and 1868, the Indian/non-Indian intermarriage rate was 24.4 percent. Further research in marriage records may determine how that rate changed over time and whether the marriages were predominantly Indian-white or Indian-black.[15]

Despite the reassurance provided by numbers, the reality of "crossblood" love and marriage is still unknown, but we can be certain that Indians determined their own criteria for whom to marry while being influenced by a growing bifurcation of race in the South and a stigma attached to blackness. For Indians, there is no "pure" past by which our authenticity and legitimacy can be accurately measured. All Indians—indeed, all people—are crossbloods in that they live with and negotiate multiple identities without degenerating culturally, spiritually, socially, or physically. Lumbees are not unique for their multiracial ancestry, even among Native Americans. The volumes of historical literature about Indians in the Southeast, the Northeast, and even the "real Indians" out West proves that the only constant in Indian history, the only thing Indians have always done, is love everyone, regardless of race. But the categories of knowledge instituted by settler societies have obscured this reality in favor of a focus on purity that makes

Indian people confused and angry. Contemporary Lumbee people take the pejorative association with multiracial ancestry very personally, not because we deny the truth of it but because we know it stigmatizes us and not other ethnic groups and Indian tribes whose ancestry is equally mixed.[16]

This resentment stretches back to the aftermath of emancipation and the rise of a different form of white supremacy. As southern whites struggled to recapture their supremacy, Indians needed new ways to affirm their identity. No longer would knowledge of one's ancestors and allegiance to one's home place suffice to mark an individual as an Indian. White southerners based their new society on the existence of two social categories, white and colored. Indians rejected whites' attempts to classify them as colored and sought ways to remind others of their Indianness. Indian families from different settlements disagreed, however, about how to approach these issues. These disagreements produced additional layers of Indian identity. For example, members of the Brooks family, who lived in what was called the Brooks Settlement, chose to articulate their Indian identity by reaching out to Native Americans from other places. They invited a group of Mohawks from Upstate New York to Robeson County to help establish a longhouse and remind surrounding Indians and non-Indians of their distinctiveness.[17] Indians in other settlements took a different approach to reinforcing their separate place in the southern racial hierarchy, embracing racial segregation and pressing for Indian-only schools.

In the creation of Indian-only schools, Indians' ideas about identity began to engage with white segregationists' ideas about the racial hierarchy. The 1835 North Carolina Constitution had labeled Indians "free persons of color" to deny their right to vote. Although the 1868 Reconstruction constitution restored the franchise, state law provided only for schools for white and black children. Under this system, Indians had no choice but to attend school with blacks. Some Indians did so, but many seemed to believe that attending "colored" schools would have undermined Indians' distinctiveness.[18] In 1885, the North Carolina state legislature passed a law that recognized Robeson County Indians as "Croatans" and provided for separate Indian schools, enabling Indians to express their separate identity through education. Native Americans also retained the ballot, in contrast to their black neighbors, whom conservative Democrats disfranchised in 1900. With white politicians recognizing Indians' tribal identity and their votes, Indians capitalized on their schools to gain political influence. This creation of a legally recognized "tribe" generated a political layer of Indian identity. Identification as a tribe formed the basis for negotiations with white supremacists and for disagreements within the group about the strategies for preserving their separate identity.

Race, Tribe, and Segregation

But adopting segregation to preserve distinctiveness proved to be a double-edged sword—excluding blacks and whites from their community assured Indians' control over their own affairs, but it also conceded whites' power to govern race relations. Indians determined their social boundaries according to what whites were willing to accept. White Democrats in the state legislature did not acknowledge Indians as Croatans and provide them with their own schools out of goodwill—whites knew that doing so would benefit them and the system of white supremacy. The origins of the name "Croatan," for example, demonstrated how recognizing Indian identity upheld white supremacy. The name stemmed from Robeson County legislator Hamilton McMillan's misinterpretation of Indian oral tradition. Elders told McMillan that their ancestors came from "Roanoke," meaning the Roanoke River region of northeastern North Carolina. McMillan, however, interpreted "Roanoke" to mean Roanoke Island, the place from which the Lost Colony, the first English settlement in America, had disappeared three centuries earlier. The colonists supposedly went to a place called Croatoan to join the Indians there. McMillan presumed that Indians in Robeson County descended from the state's first English settlers and friendly Indian tribes.

For most non-Indians at this time, being "Indian" meant belonging to a tribe; white North Carolinians saw identifying a historic lineage as necessary to be sure that these Indians were a distinct racial group, that they were not in fact African Americans. The "Croatan" label provided not only a tribal name but a noble heritage. The name embodied a legend of white ancestry, white sacrifice, and white heroism. For a society obsessed with race and the traits that blood supposedly transmitted, emphasizing the tribe's white ancestry increased support for separate schools.[19] Acknowledging a separate race of Indians based on the fact that they had white ancestry and, perhaps more important, lacked black ancestry provided a wonderful justification for white supremacy and the correctness of segregation. McMillan's history of Indian identity in Robeson County supported racial segregation, secured Indians' votes for the Democratic Party, and created new avenues for Indian leadership in the form of Indian schools.

Following their acknowledgment as Croatan, Indian settlement leaders divided over how best to secure their separate identity and autonomy. At the same time, Indians' relationships to the state continued to change, and they began to investigate the possibility of federal recognition. In 1910, Indians petitioned their U.S. senator for recognition as "Cherokee Indians of Robeson County," a name they wanted to adopt because local whites soured the name "Croatan" by shortening it to "Cro," an obvious reference to "black crows" and Jim Crow. The petition to Congress failed, but the state legislature agreed to the name change and Indians in Robeson County became known as Cherokees, over the objections of the state's Eastern Band of Cherokees. The Robeson County Indians sought federal recognition because although segregation reinforced some aspects of their identity, they feared that the state would take away their right to vote and their ability to control their schools. They desired federal recognition to shield themselves from the uncertainties inherent in the Jim Crow system.

But gaining federal recognition was a capricious and complicated political process. When a tribe petitioned Congress for acknowledgment, the House and Senate Committees on Indian Affairs remanded the proposed bill to the BIA for a recommendation. Hidden political agendas and assumptions limited Robeson County Indians' success. Native Americans' attempts to gain acknowledgment revealed the historical disagreement between the two branches of government about federal recognition. North Carolina's congressional delegation saw recognition as a political matter, seeking to please their white and Indian constituents and regarding recognition as a confirmation of North Carolina's system of segregation and white supremacy. The BIA, conversely, approached recognition from an academic perspective, seeking to verify tribal identity according to anthropological standards, particularly the presence of "Indian blood," as opposed to the absence of "black blood," which was politicians' main concern. Indians responded to these divergent purposes by splitting into political factions.

Political Divisions over Federal Recognition Strategies

One group of Indian leaders called themselves Cherokees, demonstrating their commitment to the state government's version of Indian history and their acceptance of white supremacy. In 1932, the Cherokees of Robeson County asked North Carolina's congressional delegation to introduce a bill granting them recognition and permission to attend federal Indian schools.

The BIA recommended rejecting the bill, however, and characterized the ancestry of Robeson County Indians as racially mixed. The report also cited esteemed anthropologist James Mooney, who believed that Robeson County Indians shared nothing with the Eastern Band Cherokees whom he had studied. The BIA also stated that it could find no evidence that Robeson County's Indians had a historic treaty relationship with the federal government. The "Cherokee" name did little to help Robeson County Indians—the Eastern Band of Cherokees' objections and the previous Croatan designation confused non-Indians, who depended on tribal names to help them distinguish Indians from non-Indians. Furthermore, the bureau warned that passing the bill would bring the tribe under the jurisdiction of the federal government, a situation that the BIA wanted to avoid as a consequence of the already heavy demand on federal resources dedicated to Indian tribes. North Carolina's congressmen allowed the bill to die in committee.[20]

The following year, Indians in Robeson County demanded new leadership and reinvigorated their efforts to secure congressional recognition. Since the Cherokee name had failed to impress the BIA, Indian leaders first approached the bureau for advice on a satisfactory tribal designation. John Collier, the newly appointed commissioner of Indian affairs and architect of the Indian New Deal, sent a delegation of Indians to visit anthropologist John Swanton at the Bureau of American Ethnology. Collier came into his position committed to applying anthropological theory to Indian policy. Swanton specialized in southeastern Indians, and Collier hoped he could help the Robeson County group arrive at a tribal name that would distinguish them from other Indians and from blacks. Through research in colonial records, Swanton arrived at the name "Siouan Indians of Lumber River," a label that invoked a native language family that predominated in the region where Robeson County's Indians lived. In 1933, North Carolina's senator introduced a bill recognizing these Indians as "Siouans" rather than "Cherokees." Indian leaders who retained the Cherokee identity objected to the bill and denounced the Siouan leadership to the congressional delegation, claiming that the Siouans were "enemies to white people" and that the Siouan recognition bill would damage Indians' claims to their own schools because the state recognized them as Cherokees, not as Siouans. While the Robeson County Cherokees' main concern about the Siouan bill was how it would affect the state's support of Indian schools, leaders of the Cherokee faction chose to express their concern by undermining the Siouan leadership in the eyes of Congress. Convinced that the Siouan promoters did not represent the interests of white supremacy, the congressional delegation again permitted the bill to die in committee.[21]

Those who favored keeping the name "Cherokee" believed that that designation would protect their hard-fought victories for education in the state—victories secured by white supremacists' notions of Indian identity. Those who favored the name "Siouan," however, looked to the BIA's anthropological standards of Indian identity to support their social autonomy and gain an economic base in the Jim Crow South. The primary disagreement between Cherokees and Siouans was not whether the federal government should recognize the tribe but what strategy they should use to accomplish this goal. The members of the Cherokee faction put their faith in their political contacts in Congress, the local white community, and state government, while the Siouans followed the lead of the BIA in Washington.[22]

Engaging Racial Science under the IRA

Indians perceived the failure of the recognition bills in 1932 and 1933 as a setback, but the IRA's passage in 1934 gave them new hope. To be eligible for the IRA's provisions, nonreservation Indians had to prove that they possessed at least half "Indian blood." For Robeson County's Indians, this provision became both a blessing and a curse. The half-blood criterion offered a seemingly objective standard by which Indians could establish their eligibility for federal services and circumvent the congressional politics that had doomed their previous efforts. In some ways, the criteria presented a solution to the BIA's historic conflict with Congress. Conversely, the objectivity of the criteria was an illusion. The only method the bureau used to determine an individual's blood quantum was anthropometry, a scheme that did not account for the random ways that genes combine in an individual. In most cases, this method proved inaccurate at best and destructive at worst. While the BIA's standard seemed objective on the surface, prevailing social attitudes corrupted its concept of Indian blood.

BIA staff members conferred regarding the best way for the enrollment commission to authenticate Indians' claims, exploring both genealogical and anthropometric methods. At issue was the relative reliability of the methods and how to apply abstract theoretical views of blood and culture to a concrete policy. Anthropologists respected anthropometry for its purported abilities to distinguish between people and classify the human family according to racial groups. Physical anthropologists defined a "race" as a group of individuals whose phenotypes varied around a set of well-defined physical characteristics that pervaded the group. They observed that different races possessed distinct physical features and believed that measuring those features elucidated the mental capacity and cultural advancement of each racial group. These scientists used anthropometry to distinguish between the races, but they also wanted to explain cultural differences between humans. The most obvious explanation conveniently illuminated the contemporary inequalities prevalent in urban, industrialized societies. Anthropologists linked one's physical traits to one's behavior. They believed that in a Gilded Age society full of technological advance and economic opportunity, the disadvantaged were simply biologically and physically inferior. Scientists used anthropometry to rank the races along an evolutionary scale that situated white Americans at the top of civilization and African peoples at the bottom. Indians fell in between. These views held sway in academic departments and at the Smithsonian Institution between the 1890s and the mid-twentieth century; in fact, the scientific case for the connection between race and culture encouraged lawmakers and social activists such as John Collier to apply anthropology to their social engineering efforts.[23] The scholarship that supported racial hierarchies made stereotypes into scientific "fact." Science legitimized white supremacist agendas in the academy, in government, and in popular culture by purporting that, in the words of historian of anthropology Lee Baker, "a social equality among the races is not possible because of the natural inequality between the races."[24]

Why did the BIA employ a method so loaded with social inequality? Bureau staff members might have been naive about the ways in which anthropometry supported a noxious social agenda, and they employed it because no other means seemed efficiently to provide the expert opinion they sought to shore up their policy on nonreservation Indians. The BIA was determined to apply scientific theory to policy—Collier presumed that fairness flowed from scientific objectivity.[25] However, the BIA did not apply the test equally throughout Indian Country. The bureau apparently used anthropometry only with Robeson County Indians during the New Deal, though officials had used the method in other places during the early part of the twentieth century. At the White Earth Chippewa reservation in 1916, the BIA tried to settle allotment claims by employing anthropometrist Ales Hrdlicka of the Smithsonian Institution to determine the blood quantum of tribal members. Hrdlicka believed in the promise of anthropometry to distinguish between races and to reveal mixed-race ancestry. According to Hrdlicka, "It was not only possible to detect and separate all mixed-bloods from full-bloods, but to form a fair estimate of the proportion of white blood wherever mixture existed."[26]

Although Hrdlicka cited field experience in his confident assessment of the utility of anthropometry, determining racial mixture actually had proved difficult. White Earth Ojibwes with curly hair, for example, confounded investigators, who were convinced that curly hair could never exist among full-blooded Indians. But the Ojibwes themselves recognized genetic variations better than anthropologists and told Hrdlicka that "it wouldn't make any difference if [someone] had curly hair." According to historian Melissa Meyer, the Ojibwes "objected to establishing fixed physical standards by which to differentiate among Indians because of variations they observed among themselves." The BIA determined blood status at White Earth by economic considerations more than any "scientific" biological, cultural, or social information. Hrdlicka found very few "full bloods," paving the way for the theft of allotted lands of the purported mixed-bloods as well as of some full-bloods. Indian-held economic resources were transferred to whites based on Hrdlicka's fraudulent findings of mixed blood.[27]

Twenty years later, during the Indian New Deal, not much had changed in the BIA's ability to determine blood quantum. But officials did reject anthropometry in the case of nonreservation groups in the West, such as the Chippewa-Crees of Montana. BIA policy makers did not question the Indian ancestry of the Chippewa-Crees but expressed concern that some applicants lacked the required blood quantum. BIA staff developed an "Application for Registration as an Indian," a questionnaire to determine an Indian's ancestry, tribal affiliation, relationship to the federal government, and degree of assimilation. Legal historian Paul Spruhan points out that BIA staff often relied on more than strictly blood to determine the identity of Indians under the New Deal. They frequently employed social and cultural definitions alongside evidence of blood quantum. They did not employ anthropometry to determine eligibility but instead relied on the applications, consequently rejecting some applicants who did not display what officials considered to be proper "Indian habits." For example, officials rejected applicants who were married to white men, were perceived as wealthy, or had "good jobs," sometimes against the recommendations of the BIA's Chippewa-Cree advisers. Sources indicate that these applicants were rejected because Collier determined that they did not need or deserve the economic benefits that might have accompanied land purchase. OIA officials thus employed biological criteria only loosely, and economic considerations could determine the determination of blood quantum.[28]

There may have been another reason for the BIA's exclusive use of anthropometry in Robeson County. Unlike other nonreservation Indian groups in Montana, Nevada, and California that applied for recognition under the IRA in the 1930s, Robeson County's Indians faced a systematic comparison with African Americans, the only group anthropologists considered lower on the scale of racial evolution than Native Americans. Collier probably recognized that anthropometry was the best available way to prove scientifically that Indians were biologically and hence socially separate from blacks. While the BIA ostensibly only cared about the presence of Indian blood, the absence of black blood was probably also on officials' minds, as it had been for southern whites. Using science did not eclipse a biased social agenda at the bureau.[29]

As Seltzer and the BIA set out to determine Native Americans' amounts of Indian blood, it became clear that "blood" meant different things to the BIA and to Robeson County Indians. Lumbees determined blood relationships by genealogy; if one's ancestors and their relatives belonged to the Indian community, then that community accepted one as an Indian, regardless of how many non-Indian ancestors one had.[30] When asked to describe their reasons for claiming Indian blood, Native Americans uniformly expressed themselves in terms of kinship and place. For example, one respondent said, "My parents and gra[n]dparents handed it down to me. I was born among a nest of Indians, and resided there every [sic] since." Another sixty-two-year-old participant told questioners, "My grand dad[d]y and great grand daddy said that they were Indian people."[31] Indian participants also pointed out ancestors who had signed treaties, spoken Indian languages, used traditional healing methods, or fought with or against Americans in various wars. They understood these traits as clear evidence of their distinct identity and took care to tell government officials about their past.[32] The BIA dismissed such history as "vague references" to people who could not be "positively identified as Indians" and did little documentary investigation to substantiate their view. The BIA proved unwilling to abandon preconceived notions about "Indian blood" and listen to the information that Indian respondents did impart, a situation that may have encouraged Indians to withhold knowledge of their history and internal markers of identity.[33]

Indians attempted to conform to the BIA's assumptions by declaring a percentage of Indian blood to Seltzer and his colleagues. But having never kept blood quantum records and with the overwhelming emphasis placed on kinship rather than racial ancestry, Indian calculations were hardly precise. Most Indian participants counted themselves and their spouses as half or more than half Indian, regardless of whether they had any non-Indian ancestry or how much they had. One man, for example, described his calculation of blood quantum: "To the best of my knowledge my father . . . and my mother . . . were full blood Indians, and so considered themselves, I am only making claim to be ¾ or more Indian, since they may have been a lesser degree of which I have no knowledge."[34] Few respondents indicated any non-Indian ancestry on their genealogy charts, which dated back five generations, but regardless of their apparent 100 percent Indian ancestry, most Indians declined to claim "full blood."[35]

This reluctance may have resulted from a warning the BIA issued in the first few days of the examination: "There was such a unanimity of claim to one-half or more Indian blood that we took occasion . . . to point out to [the Indians] that such claims, when not based on reasonable grounds of belief or evidence, would prove damaging to the group as a whole, on that all claims however sound might be placed under suspicion."[36] Indians increasingly began to claim half-blood status for themselves and their spouses, rather than a greater percentage. The BIA was unprepared to accept Robeson County Indians' notions of kinship, genealogy, and blood relationships. To them, it was historically and biologically impossible for the group to claim such a high proportion of Indian blood because genealogy was simply an unacceptable standard of proof. Furthermore, the BIA explicitly stated that if Native Americans employed their own identity criteria, the bureau would doubt and dismiss their claims. The agency's reliance on academic criteria for identity made it difficult for participants to pass the BIA's test. Indians told the BIA about their culture, about the ways they determined who belonged in their community. But the bureau believed that blood determined culture and sought to define Indians' relationships to one another by abstract principles that had nothing to do with the Indians' culture.

This contradictory use of science to document their identity left Indians confused and vulnerable to ridicule from the BIA. In commenting on one Indian's miscalculation of his Indian blood, officials wrote, "It will be noticed that this claimant could not write his name and the inconsistency [of his calculation] did not appear to impress him." Another participant, they reported, had "attended school only three months and presumably has small knowledge of what fractions mean."[37] As sociologist Eva Marie Garroutte has pointed out, the BIA's manner of explaining and justifying its calculations of Indian blood is complicated and had an inherent social bias. The federal government explicitly created blood quantum rules to define someone of "mixed blood," a legal and political category that determined when the federal government's responsibility to Indian people ended.[38] The complexity of determining one's percentage of Indian blood and the irrelevance of that standard to native peoples' kinship and genealogical systems ensured (1) that the blood quantum criteria retained its aura of scientific objectivity, unintelligible to the "uneducated" and "illiterate" and (2) that the BIA retained the prerogative of deciding who was Indian and who was not, over and above Indians' own criteria.[39] When the BIA exerted control over the discussion of Indian identity, as it did during the Indian New Deal in Robeson County, employees used ridicule to pressure Indians into conforming to foreign notions of identity in the name of objective science. The BIA did so in order to withhold services from most of between eight and ten thousand Indians who might otherwise have been recognized in Robeson County.[40]

While Seltzer's conclusions demonstrated the contradictions the BIA might have expected from anthropometry, the tests nonetheless accomplished their purpose. Of the 209 participants, all of whom provided evidence of their Indian identity and claimed to possess half or more Indian blood, Seltzer found only 22 whom he believed passed the anthropometric test. Highlighting the imprecise nature of the tests and the rigid character of Seltzer's analysis, he also identified 11 individuals as "borderline" and 7 as "near borderline." One might logically presume that the full siblings of these "successful" participants would also possess the same blood quantum, but Seltzer's analysis defied logic. In twelve separate cases, Seltzer identified individuals as "less than one-half Indian" while designating their full siblings as "borderline," "near borderline," or "more than one-half Indian."[41]

Blood and Identity in Robeson County

Twenty of the twenty-two recognized Indians came from one extended family that lived in the Brooks Settlement, home to the community's Haudenosaunee Longhouse. Elisha Locklear, great-nephew of a longhouse founder, Pikey Brooks (also one of Seltzer's twenty-two recognized Indians), has shared much of the Brooks Settlement history with me. Until the 1950s, the settlement was "closed like a casket," he said. "In the 1920s [settlement residents] stopped the Trailways buses from running through there," he told me. "They'd stop them on the road, and take the people out of the bus, and beat them. They left some of them dead in Uncle John Brooks's pasture there at Brooks Landing. But things like that, . . . as far as preserving blood, it was a plus."[42] Although one prominent Lumbee had said that being Indian in Robeson County is a "state of mind," Mr. Elisha disagreed strongly, arguing that this view of Indian identity "discounted any kind of blood ties." Mr. Elisha discussed his "whole blood" ancestors and validated the Siouan enrollment study's results as definitive on the question of who among Robeson County Indians has the most "Indian blood." This attitude seems to affirm the federal government's notion that Indian identity is synonymous with biology. But my conversations with Mr. Elisha over the past decade have caused me to think about what blood can mean.[43]

Many Robeson County Indians discuss blood—"good blood," "bad blood," and "It's in her blood" are common phrases in social situations. The idea behind those offhand remarks is that blood transmits certain qualities of behavior, power, and authority. This idea is nothing new—in southeastern Indian societies, the relationship to one's mother conveyed clan membership and belonging. Of course, that relationship does not exist without the mother sharing literal, visceral blood with her child. Historian Melissa Meyer has argued that the deep symbolic meanings of blood are universal and that "the metaphorical connection of blood with lineage, descent and ancestry preceded its literal physiological use."[44] Societies used blood and kinship to establish the difference between insiders (clan members in southeastern Indian groups) and outsiders (nonclan members). Lumbees and Tuscaroras discuss blood in exactly this sense—that is, as a way to distinguish between qualities the speaker wants in an insider and qualities one rejects or reserves for outsiders. The language of blood can conduct a kind of electrical current between generations that binds them together, even as it divides within a generation. Mr. Elisha's ancestors in the Brooks Settlement believed that even other Indians were outsiders; the only insiders were other members of that community.

Blood has personal power that everyone acknowledges, but blood also has political power. In the colonial context under which Indians in the United States have formed their identities, the personal symbolism of blood became linked to legitimate claims on land and resources. Indians commonly used (and still use) the language of blood. Measuring fractions of blood was intended to define cultural and biological hierarchies and deny those claims. Inequality is therefore inherent in the concept of race, a concept that emerged long after the concept of blood and that differed greatly from the meanings of kinship and connection that blood can imply. The separating discourse of blood—where it is divisible according to one's cultural ancestry and itself divides communities—is closer to what we mean in America by "race." In my experience as a Lumbee, this discourse takes place with outsiders or at least in contexts where external definitions of identity hold sway. The meaning of blood, like other identity markers, is an ongoing conversation between insiders and outsiders. Even insiders do not always have the same view. Factionalism thus breeds identity formation, and identity formation does not take place without disagreements.

Some observers might view these disagreements as destructive to the community's maintenance of its own identity markers. Indeed, such a view seems to applaud race and the Euro-American emphasis on it as legitimizing cultural affiliation. The woman who told Mr. Elisha that being Lumbee was a "state of mind" was probably not trying to be vague but rather was trying to avoid identifying herself with racialized identity definitions. However, Mr. Elisha's ancestors realized that even if they rejected race, they still could not escape its destructive consequences. The BIA would have employed blood quantum anyway.[45] Although the bureau considered Indians' criteria for identity unreliable, governmental proposals for determining Indianness rested on flawed assumptions and subjective circumstances.

Recognizing the "Original Twenty-Two"

When the secretary of the interior approved their enrollment under the Indian Reorganization Act, the BIA notified each of the twenty-two Indians Seltzer believed were half or more "Indian blood." The letters stated that the IRA entitled these men and women to educational assistance and Indian Service preference; the "Indian Service" denoted positions available at the BIA. The BIA warned, however, that funds for land acquisition were not available to these individuals, as the IRA had promised, because such funds had already been allocated to "landless tribal groups." The letters emphasized that recognition under the IRA did not entitle an individual to membership in an Indian tribe or bestow "tribal status." The IRA made it possible to recognize individual Indians without placing the heavy financial burden of a tribe onto the BIA, and the BIA staff underscored that recognition of the twenty-two individuals did not mean recognition of the community as a whole. In his letter, Collier also reminded those who were recognized that enrollment did not apply to their descendants unless Seltzer had determined that both parents possessed a blood quantum of at least half.[46]

Collier considered these twenty-two men and women to be Indians but not a "landless tribal group," so he did not permit them to organize as a tribe under a constitution, according to the IRA's provisions. The Interior Department's solicitor, Felix Cohen, opined that Indian groups could not organize unless they lived on a reservation, meaning that the BIA had to purchase land for a "landless" group, and the secretary of the interior had to proclaim that land a reservation. Funds for land acquisition went to Mississippi Choctaws, Shoshones in Nevada, the Quartz Valley Indian Community in California, and the St. Croix Chippewas of Wisconsin. The twenty-two recognized Indians in Robeson County received nothing. Legal scholar Paul Spruhan has argued that Collier did not approve organization for the twenty-two Lumbees because despite the fact that the IRA defined an Indian as an individual of "one-half or more Indian blood," Collier believed that recognized Indians should be members of cohesive communities, not individuals.[47] After several years of working with Robeson County Indians, it seems unlikely that Collier did not recognize their membership in a larger community of Indian people. He may have simply equated cohesion with reservation trust land, assuming that since the twenty-two Robeson County Indians had no such land, they did not maintain a tribal, collective existence. But this too seems like an overly simplistic explanation for Collier's decision, given his familiarity with Indian issues and with these particular situations. He may have thought that while recognizing them as individuals would do no harm, allowing them to organize under a tribal constitution would threaten the precarious resources available to help Indians whose status was not in doubt. After all, a tribal constitution provided for enrollment and membership criteria, and Collier may have imagined the recognized twenty-two writing a constitution that enrolled themselves and adopted many more Robeson County Indians—thousands more.

After Congress failed to grant Lumbees federal acknowledgment and relief from segregation, their only hope was with the BIA's criteria. The BIA had promised them a New Deal, an objective policy that would not trap them in the blood politics of white supremacy. The hallmark of the Indian New Deal was the application of science to policy, but the BIA's belief in anthropometry blinded its officials to the inconsistencies and prejudices of science. The Indian New Deal left native people in Robeson County even more vulnerable to the racial prejudices and stereotypes that white supremacy dictated. Although the values held by white supremacists in state government and Congress and by the BIA came into conflict before the New Deal, the use of science to implement policy unintentionally unified Congress and the BIA behind a determination to ignore Indians' own markers of identity. Instead, both branches of government favored criteria that kept them in control of the question of who was an Indian. Through using blood quantum to determine identity, John Collier's dream of self-government for Indian tribes became a way for the federal government to continue the domination and colonization of Indian peoples.

The BIA's pseudoscientific criteria for Indian identity formed the basis for future relationships between the bureau and Robeson County Indians and paved the way for dubious arguments against recognizing those Indians. Today, these arguments include our lack of Indian blood, our lack of Indian culture, our lack of Indian language—the same criteria Seltzer's study posed in 1936. And it is not the Office of Federal Acknowledgment at the BIA that makes these arguments—officials there know that Seltzer's and Collier's rationales failed, that times have changed. Recognition under the Federal Acknowledgment Process is not based on these criteria. Rather, politicians and lobbyists are the loudest in their accusations that Lumbees are not a legitimate tribe. Their platform is made possible by the fact that according to the Interior Department, Congress, not the BIA, must recognize Lumbees as a consequence of the termination language in the 1956 legislation that formally acknowledged our tribal status. That measure recognized the Lumbees as an Indian tribe but denied them benefits or services designated to other recognized tribes.[48] Representative Christopher Shays of Connecticut has been among the most vocal opponents to the Lumbee Recognition Act, arguing for sending the Lumbees through the Federal Acknowledgment Process. In June 2007, he said that sponsors of the Lumbee bill "don't want them to go before the Bureau of Indian Affairs because this is a tribe that had no name. It had no reservation. It had no language."[49] While the Lumbee Act passed the House in 2007 and again in 2009, it continually stalls in the Senate, where senators can arbitrarily decide the fortunes of Indian people by anonymously placing a hold on any bill and preventing it from coming to the floor for a vote.

Arbitrary, unenforceable criteria for recognition underscore the extent to which the process has little to do with identity and everything to do with power. Criteria for Indian identity continually change because Indian communities continually change. To expect them to do otherwise is to deny their humanity and pretend that colonialism never occurred. Yet this is precisely what politicians in Congress—those who have the power to make such decisions—expect of the Lumbees and by extension of other Indian tribes. Under this system, it is difficult to reconcile Indian identity with federal recognition, or at least with the process by which Indian communities have obtained such recognition. Neither the BIA nor Congress has employed methods that take full account of the realities of Indian history and identity formation. The Lumbees are a test case for how identity criteria influence a tribe's ability to determine its own future. Until politicians reconcile their policies with Indian experiences, self-determination will not be a reality for any tribe, recognized or not.

Notes

1. Vine Deloria Jr., ed., *The Indian Reorganization Act: Congresses and Bills* (Norman: University of Oklahoma Press, 2002), 20; Kenneth R. Philp, *John Collier's Crusade for Indian Reform, 1920–1954* (Tucson: University of Arizona Press, 1977), chap. 7.

2. Vine Deloria Jr. and Clifford Lytle, *The Nations Within: The Past and Future of American Indian Sovereignty* (New York: Pantheon, 1984), 150–51; emphasis added. I quote Deloria and Lytle's summary of Section 19 of the IRA because it more precisely states the status of unrecognized, nonreservation Indians, like those in Robeson County. The definition in Section 19 itself reads, "The term 'Indian' as used in this Act shall include all persons of Indian descent who are members of any recognized Indian tribe now under Federal jurisdiction, and all persons who are descendants of such members who were, on June 1, 1934, residing within the present boundaries of any Indian reservation, and shall further include all other persons of one-half or more Indian blood." The phrase "shall further include" implied that the act applied to nonreservation Indians who could meet the half-blood quantum standard. The language defining an Indian in Collier's original bill was not compressed into one section as it was in the final act but was dispersed over different titles. Title 1, "Indian Self-Government," defined an Indian to "include all persons of Indian descent who are members of any recognized Indian tribe, band, or nation, or are descendants of such members and were, as of February 1, 1934, actually residing within the present boundaries of any Indian reservation, and shall further include all persons of one-fourth or more Indian blood," but the title goes on to authorize the secretary of the interior or a tribe to prescribe additional membership criteria or offer membership to nonresidents. Title III, "Indian Lands," defined a "member of an Indian tribe" as "any descendant of a member permanently residing within an existing Indian reservation." Collier's original bill was less precise than the final act on the role of blood quantum in determining membership but still depended on the concept. See Vine Deloria Jr., *Indian Reorganization Act*, 12, 17, 23.

3. Vine Deloria Jr. and Lytle, *Nations Within*, 170.

4. D'Arcy McNickle, E. S. McMahon, and Carl C. Seltzer to John Collier, January 26, 1937, Record Group 75, Entry 121, File 64190-1935-066 General Services Part 1, National Archives and Records Administration, Washington, D.C.

5. Ibid.

6. This admittedly simplified definition of modernity is inspired most by James C. Scott, *Seeing Like a State: How Certain Schemes to Improve the Human Condition Have Failed* (New Haven: Yale University Press, 1998). For modernity's influence on segregation, see Mark Schultz, *The Rural Face of White Supremacy: Beyond Jim Crow* (Urbana: University of Illinois Press, 2005), 68; Grace Elizabeth Hale, *Making Whiteness: The Culture of Segregation in the South* (New York: Pantheon, 1998); William A. Link, *The Paradox of Southern Progressivism, 1880–1930* (Chapel Hill: University of North Carolina Press, 1992).

7. Philip J. Deloria, *Indians in Unexpected Places* (Lawrence: University Press of Kansas, 2004).

8. I am indebted to Phil Deloria's *Indians in Unexpected Places* for this language of expectation. Using "expectation" presumes not that the system of segregation or of Indian policy is normal but rather that it is expected and therefore a cultural construction.

9. See Alexandra Harmon, *Indians in the Making: Ethnic Relations and Indian Identities around Puget Sound* (Berkeley: University of California Press, 1998), 3; Fredrik Barth, introduction to *Ethnic Groups and Boundaries* (Boston: Little, Brown, 1969). For a summary of the "natural" categories on which Indian identity is based, see Raymond D. Fogelson, "Perspectives on Native American Identity," in *Studying Native America: Problems and Prospects*, ed. Russell Thornton, (Madison: University of Wisconsin Press, 1998); Joane Nagel, "American Indian Ethnic Renewal: Politics and the Resurgence of Identity," *American Sociological Review* 60 (1995): 947–65. Sociologists and legal historians who have questioned these categories are Angela A. Gonzales, "The (Re)Articulation of American Indian Identity: Maintaining Boundaries and Regulating Access to Ethnically Tied Resources," *American Indian Culture and Research Journal* 22 (1998): 199–225; Anne Merline McCulloch and David E. Wilkins, "'Constructing' Nations within States: The Quest for Federal Recognition by the Catawba and Lumbee Tribes," *American Indian Quarterly* 19 (1995): 361–87; M. Annette Jaimes, "Federal Indian Identification Policy: A Usurpation of Indigenous Sovereignty in North America," in *The State of Native America: Genocide, Colonization, and Resistance*, ed. M. Annette Jaimes (Boston: South End, 1992), 123–38; C. Matthew Snipp, *American Indians: First of this Land* (New York: Sage, 1989), chap. 2; James A. Clifton, "Alternate Identities and Cultural Frontiers," in *Being and Becoming Indian: Biographical Studies of North American Frontiers*, ed. James A. Clifton (Chicago: Dorsey, 1989), 11, 21–22. For treatments of American Indian history that encompass the view of identity as a process, see Harmon, *Indians in the Making*; Karen I. Blu, *The Lumbee Problem:*

The Making of an American Indian People (New York: Cambridge University Press, 1980); Morris W. Foster, *Being Comanche: A Social History of an American Indian Community* (Tucson: University of Arizona Press, 1991); Loretta Fowler, *Shared Symbols, Contested Meanings: Gros Ventre Culture and History, 1778–1984* (Ithaca: Cornell University Press, 1987).

10. The literature describing Lumbees as "tri-racial isolates" goes back to the 1930s. See Brewton Berry, *Almost White* (New York: Macmillan, 1963); Virginia DeMarce, "Looking at Legends—Lumbee and Melungeon: Applied Genealogy and the Origins of Tri-Racial Isolate Settlements," *National Genealogical Society Quarterly* 81 (1993): 24–45; Virginia DeMarce, "'Verry Slitly Mixt': Tri-Racial Isolate Families of the Upper South—A Genealogical Study," *National Genealogical Society Quarterly* 80 (1992): 5–35; Guy B. Johnson, "Personality in a White-Indian-Negro Community," *American Sociological Review* 4 (1939): 516–23; J. K. Dane and B. Eugene Griessman, "The Collective Identity of Marginal Peoples: The North Carolina Experience," *American Anthropologist* 74 (1972): 699; William Harlen Gilbert Jr., "Memorandum Concerning the Characteristics of the Larger Mixed-Blood Racial Islands of the Eastern United States," *Social Forces* 24 (1946): 438–47; Calvin L. Beale, "An Overview of the Phenomenon of Mixed Racial Isolates in the United States," *American Anthropologist* 74 (1972): 706.

11. For a critique, see Harmon, *Indians in the Making*, 3.

12. See, e.g., Ariela Gross, *What Blood Won't Tell: A History of Race on Trial in America* (Cambridge: Harvard University Press, 2008); Peggy Pascoe, *What Comes Naturally: Miscegenation Law and the Making of Race in America* (New York: Oxford University Press, 2009).

13. Michelle Brattain, "Miscegenation and Competing Definitions of Race in Twentieth-Century Louisiana," *Journal of Southern History* 71 (2005): 621–58; Peggy Pascoe, "Miscegenation Law, Court Cases, and Ideologies of 'Race' in Twentieth-Century America," *Journal of American History* 83 (1996): 44–69.

14. The National Museum of the American Indian has a touring exhibition, *IndiVisible: African and Native American Lives in the Americas*, that discusses multiracial perspectives on Indian and black identities. See also James F. Brooks, ed., *Confounding the Color Line: The Indian-Black Experience in North America* (Lincoln: University of Nebraska Press, 2002); Tiya Miles and Sharon P. Holland, eds., *Crossing Waters, Crossing Worlds: The African Diaspora in Indian Country* (Durham: Duke University Press, 2006).

15. Censuses taken between 1790 and 1810 did not indicate race but instead categorized people as "free white," "slave," or "all other free persons." Between 1820 and 1840, the adjective "colored" was added to "free persons." Not until 1850 did the

term "mulatto" appear in the Census. Although the terms fluctuated, none provided room to articulate an identity other than "white" or "nonwhite." If the enumerator made no mark, he assumed the individual was white, a pristine example of the extent to which the government has granted whiteness a degree of normalcy, so much so that it does not require notation. The Census rules for racial classifications changed over time, but appearance most commonly defined them; for example, enumerator instructions did not specify the proof required for an individual's racial category. An enumerator may have relied on self-identification or simply classified the individual based on appearance. In other words, the enumerator may have marked someone as mulatto not necessarily because he had definitive knowledge of that person's ancestry but because, to the enumerator's eye, that person looked mulatto. For Census questionnaires and enumerator instructions that list the racial information collected, see the website of the U.S. Census Bureau, e.g., "History: 1790," http://www.census.gov/history/www/index_of_questions/012292.html; "History: 1800," http://www.census.gov/history/www/index_of_questions/012293 .html. See also Minnesota Population Center, Integrated Public Use Microdata Series, "1850 Census: Instructions to Marshals and Assistant Marshals," http://usa .ipums.org/usa/voliii/inst1850.shtml; Minnesota Population Center, Integrated Public Use Microdata Series, "1860 Census: Instructions to Marshals and Assistant Marshals," http://usa.ipums.org/usa/voliii/inst1860.shtml. Information on 1890 census is found in Anna Bailey, "Separating Out: The Emergence of Croatan Indian Identity, 1872–1900" (Ph.D. diss., University of Washington, 2008), 104.

16. "Crossblood" is novelist and literary critic Gerald Vizenor's term that describes not only people of mixed ancestry but people of mixed social milieus, most especially rural/reservation and urban. See Gerald Vizenor, *Crossbloods: Bone Courts, Bingo, and Other Reports* (Minneapolis: University of Minnesota Press, 1990).

17. Elisha Locklear and Cecil Hunt, interview by author and Willie Lowery, tape recording, Pembroke, North Carolina, February 23, 2004, Lumbee River Fund Collection, Sampson-Livermore Library, University of North Carolina–Pembroke; Ella Deloria to Franz Boas, August 7, 1940, Franz Boas Papers, American Philosophical Society, Philadelphia; Peter H. Wood, Deborah Montgomerie, and Susan Yarnell, *Tuscarora Roots: An Historical Report Regarding the Relation of the Hatteras Tuscarora Tribe of Robeson County, North Carolina, to the Original Tuscarora Indian Tribe* (Durham: Hatteras Tuscarora Tribal Foundation, 1992), 109; Colan Brooks and Rosetta Brooks, interview by Adolph Dial, tape recording, Pembroke, North Carolina, September 2, 1969, Adolph Dial Tapes, Native American Resource Center, University of North Carolina–Pembroke.

18. Bailey, "Separating Out," 74–76, 86–88.

19. Blu, *Lumbee Problem,* 135–36; Gerald Sider, *Living Indian Histories: Lumbee and Tuscarora People in North Carolina* (Chapel Hill: University of North Carolina Press, 2003), 82, 86–90.

20. Malinda Maynor Lowery, *Lumbee Indians in the Jim Crow South: Race, Identity, and the Making of a Nation* (Chapel Hill: University of North Carolina Press, 2010), 87, 99–103.

21. Ibid., 106–10, 115–16.

22. Ibid., 120–21.

23. David Beaulieu, "Curly Hair and Big Feet: Physical Anthropology and the Implementation of Land Allotment on the White Earth Chippewa Reservation," *American Indian Quarterly* 8 (1984): 283, 305; Lee D. Baker, *From Savage to Negro: Anthropology and the Construction of Race, 1896–1954* (Berkeley: University of California Press, 1998), 35–36.

24. Baker, *From Savage to Negro,* 103, 119.

25. The Siouan Enrollment Commission expressed a hope that Seltzer's tests would enable Robeson County Indians to "feel that they have been given a fair chance." See "Investigating Siouan Claims" to John Collier, June 7, 1936, Record Group 75, Entry 121, File 45499-1937-066 General Services, National Archives and Records Administration, Washington, D.C.

26. "Conference in Mr. Herrick's Office," 18 May 1936, RG 75, entry 121, file no. 45499-1937-066 General Services, NARA.

27. Melissa Meyer, *The White Earth Tragedy: Ethnicity and Dispossession at a Minnesota Anishinaabe Reservation, 1889–1920* (Lincoln: University of Nebraska Press, 1999), 168–72. Ales Hrdlicka, founder and primary advocate of anthropometry as a definitive science, believed that nations should use anthropometry to solve modern problems, tracking the physical progression or regression of their populations, a view that became instituted in the practice of eugenics. See Ales Hrdlicka, *Practical Anthropometry,* ed. T. D. Stewart, 4th ed. (Philadelphia: Wistar Institute of Anatomy and Biology, 1952), 11.

28. Paul Spruhan, "Indian as Race/Indian as Political Status: Implementation of the Half-Blood Requirement under the Indian Reorganization Act, 1934–1945," *Rutgers Race and the Law Review* 8 (2006): 33–38.

29. Other applicants for recognition from western states can be found in Record Group 75, Entry 616, National Archives and Records Administration, Washington, D.C. See also Beaulieu, "Curly Hair and Big Feet," 305–9.

30. The White Earth Ojibwes held a similar concept of blood relationships and Indian identity, as articulated in Beaulieu, "Curly Hair and Big Feet," 288–89.

31. Carl C. Seltzer, "A Report on the Racial Status of Certain People in Robeson County, North Carolina," June 30, 1936, Record Group 75, Entry 616, Box 13-15,

North Carolina, National Archives and Record Administration, Washington, D.C., Applicants 6, 5.

32. See, e.g., Applicants 4, 19, 22, 25, 28, 30, 41, 45, 61, 68, 71, 72, 73, 78, 82, 88, 89, 91, 94, 96, 106, 107.

33. D'Arcy McNickle, E. S. McMahon, and Carl Seltzer to John Collier, January 26, 1937, Record Group 75, Entry 121, File 64190-1935-066 General Services, National Archives and Records Administration, Washington, D.C.

34. Seltzer, "Report," Applicant 4.

35. Of the 183 applicants and spouses for which data are available from 1936, 22 claimed to be "full-bloods," 74 claimed "3/4," "nearly full," or "more than 1/2," 82 claimed "1/2," 3 claimed "1/4" or "1/4 or more," 1 claimed "unknown," and 1 did not respond. Seltzer, "Report," Applicants 2–108. See also D'Arcy McNickle, E. S. McMahon, and Carl Seltzer to John Collier, January 26, 1937, Record Group 75, Entry 121, File 64190-1935-066 General Services Part I, National Archives and Record Administration, Washington, D.C.

36. "Investigating Siouan Claims" to John Collier, June 7, 1936, Record Group 75, Entry 121, File 45499-1937-066 General Services Part I, National Archives and Records Administration, Washington, D.C.

37. Ibid.

38. Eva Marie Garroutte, *Real Indians: Identity and the Survival of Native America* (Berkeley: University of California Press, 2003), 42.

39. Cf. M. Annette Jaimes, "Federal Indian Identification Policy: A Usurpation of Indigenous Sovereignty in North America," in *State of Native America*, ed. Jaimes, 123–38.

40. At least one historical researcher holds the view that the BIA implemented the tests precisely to thwart recognition for Robeson County Indians; Wesley Taukchiray argues that the BIA used anthropometry because it would decisively and "scientifically" prove Robeson County Indians to be possess blood quantums of less than half and make them ineligible for recognition. The fact that the tests were inaccurate bolstered the government's justification to use them against Indians. Phone conversation with Wesley Taukchiray, Pembroke, North Carolina, June 16, 2003.

41. Seltzer, "Report," Applicants 2–108, "Genealogical Charts of Brooks Family" file, and "Genealogical Tables with Racial Diagnoses" file. Families in which full siblings did not receive the same diagnosis include the families of Leanna Locklear Brooks and Will Brooks, Emmie Locklear Jacobs and Westley Jacobs, Boss Locklear and Mary Brooks Locklear, Beadan Locklear Brooks and Lawson Brooks, Dockery Brooks and Callie Campbell Brooks, and John David Locklear

and Lovedy Brooks Locklear. The BIA also did not include the families and siblings of the non–Brooks Settlement Indians Seltzer diagnosed as having "1//2 or more Indian blood."

42. Elisha Locklear identifies as Tuscarora, not Lumbee. His family tradition speaks to their descent from the Tuscaroras, who originally resided in North Carolina. Many left after the Tuscarora War of 1714–15 and moved north to New York to join the Iroquois Confederacy, but Mr. Elisha's elders passed down the tradition that they were descended from Tuscaroras who stayed in North Carolina. During the 1950s and 1960s, "Tuscarora" began to emerge as a separate political identity for Indians in Robeson County. See Malinda Maynor Lowery, *Lumbee Indians in the Jim Crow South: Race, Identity, and the Making of a Nation* (Chapel Hill: University of North Carolina Press, 2010), 246–49.

43. Locklear and Hunt, interview.

44. Melissa Meyer, "American Indian Blood Quantum Requirements: Blood Is Thicker Than Family," in *Over the Edge: Remapping the American West*, ed. Valerie J. Matsumoto and Blake Allmendinger (Berkeley: University of California Press, 1999), 236.

45. Cf. ibid., 241. Why and how tribes and Indian people have adopted the language of blood quantum to define community membership has been discussed in the work of Kimberly Tall Bear, "DNA, Blood, and Racializing the Tribe," *Wicazo Sa Review* 18 (Spring 2003): 89–93.

46. William Zimmerman to Joseph Brooks, December 12, 1938, Record Group 75, Entry 121, File 45499-1937-066 General Services, National Archives and Records Administration, Washington, D.C.; John Collier to Mary Lee Brooks Hammond et al., January 28, 1939, Record Group 75, Entry 121, File 45499-1937-066 General Services, National Archives and Records Administration, Washington, D.C. Other members of the twenty-two were Fannie Brooks Jacobs, Odell Brooks, Ralph Brooks Jr., Paul Brooks, Lily Jane Brooks Locklear, Rosetty Brooks Hunt, Dalseida Locklear Brooks, Henry Brooks, Lake Faddy Brooks, Ralph Brooks, Lawson Brooks, Ella Lee Brooks, Winnie Bell Locklear, Annie May Brooks Locklear, Lawrence Maynor, Lovedy Brooks Locklear, Jesse Brooks, Joe B. Locklear, and Vestia Locklear.

47. Spruhan, "Indian as Race," 40–43.

48. Lowery, *Lumbee Indians in the Jim Crow South*, 245.

49. *Congressional Record*, 110th Cong., 1st sess., June 7, 2007, H6148.

The Recognition of NAGPRA

A Human Rights Promise Deferred

JOANNE BARKER

The Native American Graves Protection and Repatriation Act of 1990 (NAGPRA) was proclaimed by many of its advocates as the first substantive piece of human rights legislation in the United States for native peoples. But the legal status on which the rights provided for by the statute are based contradicts the rights to self-determination defined within international charter and accord. This essay locates the reasons for this contradiction within the discursive and ideological work of federal recognition. This work minimizes native epistemology and expertise while reaffirming federal and scientific authority to recognize—or not—the native. It is instanced by NAGPRA's classification of native ancestry and cultural history as "culturally unidentifiable" (unknowable) and "culturally unaffiliated" (unrelated), which serves to equate repatriation rights with recognition status. The result is NAGPRA's deferral of the human rights its provisions intended to substantiate.

The Promise: The Equity in Epistemology, Expertise, and Consultation

Native claims to international human rights are often made in antagonistic opposition to the technologies of colonial, imperial, and racist power (not necessarily exclusive forms of power).[1] These claims address how historical experiences of colonialism, imperialism, and racism have been perpetuated by federal laws that rationalize native subjugation on the grounds that natives are not human, the right kind of human, or human enough.[2] The logics of lack at the heart of these rationalisms have been cultivated by the claims of some empirical scientists that native peoples are inherently inferior in all of the ways that matter to determining both the measure of their humanity and their rights to self-determination,[3] claims seemingly reinforced by empiricism's objectivity and political neutrality.[4] Native peoples rejoin with the inalienability of their human rights, reclaiming their standing as human within the legal terms of their international rights to social justice and equality.[5] These rejoinders are characterized by the assertion of the relevance and viability of native knowledge on its own terms and not as a compromised opposite of empirical or Western science.[6] One powerful instance of these debates is native peoples' work in the United States on NAGPRA (104 Stat. 3048) and its Code of Federal Regulations of 1995 (amended in 1997, 2003, 2005, 2006, 2007, and 2010).[7]

NAGPRA provides for a modest protection of native grave sites on public and tribal lands and the repatriation of native ancestors and cultural objects from federal agencies and federally funded institutions. (It does not address private lands and collections.)[8] Those that NAGPRA identifies as possessing the requisite status to make claims under its provisions include "lineal descendants," "Indian tribes," and "native Hawaiian organizations."[9] To repatriate, those with the requisite status must be determined to be "culturally affiliated" to the human remains and cultural items they claim. While this determination is reported to National NAGPRA and the *Federal Register* by those charged with fulfilling the law's mandates at federal agencies and federally funded institutions (which NAGPRA terms together as "museums"), NAGPRA directs that museums consult with all of those native people who "may be" or are "most likely" associated with the geographic sites where the remains and items originated.[10]

Through consultation, the museums produce two documents. The first document, a summary, includes a review of the "unassociated funerary objects," "sacred objects," and "objects of cultural patrimony" held at the agency or institution.[11] The summaries also note "cultural affiliation" where possible. They are intended to provide an overview of the scope of the agency or institution's collection, the kinds of objects being held, their geographic origin, and a synopsis of the records of acquisition. This information is supposed to initiate broader consultations with native peoples toward the completion of the second document, an "inventory." Inventories identify the cultural affiliation of all native human remains and cultural objects at the agency or institution and serve to establish the legal rights of "lineal descendants," "Indian tribes," and "native Hawaiian organizations" to repatriate.

The radical inclusivity of native peoples within NAGPRA's consultation provisions—irrespective of their potential legal standing as claimants—is intended to ensure that the museum has been respectful of all relevant native knowledge and experts within the determination of the cultural affiliation of the remains and objects that it holds. It is a consultation model that dramatically departs from that regularly affirmed by Executive Order

13175, first issued by President Bill Clinton on November 6, 2000, and most recently incorporated by President Barack Obama on November 5, 2009. The order charges federal agencies "with engaging in regular and meaningful consultation and collaboration with tribal officials in the development of Federal policies that have tribal implications." It requires "consultation and collaboration" with recognized tribes only. Instead, NAGPRA includes all native peoples who "may be" or are "most likely" affiliated to the remains and items at a museum irrespective of their recognition and potential claimant status. This inclusion affirms native human rights to self-determination as provided within international law and accords. It does so by affirming the relevance and respect of native knowledge about native historical experiences, cultures, genealogical practices, and geographic associations in the determination of native ancestry and the historic significance of native material culture.

This is a fairly profound shift in the practice of the U.S. federal government, which has historically relied on empirical expertise in evaluating the credibility of native knowledge—as though empiricism's promise of rigor and objectivity offered a rational perspective on matters that were, for native peoples, altogether compromised by the political. NAGPRA's inclusivity acknowledges that native knowledge is viable and relevant on its own terms and irrespective of recognition status within a legal system of government, regulation, and mediation that has historically relied on claims to objectivity to justify its programs of genocide, dispossession, and assimilation. In so doing, NAGPRA challenges the assumed authority of empirical scientists—particularly archaeologists and anthropologists—in determining the significance and value of native history and culture within federal policy.[12]

For these reasons, native and allied scholars and activists have claimed NAGPRA as long overdue human rights legislation for native peoples in the United States.[13] They assert that NAGPRA is a much-needed response to U.S. colonialism, imperialism, and racism—characteristic of a historic past when native ancestors were robbed from their graves, mutilated on battlefields, and sent off to labs for study; when cultural objects were stolen from native homes to be displayed in other homes or traded across the international antiquities market; and when native religious beliefs were criminalized and leaders assassinated.[14] They contextualize NAGPRA as answering these histories by affirming native human rights within the still colonial, imperial, and racist conditions perpetuated by acts of grave desecration; the nonconsensual curatorship, display, and study of native human remains and cultural items; and the claims still made by some empirical scientists about native historical, social, and intellectual inferiority.[15] Instead, natives perceive NAGPRA as acknowledging the relevance of their diverse ways of knowing and understanding the historic past and present meaning of native cultures. Authority on native peoples is no longer to rest solely with empirical scientists and their claims to nonpolitical, objective, and rigorous work with native dead and cultural objects. NAGPRA accomplishes this not by elevating native peoples' knowledge and expertise above those of everyone else but by establishing a legal parity between native ways of knowing and empirical science within the consultative processes of "cultural affiliation" that it mandates.[16] This is coded specifically in Section 7.4, which states that the determination of "cultural affiliation" is to be based on "a preponderance of the evidence" from "geographical, kinship, biological, archaeological, anthropological, linguistic, folkloric, oral traditional, historical, or other relevant information or expert opinion." All ways of knowing are to be treated as relevant and all experts as equals.

The Promise Deferred
The Recognition of the "Unidentifiable" and "Unaffiliated"

NAGPRA's Section 2 (Definitions) states that "cultural affiliation" is "a relationship of shared group identity which can be reasonably traced historically or prehistorically between a present day Indian tribe or native Hawaiian organization and an identifiable earlier group."[17] To establish affiliation, native groups must have federal recognition status and be able to show through a "preponderance of the evidence" that they have a "traceable" or documentable (pre)historical relationship to the "identifiable earlier group" from which the remains and items are determined to originate (geographically and assuming adequate records of acquisition are available).

Section 3 (Ownership) and Section 7 (Repatriation) explain that a "preponderance of the evidence" can originate in many different types of sources, including "geographical, kinship, biological, archeological, linguistic, folklore, oral tradition, historical evidence, or other information or expert opinion." To be considered a "preponderance," the evidence must reach a bar that "reasonably leads to such a conclusion" of affiliation. This reasonability does not require an unbroken historical record and does not have to betray ceremonial or other information considered confidential by a native group (such as the details of a specific ceremony in which a burial or sacred object is used as such).

After consideration of the evidence, if it is determined that the remains and objects originate with present-day groups that are not federally recognized or that are perceived not to be affiliated with any group because geographic origin or lineal descent is unknown, NAGPRA mandates that they be classified as "culturally unidentifiable." This classification renders them unrepatriatable and procedurally back into the control and possession of the holding museum. This holding was conclusive until the rule for the disposition of the "culturally unidentifiable" (43 C.F.R. 10.11) became effective on May 14, 2010. (The rule does not apply to associated funerary objects.)

The rule requires that museums initiate a new and presumably broader round of consultation with the recognized groups on "whose tribal lands or aboriginal occupancy areas are in the area where the remains were removed." While the regulatory aim is to determine the affiliation of all native dead, museums are directed to consult only with recognized tribes as those with potential claimant status. If this consultation does not or cannot result in a determination of affiliation as defined by NAGPRA, the rule provides that the "most likely" affiliated or neighboring recognized group "may request disposition of the remains." The museum "would then publish a notice and transfer control to the tribe." Both the request and transfer would have to be approved by the secretary of the interior, "who may request a recommendation from the Review Committee."

National NAGPRA maintains online databases of the information from completed inventories.[18] As of November 5, 2010, 4,784 inventories had been published by 445 museums that classified 42,305 "human remains" and 1,027,261 "associated funerary objects" with "cultural affiliation." Of these ancestors, only 9,144 (roughly 22 percent) had been repatriated. (No summary data is provided on associated funerary objects.) Concurrently, 17,407 inventories have been completed by 667 museums. A total of 124,534 "human remains" and 932,420 "associated funerary objects" are classified as "culturally unidentifiable."

Only time will tell if the new rule changes these results. In the interim, everyone concerned—federal agents, institution staff, scientists, and native people—understands that the classifications have resulted in the overwhelming majority of native ancestors remaining in the control and possession of museums. Everyone knows also that despite NAGPRA's provisions to the contrary, scientists at these museums are conducting collateral research on native dead and, where educational programs exist, using native ancestors in the classroom. In fact, several scientists—even while lamenting NAGPRA's tragic impact on their work and "scientific freedom" —have boasted that NAGPRA has improved their access to native human remains and material objects and thus furthered their research and advising.[19]

Self-Determination, Federal Plenary Power, and the Science That Arbitrates Them

NAGPRA's affirmation of native human rights to self-determination is immediately undercut by its restrictions against the unrecognized in two directions: first, the denial of the international legal status and rights of the unrecognized to repatriate; second, the exclusion of the unrecognized from consultation on the disposition of the culturally unidentifiable.

NAGPRA's provisions for inclusive consultation and the equality of native epistemology and expertise affirm international human rights—particularly the United Nations Charter of 1946, the International Covenant on Civil and Political Rights of 1966, and the International Covenant on Economic, Social, and Cultural Rights of 1966, to which the United States is a signatory. Article 1, Part 2, of the UN Charter states that its purpose is "to develop friendly relations among nations based on respect for the principle of equal rights and self-determination of peoples, and to take other appropriate measures to strengthen universal peace." The charter acknowledges that basic human rights to self-determination belong not merely to "nations" (as is customarily assumed) but to all "peoples"—including nonstate political entities such as indigenous groups.[20]

Article 1 of the International Covenant on Civil and Political Rights and the International Covenant on Economic, Social, and Cultural Rights, both of 1966, states that "all peoples have the right of self-determination. By virtue of that right they freely determine their political status and freely pursue their economic, social and cultural development." This provision acknowledges that "all peoples"—including nonstate political entities such as native groups—possess inherent and inalienable rights to self-determination. In fact, there are no provisions in either the charter or the covenants for states to establish policies or procedures that usurp or otherwise override the rights of all peoples to the self-determination of their governments, laws, economies, and social and cultural activities. The charter and covenants explicitly affirm a principle of consultative and procedural inclusivity of all peoples in the development and implementation of any policies that address or imply their civil and political rights.

All of these principles were affirmed by the Declaration on the Rights of Indigenous Peoples, which the UN General Assembly adopted on September 13, 2007, and which the United States voted against but has since affirmed. Article 3 of the Declaration provides that indigenous peoples—collectively and individually—possess the right of self-determination: "By virtue of that right they freely determine their political status and freely pursue their economic, social and cultural development."[21] Within the enumeration of these rights, Article 12 addresses repatriation:

1. Indigenous peoples have the right to manifest, practice, develop and teach their spiritual and religious traditions, customs and ceremonies; the right to maintain, protect, and have access in privacy to their religious and cultural sites; the right to the use and control of their ceremonial objects; and the right to the repatriation of their human remains.

2. States shall seek to enable the access and/or repatriation of ceremonial objects and human remains in their possession through fair, transparent and effective mechanisms developed in conjunction with indigenous peoples concerned.

The Declaration links the rights of repatriation to the manifestation, practice, development, and teaching of cultural beliefs and territorial integrity. It obligates states to "enable" indigenous access to and the repatriation of their ancestors and ceremonial objects from public institutions.

These links emerge from indigenous peoples' struggles for self-determination against the structures of "settler colonial" power[22] and the histories of cultural exploitation and forced assimilation that have served to operationalize that power over them.[23] Consequently, they reflect precedent that the credible redress of human rights must attend to the historical experiences of those they concern to be considered credible within the international community. Otherwise, such efforts risk being perceived as a coercive or "top-down" suppression of those experiences and their legacies.[24] Article 12 is significant thus within the context of indigenous experiences of multiple kinds of colonial and imperial practices aimed at cultural genocide, including grave desecration, property theft, land dispossession, and the use of native dead and material culture in empirically based knowledge claims that native peoples were inhumane and their societies inferior. These efforts serve the state's interests in rationalizing native genocide, land dispossession, and political subjugation.

NAGPRA and its provisions for cultural affiliation and the disposition of the culturally unidentifiable do not adhere to the principles of international human rights affirmed by the charter, international covenants, or Declaration. Instead, NAGPRA's use of "culturally unidentifiable" undermines native human rights by filtering repatriation rights through federal recognition. This filtering is not just an effect of unfortunate wording that weakens what would otherwise have been NAGPRA's unequivocal affirmation of native human rights. NAGPRA's provisions regarding cultural affiliation and the culturally unidentifiable represent an *operationalization* of federal power over the legal terms and conditions of native rights within the United States.[25] This operationalization deliberately implicates native standing and rights in the international community not only to repatriate but to all of the associated rights of repatriation, such as the manifestation, practice, development, and teaching of cultural beliefs and territorial integrity. NAGPRA thus effectively repositions native legal standing and rights under federal plenary power.

Federal plenary power has been historically challenged within native struggles for self-determination,[26] including those that informed NAGPRA's lobbying and passage.[27] A key aspect of these struggles has been native peoples' assertions of the relevance and viability of their knowledge—as mattering to understandings of native histories, cultures, and identities on their own terms and to the histories and cultures of the United States, often in regard to human rights violations by native genocide. In these ways, native peoples have insisted that their knowledge is germane to how federal law ought to be reformed to better conform to the human rights accords to which the United States is obligated as a signatory. These types of claims were potent in securing NAGPRA's passage.

But NAGPRA, situated within U.S. cultural heritage laws, likewise navigates the knowledge claims and political demands of empirical science and scientists.[28] Native claims about empirical science and scientists' historical and current roles in undermining natives' humanity and human rights are not new, but in the context of NAGPRA, these claims were focused anew on the nationalist, racist, and ethnocentric foundations of empirical science as articulated within the disciplines of archaeology and anthropology.[29] Natives charged empiricism an inherently political ideology, discourse, and research practice aimed at denying its own motivations and cultural influences in the name of objectivity and neutrality even as empirical scientists sought positions within federal policy-making processes as administrators, staff, and consultants on such politically charged matters as native governance and territorial rights and the nation's cultural heritage.[30] These criticisms—coupled with those from other disenfranchised communities, including women and nonheterosexually identified people (not necessarily mutually exclusive categories)—had a profound effect in exposing U.S. colonial-imperial histories and social legacies, changing the disciplinary contours and public perceptions of archaeology and anthropology, and revolutionizing university curricula to include critical race/ethnic, gender, and sexuality studies.

Seeking to maintain their long-institutionalized relevance in the direction and administration of U.S. cultural heritage policies and related public debates over the meaning of America's past and current national character, archaeologists and anthropologists worked hard during NAGPRA's passage and development of its regulations to protect their professional standing and authority in the academy, with the government, and in public opinion. These efforts found an especially sympathetic ear among federal agents and public officials who were challenged by the broader legal and political implications of native criticisms for understanding and redress of native treaty and territorial rights. As Laurajane Smith argues so well in *Archaeological Theory and the Politics of Cultural Heritage* (2004), it was against the veracity and implications of native knowledge claims and their persistent if modest revolution of academic spaces and federal policies that "archaeological claims to professional objectivity and neutrality found synergy with the need of policy makers to understand the politically charged claims made by American Indians about the nature of the past, and subsequently the present."[31] That "synergy" needed and found particularly useful the empirical language of "objectivity and neutrality" in negotiating and mitigating against the implications of native knowledge and political demands.[32] And this finding was not new. The utility of empirical archaeology and anthropology had long since been a feature of federal policies.[33] Empiricism had a key historical role in efforts to undermine native rights to governance, territorial integrity, and cultural autonomy, crystalizing powerfully within the development and implementation of assimilation policies in the latter half of the 1800s.[34]

The question here is how the culturally affiliated and unidentifiable instance the operationalization of federal power and the ideologies and discourses of empirical knowledge in the service of native dominance?

Essentially, they did so by articulating native human rights to federal recognition. This articulation reinforced the empirical science in which recognition had found such potent logic and rationale as an inherently objective reckoning of native legal standing. It is an authority and discourse that has been seized upon regularly: by the courts in the Ancient One (Kennewick Man) case; by public education institutions in conducting consultation; by museums in determining cultural affiliation. In each case, the aim has been to exclude the unrecognized and dismiss the veracity of native oral history and experts as politically biased, invented, and uncorroborated.[35]

The Logics of Federal Objectivity as Scientific Objectivity

From 1987 to 1990, five congressional hearings were held on the seven drafts leading to what would be the final version of NAGPRA.[36] Included in the approximately seventeen hundred pages of recorded testimony, statements, and briefs offered at the hearings, Native American Rights Foundation (NARF) attorneys addressed the fact and consequence of NAGPRA's reliance on the *Procedures for Establishing That an American Indian Group Exists as an Indian Tribe* (25 U.S.C. 83) in its language regarding "cultural affiliation" and the "culturally unidentified." While NARF was concerned with the excessive legal and economic burdens that prevented native groups from petitioning for recognition and consequently excluded them from NAGPRA's delineation of repatriation rights, I focus here on the ideological and discursive implications of NAGPRA's reliance on the promised objectivity and neutrality of the seven "mandatory criteria" for determining the recognizability of an Indian tribe.[37]

In January 1975, Senate Joint Resolution 133 (Public Law 93-580) established the American Indian Policy Review Commission (AIPRC) to study federal policy, law, and administration concerning American Indians.[38] In May 1977, the commission issued its report. In relation to recognition, the AIPRC report sharply criticized the effects of termination policy initiated by House Concurrent Resolution 108 (67 Stat. B122) of 1953 and the inconsistent and arbitrary procedures that the Bureau of Indian Affairs (BIA) used in the recognition process.

Deploying the language of objectivity and neutrality, the AIPRC recommended that the BIA develop procedures with "valid and consistent" guidelines and evaluative criteria that would be applied fairly, consistently, and purposefully to all tribes seeking recognition.[39] In response, the BIA quickly developed and released its proposed regulations on June 16, 1977 (25 C.F.R. 83). It then held "approximately 400 meetings, discussions and conversations about federal recognition with other federal agencies, state government officials, tribal groups, petitioners, congressional staff members, and legal representatives of petitioning groups."[40] Officials received more than sixty comments on the regulations, which were revised in March 1978 and published in the *Federal Register* six months later.[41] The regulations were amended in 1994, 1997, and 2000 following testimony from tribes, attorneys, and scholars at congressional hearings. These testimonies paralleled the criticisms of the BIA's inconsistent and uneven implementation of the Procedures by the General Accounting Office audits of 2001, 2002, and 2005.[42]

To administer the regulations, the BIA established the Office of Federal Acknowledgment (OFA was initially known as and is often still referred to as BAR, the Branch of Acknowledgement and Research). Deploying language about the necessity for objectivity and neutrality within recognition procedures and decisions, BAR staffers and consultants have been appointed predominantly from the predispositions of empirical science, including the disciplines of archaeology, anthropology, history, genealogy, and law.[43]

This is not a new issue. Empirical science and scientists have long since been institutionalized in federal policy development and oversight with regard to native legal standing and rights as well as within related policies regarding U.S. cultural heritage and natural resource management.[44] Science's renewed authority within the procedures' development and implementation, however, was particularly charged for native groups petitioning for recognition. As empirical science and scientists were extended authority to decide the terms of native legal standing and rights, native criticisms of the political history and consequences of empirical ideologies and discourses in native histories of colonialism, imperialism, and racism were minimized and rejected.[45] The reinstitutionalization of empiricism/scientists, then, was perceived as a dismissal of native knowledge claims and political demands for human rights redress through recognition processes.

At the same time, BAR staffers and consultants have been bribed, have received death threats, and have had their offices vandalized.[46] These incidents escalated through the 1990s to such an extent that the identities of BAR staffers and consultants were eventually made confidential, as was the move of BAR's offices to an unpublished location.[47] All of this confidentiality and anonymity reinforced the BAR's and its scientists' self-presentations of their objectivity and neutrality. Federal interests in understanding but ultimately diffusing the political force of native legal claims about U.S. histories of human rights violations—specifically on point of the recognition of those rights—were likewise served. This matters in consequential ways. These processes of empowerment and disenfranchisement are articulated specifically within the procedures to enforce the empirical ideologies and discourses of cultural authenticity.[48]

The procedures detail the process by which a tribe can receive recognition, including the submission of documentary evidence that it has satisfied the seven mandatory criteria for acknowledgment and the evaluation, public comment, and appeal phases of evaluation. Denied the right to petition for acknowledgment are terminated tribes and "splinter groups, political factions, communities or groups of any character that have been formed in recent times."[49] The seven "mandatory criteria" include "(a) The petitioner has been identified as an American Indian entity on a substantially *continuous* basis since 1900. (b) A predominant portion of the petitioning group comprises a distinct community and has existed as a community *from historical times until the present.* (c) The petitioner has maintained political influence or authority over its members as an autonomous entity *from historical times until the present.*"[50]

The procedures explain that "a criterion shall be considered met if the available evidence establishes a reasonable likelihood of the validity of the facts relating to that criterion."[51] The bar of "reasonable" evidence must be met with external sources; the procedures point petitioning tribes to the documents of federal authorities, state and county governments, parishes, churches, "anthropologists, historians, and/or other scholars," newspapers and books, recognized tribes, and native organizations. In the language of empiricism, these requirements ensure that petitioning tribes can objectively establish that they are a tribe, assuming that their own documents and expertise would be politically biased.

The mandatory criteria assume that a tribe petitioning for recognition possesses the qualities that the procedures identify as characterizing an existing Indian tribe. The Indian tribe is not taken to be configured as such within the law or through the processes of petitioning to be recognized. The Indian tribe and mandatory criteria by implication contain within them the self-evident truths—objectively observable—of what it means to be a tribe. This depoliticizes not only the policy and its regulations but the role of BIA officials, BAR staff, contracted reviewers of the applications (primarily anthropologists, historians, and genealogists), and native peoples.[52]

This is posed, of course, against the "special interests" and political biases of petitioning tribes to secure the benefits of recognition.

The procedures thus negate the politics of knowledge and interpretative practice operating within recognition, treating BAR scientists and consultants as objective and everyone else, principally native peoples, as not. The oppositions are the precondition of federal authorities being able to regenerate and even necessitate their authority over native standing and rights. By relying on the language and individuals that stand for objectivity and neutrality, they have fulfilled the spirit of the law.

But the criteria for historical and cultural continuity, distinction, autonomy, and cohesiveness are anything but neutral. They pretend the irrelevance of the histories and consequences of U.S. colonialism, imperialism, and racism for native peoples—as though these histories had not directly produced the very social conditions in which native groups are not recognized and/or have not been able to maintain their cultural practices, geographic associations, social interactions, or political cohesion.

But the expectations also pretend the authority of the empiricist sciences that so deeply inform the recognizability of native groups as native in the commitments of a liberal democracy to multicultural humanism and pluralism.[53] As I argue in *Native Acts: Law, Recognition, and Cultural Authenticity* (2011), recognition is predicated on a very particular notion of native cultural authenticity, one that is simultaneously historical (forever stuck in an authenticity and integrity of the ancient past) and without history (in the context of colonialism, imperialism, and racism).[54] The discursive and ideological circuitry between recognition and authenticity that results is important to understanding the historical, cultural, genealogical, and geographic relations that recognition articulates for native peoples—relations that federal policies have sought to destroy but that must be made continually anew so that natives can be recognized and thus made governable as authentically native. The ideologies and discourses that hold together these relations of power and knowledge are deployed in the service of federal authority, wherein native human rights to self-determination are overpowered by federal interests.

And so goes NAGPRA. The act's provisions for native "cultural affiliation" and the "culturally unidentifiable" treat native historical, genealogical, and geographic relationships as evident by the fact of recognition. The unrecognized are treated as though the absence of their legal standing results naturally from the absence of their authentic histories and cultures as native. These perceived absences—the logic of lacks—are made to be indicative of native groups having no credible or legitimate historical, genealogical, or geographic relationship to or knowledge of their ancestors or material cultures. So, inevitably, they have no right to repatriate. These relations of power and knowledge are instanced by the transposition of the unrecognized for the culturally unidentifiable—the recasting of "unrecognized" as the "culturally unidentifiable." This, of course, has broader legal implications that go to the legitimacy of native knowledge and rights claims in the context of both U.S. histories of human rights violations and the international laws that demand their redress. After all, unrecognized groups have a lot to say, and we have a lot to learn from them about the operations and functions of power in articulating the social relations and conditions of dominance.

A Conclusion

I am not saying a lot of things in this brief essay. I am not saying that recognition does not matter. It is currently the only legal venue within the United States for native peoples to secure their rights to governance, territorial integrity, and cultural autonomy. We will see, in time, if the U.S. affirmation of the Declaration on the Rights of Indigenous Peoples makes a difference in this. I am also not saying that any group claiming to be native ought to be treated as native. The severe political, economic, and cultural consequences of false claims to native identity and collective standing certainly have contributed to undermining native human rights.

I am also not arguing that the recognized are without relevant historical and cultural knowledge or that they have not challenged the final determinations of cultural affiliation on behalf of unrecognized groups. In fact, several alliances have been formed between recognized and unrecognized tribes to ensure the repatriation of those classified as being without cultural affiliation or identifiability as native.

But what those alliances for native human rights to self-determination indicate is not the unsettling of existing relations of power within recognition or repatriation or a challenge of those knowledge systems, like empiricism, that so deeply (in)form the confluence of recognition and repatriation discourses within NAGPRA. Those alliances demonstrate how native peoples have been made to navigate around and collaborate with one another because of federal authority and dominant science claims about their histories, cultures, and genealogies. It is not that empirical science is without value. But it should be accorded a similar kind of respect and role in federal policy making—whether about recognition or repatriation—as native forms and practices of knowledge, experts, and expertise. Until that happens and revolutionizes such legal categories as affiliation, identification, and recognition, NAGPRA's promise as human rights legislation will be deferred.

Notes

1. Michel Foucault, *Power/Knowledge: Selected Interviews and Other Writings* (New York: Pantheon, 1972).

2. Robert F. Berkhofer Jr., *The White Man's Indian: Images of the American Indian from Columbus to the Present* (New York: Vintage, 1979).

3. Ibid.; Robert E. Bieder, *Science Encounters the Indian, 1820–1880: The Early Years of American Ethnology* (Norman: University of Oklahoma Press, 1986).

4. Laurajane Smith, *Archaeological Theory and the Politics of Cultural Heritage* (New York: Routledge, 2004).

5. S. James Anaya, *Indigenous Peoples in International Law* (New York: Oxford University Press, 1996).

6. Vine Deloria Jr., *God Is Red: A Native View of Religion* (New York: Dell, 1973).

7. NAGPRA was developed within a complex matrix of U.S. federal laws that aim to protect "cultural heritage." These laws include the Antiquities Act (16 U.S.C. 431–33) of 1906, the Archaeological and Historic Preservation Act (16 U.S.C. 469–469c-2) of 1960, the National Historic Preservation Act (16 U.S.C. 470) of 1966, and the Archaeological Resources Protection Act (16 U.S.C. 470aa–mm) of 1979. The notion of a decidedly collective and particularly American cultural heritage in native human remains and cultural objects—one that everyone has a right to access and study—needs some serious deconstructive work, especially for its participation in configuring an idealized notion of U.S. history and nationhood.

8. NAGPRA does not stop excavations per se. The exception is in the case of "inadvertent discoveries," such as during construction projects, and then only for a thirty-day period during which coroners determine cause of death and general age of the remains; in the case of possible native affiliation, "most likely descendants" are then consulted regarding disposition. Consequently, "protection" is contingent on property title (see Section 10.4).

9. "*Lineal descendant* means an individual tracing his or her ancestry directly and without interruption by means of the traditional kinship system of the appropriate Indian tribe or Native Hawaiian organization or by the common law system of descendance to a known Native American individual whose remains, funerary objects, or sacred objects are being claimed under these regulations. *Indian tribe*

means any tribe, band, nation, or other organized Indian group or community of Indians, including any Alaska Native village or corporation as defined in or established by the Alaska Native Claims Settlement Act (43 U.S.C. 1601 et seq.), which is recognized as eligible for the special programs and services provided by the United States to Indians because of their status as Indians. . . . *Native Hawaiian organization* means any organization that: (A) Serves and represents the interests of Native Hawaiians; (B) Has as a primary and stated purpose the provision of services to Native Hawaiians; and (C) Has expertise in Native Hawaiian affairs" (NAGPRA Section 2 Definitions).

10. Sites of origin are assumed to be self-evident, indicated by records of acquisition. However, since these records are often absent, inaccurate, or incomplete, geographic origin also becomes a point of consultation.

11. NAGPRA covers "human remains" as any physical remains of a body excluding hair strands, parts that are naturally shed, and any other body parts that were freely given by an individual prior to death; "funerary objects" as objects placed with the body during a death ceremony or made specifically for mortuary purposes (such as cremation urns); "sacred objects" as objects of ceremonial significance that are needed for traditional practices; and "objects of cultural patrimony" as objects of such significance that they are considered inalienable (communally owned).

12. Smith, *Archaeological Theory*, 20–21, 102–3.

13. Suzan Shown Harjo, "Native Peoples' Cultural and Human Rights: An Unfinished Agenda," *Arizona State Law Journal* 24 (1992): 321; Jack F. Trope and Walter R. Echo-Hawk, "The Native American Graves Protection and Repatriation Act: Background and Legislative History," *Arizona State Law Journal* 24 (1992): 35; James Riding In, "Repatriation: A Pawnee's Perspective," *American Indian Quarterly* 20 (1996): 238–50.

14. See Ronald Niezen, *Spirit Wars: Native North American Religions in the Age of Nation Building* (Berkeley: University of California Press, 2000). The decriminalization of native religions did not formally occur until the passage of the American Indian Religious Freedom Act of 1978. See Christopher Vecsey, ed., *Handbook of American Indian Religious Freedom* (New York: Crossroad, 1993).

15. The debates surrounding the Ancient One, or Kennewick Man, represented a profound instance where natives were frequently represented by scientists as incapable of understanding the empirical value and social relevance of studying ancient human remains. See Roger Downey, *Riddle of the Bones: Politics, Science, Race, and the Story of Kennewick Man* (New York: Copernicus, 2000); James C. Chatters, *Ancient Encounters: Kennewick Man and the First Americans* (New York: Simon and Schuster, 2001); David Hurst Thomas, *Skull Wars: Kennewick Man, Archaeology, and the Battle for Native American Identity* (New York: Basic Books,

2001); Jeffrey Benedict, *No Bone Unturned: The Adventures of a Top Smithsonian Forensic Scientist and the Legal Battle for America's Oldest Skeletons* (New York: HarperCollins, 2003).

16. The discursive and ideological lines between native knowledge and Western science are, of course, much more complicated than this essay suggests. See, e.g., Joe Watkins, *Indigenous Archaeology: American Indian Values and Scientific Practice* (Walnut Creek, Calif.: AltaMira, 2001).

17. Since the Alaska Native Claims Settlement Act (Public Law 92-203, 85 Stat. 688) of 1971, the federal category of "Indian tribe" includes recognized American Indian tribes and Alaska Native villages. "Native Hawaiian organizations" must possess an analogous status as recognized.

18. http://www.nps.gov/nagpra/ONLINEDB/INDEX.HTM.

19. Elizabeth Weiss, "NAGPRA: Before and After" (2006), http://www.friends ofpast.org/nagpra/06WeissNAGPRA.pdf; Elizabeth Weiss, "Research & NAG-PRA," *SAA Archaeological Record* 6 (2006): 29–31; Elizabeth Weiss, *Reburying the Past: The Effects of Repatriation and Reburial on Scientific Inquiry* (New York: Nova Science, 2008); Elizabeth Weiss, "The Bone Battle: The Attack on Scientific Free-dom," *Liberty* 23 (2009): 39–44; Stephen D. Ousley, William T. Billeck, and R. Eric Hollinger, "Federal Legislation and the Role of Physical Anthropology in Repatria-tion," *Yearbook of Physical Anthropology* 48 (2005): 2–32.

20. Joanne Barker, "The Human Genome Diversity Project: 'Peoples,' 'Popu-lations,' and the Cultural Politics of Identification," *Cultural Studies* 18 (2004): 578–613.

21. For the full text of the Declaration, see http://www.un.org/esa/socdev /unpfii/documents/DRIPS_en.pdf.

22. Patrick Wolfe, *Settler Colonialism and the Transformation of Anthropology: The Politics and Poetics of an Ethnographic Event* (London: Cassell Wellington, 1999); Patrick Wolfe, "Settler Colonialism and the Elimination of the Native," *Jour-nal of Genocide Research* 8 (2006): 387–409.

23. Niezen, *Spirit Wars*.

24. Anaya, *Indigenous Peoples*.

25. Michel Foucault, *Discipline and Punish: The Birth of the Prison* (New York: Vintage, 1979).

26. Vine Deloria Jr. and Clifford Lytle, *The Nations Within: The Past and Future of American Indian Sovereignty* (New York: Pantheon, 1984).

27. Harjo, "Native Peoples' Cultural and Human Rights"; Trope and Echo-Hawk, "Native American Graves Protection and Repatriation Act"; Riding In, "Repatriation"; Devon A. Mihesuah, ed., *The Repatriation Reader: Who Owns American Indian Remains?* (Lincoln: University of Nebraska Press, 2000).

28. Smith, *Archaeological Theory*.

29. Deloria, *Custer Died for Your Sins*; Vine Deloria Jr., *Red Earth/White Lies: Native Americans and the Myth of Scientific Fact* (New York: Scribner, 1995).

30. Smith, *Archaeological Theory*; Clayton W. Dumont Jr., *The Promise of Post-structuralist Sociology: Marginalized Peoples and the Problem of Knowledge* (Albany: State University of New York Press, 2008).

31. Smith, *Archaeological Theory*, 157.

32. Ibid., 156–61.

33. Berkhofer, *White Man's Indian*; Deloria, *Custer Died for Your Sins*; Deloria, *Red Earth/White Lies*; Niezen, *Spirit Wars*; Dumont, *Promise of Poststructuralist Sociology*.

34. Niezen, *Spirit Wars*.

35. Dumont, *Promise of Poststructuralist Sociology*; Clayton W. Dumont Jr., "Contesting Scientists' Narrations of NAGPRA's Legislative History: Rule 10.11 and the Recovery of 'Culturally Unidentifiable' Ancestors," *Wicazo Sa Review* 26 (2011): 5–41.

36. Dumont, "Contesting Scientists' Narrations."

37. Alaska native villages and native Hawaiian organizations are ostensibly recognized by other legal means. See J. Kēhaulani Kauanui, "Precarious Positions: Native Hawaiians and U.S. Federal Recognition," *Contemporary Pacific* 17 (2005): 1–27; J. Kēhaulani Kauanui, *Hawaiian Blood: Colonialism and the Politics of Sovereignty and Indigeneity* (Durham: Duke University Press, 2008).

38. The resolution was passed in the same year as the Indian Self-Determination and Education Assistance Act (25 U.S.C. 450), which reversed termination policy initiated by House Concurrent Resolution 108 of 1953. It was addressed to American Indian tribes and not Alaska natives, whose status and rights had been addressed by the Alaska Native Claims Settlement Act of 1971.

39. American Indian Policy Review Commission Final Report, May 17, 1977, 2 vols., http://www.eric.ed.gov/.

40. *Federal Register*, 1978, 39361.

41. Ibid.

42. See Peter Beinart, "Lost Tribes: Native Americans and Government Anthropologists Feud over Indian Identity," in *American Indians and U.S. Politics: A Companion Reader*, ed. John M. Meyer (Westport, Conn.: Praeger, 2002), 143–54; Mark Edwin Miller, *Forgotten Tribes: Unrecognized Indians the Federal Acknowledgement Process* (Lincoln: University of Nebraska Press, 2004). Antigaming constituencies and elected officials have frequently called for audits based on the on erroneous concern that tribes seek recognition status merely to open up lucrative

gaming operations. See Joanne Barker, "Recognition," *Indigenous Nations Journal and American Studies* 46 (2005): 117–45.

43. Beinart, "Lost Tribes"; Miller, *Forgotten Tribes.*

44. Smith, *Archaeological Theory.*

45. Ibid.

46. Beinart, "Lost Tribes."

47. Ibid.

48. Joanne Barker, *Native Acts: The Law of Cultural Authenticity* (Durham: Duke University Press, 2011).

49. 25 C.F.R. 83.3, *Scope.*

50. Bureau of Indian Affairs, 25 C.F.R. 83, *Procedures for Establishing That an American Indian Group Exists as an Indian Tribe.*

51. 25 C.F.R. 83.6d, *General Provisions.*

52. Miller, *Forgotten Tribes.*

53. Elizabeth Povinelli, *The Cunning of Recognition: Indigenous Alterities and the Making of Australian Multiculturalism* (Durham: Duke University Press, 2002); Patchen Markell, *Bound by Recognition* (Princeton: Princeton University Press, 2003).

54. Barker, *Native Acts.*

State Recognition of American Indian Tribes

A Survey of State-Recognized Tribes and State Recognition Processes

K. ALEXA KOENIG & JONATHAN STEIN

This chapter analyzes the legal status of state-recognized American Indian tribes—those tribes that have been recognized by their respective states but not by the federal government. State recognition[1] is a widely practiced but poorly understood aspect of the U.S. federalist system that has been increasingly employed in relations between tribal nations and individual states as a counterpart to the unwieldy federal recognition process. Thus, there is a pressing need to clarify and better understand the panoply of state recognition processes and their results as well as their implications for the rights of tribal nations. Internet sources that list state-recognized tribes vary dramatically in quality and too often offer little explanation of their standards or methodology. These sites also do not detail the widely disparate state recognition processes.[2] Even a leading Indian law text, *Cohen's Handbook of Federal Indian Law*, offers only a cursory overview of state recognition and fails to include a comprehensive list of state-recognized Indian tribes.[3] This chapter fills these gaps by documenting the results of one of the first systematic efforts to survey, categorize, and analyze the complexity of state recognition of American Indian tribes. We highlight particular contexts in which tribal-state relations emerged and examine the diversity of state recognition processes to more precisely define state recognition within the context of the federalist system and to address the ways in which it functions to facilitate state-tribal relations. Finally, we consider the ways in which state recognition contributes to indigenous governance and self-determination in the international arena.

State versus Federal Recognition

The federal government recognizes 566 tribes, but dozens of other tribal nations are recognized solely by the states in which they reside.[4] According to our research, twenty-one states—Alabama, California, Connecticut, Delaware, Georgia, Hawai'i, Kentucky, Louisiana, Massachusetts, Michigan, Missouri, Montana, New Jersey, New York, North Carolina, Ohio, Oklahoma, South Carolina, Texas, Vermont, and Virginia—recognize a total of 73 tribes that are not federally recognized.[5] An additional four states—Florida, Kansas, Maryland, and Tennessee—have considered or recently employed some form of state recognition.[6] Because this area of law and practice is changing rapidly, this chapter is meant to be a starting place for further research, not a static overview of recognition states and state-recognized tribes.

Over the past few decades, states and tribes have increasingly realized that state recognition can serve as an important albeit limited alternative to federal recognition. State recognition can facilitate communication between state and tribal governments, encourage diversity in state institutions, enable the provision of state services to underserved populations, and increase tourism.[7] State recognition can also support tribes' rights and provide important benefits in their relations with state and federal governments[8] as well as clarify which tribes are exempt from the purview of legislation that explicitly excludes "Indians."[9] This emergent state-tribal rapprochement is evidenced by the many states that have recently codified their state recognition processes, are planning to implement new recognition processes, or are working to enhance their state recognition processes.[10]

An important example in analyzing the historical and political significance of state recognition lies within the continuing relationship between tribal nations and what is now the Commonwealth of Virginia. While the region has been a native homeland for at least twelve thousand years, none of the tribal nations within the commonwealth today are recognized by the U.S. federal government. Although the histories of the indigenous peoples of Virginia have been richly documented since the colonial period, they have also been appropriated and obscured by Euro-American conquest mythology and its voracious appetite for caricatures of Pocahontas. Racial ideology and racist legislation in the twentieth century also worked to obfuscate the identities and histories of Indian people in Virginia. The 1924 Racial Integrity Act is a case in point: It declared that only two racial categories—"white" and "colored"—existed in Virginia.[11] Until this legislation was declared unconstitutional by the U.S. Supreme Court in 1967[12] and repealed in 1975,[13] Census records identified individual tribal members as "colored" rather than as American Indian.[14] Despite the destructive impact of both racism and popular mythology, the tribal nations in Virginia endure.

Members of the Mattaponi Indian nation and the Pamunkey nation, for example, continue to live on their respective reservation lands, which were established in the mid-seventeenth century and are among the oldest in the United States.[15] As of 2010, Virginia recognized eleven tribal nations.

Such instances of state recognition raise several questions about the federal government's inability or refusal to recognize many tribal nations that have long-standing relationships with individual states and suggest that this lack of recognition is not so much a policy failure as a policy choice. In Los Angeles County, for example, more than twenty-eight hundred archeological sites, thousands of pages of Spanish Mission and Catholic Church records, and hundreds of early photographs delineate the history and culture of the Gabrielino-Tongva Indians.[16] Nonetheless, the Gabrielino-Tongva tribe is not recognized by the federal government, despite a treaty signed with the United States in 1851.[17] The Gabrielinos cannot expect federal recognition by the Bureau of Indian Affairs (BIA) any time soon, since, like other tribal nations that have sought recognition through the BIA administrative process, their petition remains on a waiting list, with a decision as long as decades away: The tribe is currently 141 on the BIA's list of Indian tribes seeking recognition, moving up just one or two positions each year.[18]

The Shinnecock nation of New York, whose reservation is adjacent to the Shinnecock Hills PGA Golf Course and the tony residences of Southampton, Long Island, became the 565th federally acknowledged tribal nation in October 2010, nearly four decades after the group's struggle to secure federal recognition through the BIA began.[19] In 2007, after years of litigation in the U.S. District Court, a federal judge declared the Shinnecock nation recognized based on overwhelming evidence of their long-standing presence within and recognition by the State of New York.[20] Although the BIA initially argued that the court's judgment did not bind the federal government and refused to acknowledge the Shinnecocks, the bureau subsequently relented.[21]

While these examples strongly suggest the federal government's inability and/or unwillingness to recognize long-standing indigenous groups and thus the potential importance of state recognition within the federalist system, the federalist approach itself warrants continuing scrutiny, since many of the most egregious abuses enacted by states on tribes were done in the name of federalism. As Deborah A. Rosen has pointed out, states have historically "placed questions of their authority over Indians within the framework of federalism," which provided states with considerable leverage to assume authority over Indian lands and resources and to challenge federal interference.[22] Moreover, states have long relied on the discourse of conquest to validate their abuses, acting as though tribal sovereignty and indigenous rights were nonexistent.[23] Historically, states too frequently recognized only the federal government as a valid barrier to acquiring Indian lands and resources. All current state efforts to recognize tribes must be understood within that contentious context.

The Significance of State Recognition within the Federalist System

The sovereignty of American Indian tribes is unquestionably inherent. Yet the U.S. federal government has claimed to have "plenary power" over Indian tribes: primary authority to recognize Indian tribes' sovereign status.[24] But state recognition is an alternative legal and political status to this formal federal recognition.[25] Much like federal recognition, state recognition operates as a means for states to acknowledge the long-standing existence of specific, inherently sovereign Indian tribes within state borders and can be a means to address and rectify centuries of oppressive policies and practices with regard to tribal nations.[26] Reflecting the diverse approaches of different states, state recognition can establish a government-to-government relationship based on law or merely grant official acknowledgment of a tribe's continued existence. State recognition can also be a formal prerequisite to certain federal and state benefits earmarked for indigenous communities. Alternatively—and perhaps more strategically from the perspective of some state officials—state recognition may simply be employed by a state government to assert its support for cultural diversity, enhance tourism, and commemorate historical locales.

The federal government has endorsed and legitimized state recognition by, among other things, providing certain federal rights or benefits (such as scholarships, grants, or health services) based on the legal status of state recognition.[27] Through its decision to bestow particular federal rights or benefits to state-recognized Indian tribes, the United States has repeatedly acknowledged the constitutional authority of states to recognize tribes.[28] What becomes debatable from the perspective of the federal government is the source of that authority—specifically, whether that authority is delegated to states by Congress or is inherent in the states themselves.

Indian law treatises and case law agree that state authority to recognize tribes is historically grounded in relationships formed between American

Indian tribes and British, Dutch, and French colonies prior to the establishment of the United States. But this is the point of departure for current theories regarding the basis of that authority. One approach would limit state authority to powers delegated by the United States, on the assumption that the United States holds plenary power over all Indian tribes, whether or not they are federally recognized.[29] Because of this claim to plenary authority, federal laws involving Indian tribes are often presumed to preempt state laws regardless of whether the United States has recognized a particular tribal nation. This plenary approach is founded on a historical paradigm of federal supremacy and the colonially rooted notion that U.S. Indian law "protects" tribes from states and individuals and thus purportedly prevents state or individual infringement on tribal affairs.[30]

We favor what we label the "federalist" approach, which is supported by the actions of the twenty-one states that have recognized Indian tribes without federal authorization. The federalist approach proposes that inherently sovereign Indian tribes do not require federal "protection" from state authority in all contexts and recognizes that many tribal nations want state recognition. In such cases, state recognition does not conflict with the federal government's goal of furthering tribal self-governance: State and tribal authority may be viewed as complementing federal authority. Under this federalist approach, federal supremacy does not reach all matters regarding Indian tribes: State and tribal authority operate on their own where the United States has refused or failed to act and thus where the federal government does not have a government-to-government relationship with a particular tribe.

Under the federalist approach, states' authority to recognize tribes is based on the reservoir of state powers preserved by the Tenth Amendment, which guarantees that powers not specifically enumerated in the U.S. Constitution as powers of the federal government are reserved to the states. Tribal nations' right to such recognition is based on their inherent sovereignty. When state recognition is desired by an Indian tribe and furthers the goal of tribal sovereignty, promoting federal and state objectives favoring tribal self-sufficiency, federal power does not preempt state or tribal authority.

When the federal government fails or refuses to address a policy problem, state governments often will seek to fill that gap. Under this federalist construct, state authority (as long as it does not conflict with federal or tribal interests in tribal self-determination) complements federal authority, encouraging experimentation and the flexibility to meet local needs.

According to legal scholar Felix Cohen, "State-recognized tribes are, by definition, not considered federally recognized tribes, and the legal status of their reservations and the scope of their governmental authority, if any, is a matter of state—not federal—law."[31]

Traditional Euro-American notions of federalism gird this limitation. As Cohen explains, "State-recognized tribes are generally not the subject of federal legislation and concern. Hence, there would not appear to be any conflict with federal law when states administer their own programs of respect and protection."[32] This statement should hold true not only under a Tenth Amendment analysis but also under the "canons of construction" in U.S. Indian law, a federal doctrine that holds that "all ambiguities [in the law] are to be resolved in favor of the Indians."[33]

According to both the plenary and federalist approaches, the U.S. federalist framework places one fundamental limitation on state authority: "State law addressing state-recognized tribes may not conflict with any rules of federal Indian law."[34] This limitation does not necessarily mean that there is federal preemption of the field of tribal recognition, however, because federal recognition and state recognition apply to different tribes and, from the perspective of U.S. law, confer different rights and powers. In the context of U.S. federal law, state recognition does not confer federal sovereign immunity, nor does it create a government-to-government relationship with the United States.[35] And since state recognition addresses the rights of tribal nations that are not federally recognized, it becomes a significant means of bringing the "unrecognized" rights of many native peoples to public attention.

A federalist approach to tribal-state relations is controversial, and potential opponents of state recognition have raised valid concerns. Most notably, Jeff Corntassel and Richard C. Witmer II have warned of the dangers of "forced federalism," a term they have used to describe an era reaching from 1988 (and the onset of the Indian Gaming Regulatory Act) to the present.[36] Corntassel and Witmer posit that during the past couple of decades, "the federal policy of self-determination has been replaced by a policy of forced federalism, which compels indigenous polities to participate in the federal order at a subnational level"[37] by requiring tribes to enter into relationships with states. Because we agree that the subjugation of tribal interests to state ones (and the corresponding infringement on tribal sovereignty) is a potential danger, our arguments include the caveat that state recognition should be an option for tribes and states as long as they are specifically not forced—by the federal government or by anyone else—to enter into a government-to-government relationship.[38] Thus, as long as state recognition does not attempt to (1) interfere or conflict with federal recognition of an Indian tribe, (2) confer federal sovereign immunities, (3) confer a government-to-government relationship with the United States, or (4) compel a tribe to enter into a relationship with a state without that tribe's full, informed, uncoerced consent, then state recognition should be understood to comport with constitutional requirements, having the potential to foster tribal interests and to provide a means for tribal nations to defend their inherent sovereignty.[39]

Another critique of state recognition focuses on fraud—specifically, a concern that "fraudulent" tribes will secure state recognition to the detriment of "legitimate" tribes. This concern underlies both the federal and state recognition schemes and has frequently been raised as a counter to the call for state recognition. For example, one of the most vocal critics of state recognition has been the Inter-Tribal Council of the Five Civilized Tribes, which passed a 2009 resolution formally objecting to the recognition of "Indian heritage groups and cultural clubs" by states and calling on Congress to limit all federal funding to federally recognized tribes.[40] The concern with fraud has prompted the federally recognized Cherokee nation to dedicate millions of dollars to fight the development of state recognition processes in several states, including Tennessee[41] where the effort to reinstate state recognition devolved in 2010 into a contentious and costly battle that ultimately derailed the proposed state recognition process. The Cherokee nation has also developed promotional materials and lobbied to protest state recognition,[42] framing such recognition as a threat to federal recognition and federally recognized tribes by draining resources, distorting Indian history, perpetuating identity theft, and otherwise harming the interests of federal tribes and surrounding populations.[43]

While we certainly agree that fraud can occur and has the potential to undermine the rights of tribal nations—and that stringent efforts to thwart fraud may be needed—we do not agree that the best way to prevent such fraud is to automatically prohibit states from recognizing the inherent authority of tribes. We also do not agree with the Cherokee nation that "state recognition requires no process for documentation as a legal historic tribal government."[44] Rather, as our research establishes, many states employ quite detailed recognition processes to combat the potential for fraud. Several of these approaches could provide workable models for the future, especially in lieu of major revisions to eradicate the very real on-the-ground injustices that have, in some cases, been fostered by the federal administrative recognition process.

While state recognition can support the rights of tribal nations not recognized by the federal government, its powers ultimately are relatively limited. State-recognized tribes lack the immunities from state law that federal tribes possess and have no sovereign immunity from federal enactments.[45] Instead, they are viewed as having only those rights recognized by that state's laws, legislative resolutions, administrative regulations, and other documents that collectively help to clarify and define the relationship.[46] These rights vary dramatically among states. They may range from powers of self-government analogous to that of a municipality, such as the right to operate a police force, to exemptions from paying state and local taxes, to merely offering official acknowledgment of a tribe's long-standing presence within a state.[47] At a minimum, state recognition can connote official acknowledgment of an Indian tribe and establish a political relationship that can assist tribes in the face of federal intransigence. This power is especially critical should states decide to provide rights or services for tribes that are not provided for the rest of the population, since, as Cohen notes, "the fact that states maintain a political relationship with the tribes that they recognize may insulate state legislation directed at such tribes from legal challenge under principles of equal protection."[48]

Three Eras of State Recognition

State recognition has a significant history, enjoying several centuries of precedent and evolution. In some states (for example, Connecticut, New York, and Virginia), recognition was secured in colonial times and has continued into the present. In other states, official recognition of individual tribes first occurred in the twenty-first century.[49] The history of state recognition can be divided into at least two periods, demarcated by the American Revolution and the founding of the United States.[50] However, we suggest that there have been three periods.

The first, colonial recognition period, has its basis in treaties negotiated by administrators of the British, Dutch, and French colonies prior to the formation of the United States. These treaties generally recognized indigenous Indian nations as possessing a government status equal to that of the colonies and were considered agreements between sovereigns.[51] These treaties predate the U.S. Constitution and the imposition of the constitutional authority of states. In many cases, such colonial enactments were never superseded by federal or state enactments. With the formal adoption of colonial law by the nascent states after formation of the United States, the government-to-government relationship between colony and tribe became the government-to-government relationship of state and tribe. As a result, today, the colonial recognition period provides the foundation for recognition in several of the nation's original states, including New York, Connecticut, and Virginia.[52]

The second era, the postrevolutionary recognition period, began only after formation of the United States. The years immediately following the end of the Revolutionary War are characterized by efforts to clear the continent of indigenous peoples, usually by force of arms, to expand the sovereignty and reach of the United States. When the U.S. Constitution was adopted, the federal government was charged with creating and defending an expanded footprint by subjugating numerous Indian nations. As Thomas Jefferson chillingly concluded, the task of the United States was to eradicate the original peoples of the continent and impose federal authority to serve the interests of a largely European constituency.[53] This claim to federal supremacy is modeled on an earlier British enactment, the Proclamation of 1763, by which the British Parliament sought to overtake the North American colonies' claimed right to deal with tribal nations.[54]

Authorities during the postrevolutionary period reinforced and expanded on that paradigm, using two clauses of the U.S. Constitution. The Commerce Clause of Article I has been repeatedly interpreted as granting the federal government "plenary power" to recognize tribes as sovereign entities,[55] with its declaration that Congress has the power to "regulate commerce with foreign Nations, and among the several States, and with the Indian Tribes."

The Supremacy Clause of Article VI similarly confirms the superior power of the federal government over state governments.[56] The Supremacy Clause declares that the "Constitution, and the Laws of the United States which shall be made in Pursuance thereof; and all Treaties made, or which shall be made, under the Authority of the United States, shall be the supreme Law of the Land; and the Judges in every State shall be bound thereby, any Thing in the Constitution or Laws of any State to the Contrary notwithstanding." Because of the Commerce Clause and the Supremacy Clause, conventional approaches to Indian law have taken it as axiomatic that federal laws relevant to Indian tribes generally trump state laws.

The Indian Nonintercourse Act of 1790 served as another foundational legal authority during this period in the history of state recognition.[57]

Under the Nonintercourse Act and its subsequent amendments, the right to acquire Indian land was reserved exclusively for the U.S. government; Indian tribes and states were prohibited from engaging in tribal land transactions without federal approval.[58] While the act slowed the rampant theft of Indian lands by nontribal individuals, as it was designed to do,[59] it did nothing to stop appropriation of the North American continent by the federal government. Consequently, the Nonintercourse Act declared that Indian tribes' most valuable asset—land—would be controlled and managed by the federal government and not by the various states.[60]

The legal doctrine of federal supremacy was most fully articulated during the postrevolutionary recognition period by the three Supreme Court cases that comprise the "Marshall Trilogy." These cases, dated from 1823 to 1832 and authored by Chief Justice John Marshall, established a federal trust responsibility over Indian affairs that significantly increased federal authority over Indian tribes.[61] The Marshall Trilogy established fundamental parameters for the federal government-to-government relationship with individual tribes and was formulated to promote the widely accepted paradigm of European colonization and indigenous removal. The Marshall Trilogy recognized Indian tribes as indigenous nations with inherent sovereign rights but declared that as indigenous nations conquered by "force of arms," their inherent sovereign rights were subordinate to the United States and its lawmaking authority. By "conquering" these indigenous populations, the federal government purported to have converted them into "domestic dependent nations."[62] The Marshall Trilogy also established the legal fiction that Indian title was possessory or "occupancy" only; therefore, like tenants, Indian tribes could be removed from their historic lands by the United States, whether by force of arms, treaty agreement, or legal fiat.[63]

Over time, the Marshall Trilogy has been used to justify disturbing exercises of plenary power, such as the forced removal of tribal nations from their ancestral homelands in the nineteenth century. The Cherokee Trail of Tears, which occurred in 1838, was only one of many and an especially egregious example of the large-scale use of emergent federal powers to design, organize, and execute a genocidal march of men, women, children, and the elderly from southern Georgia to Indian Territory (later the state of Oklahoma) in the dead of winter.[64]

With federal plenary authority driving Euro-American expansion and the systematic removal and marginalization of indigenous peoples in the nineteenth century, very little state recognition occurred during the postrevolutionary period. However, Delaware and Kentucky came to recognize

Indian tribes on their own authority during this period.[65] In 1881, Delaware passed the Act to Better Establish the Identity of a Race of People Known as the Offspring of Nanticoke Indians, which declared that descendants of the Nanticokes would thereafter be "recognized as such" within the state.[66] While this legislation provided (and continues to provide) critical evidence of state recognition, no regulatory scheme was established to facilitate any sort of government-to-government interaction. Kentucky's recognition of the Southern Cherokee nation proved even more tenuous: while Governor John Young Brown sent a letter to the Southern Cherokee nation in 1893 welcoming the tribe to the Commonwealth's state fair and noting that the Commonwealth "recognize[d] the Southern Cherokee Nation as an Indian tribe"[67] (recognition that would be underscored by a 2006 proclamation by Governor Ernie Fletcher),[68] Kentucky currently claims to have no state-recognized tribes and disputes that any kind of government-to-government relationship was established. Thus, even those recognitions that did occur during this period were more ambiguous and uncertain than many that took place during earlier and later periods.

In the post–World War II era, after the devastation wrought by forced removals and Euro-American "settlement" of the West, a third paradigm for state recognition emerged that we identify as the modern recognition period. Beginning in the 1950s and continuing to the present day, the federalist paradigm underlying this period reflects a contemporary mind-set that may be viewed as a departure from the traditional federal approach.[69] This period is informed by contemporary ideals characterized by the civil and human rights movements as well as improvements in public recognition of the rights of indigenous peoples in the United States. Although the aspirations of justice, antiracism, and freedom embodied in these movements are yet to be fully realized in the United States, and while racism and oppressive federal laws directed at tribal nations continue to have a destructive impact on their inherent right to self-determination, the resurgent wave of state recognition suggests a shift in attitudes and policies that may result in the creation of greater opportunities for tribal nations to assert and defend their sovereignty and achieve greater justice within the U.S. system. In addition, as Corntassel and Witmer explain, a "devolution of federal powers to state governments" has occurred during recent decades, and thus it is perhaps not surprising that the number of instances of state recognition has increased.[70]

The modern recognition period can especially be distinguished by the fact that tribal nations and individual states are actively shaping and redefining their relationships to each other. These new tribal-state relationships emphasize the central principle of federalism—that federal authority is in fact limited by both inherent tribal sovereignty and constitutionally based state authority.[71] Indeed, twenty of the twenty-one states that recognize tribes have employed some form of recognition process during the modern recognition period, and they have engaged in relationships with tribal nations for a variety of reasons. Several have substantiated prior state recognition, either by establishing new state laws or more formal recognition processes. Others have recognized one or more Indian tribes for the first time. And finally, many have expanded the number of Indian tribes previously recognized. This state recognition of Indian tribes covers a broad range of legal forms: state laws, resolutions passed by state legislatures, gubernatorial proclamations, regulations promulgated by state executive agencies, and a new round of increasingly detailed state statutes with explicit recognition criteria.[72]

Because of the recent volume and variety of recognition activities by states, the modern recognition period potentially delineates an era within which state and tribal authority have begun to shift back into balance with federal authority. While state recognition does not provide federal sovereign immunity, a direct government-to-government relationship with the United States, or many federal benefits, it does enable state-recognized tribes to secure some degree of legal status and broader public recognition. In this sense, the federalist paradigm has yielded possibilities for establishing and validating legal pluralism and diversity in governmental relationships and institutions, which can support the interests and the rights of tribal nations. This federal-state-tribal dynamic demonstrates the elasticity of the U.S. federalist system as well as the effectiveness of tribal nations' efforts to resist impositions of federal authority and transform relations with Euro-American governments. And states are increasingly recognizing that working with local indigenous communities can benefit tourism, encourage greater acknowledgment of their regions' culturally diverse histories, and contribute to diversity in education and other aspects of social life.[73] The present state recognition paradigm, then, indicates that some tribes and state governments discern advantages in fostering positive relations now and in the future.[74]

If the uniqueness of the U.S. federalist system is its "flexibility,"[75] it should be expected that the system will enable the establishment of such relationships between tribal nations and states, particularly when the federal government fails or refuses to recognize an Indian tribe.

The Four Types of State Recognition

The federal recognition process is painfully unwieldy,[76] often takes decades to resolve, and has left hundreds of indigenous communities without the legal status necessary to enhance their self-governance, secure valuable federal support, or defend their sovereignty and their rights to their ancestral lands. State recognition processes offer the potential for another official status, allowing tribes and states to work together for mutual benefit. Thus, state recognition has become a living, breathing alternative to the federal recognition process.

For tribal nations, one potentially positive aspect of the U.S. federalist system lies in the flexibility and experimentation made possible by fifty different state governments, each having to respond to local needs and particular histories. With regard to political relationships between individual states and Indian tribes, including the establishment of government-to-government relationships, regulatory schemes are as diverse as the federalist system itself.

In some states, numerous agencies coordinate interaction between tribes and the state, while in others, one entity is vested with sole responsibility. Some states have passed detailed legislation to determine the nature and extent of government-to-government relationships, while others use legislative resolutions to acknowledge historic tribes, offering surface recognition but no more. In the interest of providing a framework for describing the diversity of state governmental policies and practices that have been established, we group them into four categories: (1) state law recognition, (2) administrative recognition, (3) legislative recognition, and (4) executive recognition.

State Law Recognition

State law recognition is official recognition of an Indian tribe by merit of a new state law. State law recognition typically requires the origination of a bill in one house of the state legislature, passage of the bill by both houses, and approval by the governor. State law recognition is the most formal type of state recognition and unambiguously carries the force of law. State law recognition may establish either a government-to-government relationship between the state and the Indian tribe or a lesser political relationship.

Twelve states—Alabama, Connecticut, Delaware, Georgia, Hawai'i, Montana, New Jersey, New York, North Carolina, South Carolina, Vermont, and Virginia—have employed state law recognition for at least one state-recognized Indian tribe. Among these states, acts were passed as early as 1881 in Delaware and as recently as 2010 in Virginia.

Virginia has one of the most detailed state recognition processes and is a particularly good example of how state recognition operates. While Virginia has historically utilized executive and legislative recognition processes, since 1983, state tribes must be officially recognized through an act originated in the General Assembly.[77] To date, Virginia has recognized eleven tribal nations, including the Chickahominy tribe, Eastern Chickahominy tribe, Mattaponi Indian nation, Pamunkey nation, United Rappahannock tribe, Upper Mattaponi tribe, Nansemond Indian tribal association, Monacan Indian nation, Cheroenhaka (Nottaway) tribe, Nottoway of Virginia, and Patawomeck tribe.[78]

Virginia's tribal-state relations are generally coordinated through the Virginia Council on Indians.[79] The council's powers include establishing tribal recognition criteria and recommending to the governor and the General Assembly any tribes that should be granted official state recognition.[80]

The recognition criteria have been summarized as follows:

(1) members must have retained a specifically Indian identity through time;

(2) members must have descended from a historical Indian tribe that lived within Virginia's current boundaries at the time of that tribe's first contact with Europeans;

(3) the tribe must be able to trace its continued existence within Virginia from first contact to the present;

(4) the tribe must provide a complete genealogy of current group members, traced as far back as possible;

(5) the tribe must show that the community has been socially distinct—at least for the twentieth century, farther back if possible—from other cultural groups, preferably by organizing separate churches, schools, political organizations, and the like;

(6) the tribe must provide evidence of contemporary formal organization, with full membership restricted to people genealogically descended from the historical tribe(s).[81]

The council consists of sixteen members. According to Virginia statutory law,

Four legislative members, eleven nonlegislative citizen members, and one ex officio member [including] the eight Virginia tribes officially recognized by the Commonwealth shall be entitled but not required to be represented by one member from each tribe, two members at large from the Indian population residing in Virginia, and one member from the Commonwealth at large, all of whom shall be appointed by the Governor; three members of the House of Delegates appointed by the Speaker of the House ... one member of the Senate ... and the Secretary of Health and Human Resources, or his designee, shall be an ex officio voting member.[82]

Virginia's tribes have had an especially difficult time proving their continued existence—and thereby meeting the BIA's criteria for federal recognition—as a consequence of the fifty-year reign of Virginia's Racial Integrity Act of 1924 and Virginia officials' destruction of American Indian–related state and courthouse records during that period.[83] The act, which was a by-product of the eugenics movement,[84] was promulgated by Walter Plecker, the registrar at Virginia's Bureau of Vital Statistics, who believed that tribes should be "assimilated" into the mainstream culture and that the "races" should be kept "pure" by prohibiting intermarriage.[85] He made it his personal mission to ensure that no one could register as an Indian and that people who gave their children Indian names would be jailed.[86] In addition, vital records were altered to indicate that Native Americans were "colored" instead of Indian, effectively erasing "Indian" from the Virginia lexicon.[87] The act remained in effect until 1975, and during the five decades during which it was in force, many Native Americans moved out of state to marry and/or give their children Indian names.[88]

Because of these challenges to securing federal recognition, state recognition has proved an important alternative to help ensure that the tribes' rights continue to be acknowledged and honored, at least by the Commonwealth of Virginia.[89]

Administrative Recognition

Under administrative recognition, state executive agencies are empowered by a previously adopted state statute to create recognition standards for tribal applicants. This is in many ways a state analog to the federal administrative recognition process conducted by the BIA. With administrative recognition, an executive agency is empowered to acknowledge or recognize Indian tribes administratively. For example, in 2003, South Carolina amended its existing statutes to grant new authority to the State Commission for Minority Affairs to "determine, approve, and acknowledge by certification state recognition for Native American Indian entities."[90] The statute also provided authority to "promulgate regulations as may be necessary to carry out the provisions of this article including, but not limited to, regulations regarding State Recognition of Native American Indian entities in the State of South Carolina; and . . . perform other duties necessary to implement programs."[91] According to the SCIway, a website dedicated to information on South Carolina with a special section on the state's tribes, "State recognition of tribes varies but is generally similar to federal recognition in that it acknowledges the right of tribes to govern themselves."[92]

Unlike many states, South Carolina grants recognition to three different kinds of tribal entities. These include the traditional "Native American Indian tribe," but also "Native American Indian group," and "Native American special interest group."[93] South Carolina's Criteria for State Recognition, designed to identify these three entities within the state, were created in conjunction with several Native American leaders and have begun to serve as a model for other states that are considering administrative recognition. These criteria are as follows:

(1) The tribe is headquartered in the State of South Carolina and indigenous to this State. The tribe must produce evidence of tribal organization and/or government and tribal rolls for a minimum of five years.

(2) Historical presence in the State for past 100 years and entity meets all of the characteristics of a "tribe" as defined in R.139-102(D).

(3) Organized for the purpose of preserving, documenting and promoting the Native American Indian culture and history, and have such reflected in its by-laws.

(4) Exist to meet one or more of the following needs of Native American Indian people—spiritual, social, economic, or cultural—through a continuous series of educational programs and activities that preserve, document, and promote the Native American Indian culture and history.

(5) Claims must be supported by official records such as birth certificates, church records, school records, U.S. Census records, and other pertinent documents.

(6) Documented kinship relationships with other Indian tribes in and outside the State.

(7) Anthropological or historical accounts tied to the group's Indian ancestry.

(8) A minimum of one hundred living descendants who are eighteen years of age or older, whose Indian lineage can be documented by a lineal genealogy chart, and whose names and current address appear on the Tribal Roll.

(9) Documented traditions, customs, legends, etc., that signify the specific group's Indian heritage.

(10) Letters, statements and documents from state or federal authorities, which document a history of tribal related business and activities that specifically address Native American Indian culture, preservation, and affairs.

(11) Letters, statements, and documents from tribes in and outside of South Carolina which attest to the Indian heritage of the group.[94]

Points 1–9 are mandatory for tribal entities seeking recognition as a Native American Indian tribe, while 10 and 11 are optional but can support the petition for recognition.[95] Native American Indian groups must establish criteria 1–6, with 7 optional, and Native American special interest groups must establish criteria 1–4, with 5 optional.[96]

Only Indian tribes and Indian groups appear to enjoy a government-to-government relationship with South Carolina. Special interest groups may register as nonprofit organizations.[97] Limitations are imposed on the sovereignty of state tribes to meet local political concerns. Specifically, the tribes are subject to civil, criminal, and regulatory jurisdiction and laws of South Carolina to the same extent as others within the state.[98] Indian gaming is currently forbidden by regulation: "Notwithstanding their state certification, Native American Indian entities have no power or authority to take any action that would establish, advance or promote any form of gambling in the State of South Carolina; nor does this provision of law confer power or authority to take any action which could establish, advance or promote any form of gambling in the State."[99]

Like state law recognition, and as evidenced by the South Carolina example, administrative recognition may ultimately create a government-to-government relationship or merely provide for official acknowledgment of an Indian tribe, depending on the state process and its underlying enactment. Alabama, Massachusetts, Michigan, Oklahoma, and South Carolina employ administrative recognition, although many of these states' recognition criteria are far less developed than those of South Carolina and their legal parameters far more uncertain.[100]

Legislative Recognition

The third category, legislative recognition, refers to cases in which the state acts only through its legislature, without signature or other approval by the governor or the passage of a new state statute. Instead, a joint or concurrent resolution by one or both houses of the state legislature creates an official relationship with the Indian tribe. Legislative recognition has been used in California, Louisiana, New Jersey, Ohio, Texas, and Virginia. In most cases it is questionable whether legislative recognition possesses the force of law and therefore carries any legal rights for tribes. Each state's constitution determines whether legislative enactments, without approval by the governor, have any legal significance. While legislative recognition constitutes official recognition of an Indian tribe, it is less clear whether legislative recognition creates any kind of government-to-government relationship. By comparison to state law recognition and administrative recognition, legislative recognition is a less formal, more uncertain, but often more easily accomplished process for achieving some measure of "official" recognition.

Despite these weaknesses, however, legislative recognition should be viewed as sufficient to express official recognition of an Indian tribe for at least two reasons. First, federalism permits various methods to be used to grant state recognition, since the federal government allows individual states to decide whether and how to recognize Indian tribes.[101] Second, an abundance of legal precedents establishes joint legislative resolutions as an accepted method for garnering state recognition.

Turning to federalist principles first, the Tenth Amendment guarantees sovereign powers to individual states, and each state is free to decide how best to exercise its powers within the purposefully broad parameters of the U.S. Constitution. The Constitution certainly does not require states to recognize Indian tribes, let alone mandate that state recognition be pursued in any particular manner. That said, joint resolutions effectively express the state legislature's intent to acknowledge an Indian tribe, which, absent an express limitation in the state constitution, should be sufficient to officially recognize an existing Indian tribe for state purposes. As long as the state legislature acts in its official capacity, through resolution or other officially recorded vote, and the legislative act falls within the powers and limitations placed on the legislature by the state's constitution, then legislative recognition would constitute official acknowledgment of an Indian tribe[102] even if such recognition falls short of establishing a government-to-government relationship.

This issue has emerged in California, where two Indian tribes have been recognized by joint legislative resolution: the Gabrielino-Tongva tribe, historically known as the San Gabriel band of Mission Indians,[103] and the Juaneno band of Mission Indians, located in Orange County.[104] The Gabrielino-Tongva tribe was recognized by legislative resolution in 1994 as part of a "measure [to] recognize the Gabrielinos as the aboriginal tribe of the Los Angeles Basin" and "memorialize the President and Congress to give similar recognition to the Gabrielinos."[105] The legislature used the term "recognize" and noted its desire that the federal government "give similar recognition."[106] Based on authority granted by the California Constitution, Article IV, joint legislative resolutions do not need to be signed or otherwise approved by the governor to go into effect.[107] But by the same token, such resolutions do not carry the force of law but instead are "initiated when the Legislature wants to comment to Congress and/or the President on a federal matter of concern to the state."[108] Thus, as long as the California Legislature had the authority under its state constitution to grant official recognition to the Gabrielinos through a joint legislative resolution, the resolution should suffice to "officially recognize" the Gabrielino-Tongva tribe. However, nothing in the resolution's language points to a single government for the tribe or mentions with specificity that a government-to-government relationship is intended. Thus, whether legislative recognition by California creates a government-to-government relationship with the Gabrielino-Tongva tribe remains an open question.

The second reason that legislative recognition should suffice to officially recognize an Indian tribe is precedent. Of the twenty-one states that have acknowledged tribal nations, six have recognized tribes through joint legislative resolutions. Louisiana offers perhaps the best example of a state that offers legislative recognition to Indian tribes. Louisiana's nine state tribes are solely recognized through joint or concurrent resolutions passed by the state legislature. In Louisiana as in California, joint or concurrent resolutions do not require the signature or other approval of the governor and so would appear not to carry the force of law.[109] Nonetheless, Louisiana's state officials widely acknowledge the state's government-to-government relationship with the nine tribal nations within the state's borders.[110] Thus there is no ambiguity in the official recognition of Louisiana's Indian tribes by legislative recognition.

Indian law scholar Felix Cohen has observed that "the legal status of [state-recognized tribes'] reservations and the scope of their governmental authority, if any, is [ultimately] a matter of state—not federal—law."[111] Cohen refers to the legislative recognition of the Gabrielinos as the aboriginal inhabitants of the Los Angeles Basin as crucial evidence for his argument.[112] This provides further evidence that a state legislative resolution may be both sufficient and appropriate to officially recognize an Indian tribe and thereby support tribal sovereignty in a substantial way. This type of acknowledgment can also become a critical stepping-stone for later federal recognition and/or otherwise enhance relations between tribes and nontribal institutions within the state by making such tribes more visible to nontribal populations.

Executive Recognition

Executive recognition results from gubernatorial proclamation or executive order from the state's top executive official. No action by the state legislature is required; no objective administrative procedure is employed. Like legislative recognition, executive recognition by a state's governor or executive branch alone will usually not possess the force of law—whether it does can only be answered definitively by the state constitution and the scope of the governor's authority. Only Kentucky, Missouri, and Montana have solely employed executive recognition.

Executive recognition is the weakest category of state recognition. Gubernatorial proclamations or executive orders are often worded ambiguously, and/or move away from the question of official recognition into different policy questions. For example, in Missouri, recognition took the form of a 1983 gubernatorial proclamation "acknowledg[ing] the existence of the Northern Cherokee Tribe as an American Indian Tribe within the boundaries of the State of Missouri."[113] The governor's proclamation noted that the tribe had "continued a form of tribal government for the past 140 years."[114] But even though Missouri "recognized" the tribe by gubernatorial proclamation, officials presently claim that Missouri has no state-recognized tribes[115] Thus, several resolutions and bills have been introduced in the state Senate and House of Representatives in recent years to try to provide the tribe with a more secure form of recognition; however, none has yet passed.[116] Similarly, in Montana, any official recognition is based on a series of gubernatorial declarations from 2000.[117] Recognition in Kentucky, too, is based on a gubernatorial acknowledgment that was documented in 1893 and confirmed and enhanced in 2006.

While state officials may or may not consider executive recognition to establish "official" state recognition, on its face executive recognition would appear to be a form of official recognition (which is why we have included Montana, Missouri, and Kentucky on our primary list of recognition states, despite interviews with state officials who claim that the tribes remain unrecognized). We believe the ambiguity in how these gubernatorial proclamations are interpreted arises because Missouri and Kentucky have not established government-to-government relationships with tribes. However, that is a separate issue from whether the tribes have, in fact, been recognized. Further, Missouri, Montana, and Kentucky are included on several Internet lists of recognition states, suggesting that other observers consider their executive recognition processes sufficient to officially recognize tribes. Perhaps most important, however, the cases of Missouri, Montana, and Kentucky emphasize the ambiguity inherent in executive recognition and why we consider it the weakest (and therefore least desirable) of the four processes.

These four categories ultimately offer a diverse array of federalist models for facilitating cooperation and communication between tribal governments and states and potentially for supporting the inherent sovereignty of tribal nations that are not federally recognized.[118]

Conclusion

While state recognition is playing an increasingly important role in establishing formal government-to-government relationships, validating tribal histories and facilitating state-tribal interaction, more is needed, both to clarify state-tribal relationships and to address the concerns of state recognition opponents. First, states that have eligible tribes but no state recognition process should implement recognition schemes for state and tribal benefit that are carefully designed with local tribal input. Especially in states such as Michigan and Oklahoma, where the state government is already working with Indian tribes, the implementation of a formal state recognition process would constitute a significant step forward in clarifying and formalizing such relationships.

Second, states that have recognition processes that remain uncodified would benefit from the passage of legislation to confirm and clarify their state recognition schemes. For example, while joint resolutions used in legislative recognition and gubernatorial proclamations used in executive recognition processes can be sufficient to establish official state recognition (as evidenced by Louisiana and other states), the detailed state law recognition processes of states such as South Carolina can and should be used as models for the future—albeit modified to respond to local histories and state-specific impediments to federal recognition. Although joint legislative resolutions and gubernatorial proclamations can provide the basis for official recognition, the scope of these official acts and their meaning often remain ambiguous, leaving the official status of state-recognized tribes vulnerable to legal challenges. Thus, as in Missouri and Oklahoma, state officials may declare unrecognized Indian tribes that might otherwise be considered recognized, probably because such officials are concerned about the ramifications of entering into government-to-government relationships. Statutes that clearly spell out the criteria for recognition or explicitly recognize specific tribes with the force of law provide little room for questioning tribal status.

Deanna Beacham of the Virginia Council on Indians similarly believes that it is important for states to clarify their recognition processes.[119] Through legislation, bona fide tribal nations can finally achieve the benefits of a government-to-government relationship, and states can develop relationships with tribes with which they can consult on matters of tribal concern.[120] By drawing a line demarcating which Indian groups achieve recognition and which do not, state governments give greater meaning and validity to state recognition. For tribal nations working to preserve and defend their inherent rights, state recognition may thus grow as a complement or even an alternative to the federal recognition process. Beacham has also stressed the importance of seeing more state-recognized tribes represented in the National Congress of American Indians and on the National Governor's Interstate Indian Council, an organization within the National Governors' Association, to encompass a wider range of tribal voices and perspectives.[121] But this expansion can occur only when it is clear which tribal nations have state recognition and which do not.

It is also important that states provide greater funding for recognized tribes. The federal government does not acknowledge the full extent of the inherent rights of state-recognized tribal nations,[122] even though their needs may be just as great as or greater than those that qualify as federally recognized. Colonel Joey Strickland, director of the Louisiana Governor's Office of Indian Affairs, has expressed similar sentiments, noting the importance of having state governments make a concerted effort to support tribes.[123] While state recognition is a positive first step, it is critical to put enough money into the various offices of Indian affairs and other coordinating agencies to grant tribes a greater voice in their future and to give such recognition greater weight. For example, states can hire genealogists and archaeologists to help establish tribal ties to each state and can formalize state recognition processes to ensure that the proper tribes are acknowledged.[124] Of course, one danger is that state processes may become as complex, unwieldy, and oppressive as the BIA's federal acknowledgment process. To truly serve tribes and states, that pattern must be carefully avoided. One means of doing so is for states to work closely with local tribes—both recognized and not—to determine the most appropriate, pragmatic, and just ways to recognize tribes within each state.

Finally, as explained by Harold Hatcher, chief of South Carolina's Waccamaw tribe, fiscal agent for the South Carolina Indian Affairs Commission, and contributor to the development of South Carolina's recognition process, there is yet another important reason to clarify the recognition process. Since many states expressly exclude Indian tribes from the ambit of particular laws, it is "imperative [to] define who [the] Indians are."[125] As Hatcher points out,

Thousands of people [in South Carolina, as elsewhere] are undoubtedly of Indian descent. Some have the stereotypical appearance and some do not. Some hold and practice the ancient beliefs, and some do not. Some have the cultural knowledge of their ancestors, and some do not. Some have passed as Black and some have passed as White. Here again, some have not! . . . Black and White youth are seldom challenged as to their ethnic ties. Indians always are! . . . Indians . . . are compelled to prove who they are and to do so based upon "White" acceptance. . . . This leaves the legitimacy of the application to the discretion of the reviewer.[126]

When states set no standards, "subjective decisions foster a process open to every prejudice imaginable, and one where fraud will inevitably abound."[127]

While the federal government takes an unreasonably long time to acknowledge the inherent sovereignty of many tribal nations with U.S. borders, often requiring decades to review applications and subjecting those applications to painstakingly detailed and prejudicial criteria, some states have employed their inherent federalist powers actively to counter this injustice. For non-federally acknowledged tribal nations, a central positive aspect of the U.S. federalist system lies in its flexibility: With gridlock at the federal level, states and tribes should adopt their own forms of governance to address local needs, conditions, and rights that matter to tribal communities. By recognizing the existence, contributions, and inherent rights of Indian tribes within their borders and creating government-to-government relationships with tribes, states may demonstrate their genuine support for cultural diversity and public acknowledgment of indigenous history, enrich intercultural understanding and communication among communities, address distorted historical records, and make more concrete strides toward correcting historical injustices. In the long run, this is a federalist process that should be encouraged as potentially beneficial for both tribes and states.

Notes

1. Tribes that have been acknowledged by the U.S. federal government are also usually recognized by states and are therefore also technically state-recognized. However, to minimize confusion, we refer to tribes that are recognized by both state and federal governments as "federally recognized."

2. See, e.g., National Conference of State Legislatures, "Federally Recognized Tribes," http://www.ncsl.org/programs/statetribe/tribes.htm; Access Genealogy Indian Tribal Records, "State Recognized Tribes," http://www.accessgenealogy.com/native/staterectribes.htm; Native Data, "State Recognized Tribes," http://www.nativedata.com/statetribes.htm.

3. Felix S. Cohen, *Cohen's Handbook of Federal Indian Law* (Newark, N.J.: Lexis-Nexis, 2005), 168–71 (providing five paragraphs on state-recognized tribes).

4. Throughout this chapter, we refer to the states that recognize tribes independent of federal recognition as "recognition states."

5. This list was compiled through statutory research, a review of primary and secondary sources, and phone interviews with numerous state and tribal organizations. For an overview of each state's tribal-regulatory scheme, see K. Alexa Koenig and Jonathan Stein, "Federalism and the State Recognition of Native American Tribes: A Survey of State-Recognized Tribes and State Recognition Processes across the United States," *Santa Clara Law Review* 48 (2008): 79–153.

6. See, e.g., National Conference, "Federally Recognized Tribes"; Access Genealogy, "State Recognized Tribes"; Native Data, "State Recognized Tribes"; "State Recognized Tribes," http://en.wikipedia.org/wiki/State_recognized_tribes.

7. Koenig and Stein, "Federalism."

8. Cohen, *Cohen's Handbook*, 169–71.

9. For example, tribes are exempt from many states' fishing and hunting regulations. See, e.g., Fla. Stat. Ann. 285.09 (West 2003), Op. Att'y Gen. 358 (1953–54).

10. Deanna Beacham, telephone interview by K. Alexa Koenig, July 14, 2006.

11. See Virginia Racial Integrity Act of 1924, An Act to Preserve Racial Integrity, http:://www.vcdh.virginia.edu/lewisandclark/students/projects/monacans /Contemporary_Monacans/racial.html.

12. *Loving v. Virginia*, 388 U.S. 1 (1967).

13. See, e.g., Nikki L. M. Brown and Barry M. Stentiford, *The Jim Crow Encyclopedia: Greenwood Milestones in African American History* (Westport, Conn.: Greenwood, 2008), 275.

14. For an overview of Virginia's ancestry classifications, see Carolyne Gould, "Virginia Records: Deciphering Indian versus African Heritage," *Genealogy Today*, http://www.genealogytoday.com/articles/reader.mv?ID=629.

15. Beacham, interview.

16. Ibid. See also "Tribal History—Lost Treaty Rights and Current Status," Gabrielino Tongva website, http://www.gabrielinotribe.org/TribalHistory/tribal _history.cfm.

17. See K. Alexa Koenig and Jonathan Stein, "Lost in the Shuffle: State-Recognized Tribes and the Tribal Gaming Industry," *University of San Francisco Law Review* 40 (2006): 331–37. For additional background on the California treaties, see Francis Paul Prucha, *American Indian Treaties: The History of a Political Anomaly* (Berkeley: University of California Press, 1994): 243–46.

18. Cohen, *Cohen's Handbook*, 159 (discussing the BIA's recognition rate). As of April 2011, 350 petitions remained outstanding. See U.S. Department of the Interior, Bureau of Indian Affairs, Office of Federal Acknowledgment, "Number of Petitions by State as of April 29, 2011," http://www.bia.gov/idc/groups/xofa /documents/text/idc013621.pdf.

19. http://www.shinnecocknation.com/history.asp.

20. *New York v. Shinnecock Indian Nation*, 400 F. Supp. 2d 486, 489 (E.D.N.Y. 2005).

21. John Moreno Gonzales, "Shinnecocks Waiting to Be Recognized," *Newsday*, January 15, 2007.

22. Deborah A. Rosen, *American Indians and State Law: Sovereignty, Race, and Citizenship, 1790–1880* (Lincoln: University of Nebraska Press, 2007): ix–x.

23. Ibid.

24. Cohen, *Cohen's Handbook*, 140–41.

25. For an overview of additional tribal statuses beyond state and federal recognition, see Noelle M. Kahanu and Jon M. Van Dyke, "Native Hawaiian Entitlement to Sovereignty: An Overview," *University of Hawai'i Law Review* 17 (1995): 430–38.

26. In a recent e-mail, Ken Johnson explained what the lack of state recognition has meant for the members of his tribal community: "Since the 2001 abolition of Florida's state recognition laws, tribes, such as mine, have been unable to assert our tribal authority, in certain circuits, regarding the American Indian Child Welfare Act cases. Native American burial sites have been made into parks and subdivisions. Artisans have been legally prohibited from calling their artwork 'American Indian Made.' We have lost the right to protect the wilderness that we gain our cultural identity from. And, our children and elderly have lost access to valuable resources" (Ken Johnson to author, February 1, 2011).

27. Cohen, *Cohen's Handbook*, 169–70 (noting several federal statutes that extend services to state tribes); Koenig and Stein, "Lost in the Shuffle," 368–69 (arguing that the federal government has validated state recognition by extending services to such tribes). Federal legislation that extends benefits to state tribes includes 45 C.F.R. 96.44(b), *Health and Human Services Block Grants*; 7 C.F.R. 281.2(a)(1), *Administration of Food Stamp Program on Indian Reservations*; 10 C.F.R. 455.2, *Energy Conservation Grant Programs*; and 45 C.F.R. 1336.10, *Native American Welfare Programs*.

28. Cohen, *Cohen's Handbook*, 169–71. But see Cherokee Nation, "Support the Federal Recognition Process to Protect All Tribal Citizens" (2009; in possession of the authors) (arguing that state recognition violates the U.S. Constitution); Vine Deloria Jr. and Clifford M. Lytle, *The Nations Within: The Past and Future of American Indian Sovereignty* (Austin: University of Texas Press, 1998) (explaining that "there is no inherent power in any of the fifty states to deal with Indians at all").

29. Cohen, *Cohen's Handbook*, 116–18, 168.

30. Ibid., 118.

31. Ibid., 169.

32. Ibid.

33. Ibid., 119.

34. Ibid., 171.

35. Ibid., 169.

36. Jeff Corntassel and Richard C. Witmer II, *Forced Federalism: Contemporary Challenges to Indigenous Nationhood* (Norman: University of Oklahoma Press, 2008).

37. Ibid., ix (foreword by Lindsay G. Robertson).

38. A major difference between forced federalism and federalism in the context of state recognition is that with the former, tribes are mandated to enter into such

agreements; with state recognition, that relationship is potentially far less coercive, since tribes are not required to seek state recognition. Instead, each tribe can determine for itself whether, based on its unique circumstances, it is in its best interest to pursue such a relationship. For additional criticism of the Indian Gaming Regulatory Act and the potential coerciveness of its compacting scheme, see Corntassel and Witmer, *Forced Federalism*. See also K. Alexa Koenig, "Gambling on Proposition 1A: The California Indian Self-Reliance Amendment," *University of San Francisco Law Review* 36 (2002): 1033–66.

39. Koenig and Stein, "Federalism," 79.

40. Inter-Tribal Council of the Five Civilized Tribes, Resolution FY09-07 (May 21, 2009) (in possession of the authors).

41. See, e.g., *Greene v. Tennessee Commission of Indian Affairs*, Verified Complaint, No. 10-1053-III (Chancery Court for Davidson County, Tennessee) (filed February 16, 2010); Ken Johnson to author, February 1, 2011.

42. Cherokee Nation, "Support the Federal Recognition Process."

43. See also Joint Council of the Cherokee Nation and the Eastern Band of Cherokee Indians, "A Resolution Opposing Fabricated Cherokee 'Tribes' and 'Indians,'" Resolution 00-08 (in possession of the authors).

44. Cherokee Nation, "Support the Federal Recognition Process."

45. Cohen, *Cohen's Handbook*, 169 (noting that state law generally determines the governmental authority of state-recognized tribes).

46. Ibid.

47. Ibid., 170–71, 169 n. 235.

48. Ibid., 171.

49. Ibid., 169.

50. Ibid.

51. Wilcomb E. Washburn, "Indians and the American Revolution," http://www.americanrevolution.org/ind1.html.

52. In Virginia, both the Mattaponi Indian nation and the Pamunkey nation continue to operate under treaties that were first ratified in the mid-1600s. See Beacham, interview. See also "Treaty between Virginia and the Indians, 1677," http://www.baylink.org/treaty (providing the text of the 1677 treaty between the Virginia Colony and the Pamunkey nation); "Virginia's First People Past and Present," http://virginiaindians.pwnet.org/today/reservations_mattaponi.php (discussing the tributes made annually to the governor on the fourth Wednesday of November).

53. See "President Jefferson and the Indian Nations," http://www.monticello.org/jefferson/lewisandclark/presidentindian.html.

54. Cohen, *Cohen's Handbook*, 117.

55. Ibid., 140.

56. Cohen, *Cohen's Handbook,* 118.

57. 1 Stat. 137 (July 22, 1790) (since modified as 25 U.S.C. 117). See also "Indian Lands," http://library.findlaw.com/1999/Jan/1/241490.html.

58. 25 U.S.C. 177.

59. See *Cass County Joint Water Resource District v. 1.43 Acres of Land in Highland Township,* 643 N.W. 2d 685, 695 (N.D. 2002) (noting the act's intent "to protect Indian tribes by ensuring Indian lands were settled peacefully and Indians were treated fairly, and to protect them from the 'greed of other races' and 'artful scoundrels inclined to make a sharp bargain'").

60. Ibid.

61. *Worcester v. Georgia,* 31 U.S. 515 (1832); *Cherokee Nation v. Georgia,* 30 U.S. 1 (1831); *Johnson v. M'Intosh,* 21 U.S. 534 (1823).

62. See Koenig and Stein, "Lost in the Shuffle," 343–47 (detailing the jurisprudence that recognized Indian tribes as "dependent" sovereigns).

63. *Johnson v. M'Intosh;* Cohen, *Cohen's Handbook,* 420.

64. Gerard N. Magliocca, "The Cherokee Removal and the Fourteenth Amendment," *Duke Law Journal* 53 (2003): 875–965; "Indian Territory," http://en.wikipedia.org/wiki/Indian_Territory.

65. See "Tribe History," http://www.nanticokeindians.org/history.cfm? (stating that the Nanticoke tribe was recognized by the state of Delaware on March 10, 1881); John Brown to Mr. Martin, December 26, 1893, http://www.southern cherokeenation.net/images/commonwealth.jpg.

66. Delaware State Laws XX, ch. 470, p. 986; "Tribe History," http://www .nanticokeindians.org/history.cfm; Jean Norwood to author, August 1, 2006.

67. John Brown to Mr. Martin, December 26, 1893, http://www.southern cherokeenation.net/images/commonwealth.jpg.

68. See Proclamation by Ernie Fletcher, November 20, 2006, http://www .southerncherokeenation.net/.

69. Cohen, *Cohen's Handbook,* 118.

70. Corntassel and Witmer, *Forced Federalism,* 134.

71. Rosen has noted the ways in which federalist claims have been used historically to subjugate tribes (*American Indians and State Law,* x). Such federalism must be viewed in light of the federal goal of favoring tribal self-determination, and tribal-state agreements must be based on consent rather than coercion.

72. See Koenig and Stein, "Federalism."

73. Again, the potential for coercion—for forced federalism—is a risk. This risk is especially evident in the sudden increase in state recognition schemes that

attempt to place limits on particular practices, such as opening tribal gaming facilities. However, as long as such provisions do not conflict with tribal rights that are recognized by the federal government, such provisions arguably do not impose any new legal constraints on tribes.

74. Matthew L. M. Fletcher, "Retiring the 'Deadliest Enemies' Model of Tribal-State Relations," *Tulsa Law Review* 43 (2007): 1–26.

75. See generally James Madison, "The Federalist No. 46: The Influence of State and Federal Governments Compared," January 29, 1788, http://www.constitution .org/fed/federa46.htm (comparing the respective powers that would be reserved for the state and federal governments if they were united under one federalist system).

76. Barry T. Hill, "Comments before the Subcommittee on Energy Policy, Natural Resources and Regulatory Affairs, Committee on Government Reform, House of Representatives, 'More Consistent and Timely Tribal Recognition Process Needed,'" February 7, 2002, 107th Cong. 2 (2002), available at http://www .gao.gov/new.items/d02415t.pdf (noting that it could take more than fifteen years to resolve all completed recognition petitions currently on file with the BIA); Alva C. Mather, "Old Promises: The Judiciary and the Future of Native American Federal Acknowledgment Litigation," *University of Pennsylvania Law Review* 151 (2003): 1827–60 (discussing the difficulties inherent in acquiring formal federal recognition).

77. "State Recognition of Indian Tribes," http://indians.vipnet.org/state Recognition.cfm.

78. See "Virginia Tribes," http://indians.vipnet.org/tribes.cfm. See also Virginia Joint Resolution 54, March 25, 1983, available at Virginia General Assembly Legislative Information System at http://leg1.state.va.us (recognizing six of the eight federally recognized tribes in Virginia: the Chickahominy tribe, Eastern Chickahominy tribe, Mattaponi Indian nation, Pamunkey nation, United Rappahannock tribe, and Upper Mattaponi tribe). Additional joint resolutions were passed in 1985 (recognizing the Nansemond Indian Tribal Association) and in 1989 (recognizing the Monacan Indian tribe).

79. See Va. Code. Ann. 2.2-2628 (establishing the council). Notably, at the end of 2011 the governor of Virginia recommended eliminating the Council on Indians. See Report of the Governor: Proposed Reorganization of State Government (Commonwealth of Virginia 2011), available at http://dhrm.cache.vi.virginia.gov /documents/GovernmentReorganizationPlan.pdf.

80. Ibid., 2.2-2629(C).

81. "State Recognition of Indian Tribes."

82. Va. Code. Ann. 2.2-2628(A).

83. Racial Integrity Act of 1924, Va. Code Ann. 20-53 et seq. (1960) (repealed 1975). See Bobbie Whitehead, "House Approves Virginia Tribes' Federal Recognition Bill," *Indian Country Today*, June 5, 2010.

84. The eugenics movement of the late nineteenth to mid-twentieth century aimed at "improving the quality of the human population by selecting for desirable traits." This manifested in numerous discriminatory practices, including sterilizing nonwhite, poor, and/or handicapped individuals as well as other tactics aimed at marginalizing populations categorized as unfit. See Karen Norrgard, "Human Testing and the Eugenics Movement, and IRBs," *Nature Education* 1 (2008), http://www.nature.com/scitable/topicpage/human-testing-the-eugenics-movement-and-irbs-724.

85. Paul Lombardo, "Eugenic Laws against Race Mixing," http://wwww.eugenicsarchive.org/html/eugenics/essay7text.html. See also "Battles in Red, Black, and White, Virginia's Racial Integrity Law of 1924," http://xroads.virginia.edu/~CAP/POCA/POC_law.html; Beacham, interview; W. A. Plecker, "The New Family and Race Improvement," *Virginia Health Bulletin* 17 (1925), select pages available at http://www.eugenicsarchive.org/eugenics/image_header.pl?id=1314&detailed=1.

86. Beacham interview.

87. Ibid.; Whitehead, "House Approves."

88. Beacham, interview; Peter Hardin, "Documentary Genocide, Families' Surnames on Racial Hit List," *Richmond Times-Dispatch*, March 5, 2000. The act suffered a major blow with the U.S. Supreme Court's decision in *Loving v. Virginia* (1967), which concerned a black woman and white man who married in Washington, D.C., and then moved to Virginia, only to be indicted for violating the act. Although the Virginia state courts ruled against the couple, the U.S. Supreme Court unanimously found for the couple, thereby striking down the Racial Integrity Act and similar laws in fifteen states. See Lombardo, "Eugenic Laws."

89. Many of Virginia's tribes are still trying to secure federal recognition through the U.S. Congress even though they have been participating in an unsuccessful bid for congressional recognition for more than a decade (Beacham, interview). See also Whitehead, "House Approves."

90. S.C. Code 1-31-40(6) (2003).

91. S.C. Code Ann. Regs. 1-31-40(10) (2003).

92. http://www.sciway.net/hist/indians/terms.html.

93. S.C. Code Ann. Regs. 139-101 (2005).

94. Ibid., 139-105.

95. Ibid., 139-105(A).

96. Ibid., 139-105(B), (C).

97. Ibid., 139-102.

98. Ibid., 139-104(A).

99. Ibid., 139-104(B).

100. Please contact the authors for a state-by-state overview.

101. Cohen, *Cohen's Handbook*, 170.

102. Ibid.

103. Cal. Jt. Res. 96, ch. 146, 1993–94 Reg. Sess. (September 13, 1994).

104. Cal. Jt. Res. 48, ch. 121, 1993–94 Reg. Sess. (September 22, 1993). The BIA issued a proposed denial of federal recognition against the tribe in 2007. See "BIA Denies Recognition to Juaneno Band," November 27, 2007, http://64.38.12.138 /News/2007/006039.asp.

105. Cal. S.J. Res. 96, 1993–94 Leg. Spec. Sess., ch. 146 (Cal. 1994), http://leg info.public.ca.gov/pub/93–94/bill/asm/ab_0051–0100/ajr_96_bill_history.

106. Ibid.

107. See State of California Administrative Manual, http://sam.dgs.ca.gov /TOC/6000/6925.htm.

108. Ibid.

109. Joey Strickland to author, July 18, 2006.

110. Strickland, interview; Joey Strickland to author, July 18, 2006.

111. Cohen, *Cohen's Handbook*, 169.

112. Ibid., 171 n. 249.

113. Proclamation of Christopher S. Bond, http://www.angelfire.com/mo2 /ncnolt/Missouri_Bond.html.

114. Ibid.

115. Ibid.

116. Northern Cherokee Nation, "Urgent and Important," http://ncnolt1 .homestead.com.

117. Russell Boham, telephone interview by author, July 31, 2007; *Koke v. Little Shell Tribe of Chippewa Indians of Montana, Inc.*, 315 Mont. 510 (2003).

118. For additional information regarding the twenty-one recognition states and the tribes recognized by each state, please contact the authors. An expanded version of this chapter identifies four other states that accord Indian tribes some type of status short of official recognition, have a recognition scheme in place but have yet to recognize any tribes, or have recently engaged in a heated debate about whether to recognize tribes.

119. Beacham, interview.

120. Such consultation is especially important in states that have no federally recognized tribes.

121. See http://www.ncai.org; http://www.nga.org.

122. Examples include the exercising of self-governance over tribal members, eligibility for most federal grants, the right to conduct Las Vegas–style gaming under the Indian Gaming Regulatory Act, and more. See, e.g., Cohen, *Cohen's Handbook*, 169.

123. Strickland, interview.

124. Ibid.; John Werner, telephone interview by author, May 29, 2007.

125. Harold D. Hatcher to author, July 18, 2006.

126. Harold D. Hatcher, report (in possession of the authors).

127. Ibid.

Part II
State and Federal Recognition
in New England

State Recognition and "Termination" in Nineteenth-Century New England

JEAN M. O'BRIEN

Over the course of two and a half centuries of colonialism in southern New England, colonial polities developed a system of guardianship that bore striking parallels to the "trust relationship" that stands at the center of federal recognition of Indian nations in the United States. But over the course of the nineteenth century, and in dialogue with debates over abolition, enfranchisement, and citizenship, Connecticut, Massachusetts, and Rhode Island took steps to "terminate" those relationships (a process they called "detribalization," which for them carried the notion of "liberating" Indians from the perceived shackles of tribalism). This chapter raises questions about the complexities of the political position of tribal nations under settler colonialism more broadly. How has the relationship of citizenship to Indian nationhood been imagined historically? What possible political relationships might be negotiated in this context? How might a historical perspective on the tension between state and federal recognition help illuminate important questions about the nature of the trust relationship?

In the last half of the nineteenth century, the state legislatures of Connecticut, Massachusetts, and Rhode Island took measures that purported officially to "terminate" the ongoing legal recognition of Indian peoples still present in their own homelands, echoing the gesture Connecticut had made to legislate the Pequots out of existence in the wake of the Pequot War in 1637. These actions and others paralleled a mythology that New Englanders had been haphazardly forging in cultural production throughout the nineteenth century—that Indian peoples in New England had ceased to exist as such. Indeed, these forces interacted with notions about racial purity and blood, importantly influencing debates regarding the status of Indian communities. This self-serving process amounted to an abandonment of the trust responsibility implicit in the notion of guardianship as it had organically developed in New England, and this change carried grave consequences for Indian people.[1]

Although the process transpired in various ways throughout New England—and was linked to the national struggle over race, slavery, citizenship, and equality—all of these movements toward "terminating" New England tribes were rooted in the failure of non-Indian New Englanders to recognize Indian peoples *as* Indians. The best evidence that this project was deeply flawed can be found in the still unfinished process of rerecognizing New England Indian peoples through federal processes beginning in the 1970s.[2] Thus, long before the U.S. Indian policy of the 1950s of "terminating" the federal relationship with tribes turned out to be a colossal case of wishful thinking, New Englanders embarked on official state-level actions to legislate Indian peoples out of existence that were doomed to failure.[3] Indeed, predictions of the vanishing Indian that can be dated at least as early as the now-iconic Squanto, "Last of the Patuxets," are among the oldest and most stubborn tropes in Indian America that continue to be revealed as mythological.

Discussions of the status of native peoples in the United States frequently conflate the categories of race and political status in ways that have fundamentally distorted the actual political terrain of the United States as a settler colonial state. What sets American Indians apart from other peoples in the United States is Indian nationhood. In the words of Lumbee political scientist David E. Wilkins, "Indian peoples are nations, not minorities."[4] Fundamental to this distinction is the indigeneity of Indian nations, which can be distinguished from other so-called minorities in the United States because of the long history of diplomacy and treaty making with European intruders that lies at the center of their political status as inherent sovereigns. Tribes possess the inherent power to determine tribal citizenship, which historically has been determined by ancestry and belonging, typically defined with reference to social, cultural, territorial, and other criteria.[5] By the late nineteenth century, the federal government began to use dubious notions of "blood quantum" rooted in erroneous ideas about the science of race to reduce federal responsibility for tribes. In this formulation, Indians must meet blood quantum requirements to be recognized by the federal government. Tribes, too, frequently but not always use blood quantum for determining tribal citizenship.[6]

Issues of recognition move beyond the "problem" of race in New England in additional ways. The United States came into existence long after English colonialism largely dispossessed New England Indians, much like most tribes in what became the original thirteen states, and tribes there lack a treaty relationship with the United States. In 1978, the federal government created the Branch of Acknowledgment and Research within the Bureau of Indian Affairs to extend recognition, or acknowledgment, to tribes who, for a variety of reasons, lacked this status. Congress also possesses the power to recognize tribal nations. Some states, including Connecticut and Massachusetts, also acknowledge tribes as political entities within their bounds.

Looking back to the nineteenth century, the federal government regarded members of tribes that were not federally recognized in the former English colonies as citizens and thus the responsibility of the states that encompassed them. But not until the mid- to late nineteenth century did the issue of Indian citizenship arise, and in the case of Connecticut, state citizenship for Indians was not fully resolved until the late twentieth century.[7] In the case of Connecticut, Indians required a specific granting of state citizenship.[8] According to Indian policy as it emerged in the nineteenth century, New England Indians were thus not regarded as a federal responsibility even when states did not consider individuals in tribes within state guardianship relationships to be state citizens. The federal government took this stance even when it knew of the existence of tribes that officials did not acknowledge as falling within the purview of federal responsibility.[9]

A policy of termination would take hold in southern New England via debates over citizenship and the franchise. Even as the federal and state governments might hold divergent views of the political situation of Indians in Connecticut and elsewhere, the agitation over race, slavery, and citizenship brought the question to the fore across southern New England. In the end, arguments about the extension of citizenship as it transpired there implemented a policy of terminating the official recognition of the separate political status of many tribal nations in southern New England in the mid- to late nineteenth century. This political reformulation found its expression in the liberatory vocabulary of "equality." "Citizenship" and "enfranchisement" served the larger non-Indian aims of eliminating the political and legal distinction between Indian peoples as inherent sovereigns and their non-Indian neighbors. Thus, the extension of citizenship and enfranchisement meant for southern New England Indians "termination" of the recognition of their political separation as tribal nations recognized by the states within which they had become encompassed. This outcome need not have resulted. In the long and immensely complex history of the political status of Indian nations within the United States, case law came to define Indians as "dual citizens." That is, Indians are considered as citizens of their own tribal nations even after the guarantee of citizenship in the United States came in the early twentieth century.

States of Recognition

Even while non-Indians failed to understand the Indianness of still-present Indian peoples—which translated into a failure to recognize Indians as such—the states of Connecticut, Massachusetts, and Rhode Island did indeed extend official recognition to tribes.[10] While the relationship between each state and tribe varied in particular details, parallels can be drawn among them and between these relationships and those that existed on the federal level. The situation in New England (and generally speaking in other former English colonies) differed from elsewhere in the United States in that federal Indian policy as developed in the new nation did not specifically govern Indian affairs.[11] Nonetheless, state bureaucracies gave shape to Indian affairs in nineteenth-century New England. These bureaucracies grew organically from colonial policies, so straightforward and comprehensive blueprints for these relationships do not exist.[12] Instead, the general shape of Indian policy and its bureaucracy can be understood only by taking into account the actual state of affairs and the periodic legislation that took up Indian relations from time to time. Indian affairs in this context often seem tremendously haphazard, as officials involved with tribes rarely concerned themselves much with those tribes under their oversight, and Indian peoples frequently sought to avoid that oversight.[13] Rhode Island created an office of commissioner of the Narragansett Indians in 1840, but neither Connecticut nor Massachusetts developed even this modicum of regularized bureaucracy regarding Indian affairs.[14]

An 1859 report filed by John Milton Earle, appointed to investigate the condition of Indian peoples in Massachusetts, offers an excellent snapshot of Indian affairs that can be applied to Connecticut and Rhode Island as well:

> There has been neither order, system, nor uniformity of purpose in our legislation concerning the Indians. The subject has not been studied, nor the facts ascertained, or the relations correctly understood by successive legislatures and consequently much of the legislation has been special in its character, and too often dictated by mere expediency for the occasion, to get over a present difficulty . . . and the whole matter has become so complicated, that he must be a patient man who will trace out the legislation and digest it, and a wise one if he can tell when he has done it, precisely what the legal relations of the Indians are, and what their various rights, in relation to property, whether

held in severalty or in common, having reference as well to the Indian traditional law as to the statutes of the Commonwealth.[15]

Among Earle's recommendations for rectifying the situation was the appointment of a single commissioner for Indian affairs in the commonwealth so that some more comprehensive vision and understanding might be achieved. This recommendation was not implemented.[16]

So what were the constituent elements of official state recognition? Although exceptions can be found to nearly every generalization one might wish to draw, some fundamental points can be made. The relationship between the states and the tribes, developed organically beginning in the seventeenth century, can be characterized as that of a guardian to a ward, a concept famously summarized in Chief Justice John Marshall's majority opinion in the landmark 1831 decision, *Cherokee Nation v. Georgia*, that gave shape to the federal definition of Indian affairs.[17] Based on colonial and then state statutes—sometimes general and other times specific to tribes and even individual Indians—the state acted as a guardian over Indian peoples and their property. The state held reservation lands and other resources that remained in Indian hands in trust—with a theoretical system of oversight that prohibited the sale of Indian lands and resources without the approval of official guardians or overseers appointed by the legislature. Indian lands and other resources held in common remained exempt from taxation. Furthermore and specifically related to their tax-exempt status as wards of the state, Indians were not guaranteed citizenship in their localities, the state, or the United States. Although, as Earle found in his rather extensive investigations, some Indians in Massachusetts paid taxes and exercised the franchise, such arrangements were highly individualized.[18] The Deep Bottom Indians on Martha's Vineyard, he noted, "have never been under guardianship, *and* are not considered as entitled to the rights of citizenship."[19] No New England state guaranteed Indians citizenship prior to the 1869 passage of the Massachusetts Indian Enfranchisement Act after more than two decades of agitation. Indeed, Connecticut did not extend citizenship to any tribes except the Mohegans and Niantics until 1973.[20]

The historical relationship between the Eastern Pequots and Connecticut demonstrates strong similarities in Indian policy to that of the tribes and Massachusetts. First as a colony and subsequently as a state, Connecticut treated them as a distinct tribe from the time their lands received official recognition, an implicit acceptance of a relationship between distinct political bodies.[21] This relationship defined the Eastern Pequots as a group and as different from all non-Indian groups in the state, "based on their status as a group rather than being a racial classification of individuals. By contrast, Connecticut treated individual, non-tribal Indians the same as the remainder of the population."[22]

Connecticut's Indian policy, again epitomized by the example of the Eastern Pequots, paralleled that of Massachusetts in defining a distinct political status within a system of guardianship and rooted in the at least theoretical protection of Indian land. The colony recognized the land base of the Eastern Pequots in 1683, a recognition that continues into the present. As in Massachusetts, Indian lands were exempt from taxation, and the lands themselves as well as any income derived from them were treated as tribal rather than individual possessions. Connecticut appointed overseers for the Eastern Pequots beginning in 1764 (and earlier for other tribes) and entrusted them with supervising and holding authority over tribal lands and funds and with responsibility "for the welfare of [tribe] members," though the precise roster of responsibilities varied over time. As in Massachusetts, Indians did not exercise the attributes of state citizenship such as the franchise. And further,

> The earliest laws reflect the idea that the tribes had a distinct political status in that it was considered necessary to explicitly legislate that certain of the Colony's laws, such as criminal laws, applied to the Indians—*i.e.* they were not considered to apply otherwise. This legislative treatment reflects the tribes' origins as distinct polities outside the Colony. . . . This idea is expressed in law until 1808. After that point, the tribes' distinct status continues in the form of the overseers' protection and responsibility, the distinct status of the land, and the noncitizenship of the members of these tribes.[23]

As this passage suggests, Earle's observations about the haphazard nature of Indian policy would have been apt in nineteenth-century Connecticut as well, in that much of the relationship here described never received coherent articulation.

The Problem of Citizenship in Nineteenth-Century New England

Throughout southern New England, abolitionism and the mounting crisis of the Civil War precipitated debates regarding the status of Indian peoples, although these debates varied in their particulars from place to place. Earlier, in connection with the events that collectively composed the Mashpee Revolt and the activism of William Apess, media attention had "forced Massachusetts to acknowledge that Christiantown, Chappaquiddick, Gay Head, Mashpee, and Herring Pond were 'five communities within the state, but not of it, subject to its laws, but having no part in their enactment; within the limits of local municipalities, yet not subject to their jurisdiction; and holding real estate in their own right, yet not suffered to dispose of it except to each other.'"[24] In Massachusetts, agitation regarding the status of Indian peoples began in earnest in 1849 and continued until the passage of the Massachusetts Indian Enfranchisement Act in 1869.[25] Within this twenty-year span, the legislature commissioned three investigations, headed by men committed to abolition and the Radical Republican agenda, on the status and situation of Indians in Massachusetts. All of these investigations "were explicitly charged with determining when and how the Indians could be made full citizens of the Commonwealth."[26] After the passage of the Civil Rights Act of 1866, legislators voiced concerns that Massachusetts would be in violation of federal statutes if it did not extend citizenship to Indians.[27] In the midst of this decades-long debate, Earle compiled his report, offering specific recommendations on the pace of enfranchisement: He suggested gradual action in keeping with the particular situations in different communities rather than incorporating all Indians immediately.[28]

The debates over citizenship in New England took up the political status of Indians from the perspective of rights and responsibilities. As suggested in the language narrating the situation of Christiantown, Chappaquiddick, Gay Head, Mashpee, and Herring Pond, Earle and other observers regarded those Indians as political anomalies. Not explicitly empowered with the franchise, they had no role in the enactment of legislation to which they were subjected, a political disability that had been a central political preoccupation regarding the institution of slavery for decades. Earle and others likewise narrated the trust protections governing Indian common lands as a shackle on the possibility of full participation in the market economy, or what might be thought of as economic citizenship, since only other Indians could be parties to transactions of their common property. The tax-exempt status of their lands signaled both their standing as peoples apart from the citizenry and their failure to fulfill a fundamental responsibility of citizenship.

As Ann Marie Plane and Gregory Button have noted, enfranchisement in Massachusetts bore remarkable similarities to the General Allotment

Act of 1887, sponsored by Massachusetts senator Henry Dawes, in removing Indian lands from trust protection and rendering it a taxable resource as well as in the legislation's citizenship objectives. The measure echoes equally with the termination policy initiated in 1953 in its language of liberation that cloaked the real intent: that of ending the recognition of Indian nationhood in a definitive legislative action, which went further than policy as it unfolded after the Dawes Act. This language from the 1848 Bird report could have been entered into the *Congressional Record* in 1953: "The progress of civil and ecclesiastical liberality has released all but the Indian from these disabilities [disenfranchisement]. The African, the Turk, the Japanese, may enjoy, in Massachusetts, all the privileges of American Citizenship. The Indian alone, the descendant of monarchs, is a vassal in the land of his fathers." Enfranchisement in nineteenth-century New England thus both prefigured federal Indian policy nearly a century later and constituted a separate and disjointed set of policies concocted at the state level in a time of political ferment regarding the extension of citizenship or democratic participation more generally.

Enfranchisement in Massachusetts entailed the end of the guardianship relationship that recognized the separate nationhood of Indian peoples in southern New England. It would have been possible, as subsequent history tells us, for Massachusetts and other states to extend citizenship to Indians without ending guardianship, which is precisely what happened with the passage of the Indian Citizenship Act of 1924. That measure finally guaranteed citizenship to Indians without obliterating the trust status and the nation-to-nation relationship that characterizes tribal nations within the United States.[29] Moreover, a distinction exists between the exterior recognition of Indian separateness and its actual existence. Recognition in this context refers to the diplomatic relationship between separate nations.

Responding to the Earle Report, the Massachusetts legislature passed the 1862 Act Concerning the Indians of Commonwealth. The first provision addressed the legal status of Indians: "All Indians and descendants of Indians in this State are hereby placed on the same legal footing as the other inhabitants of the Commonwealth, except such as are or have been supported, in whole or in part, by the State, and except also those residing on the Indian plantations of the Chappaquiddick, Christiantown, Gay Head, Marshpee [sic], Herring Pond, Fall River, and Dudley tribes, or those whose homes are on some one of said Plantations and who are only temporarily absent."[30] By this act, Massachusetts extended citizenship to nearly 400 Indians while continuing the guardianship relationship with the seven enumerated tribes whose membership totaled 1,241 by Earle's accounting procedures. In effect, this measure terminated the commonwealth's official recognition of these Indian people. An additional provision made citizenship a possibility for any other Indian "or person of color" upon application to the town clerk where they resided and the paying of a poll tax, which would terminate their recognition as Indian.[31] Additional alterations followed this legislation, such as, in the words of the Aquinnah federal recognition petition, "the imposition of district status on Gay Head [which] augured profound changes for the community. By increasing the power of elected officials and denying women the right to vote, it disrupted the egalatarian [sic] traditions of the Indians. It also established the groundwork for terminating their communal system of land tenure by hastening the development of a system of codified laws and recorded deeds."[32]

Agitation for terminating the official recognition of Indians categorically excluded from the enfranchisement continued after the passage of the act in 1862. The Massachusetts House of Representatives appointed additional committees to "study the feasibility 'of removing the civil and political disabilities under which they are placed, and of merging them in the general community as citizens.'"[33] Finally, the legislature passed the 1869 Massachusetts Indian Enfranchisement Act, which purported to eliminate what Governor William Claflin declared a "political anomaly": "These persons are not Indians in any sense of the word. It is doubtful there is a full-blooded Indian in the State. . . . A majority have more or less the marked characteristics of the aboriginal race, but there are many without a drop of Indian blood in their veins. The marriage of a foreigner with a member of a tribe transforms the foreigner into an Indian. The result of this singular system has been a heterogeneous population, in which the characteristics of the white and negro races have already nearly obliterated all traces of the Indian."[34] Steeped in the nineteenth-century language of blood, this declaration brought together the mythology of blood with the political project of termination, justifying the ending of trust status by trucking in racist assumptions about Indians.

"Termination" and Its Refusals[35]

Not surprisingly, enfranchisement and the duties and liabilities that accompanied that change in legal status engendered controversy and rancor within Indian communities. Earle reported opposition to the change in every community where he inquired—Chappaquiddick, Christiantown,

Gay Head, and Mashpee—and he opposed changes in those communities as well as in Herring Pond. At Chappaquiddick, the "older members of the tribe, thoughtful, considerate, and prudent persons . . . believed . . . it would operate disastrously on the tribe; that most of them would soon become the prey of the shrewder and sharper men outside, that the little property they possess would be wrested from them."[36] At Gay Head, wrangling over land and the status of the community had begun early in the century and continued through the enfranchisement struggles.[37] At Chappaquiddick and Christiantown, the land loss that followed the ending of legal protections fractured the communities, and residents moved to Gay Head or elsewhere.[38]

The administration of Indian affairs in Connecticut unfolded equally organically, and discussions about citizenship may have also been precipitated by events of the civil war.[39] Connecticut terminated its guardianship of the Mohegans in 1872, apparently at the tribe's request, and extended them citizenship and removed restrictions on land allotments that had been made to individuals in 1861.[40] According to tribal historian Melissa Jayne Fawcett, Mohegans requested this alteration in response to the corruption of their overseers, who allowed "desecrations and theft of tribal land" to undermine the people.[41] Connecticut later acted similarly to terminate the Niantics. No other Connecticut tribes were terminated in the nineteenth century—state recognition of the tribes has extended continuously into the present.[42] But the issue of termination resurfaced in 1953, when a bill was introduced into Congress "to end the second class citizenship of Connecticut's few remaining Indians," specifically the Eastern Pequots.[43] The bill's language (quoting from the Eastern Pequot federal recognition petition) "was identical to the language in the 1872 Mohegan bill."[44] The effort failed. Debate over the status of Connecticut Indians continued until the 1973 legislation that created the Connecticut Indian Affairs Council, which "granted all the rights and privileges afforded by law, that all of Connecticut's citizens enjoy. It is further recognized that said Indians have certain special rights to tribal lands as may have been granted to them in the past by treaty or other agreement."[45]

Reconciling the rights issue also provided the pretext for addressing the situation of the Narragansetts in Rhode Island in the Civil War era. But Rhode Island employed a different vocabulary in its drive to obliterate the Narragansett nation, casting debates about the problem of civil rights and the special privileges entailed in the guardianship relationship in the language of "detribalization." By "detribalizing" the Narragansetts, Rhode Island acted in exactly the same fashion in extending the franchise to Indians made citizens and did so by illegally terminating recognition of the Narragansetts' separate status.[46]

The idea of terminating guardianship and thus the Narragansetts' sovereign status received a public hearing as early as 1832.[47] In 1866, the Rhode Island Legislature appointed a committee to look into the possibility of terminating the state's guardianship relationship to the tribe and liquidating their lands on the premise that the state was not "bound to extend to the members of the tribe any peculiar or special privileges not enjoyed by all the inhabitants of the State," in spite of the long history of treaty relations inaugurated in the colonial period that protected tribal jurisdiction over their lands.[48] The committee met with the tribe and "sundry citizens of Charlestown" and informed the assembled group that equality before the law "without regard to race or color" had culminated in the civil rights amendments. These developments prompted a "concern" on the part of the legislature and citizens of the state "that this tribe, to whose ancestors our ancestors were under so many obligations, should still claim to owe allegiance to their tribe, rather than to the State, and to maintain even a semblance of another jurisdiction amongst us." Furthermore, the committee members opined, no one should be part of a "privileged class in the State." But the committee had approached the tribe to "hear the views of others," including the "officers and members of the tribe."[49]

The Narragansetts obliged. According to the newspaper account of the gathering, they delivered their reply "with dignity and propriety of manner," informing the committee that they had not initiated the meeting, and as far as they knew, they were living in peace and prosperity, thus calling into question the purpose of the whole affair. They continued by taking up the idea of citizenship, informing the committee that they had traveled the country and "heard much said about the rights of the negro; of negro citizenship and negro equality; but we have not found the place where this equality and these rights exist, or the negroes who enjoy them."[50] Astutely pointing out the law's failure to guarantee African American equality, the Narragansetts rejected the possibility that the law could similarly insure their rights. Furthermore,

We are not negroes: we are the heirs of Ninigret, and of the great chiefs and warriors of the Narragansetts. Because, when your ancestors stole the negro from Africa, and brought him amongst us, and made a slave of him, we extended to him the hand of friendship, and permitted his blood to be mingled with ours, are we to be called negroes, and to be told that we may be made negro citizens? We claim that while one drop of Indian blood remains in our veins, we are entitled to the rights and privileges guaranteed by your ancestors to ours by solemn treaty, which, without a breach of faith, you cannot violate. We did not go to the white man, but the white men came to us. When we were powerful and he was weak, he claimed our protection and we extended it. We are now weak, and our grasping neighbors, of a grasping race, are seeking the remaining remnant of our inheritance, and will not give over while an inch of our territory remains to us, and until the members of our tribe are beneath the soil, or are scattered to the winds of heaven. . . . We deny your right to take from us that which never came from you.[51]

The Narragansetts asserted their sovereignty as an inherent right not subject to termination by the state. They predicted that if those rights were subject to termination, Narragansett lands, held mainly by the women, would be steadily eroded through taxes, and the people would be left impoverished. Furthermore, "your imperious draft cannot touch us now; we may volunteer to fight your battles, but now you cannot force us into the ranks of your army to be shot down without our consent."[52] The right to vote amounted to nothing. The effort to terminate the Narragansetts similarly came to nothing at that time.

Thirteen years later, Rhode Island renewed its efforts to abolish the tribe. During hearings on the issues in 1879, all five Narragansett tribal council members lodged their disapproval, even though they agreed to have their school closed. Later that year at an undocumented meeting and for reasons that are not clear, the council agreed to sell tribal lands. This action, perhaps based on a misunderstanding of what was at stake, did not involve the full membership of the tribe. Indeed, tribal members protested the action in 1881, and a close reading of the documentary record reveals opposition during the hearings on the matter.[53] A year earlier, the state of Rhode Island passed legislation "which purported to abolish tribal authority and tribal relations, declared tribal members citizens, ended the state's relationship with the tribe, and which authorized the sale of all land held in common."[54] With this act of "detribalization," the state of Rhode Island legislated the Narragansetts out of existence. Virtually all of the remaining 927 acres belonging to the tribe fell into non-Indian hands, leaving only 2 acres surrounding the Narragansett Church, which retained special status and continues to do so.[55]

In effect, New England pursued termination to eliminate the claims that can be made by Indians by virtue of being nations, such as the protection of Indian homelands. Individual Indians could remain and be recognized as individuals, but such actions removed Indian survivors, usually cast as "colored," "mixed," or "black," from an Indian nationhood recognized by the state and subjected them to a narrative that insisted that Indian populations were "degenerate" and disappearing.

Legacies

The emphasis on incorporating Narragansett individuals as citizens found expression in the creation of a tribal roll listing those who would benefit from the liquidation of tribal lands. Ironically, the existence of this roll became a crucial piece of evidence in the Narragansetts' successful effort to reverse the illegal detribalization through the federal recognition process. That 1983 decision recapitulated the history of colonialism experienced by the Narragansetts after English invasion. It pointed out Rhode Island's development of the guardianship system, which began in 1709 and "continued until 1880, when the state legislature of Rhode Island enacted the so-called 'detribalization' act." The decision acknowledged the fact that the Narragansetts continued their measured separatism as a social, cultural, and political community in spite of their detribalization and the fact that "essentially all of the current membership are believed to be able to trace to at least one ancestor on the membership lists of the Narragansett after the 1880 Rhode Island 'detribalization' Act."[56] Thus, the historical record that sought to bring an end to the Narragansett nation served instead as crucial evidence of Indian resistance, survival, and refusal to be terminated.

The process of recognition in New England is highly contested terrain and will in all likelihood remain so into the future. Following the Narragansett decision, four more tribal nations gained acknowledgment. The Mashantucket Pequots achieved congressional recognition in 1983, while the Aquinnahs (1987), Mohegans (1994), and Mashpee Wampanoags (2007) successfully navigated the federal acknowledgment process. In the case of the Mashpees, their recognition reversed the controversial and highly visible rejection of their nationhood in federal district court in 1977. Their triumph thirty years later attests to their resilience and determination to remain an Indian people apart.

Other New England tribal nations have different stories to tell. The Hassanamisco Nipmucs, Golden Hill Paugussetts, Eastern Pequots, and

Schaghticokes all have been denied federal recognition in highly politicized, fiercely contested, and ongoing battles. In the case of the Nipmucs, delays in issuing an anticipated positive finding under the Clinton administration allowed the new Bush administration to deny them. Both the Eastern Pequots and the Schaghticokes gained federal recognition in 2002 and 2004 respectively, only to have it rescinded in October 2005 following the determined opposition of grassroots organizations and the lobbying efforts of Connecticut's attorney general, Richard Blumenthal. The tribes suffered this denial in spite of the continuous recognition of their status by the State of Connecticut, which the Bureau of Indian Affairs rejected as insufficient evidence of their continuous existence. Both groups are fighting the ruling in the courts. So in ironic juxtaposition for the "terminated" Narragansetts and Mohegans, ongoing relationships to the state failed to secure federal recognition for the Eastern Pequots and the Schaghticokes.

The debates over Narragansett detribalization illuminate the underlying logic that characterizes New England recognition battles more generally. Nineteenth-century New Englanders sought to erase the distinctions between Indians and themselves by essentially rescinding the centuries-long recognition of the Indians' separate political status. New England officials did so using the language of liberation and equality, treating Indian peoples as racial minorities rather than as political units whose recognition rested on a legacy of diplomacy and the trust relationship. In the immediate aftermath of these recognition struggles and in the long term, all of these tribal nations engaged in what Jessica R. Cattelino has characterized as a refusal to be terminated, an implicit and often explicit argument that their nationhood survives whether or not official recognition by the United States has been extended. New England tribal nations and other indigenous people "enact sovereignty" through lived practices of their uniqueness.[57]

This brief synopsis of Indian affairs as the nineteenth century drew to a close cannot possibly do justice to the extraordinary complexity of the situation. This story is still being reconstructed, and each tribal history contains its own crucially unique elements. But the collective actions of the state governments in the era surrounding the Civil War, steeped in the scientific racism of the nineteenth century, sought to terminate the separate existence of the astonishingly resilient Indian peoples of southern New England. As the eloquent synopsis supplied by the Narragansetts demonstrates, as long as they retained even one drop of metaphorical "Indian blood," they would defend their nationhood. So, as for termination and so much more, Indians, then and now, had other ideas.

Notes

1. Jean M. O'Brien, *Firsting and Lasting: Writing Indians Out of Existence in New England* (Minneapolis: University of Minnesota Press, 2010). See also Daniel R. Mandell, *Tribe, Race, History: Native Americans in Southern New England, 1780–1880* (Baltimore: Johns Hopkins University Press, 2008), 195–217.

2. On the federal acknowledgment process, see, e.g., Renée Cramer, *Cash, Color, and Colonialism: The Politics of Tribal Acknowledgment* (Norman: University of Oklahoma Press, 2005); Anne Merline McCulloch and David E. Wilkins, "Constructing Nations within States: The Quest for Federal Recognition by the Catawba and Lumbee Tribes," *American Indian Quarterly* 19 (1995): 361–88; William A. Starna, "'We'll All Be Together Again': The Federal Acknowledgment of the Wampanoag Tribe of Gay Head," *Northeast Anthropology* 51 (1996): 3–12.

3. As of 2005, the United States had restored recognition to thirty-seven tribes that had been "terminated" (Cramer, *Cash, Color, and Colonialism*, 44).

4. David E. Wilkins, *American Indian Politics and the American Political System* (Lanham, Md.: Rowman and Littlefield, 2002), 41.

5. Ibid., 49.

6. Ibid., 23. See also Kimberly TallBear, "DNA, Blood, and Racializing the Tribe," *Wicazo Sa Review* 18 (2003): 81–107, for an excellent discussion of the complex interplay of "blood talk," belonging, and the political determination of Indian citizenship.

7. U.S. Department of the Interior, Bureau of Indian Affairs, Office of Federal Acknowledgment, *Summary under the Criteria and Evidence for Final Determination in Regard to Federal Acknowledgment of the Eastern Pequot Indians of Connecticut as a Portion of the Historical Eastern Pequot Tribe* (2002), 75.

8. Ibid., 61.

9. Ibid., 75.

10. See Jedidiah Morse, *A Report to the Secretary of War of the United States, on Indian Affairs* (New Haven, Conn.: Converse, 1822), 24; Jack Campisi, "The Emergence of the Mashantucket Pequot Tribe, 1637–1975," in *The Pequots in Southern New England: The Fall and Rise of an American Indian Nation*, ed. Laurence M. Hauptman and James D. Wherry (Norman: University of Oklahoma Press, 1990), 117–40; Jack Campisi, *The Mashpee Indians: Tribe on Trial* (Syracuse: Syracuse University Press, 1991), 99–118; James Clifford, "Identity in Mashpee," in *The Predicament of Culture: Twentieth-Century Ethnography, Literature, and Art* (Cambridge: Harvard University Press, 1988), 277–348; U.S. Department of the Interior, Bureau of Indian Affairs, Office of Federal Acknowledgment, *Summary under the Criteria and Evidence for Final Determination in Regard to Federal Acknowledgment of the Eastern Pequot Indians*, 29.

11. For an overview of these relationships, see Wilkins, *American Indian Politics*, 21–23.

12. For a useful overview of the colonial roots of this situation, see Dorothy V. Jones, "British Colonial Indian Treaties," in *Handbook of North American Indians*, ed. Wilcomb E. Washburn (Washington, D.C.: Smithsonian Institution Scholarly Press, 1988), 4:185–94.

13. See, e.g., David Silverman, *Faith and Boundaries: Colonists, Christianity, and Community among the Wampanoag Indians of Martha's Vineyard, 1600–1871* (New York: Cambridge University Press), 258; John Milton Earle, *Report to the Governor and Council, Concerning the Indians of the Commonwealth, under the Act of April 16, 1859* (Boston: White, 1861), 38.

14. Paul R. Campbell and Glenn W. LaFantasie, "Scattered to the Winds of Heaven—Narragansett Indians 1676–1800," *Rhode Island History* 37 (1978): 77.

15. Earle, *Report*, 134. For a discussion of the problems associated with the Earle Report, see Christopher J. Thee, "Massachusetts Nipmucs and the Long Shadow of John Milton Earle," *New England Quarterly* 79 (2006): 636–54; Gould, this volume.

16. He also lamented the state of record keeping, which hindered his task tremendously. He suggested that measures be taken to keep regular records regarding Indians, including vital records (Earle, *Report*, 46, 49). The final act did not create a commissioner, but its fifth section called for "the clerks of the Districts of Mashpee and Gay Head and the guardians of the other tribes" to make registers of members and to keep vital records and land registers and to track any changes in land holdings. See Massachusetts General Court, Council, *Acts and Resolves, Passed by the General Court of Massachusetts, in the Year 1862* (Boston: White, 1862), 150–51.

17. *Cherokee Nation v. Georgia*, 30 U.S. 1 (1831).

18. Earle, *Report*, e.g., 20, 76, 102, 104–5, 118, 115.

19. Ibid., 116.

20. U.S. Department of the Interior, Bureau of Indian Affairs, *Summary under the Criteria and Evidence for Final Determination in Regard to Federal Acknowledgment of the Eastern Pequot Indians*, 78.

21. Ibid., 29.

22. Ibid.

23. Ibid., 29–30.

24. Silverman, *Faith and Boundaries*, 257.

25. For a useful overview of this legislation and its relationship to the Indian community at Mashpee and race relations more generally, see, e.g., Ann Marie Plane and Gregory Button, "The Massachusetts Enfranchisement Act: Ethnic Contest in Historical Context, 1849–1869," in *After King Philip's War: Presence and*

Persistence in Indian New England, ed. Colin G. Calloway (Hanover, N.H.: University Press of New England, 1997), 178–206.

26. Plane and Button, "Massachusetts Enfranchisement Act," 183.

27. Ibid., 183.

28. Ibid., 181–82.

29. The Indian Citizenship Act reads, "Be it *enacted* . . . That all non citizen Indians born within the territorial limits of the United States be, and they are hereby, declared to be citizens of the United States: Provided That the granting of such citizenship shall not in any manner impair or otherwise affect the right of any Indian to tribal or other property" (Francis Paul Prucha, ed., *Documents of United States Indian Policy* [Lincoln: University of Nebraska Press, 1975], 218).

30. Massachusetts General Court, Council, *Acts and Resolves*, 149.

31. Ibid., 149–50.

32. U.S. Department of the Interior, Bureau of Indian Affairs, Office of Federal Acknowledgment, *Evidence for Proposed Finding against Federal Acknowledgment of the Wampanoag Tribal Council of Gay Head, Inc.* (1985), 27.

33. Ibid., 28 (quoting from House documents).

34. Ibid.

35. This section heading gestures toward Jessica R. Cattelino's argument in "The Double Bind of American Indian Need-Based Sovereignty," *Cultural Anthropology* 25 (2010): 235–62. This double bind, she argues, can be figured generally as the problem that "American Indian tribal nations (like other polities) require economic resources to exercise sovereignty, and their revenues often derive from their governmental rights. However, once they exercise economic power, the legitimacy of tribal sovereignty and citizenship is challenged in law, public culture, and everyday interactions within settler society" (235–36). She analyzes the 2007 Seminole celebration of the fiftieth anniversary of the tribe's governmental organization as more accurately not lauding "the founding Seminole political moment" (249) but rather as a "refusal of termination" that the U.S. government had sought to impose on them in the 1950s under the official termination policy.

36. Earle, *Report*, 24.

37. Silverman, *Faith and Boundaries*, esp. 223–73.

38. Ibid., 270.

39. U.S. Department of the Interior, Bureau of Indian Affairs, Office of Federal Acknowledgment, *Summary under the Criteria and Evidence for Final Determination in Regard to Federal Acknowledgment of the Eastern Pequot Indians*, 55. On the origins of the guardianship system in Connecticut, see Wendy B. St. Jean, "Inventing Guardianship: The Mohegan Indians and Their 'Protectors," *New England*

Quarterly 72 (1999): 362–87; U.S. Department of the Interior, Bureau of Indian Affairs, Office of Federal Acknowledgment, *Summary under the Criteria and Evidence for Final Determination in Regard to Federal Acknowledgment of the Eastern Pequot Indians*, 61.

40. Some Mohegans protested the sale of lands at this time, fearing that they would lose the land. See U.S. Department of the Interior, Bureau of Indian Affairs, Office of Federal Acknowledgment, Anthropological Report, *Summary under the Criteria and Evidence for Proposed Finding against Federal Acknowledgment of the Mohegan Tribe of Indians of the State of Connecticut: Anthropological Report* (2000), 32, 30. The membership list prepared for the land distribution that occurred in 1861 ironically "now serves as the primary historic roll for the petitioning group" (U.S. Department of the Interior, Office of Federal Acknowledgment, *Summary under the Criteria and Evidence for Proposed Finding against Federal Acknowledgment of the Mohegan Tribe of Indians of the State of Connecticut: Genealogical Report*, 31).

41. Melissa Jayne Fawcett, *The Lasting of the Mohegans*, Part 1, *The Story of the Wolf People* (Uncasville, Conn.: Mohegan Tribe, 1995), 22.

42. U.S. Department of the Interior, Bureau of Indian Affairs, Office of Federal Acknowledgment, *Summary under the Criteria and Evidence for Final Determination in Regard to Federal Acknowledgment of the Eastern Pequot Indians*, 61. Continuous state recognition is contested.

43. Ibid., 62.

44. Ibid., 63.

45. Ibid.

46. Ruth Wallis Herndon and Ella Wilcox Sekatau, "The Right to a Name: The Narragansett People and Rhode Island Officials in the Revolutionary Era," in *After King Philip's War*, ed. Calloway, 114.

47. Patricia E. Rubertone, *Grave Undertakings: An Archaeology of Roger Williams and the Narragansett Indians* (Washington, D.C.: Smithsonian Institution Press, 2001), xx; Campbell and LaFantasie, "Scattered to the Winds of Heaven," 76–79. For an early study of Narragansett detribalization that bears the marks of terminationist thinking in the 1950s, see Ethel Boissevain, "The Detribalization of the Narragansett Indians: A Case Study," *Ethnohistory* 3 (1956): 225–45.

48. Frederic Denison, *Westerly (Rhode Island) and Its Witnesses, for Two Hundred and Fifty Years, 1626–1876, Including Charlestown, Hopkinton, and Richmond, until Their Separate Organization with the Principal Points of Their Subsequent History* (Providence, R.I.: Reid and Reid, 1878), 82. This text reproduces an account of these events published in the *Providence Journal*, October 17, 1866.

49. Denison, *Westerly*, 83.

50. Ibid., 83–84.

51. Ibid., 84.

52. Ibid.

53. Paul Robinson, "A Narragansett History from 1000 B.P. to the Present," in *Enduring Traditions: The Native Peoples of New England,* ed. Laurie Weinstein (Westport, Conn.: Bergin and Garvey, 1994), esp. 85–86.

54. U.S. Department of the Interior, Bureau of Indian Affairs, Office of Federal Acknowledgment, *Recommendation and Summary of Evidence for Proposed Finding for Federal Acknowledgment of the Narragansett Indian Tribe of Rhode Island Pursuant to 25 CRF 83* (1982), 4.

55. Ibid.

56. *Federal Register,* February 10, 1983, 6177.

57. Cattelino, "Double Bind," 252.

Altered State?

Indian Policy Narratives, Federal Recognition,
and the "New" War on Native Rights in Connecticut

AMY E. DEN OUDEN

If there is one important lesson to be derived from Connecticut's Indian policy as it has been developed and articulated in response to tribal nations' federal acknowledgment struggles in the late 1990s and early 2000s, it is that the ancestry of the state's Indian policy should be investigated. This history is indeed long, and its contemporary narratives—that is, the public stories it tells about Indians and their rights—are rooted in the colonial period. One of Connecticut Indian policy's most politically powerful and ancient tales might be titled "Fairness to the Indians." That narrative is as old as Connecticut's tales of the so-called Pequot Conquest of 1637. In the 1700s, as native peoples within the colony's borders struggled against relentless encroachment and pillaging of their reservation lands by Anglos, stories of the "just" English conquest of the Pequot nation (in fact, it was a massacre) were evoked to counter Mohegans' and Pequots' defense of their land rights expressed in their formal petitions to the Connecticut government. In effect, the "Pequot Conquest" was born again in the eighteenth century as Connecticut officials grappled with the unanticipated problem of indigenous resistance to theft of reservation lands and with the troubling fact that there were seventeenth-century colonial laws on the side of the resisters. The "new," or recycled, Indian policy narrative that was emerging around the issue of indigenous land rights in the eighteenth century was to a great extent successful, and the theme of an "original" conquest by which indigenous lands could be "justly" appropriated found renewed political efficacy as a means of masking the illegality of colonial encroachment on Indian reservations. The "fairness" of dispossessing Indians in eighteenth-century Connecticut depended on good storytelling.[1]

Contemporary Indian policy narratives constitute good storytelling as well and have also worked to deflect attention from the rights of tribal nations in Connecticut that have petitioned for and been denied federal recognition. While the native people of Connecticut have a long history of engagement with and resistance to the state's Indian policy, their historical narratives—including those that have been recounted in federal acknowledgment petitions—must contend with the pronouncements of government officials whose political motives have for the most part escaped careful public scrutiny. While the state's assessments of federal acknowledgement cases have been proffered as "objective," tribal nations' accounts of their histories and indeed their existence as Indian peoples have often been readily dismissed as "invented." Having worked for more than a decade as a researcher, writer, and oral history interviewer for the Eastern Pequot tribal nation's federal acknowledgment project, and having listened to elders talk about their tribal nation's history and its centrality in Eastern Pequot community life, I know well that their knowledge of the past has power in the present. Yet the state's Indian policy narratives have had the advantage of public platforms that lend them credibility without question. I begin this essay by assessing how particular claims and themes of Indian policy are employed to replace or silence history; I then track important moments in the formation of Indian policy narratives in early twenty-first-century Connecticut, as some state officials became more strident in their opposition to the federal acknowledgment of the Eastern Pequot, Golden Hill Paugussett, and Schaghticoke tribal nations. I argue that the state's formation of an antirecognition Indian policy has troubling implications for public perceptions of the rights of tribal nations, and that those implications extend beyond local debates over federal acknowledgment cases. Indeed, the articulators of the state's Indian policy have made such claims themselves in national political settings, insisting that Connecticut is a crucial site of precedent-setting battles against forces that threaten its "legitimate" citizenry as well as the sovereignty of states. In an ironic and compelling fashion, these claims point to the ways that native rights issues in Connecticut merge with global articulations of indigenous rights embodied in the United Nations Declaration on the Rights of Indigenous Peoples. As the Declaration makes clear, recognition of the specificity and diversity of indigenous histories and cultural identities is necessary for the establishment of just and democratic relations between the governments of nation-states and indigenous peoples. For the historically state-recognized, but now federally unacknowledged, tribal nations in the state, Connecticut's antirecognition narratives have worked to obscure and to denigrate the distinct history and identity of the Eastern Pequot, Golden Hill Paugussett, and Schaghticoke tribal nations.

Indian Policy versus History

In his voluminous introduction to *Indian Land Cessions in the United States* (1899), Bureau of American Ethnology archaeologist Cyrus Thomas begins a segment on colonial Indian policy as follows: "The policy of the settlers of Connecticut in their dealings with the natives regarding their lands forms one of the brightest chapters . . . of the early history of our country."[2] This statement and an extensive excerpt from Thomas now appear on the website *Native American Nations: Your Source for Indian Research* under the heading "Connecticut Indian Land Cessions."[3] The resuscitation of Thomas's account, commending colonial leaders for their "just and humane policy," is an important example of the way Indian policy and claims about its legitimacy are interwoven with historical narratives that have become part of the common knowledge of Indianness in the region. As is often the case with such common knowledge, it deflects scrutiny of the actual historical processes of conquest and colonization as they were endured and resisted by indigenous people.[4] Thomas's conclusion that the colony's Indian policy was benevolent is based on the accounts of nineteenth-century local historians. As historian Jean O'Brien explains in her study of New England narratives of Indian erasure, *Firsting and Lasting: Writing Indians Out of Existence in New England*, chroniclers of that era insisted that the region was the cradle of American civilization and that the triumph of Euro-American modernity was to be measured against the inevitable and necessary demise of New England Indians.[5] As one orator proclaimed at the 1889 unveiling of a monument honoring Major John Mason, leader of the 1637 massacre of Pequots in Mystic, Connecticut, Mason's actions initiated "the march of human progress" across lands "reclaimed from savagery and waste." In presumed historical effect, Mason was "abundantly vindicated by the process of time, the award of history, and the judgment of posterity."[6] Thus, one might dismiss Thomas's rosy version of the colony's Indian policy as a superficial repetition of the politically expedient sentiment of the period. But the appearance of Thomas's account on an "Indian Research" website points to the way arcane or "specialized" knowledge of Indian policy issues are disseminated to a wide public audience today. This is a key means by which the foundational claims of Euro-American Indian policy are recycled, legitimized, and now "democratically" distributed via the Internet, and offered as objective history to a nonnative public hungry for "expert" opinions on Indians. If these policy narratives are enmeshed with a broader, popular discourse on Indianness, how will they influence public recognition of present-day native peoples and their rights? Do such narratives end up standing in for history? Do they silence other narratives about colonial law and policy and their impact on indigenous peoples?

One way to begin to address these questions is to consider how Indian policy has been defined—"officially," or sanctioned by government—in the twentieth century. A key example is the definition of Indian policy articulated in the early 1970s as a part of the U.S. federal government's narrations on its newly formulated self-determination policy. In a 1973 U.S. Department of the Interior publication, *A History of Indian Policy*, historian S. Lyman Tyler explains, "Indian policy shall be considered a course of action pursued by any government and adopted as expedient by that government in its relations with any of the Indians of the Americas. By expedient, we mean action that is considered by government to be advantageous or advisable under the particular circumstances or during a specific time span."[7]

As Secretary of the Interior Rogers C. B. Morton stated in the foreword to this text, Tyler's account was intended to "help Indian and non-Indian alike understand what happened when two cultures collided on the land that has become the United States." That is, this history of Indian policy was intended to explain both the history of conquest and colonization ("collision") and the policies formulated and enacted throughout that history—a dual intent of critical significance at a time when federal Indian policy had purportedly been transformed in connection with dramatic national political change, with the resulting policy trajectory to reflect a more willing and sincere U.S. recognition of indigenous nations' right to self-determination. Morton proclaimed not only that Indian policy had changed but that the new "self-determination policy" would unfold with the active participation of Native American people as policy shapers. Tyler's history—his "looking backward" at policies and practices—was meant to ensure "that mistakes of the past are not repeated."[8] Here, then, is a compelling example of the interweaving of claims about Indian policy and history in which the two seem almost indistinguishable. Morton points toward a new era but implies that the interpretation of Indian history—and indeed, Indians' future—is inevitably tied to if not defined by U.S. Indian policy. Tyler's definition, a rather honest one, indicates that Indian policy is a form of governmentality, a strategy of management and control driven by the will of "the government" (itself a complex and internally fragmented entity) as it maneuvers through historical "circumstances" and "spans of time" in ways that are "expedient" and "advantageous" (that is, serving the interests of the established power structure).[9] These are useful starting points for an analysis of the discourse of Indian policy as a rich, diffuse, and fraught narrative field, one including but extending well beyond "official" policy statements and through which we might track particular visions and narrations of history as they are tied to claims about Indian policy's legitimacy and the rights of native peoples.[10]

Whose vision of history and of the possible future of relations between native peoples and nonnative governments is privileged in specific artic-ulations of Indian policy? While Morton's foreword suggested a genuine optimism about the ending of a dismal policy history and the emergence of a new period "in which Indians are full partners in planning, developing and administering programs and services,"[11] in the 2011 State of the Indian Nations Address, "Sovereign Indian Nations at the Dawn of a New Era," National Congress of American Indians president Jefferson Keel com-mented on the continuing exclusion of indigenous people from important decision-making processes that affect the present and future of their tribal nations and communities.[12] As Keel plainly puts it, "Words are one thing, but actions are another": "Even the recent promise of the self-determina-tion era," he reminds us, was nonetheless "defined by what the federal gov-ernment chose to do. . . . But this new era is defined by what we, as Indian nations, choose to do for ourselves."[13] Keel's assessment urges us to consider that even ostensibly pro-Indian Indian policy is imperial in a most literal sense—that is, commanding or seeking to dictate the course of indigenous lives and historical possibilities from an external center of power. The offi-cial discourse of those who assume the right to command the affairs of oth-ers not only masks the actual practices by which power over others and over their lands and resources has been exerted and maintained but also may sustain the notion that those in power are the primary agents and legitimate interpreters of history.

While it may now be a truism to state that destructive discrepancies have always existed between the grand claims of Indian policy and real-world practices and that statements heralding major historical changes or "high points" in Indian policy do not necessarily mark moments of significant change in the political practices and historical processes that affect native peoples and their rights, the dogma of Indian policy constitutes something much more complicated and problematic than a collection of historical falsehoods that might easily be revealed and expunged from public con-sciousness.[14] Indeed, Indian policy's foundational historical myths can have a long public life, as is evident in the reiteration of the timeworn "just and humane" theme to describe colonial Indian policy in Connecticut. One of Connecticut's eighteenth-century makers of Indian policy, Governor Joseph Talcott, would likely be pleased to see that theme live on. As he insisted in a February 1736 letter to one of the commissioners of the Society for the Propagation of the Gospel in New England—written while Mohegans, Pequots, Niantics, and other native people in Connecticut struggled to preserve their remaining reservation lands—"this Colony hath been a candid protector of the Indians."[15] Because the discourse of Indian policy has been entangled with the discourse of American history, each validating the other as core sources of information on the history and the rights of Indians, its public audience (for example, those engaged in research on Indians) may be unlikely to consider that the official slogans of Indian policy obscure the histories of indigenous struggles to reject it.

Thus I frame my discussion of Connecticut's early twenty-first-century Indian policy within multiple historical and political contexts in which "new" Indian policies have emerged (in the eighteenth and twentieth centuries) and in which the impacts of policy dictums are not readily discernible or predictable. Morton, for example, lauded Richard M. Nixon's "historic message to Congress" in July 1970, in which the president proclaimed that "the time has come to break decisively with the past and to create the conditions of a new era": "Both as a matter of justice and as a matter of enlightened social policy," Nixon declared, "we must begin to act on the basis of what the Indians themselves have long been telling us."[16] Potent words to be sure, they emphasize that acknowledgment of policy failures in the past—of the "centuries of injustice" during which "American Indians have been oppressed and brutalized"—is essential to establishing just relations in the present.[17] In that sense, Nixon's message is a kind of recognition narrative, acknowledging that there has "long been" another narrative talking back to the originators and purveyors of official Indian policy.[18] Keel's State of the Indian Nations address articulates an enduring counternarrative, underscoring the discrepancies between the discourse of Indian policy—in this case, that of the "self-determination" policy launched four decades ago—and indigenous peoples' historical experiences. And as Keel's address makes clear, this critique is now linked to a globalized indigenous narrative that "formally affirms our fundamental human rights": the UN Declaration on the Rights of Indigenous Peoples.[19] Thus, Keel announces that the U.S. government's recent endorsement of the Declaration is "a great step forward." Does the endorsement herald the emergence of new practices and discourses that may break decisively with Indian policy of the past? As a form of governmentality forged in a colonial situation,

Indian policy cannot be decolonized. But might the U.S. endorsement of the Declaration, an action that introduces into Indian policy's history a new guideline for the recognition and protection of indigenous peoples' human rights, open up possibilities for unsettling the popular narratives of Indian policy and its claims on history that have delimited indigenous rights in the United States?

Such questions must now be brought to bear on Indian policy in Connecticut, particularly in light of recent arguments by legal scholars that a transformation is indeed under way in the history of relations between indigenous nations and the United States in that the Indian policy of individual states is becoming increasingly influential in the national arena of Indian affairs. Matthew L. M. Fletcher has observed that "a new and dynamic relationship between *states* and Indian tribes is growing" in which "cooperation and agreement" is fundamental.[20] Fletcher points to gaming compacts between tribal nations and states as a central example of these new relationships, but he also explains that the broader legal and historical significance lies in the fact that these relationships signal the eventual demise of what he identifies as "the 'deadliest enemies' model of tribal-state relations."[21] Rooted in "the early history of federal Indian law and policy," the "deadliest enemies" designation refers to states' "never-ending quest" over the past two centuries "to take Indian lands and resources and, in some circumstances, to eliminate Indians and Indian tribes."[22] Fletcher argues that this quest diminished in the last few decades of the twentieth century and that "it no longer appears to be the goal or policy of state governments to eliminate Indian tribes and Indian people. The 'Indian Problem' [for states] is now political and legal."[23]

Connecticut's strident opposition to the federal acknowledgment of the Eastern Pequot and Schaghticoke tribal nations offers an important test case. The Eastern Pequot and Schaghticoke recognition struggles garnered a great deal of public interest and media attention between 2000 and 2005, as did those who articulated the state's turn-of-the-century Indian policy. Government officials in Connecticut who have opposed their federal acknowledgment claimed that they are not the Indians' enemies but rather defenders of "legality" and "fairness" against a "flawed" and "corrupt" federal acknowledgment process and antidemocratic desires for "special rights." As Connecticut attorney general Richard Blumenthal said at a July 2000 meeting in Shelton, Connecticut, with "leaders from 10 Connecticut cities and towns" who "join[ed] forces to fight federal recognition petitions," he was concerned that "the [federal acknowledgment] process basically is broken and we need to fix it": "This is not about being for or against Native Americans," he said. This notion of "fairness in the process" was repeated by a town official at the meeting who emphasized another key theme of antirecognition arguments: "If they are a legitimate tribe, we're willing to deal with whatever comes after that."[24] In the wider context of the productive political change that the U.S. endorsement of the Declaration suggests, and in light of the development of more equitable tribal-state relations as described by Fletcher and by Koenig and Stein in this volume, it is important to consider where Connecticut's antirecognition arguments figure in the complex trajectory of U.S. Indian policy.

Analysts of ongoing and potential transformations in tribal-state relations should not assume too readily that ancient models and themes that resonate in Connecticut's Indian policy today will be significantly affected by the new indigenous rights narrative embodied in the Declaration, or that the new histories of tribal-state relations under way elsewhere will influence official attitudes toward federally unrecognized native peoples in the state. Opposition to federal acknowledgment has entailed the repetition of a supposed goal of instilling "fairness" in the Bureau of Indian Affairs (BIA) process of evaluating and making determinations on petitions. This argument suggests that government officials are "just and humane" in their attitudes toward Indians, seeking only to protect the state from external federal interference (the "broken" BIA acknowledgment process) and from internal troublemakers—those targeted as conveyors of fraudulent tribal histories and identities—who are now the "enemies" of both the state and "legitimate tribes." Here, I do not argue the case of any particular federal acknowledgment petition but instead offer an overview of Connecticut's most prominent Indian policy statements and claims between 2000 and 2005, a critical period in Indian policy formation in the state, with the May 12, 2005, decisions of the Interior Board of Indian Appeals (IBIA) to vacate the BIA's final determinations to acknowledge the Eastern Pequot and Schaghticoke tribal nations (in June 2002 and January 2004, respectively) constituting a major turning point in state and town officials' long-running effort to prevent the two tribes from gaining recognition.[25] Blumenthal lauded the 2005 IBIA decision as a "historic" and "victorious" moment for the state and for his own policies and arguments against the federal acknowledgment of these tribal nations. In October 2005, when BIA issued its Reconsidered Final Determination to Decline Acknowledgment of the Eastern Pequots and Schaghticokes, the *New York Times* reported that the former attorney general construed the IBIA decision as a gesture reflecting a strategic state-federal government alliance against the recognition of tribal sovereignty in these cases and as indicating that potential legal challenges to the decision would fail: "Where the [Eastern Pequot and Schaghticoke] tribes were previously petitioning the federal government, with the State of Connecticut opposing the petitions, now the federal government had joined with the state in opposing the sovereignty of the tribes. . . . 'They will confront both the United States of America and the State of Connecticut on the other side of the courtroom,' Mr. Blumenthal said. . . . 'We will be united in defending the Bureau of Indian Affairs decision, and they will have the full weight against them of both federal and state governments, with all the resources we can muster.'"[26]

The "new era" in Connecticut's Indian policy as expressed in antirecognition efforts between 2000 and 2005 does not bode well for the future of native rights in the state or for a deepened public understanding of the historical and legal grounding of indigenous sovereignty. Linking policy making with history making (and history ending) in grandiose claims of an absolute power to determine the fate of unrecognized native peoples, the discourse of Indian policy in early twentieth-first-century Connecticut presents major obstacles to public recognition of the basic human rights of tribal nations and communities, which include the right to exist and to have a future as peoples.

Claiming a "Monumental and Momentous Victory": Connecticut's Indian Policy Narratives, 2000–2005

On May 13, 2005, a press release from the Connecticut Attorney General's Office declared a turning point in the state's effort to thwart the federal acknowledgment of the Schaghticoke and Eastern Pequot tribal nations. Though both were acknowledged by the BIA, Blumenthal appealed those decisions to the IBIA, and in May 2005, the IBIA overturned the recognition of both tribal nations. The May 13 press release described this action as a "landmark decision," "huge and historic":

Today's ruling is the first time the IBIA has overturned a BIA decision granting tribal recognition. . . . The IBIA agreed with Blumenthal that the Bureau of Indian Affairs violated its own rules by using state recognition to fill in huge gaps in the Schaghticoke and Eastern Pequot federal acknowledgment petitions. . . . "It is a knockout punch, a monumental and momentous victory for Connecticut," Blumenthal said. "The net result: Federal recognition for these two groups is virtually impossible, because they cannot rely on state recognition to overcome key flaws or gaps in evidence. Our long fight against a fatally flawed process has produced this powerful result. The IBIA agreed with our argument that the BIA acted illegally when it ignored its own rules—relying on state recognition—to grant recognition to these two groups. Equally important, the IBIA has created a critically important standard: state recognition cannot establish federal recognition. The IBIA has restrained and rebuked this out-of-control, lawless and capricious agency."[27]

The following day, the *Hartford Courant* article "Gaps in History Trip Up Tribes: Eastern Pequots, Schaghticokes Lose Status" continued Blumenthal's celebratory refrain on the rescinding of federal acknowledgment in these cases as a victory for the state and for legality; on the demise of state recognition as valid evidence of what has been referred to in governmental rhetoric as "tribal existence"; and on the decision as an instance of just and fair treatment for two groups whose federal acknowledgment petitions were purportedly filled with "gaps." The *Courant* presented the IBIA decision as a death sentence for Eastern Pequot and Schaghticoke histories and an undeniable triumph for the state's primary policy maker in the realm of unrecognized Indian affairs:

> In a stunning reversal, the Department of the Interior Friday overturned the federal recognition of the Eastern Pequots and the Schaghticokes, telling the tribes to come up with new evidence to prove they didn't fade away during the 19th and 20th centuries. The rulings bolster arguments long made by the state and municipalities that these native groups long ago ceased to live as formal Indian tribes. Both still have reservations, but the Interior Board of Indian Appeals said hundreds of years of state recognition fails to prove they have survived as intact Indian tribes with a government, culture and community. "What is amazing is that they listened to the arguments that we made. They adopted virtually verbatim the arguments that we made over the years," said Attorney General Richard Blumenthal, who called the ruling "one of the biggest victories in my 14 years as attorney general."[28]

Blumenthal told the Associated Press that he was "absolutely elated" about the IBIA's decision because "the recognition would have impacted our state in hugely significant and lasting ways." Christopher Shays, a member of the U.S. House of Representatives from Connecticut and a long-standing opponent of these federal acknowledgment cases, asserted that the decision "is a huge victory for the communities threatened by casino expansion and the entire state of Connecticut" and that "granting federal recognition means creating sovereign nations and it must be conducted in a fair, objective and transparent manner."[29]

These public commentaries point to the colonial lineage of the state's Indian policy and reflect the emergence of new policy themes and strategies that elaborate the "deadliest enemies" model and thus have ramifications for native rights in Connecticut and potentially beyond. They constitute important examples of the internal political complexity and the semantic density of Indian policy discourse, which is packed with multiple claims about law and legality; about Indian history, identity, rights, and sovereignty; about what constitutes "intact tribes"; and about external (federal/BIA) and internal (Indian tribal) threats to the state, its ("legitimate") citizenry, and its governmental "territory." Such statements reveal that Indian policy is also a discourse of sentiment, of expressions of emotion (for example, elation and outrage) that work to convey the idea that the makers and implementers of the state's Indian policy are driven not by politics or personal prejudices but by a basic, commonly shared desire for "fairness" and "justice." Looking carefully at the claims and themes of Indian policy as they are articulated in such statements, we find that they not only make an emotional appeal to their public audience in Connecticut but also beckon national attention and assert a legal significance that extends beyond the realm of the state. As Blumenthal told the *New York Times* in June 2002, "The ramifications [of Eastern Pequot and Schaghticoke recognition] will be profound and far reaching, not only for Connecticut but for the whole country."[30] In a September 2002 press release, Blumenthal argued that "the Eastern Pequot recognition is unsupported and unlawful, denying fairness and fact" and "if not reversed, will have ramifications across the state and country, supporting other deficient decisions." That press release also quoted town officials who had allied with the attorney general in this effort to overturn the BIA's determination: These officials, too, asserted the broad significance of their actions and their claims to be protectors of a native and nonnative public. The mayor of Ledyard commented that the "decision affects not only our three towns [Ledyard, Preston, and North Stonington, which surround the Eastern Pequot reservation,] but the entire state of Connecticut and also legitimate Indian tribes"; a Preston town official also lamented "this flawed [BIA] decision," adding, "I hope that both Native Americans and non–Native Americans alike will support our appeal and efforts to create a process that is objective and not influenced by money and politics."[31]

Such statements must be examined as part of the archive of the state's Indian policy, by which I mean the corpus of formal or official as well as informal, textual embodiments of Indian policy and the particular truths it constructs and disseminates to legitimize its authority to govern Indians and determine the course of Indian affairs (and Indian histories). Here I build from historical anthropologist Ann Laura Stoler's argument that an analysis of colonial governmentality requires an ethnographic investigation of its archive, which is not a mere repository of accumulated documents from which objective information can be retrieved but rather a site of knowledge production—of the construction of what is to count as fact, of the inscriptions that convey what government has deemed should (and should not) be known.[32] Thus, the archive of Indian policy is a source as well as a product of the state's power as it intervenes in and attempts to control matters of federal recognition and native rights. The documents electronically archived under the category "Indian Issues" on the "Press Releases" section of the website of Connecticut's Office of the Attorney General, for example, do not serve simply to inform a public audience interested in "Indian Issues"; rather, as is evident from various statements and claims, these documents dictate what is to be considered valid, credible knowledge of those issues and who is to be deemed qualified or not qualified to explain them and determine their outcome. Who gets to speak with authority and credibility is decided by the state, making that archive an exercise as well as an artifact of governmentality. Those in the archive who are presented as the rightful and objective interpreters of "Indian Issues"—the makers and enforcers of state Indian policy—likewise assert and normalize the notion that those issues are and must be under the jurisdiction of the state.[33]

The power of Connecticut's Indian policy at the turn of the century and the emergence of particular government officials as the widely recognized credible voices or "experts" in the realm of Indian issues, must be understood in the context of the enormous economic success of the casino ventures of the Mohegan and Mashantucket Pequot tribal nations (both federally acknowledged prior to 2000). Negative public and official reactions to native-operated casinos in the state—directed primarily at the Mashantucket Pequots—received much media coverage, and state officials targeted federal acknowledgment as the new "Indian problem" that had produced Indian casinos. This view was neatly encapsulated in a July 2000 statement by Blumenthal in a *New London Day* article: "There are huge ramifications of recognition . . . such as removal of land from the taxing power of local municipalities, and potential property or land claims by tribal members—not to mention the establishment of a gambling casino." The attorney general and town officials continuously reiterated the idea of tribal recognition as an economic and political threat to the state's citizenry—with casinos cast as the resultant blight—and it became a central "truth" of Indian policy discourse that worked to trivialize and obscure the points of view expressed publicly by petitioning tribal nations. Their right to petition for federal acknowledgment was not conveyed as a significant Indian issue, and the inciting of suspicions about the legitimacy of particular Indian identities in the state bolstered antirecognition sentiments and sanctioned racist attitudes about Indianness.[34]

As Kevin Bruyneel has pointed out, the "casino tribes" (a term frequently applied to the Mohegans and Mashantucket Pequots) have been "at the center of many of the most public debates and conflicts over tribal sovereignty in contemporary American politics."[35] Indeed, in Connecticut, where federal acknowledgment cases and casinos have been consistently posited as inextricably linked since 2000—Indians' desire for the latter is supposedly the sole motivation for pursuit of the former—debates about casinos have been interwoven with charges of fraudulent or insufficient Indian identity and have influenced the extent to which serious considerations of the histories and the rights of native peoples petitioning for federal acknowledgment could be introduced into public discussions.[36] But as state and town officials launched efforts to oppose the federal acknowledgment of Eastern Pequots and Schaghticokes in 2000, experts who challenged their arguments entered into the realm of public debate. Nell Jessup Newton, who was about to become dean of the University of Connecticut School of Law, made an initial public foray into the federal acknowledgment issue in June 2000, just as the statements and activities of opponents of federal acknowledgment—among them town officials who formed an antiacknowledgment coalition—gained steady press coverage.[37] Asked to comment on "Connecticut Indian legal issues," Newton responded that "here, as in many other states, the real issues are obscured by being 'racialized'" and that disputes focusing "on whether or not Indians are really Indians" can "become very vicious." Newton also made a point crucial to enlightening the public about one of the fundamental obstacles faced by tribal nations petitioning for federal acknowledgment: Native peoples are often invisible to nonnatives because "their informal tribal structures may not conform at all to the Western European model of government that most Americans identify with."[38] Here, then, at the outset of a "new" war against unrecognized Indians in the state, a well-known and highly respected scholar within the field of Native American law broached the intertwined problems of white racism and externally imposed, false characterizations of tribal legitimacy, both of which were obfuscated in the rhetoric of the state's most prominent opponents of federal acknowledgment.

Other notable critiques of antiacknowledgment and anti–Indian gaming efforts entered the public domain at the time, responding directly to government officials who sought to impose a moratorium on federal acknowledgment. In a 2001 report for the National Indian Gaming Association that was posted online at the group's website, anthropologist Kate Spilde explained that "the linking of federal recognition with gaming in the popular imagination and among policy makers" reflected anti-Indian sovereignty sentiments as well as a denial of the history of "Indian nations [that] have been fighting to retain their rights since the first Europeans arrived on this continent."[39] She argued that those officials who demanded an investigation into the federal acknowledgment process in 2000 not only falsely characterized petitioning tribal communities as "pawns for powerful gambling interests," as Representative Frank Wolf of Virginia claimed, but also sought to "delay and deny Indian nations their inherent right to self-government":

> Congressman Wolf and others wrongly believe that there is a necessary relationship between recognition and gaming and so skew political opinion against the Federal acknowledgment process. . . . Linking the process of federal recognition to Indian gaming . . . masks the injustices endured by unrecognized tribes in the United States [that] undertake the grueling [federal acknowledgment process] for myriad reasons, including a desire to enhance their ability to maintain their language, culture and ways of life.

Spilde also noted that "only one Indian nation that received federal recognition by the BIA since 1988 has pursued gaming"—the Mohegan tribe of Connecticut—and that "the impact of a moratorium . . . will be to delay and ultimately deny Indian people their inherent rights." Citing a 1976 federal report, Spilde further explained that "tribal members who belonged to unrecognized tribes were far more likely to suffer from poor health, inferior education and inadequate housing than members of federally recognized tribes."[40]

While alternative and authoritative analyses of ongoing federal recognition issues and criticisms of antiacknowledgment policy makers entered the public debate, the specific concerns they raised—racism, categorizations that falsely denied tribal existence and silenced native histories, and the failure to acknowledge the sociopolitical and economic inequalities endured by tribal nations in the United States—were not identified as relevant concerns by government officials in Connecticut, whose arguments against Eastern Pequot and Schaghticoke federal recognition gained ascendancy in the public sphere. The adjoined "threat" of casinos and a corrupt federal acknowledgment process became the reverberating theme of anti-recognition oratory, which solidified the notion that tribal sovereignty was something bureaucratically manufactured and, worse, that it produced "a whole different set of rights," as one town official put it in June 2000, from which the state and its citizenry must be protected.[41] In the context of the broader field of public discourse on federal acknowledgment and casinos, commentaries by scholars like Newton and Spilde were overshadowed by the state-as-protector theme, in which governmental authority was ranked as superior to any other arguments precisely because of the (posited) stakes: "In my view," Blumenthal said in June 2000, "the state attorney general has a clear obligation to protect local and state interests that may be severely and lastingly impacted by granting federal recognition to a tribe." Blumenthal added that these effects included the removal of reservation land from "the taxing and land-use powers of local government" and "the tremendous ramifications for enforcement of civil and criminal laws and other forms of citizen protection."[42] Thus was an ancient colonial notion of an Indian menace effectively recycled and reintroduced to a twenty-first-century audience via the new notion of BIA-created "illegitimate" tribes. Federal recognition was conveyed as something to be feared by the public at large, and charges of racism could be readily dismissed in the face of such a threat. Moreover, the explicit description of this threat was aided by the repetition of the idea that "legitimate tribes" (whose identity and existence could now be validated only by the state) were among those who would benefit from the "state protection," itself a new and effective governmental manipulation of Indian recognition.

The transcript of the May 2004 hearing before the U.S. House of Representatives Committee on Government Reform might now be considered a classic text of Connecticut's official Indian policy archive as it was produced between 2000 and 2005. Perhaps more important, *Betting on Transparency: Toward Fairness and Integrity in the Interior Department's Tribal Recognition Process* has now become a part of national Indian policy discourse.[43] Focused on the federal acknowledgment cases of the Eastern Pequot and Schaghticoke tribal nations and serving as a forum for the elaboration and public dissemination of Connecticut officials' arguments against the tribes' recognition, the hearing is extraordinary for the range of "Indian problems" it evoked, and some government officials testified that what was at stake in these recognition cases went far beyond the concerns of Connecticut alone. Indeed, a main theme of testimony was that these tribal recognition cases posed a national threat.

Among the Connecticut officials who testified at the hearing were Representatives Shays (vice chair of the committee) and Nancy Johnson; Nicholas Mullane, first selectman of North Stonington; and Blumenthal, who gave testimony and responded to numerous questions. Marcia Flowers, chair of the Eastern Pequot Tribal Council, read a prepared statement; however, the committee did not question her about the substance of her statement, as they did with others who gave testimony. Shays told Flowers, "I don't want you to interpret our lack of questions as a lack of respect." As she read her statement, Shays also directed her to "read a little faster": "I don't usually do that," he said, "I usually tell people to slow down."[44] The opening statement of the committee chair, Representative Tom Davis of Virginia, explained that the congressional delegation from Connecticut "recently brought to my attention two BIA recognition petitions filed by Connecticut tribes and asked the committee to hold a hearing to explore questions about the objectivity and transparency of the BIA recognition process in connection with decisions to recognize the Historical Eastern Pequot and the Schaghticoke tribes." Shays opened by restating the central antiacknowledgment arguments already well publicized in Connecticut but now provided with a national stage. The rhetorical flourishes of Shays and other tribal acknowledgment foes who testified suggested a political strategy intended to garner a wide audience. Shays's initial commentary, for example, explained that the BIA's "flawed system" had "a truly national impact, affecting the sovereignty, social policy, and fiscal health of every State," and that the federal acknowledgment petitions in question were driven by "the lure of casino revenues."[45] Paramount in Shays's testimony was his description of the BIA as "adrift in a sea of guilt, paternalism, and greed, [its] procedures beyond the view of interested parties and communities whose rights hinge on the opportunity to participate meaningfully in a transparent, fair process." It is unclear whether Shays's reference to the rights of "interested parties and communities" was meant to include the rights of native peoples petitioning for federal acknowledgment, but the rhetoric nonetheless points to a looming enemy against which the citizenry, as he envisions it, must rally.

The BIA is more than a convenient enemy here. Its infamous history as an intractable, corrupt federal bureaucracy—most evident in the early twenty-first century in the context of the *Cobell* case[46]—makes the linking of the "corrupt BIA process" argument with popular anti–big government and pro–state's rights sentiments appear quite reasonable. The charges of corruption were compellingly phrased during the hearing and included depictions of the state of Connecticut as engaged in a struggle of mythological proportions. Johnson, for example, asserted collusion between the BIA and a gaming "Goliath" that was bludgeoning the state with its economic power and political influence. She charged the BIA with having committed willful "subversion and distortion" of evidence that resulted in an "extremely destructive" decision to acknowledge the Schaghticokes and Eastern Pequots: "This isn't a recognition about tribal history. This is about casinos; it is about big, big money; it is about gambling. It is a David and Goliath Battle, and David is losing."[47]

Connecticut's "momentous victory" in 2005 was thus won against a federal agency as much it was against two tribal nations. The potential impact of Johnson's claim that the state and its citizenry were in essence a David under siege should not be underestimated, particularly with regard to the Schaghticoke and Eastern Pequot tribal nations' rights to their reservation lands, which are among the oldest in the United States. Johnson also implied that the legal status of those reservations might be disregarded: "The existence of a reservation is a historic preservation type decision, it is not a tribal recognition decision, and it doesn't meet tribal recognition criteria."[48] Given Connecticut officials' overt efforts to thwart the Eastern Pequot and Schaghticoke tribal nations' federal acknowledgment, such a notion—that is, the idea that the legal status of the reservation lands of state-recognized tribal nations can be rendered ambiguous when state officials deem it necessary—might yet be employed to "unrecognize" the Eastern Pequots' and Schaghticokes' land rights.

The reservation lands of state-recognized (but as of yet non–federally recognized) tribal nations in Connecticut have long been sites of native struggles to defend ancient and enduring rights. But politicians in Connecticut as well as media accounts have effectively distorted or wholly obscured the historical underpinnings of native rights struggles in the state and their direct connection to federal acknowledgment cases. It was not simply the "lawless, out of control, arbitrary, capricious" BIA federal acknowledgment process that posed a threat to both "the State and the Nation," as Blumenthal testified in the 2004 hearing.[49] As Representative Wolf claimed, it was a failure to adhere to an earlier Indian policy model. His personal outrage at the BIA was expressed through a salute to former secretary of the interior Morton, under whom Wolf worked at the Department of Interior for five years. Speaking directly "to the Department," Wolf opined that if Morton "could see what you are doing . . . you would be held in disgrace. I ask you as a Republican member of the Congress who supports [the Bush] administration on most issues, go back and clean up your house. . . . This whole town, and now the whole country, knows about the corrupt [BIA] process."[50] Whether "the whole country" possesses much knowledge of the history of U.S. Indian policy or of the specific histories of native peoples in Connecticut was not in question during the hearing. The BIA acknowledgment process and "big [casino] money" were tantamount to an attack on the integrity of the country itself, and Connecticut had become the front line in a battle against those forces, purported creators of illegitimate tribes that would undermine state sovereignty.

Ironically, Morton's statement of support for self-determination policy in the early 1970s would have offered some relevant contrast to the claims made by Connecticut officials at the hearing that day and perhaps would have allowed for a more informed public assessment of the history of federal acknowledgment and the specific cases at issue during the hearing. However, that aspect of Morton's Indian policy legacy was effaced. So too, ultimately, did testimony at this hearing work to deflect the question of what legacy might be left by these contemporary Indian policy makers and whether their claims about history or their motives and legitimacy as interpreters and implementers of Indian policy would be subjected to scrutiny. Testimony during the hearing suggests that opponents of Eastern Pequot and Schaghticoke tribal nations' federal acknowledgment sought to avoid scrutiny of their motives by offering expressions of support, albeit superficial, for native rights. While Connecticut officials asserted that the BIA had fabricated tribal histories they also insisted "we don't deny the rights of Native Americans to seek recognition if they so deserve," as the mayor of one Connecticut town testified.[51]

The hearing was undoubtedly a factor in the IBIA's decision to vacate the BIA's acknowledgment of the Eastern Pequot and Schaghticoke tribal nations and to remand the two cases to the BIA for reconsideration. Testimonies of Connecticut officials conveyed a sense of urgency in stopping an unprecedented attack that was presented as well under way and moving toward a dire outcome for the state, its citizens, and even the broader United States—the entities whose history and claim to rights over tribal nations required no proof of legitimacy in this hearing. Mullane's final commentary perhaps most honestly displays the refusal to address the disruptive questions raised by native histories and struggles for federal acknowledgment, evoking the tenets of a master narrative that defines legitimacy for the sole nation he recognizes: "There are two things that have always been bread [sic] into me: one nation under God and all men are created equal. Yes, there is an issue with the Native Americans, and I am not going to answer that question."[52] But why?

Toward a New Counternarrative: Connecticut's Indian Policy in Light of the Declaration

The discourse of Indian policy in early twenty-first-century Connecticut revitalizes the "deadliest enemies" model of tribal-state relations, and the implications of this revitalization are yet to unfold. Of major concern is that the overturning of the Eastern Pequots' and Schaghticokes' federal acknowledgment decisions constitutes a form of historicide, which, as anthropologist Jonathan D. Hill defines it, entails "the removal of peoples from their histories," a "radically disempowering" act that "obscures the historical processes that have produced the racial hierarchies that prevail in the Americas today."[53] An examination of the discourse of Indian policy in Connecticut offers insight into how such hierarchies and limitations on justice are reproduced and normalized via the repetition and reaffirmation of familiar public themes and ancient narratives that overwrite questions of rights and justice. To deny that the Eastern Pequot and Schaghticoke tribal nations have a valid history, to deny that they may serve as credible sources on their own pasts, is to deny them a means to articulate and defend their rights. Connecticut officials have claimed the authority to determine whether these tribal nations "deserve" recognition. However, the "historic victory" of Connecticut's Indian policy must now be assessed from a human rights perspective in light of the minimum standards of justice and equity outlined in the UN Declaration on the Rights of Indigenous Peoples. Legal scholar Nicholas Robinson has argued that the Declaration compels us to "return to events long forgotten by most" so that we might understand how to build just relations and preserve human rights.[54] The federal acknowledgment struggles of the Schaghticoke and Eastern Pequot tribal nations bring our attention to the means by which state Indian policy determines what histories are to be forgotten, thus urging us to address the human rights questions that Indian policy continues to deflect.

Notes

1. See Amy E. Den Ouden, *Beyond Conquest: Native Peoples and the Struggle for History in New England* (Lincoln: University of Nebraska Press, 2005).

2. Cyrus Thomas, "Introduction," in *Indian Land Cessions in the United States*, comp. Charles C. Royce, Annual Report of the Bureau of American Ethnology, Part 2 (Washington, D.C.: U.S. Government Printing Office: 1899), 611.

3. www.nanations.com/land/connecticut_land_cessions.htm.

4. In light of the historical details regarding colonial antagonism toward native peoples living on reservation land in eighteenth-century Connecticut, for example, and considering the colonial documentary record that attests to the grinding poverty endured by reservation-based indigenous communities in the colony of Connecticut, this declaration is troubling to say the least. See Den Ouden, *Beyond Conquest*.

5. Jean M. O'Brien, *Firsting and Lasting: Writing Indians out of Existence in New England* (Minneapolis: University of Minnesota Press, 2010).

6. Major John Mason's status in history and the policy he implemented are still offered as a matter of "perspective." See, e.g., "Connecticut History on the Web" (www.connhistory.org/), which includes teacher guides on a number of topics in Connecticut history. The Pequot War is first in its list of eleven topics, and there are links to a set of student readings under the heading "Differing Views of the Outcome: Four Different Perspectives on the Pequot War, Ranging from Seeing Captain John Mason as a Hero to Seeing the Pequots as Tragic Victims of Exploitation and Greed."

7. S. Lyman Tyler, *A History of Indian Policy* (Washington, D.C.: U.S. Government Printing Office, 1973), 1–2.

8. Rogers C. B. Morton, foreword to ibid., v–vi.

9. Michel Foucault, "Governmentality," in *The Foucault Effect: Studies in Governmentality*, ed. Graham Burchell, Colin Gordon, and Peter Miller (Chicago: University of Chicago Press, 1991), 87–104. See also Colin Gordon, "Governmental Rationality: An Introduction," in *Foucault Effect*, ed. Burchell, Gordon, and Miller, 1–48. One of the main concerns of my analysis of Indian policy as a form

of governmentality is the formation and dissemination of the rhetorical strategies by which governmental authority is enforced, masked, and legitimized. Robert L. Bee has commented on the assumption that late twentieth-century Connecticut had no clearly established Indian policy ("Connecticut's Indian Policy: From Testy Arrogance to Benign Bemusement" in *The Pequots in Southern New England: The Rise and Fall of an American Indian Nation*, ed. Laurence Hauptman and James Wherry [Norman: University of Oklahoma Press, 1990], 194–212). The policy agenda that emerged at the turn of the century, however, suggests that very old themes of the necessity and naturalness of governmental control over Indians and of "fairness to the Indians" could be merged with new stated policy concerns (federal recognition and casinos) in ways that deflect attention from the rights and the histories of tribal nations in the state.

10. Vine Deloria Jr. observed that "state, federal and Supreme Court decisions" in the realm of Indian law "contain a fictional view of American history that would shame some of our country's best novelists" ("Laws Founded in Justice and Humanity: Reflections on the Content and Character of Federal Indian Law," *Arizona Law Review* 31 [1989]: 203–23). Bethany Berger provides an example with respect to the 1846 U.S. Supreme Court decision in *U.S. v. Rogers* (45 U.S. 567), in which the Court's "vision of the history of Indian–United States relations" was embodied in the claim that "from the very moment the general government came into existence to this time, it has exercised power over this unfortunate race in the spirit of humanity and justice." The narrative of the United States as benevolent caretaker of "subjects in need of guidance" remains a powerful U.S. policy theme well known to a broad public ("'Power over This Unfortunate Race': Race, Politics, and Indian Law in *United States v. Rogers*," *William and Mary Law Review* 45 [2004]: 1957–2052). Robert Williams demonstrates that a "long-established language of racism . . . can be found at work throughout the leading Indian law decisions of the nineteenth century U.S. Supreme Court" (*Like a Loaded Weapon: The Rehnquist Court, Indian Rights, and the Legal History of Racism in America* [Minneapolis: University of Minnesota Press, 2005], 33, 39).

11. Morton, foreword, v.

12. Jefferson Keel, "State of Indian Nations Address," http://indiancountry todaymedianetwork.com/2011/01/2011-state-of-the-indian-nations-address-by -jefferson-keel.

13. Ibid. President Obama's remarks at the opening of the November 2009 Tribal Nations Conference acknowledged the discrepancy between the promises of U.S. Indian policy and the ongoing practices that have "marginalized and ignored . . . our First Americans." Obama acknowledged "a history marked by

violence and disease and deprivation" during which "treaties were violated. Promises were broken"; in "our more recent history, Washington thought it knew what
was best for you. There was too little consultation between governments" (http://
www.whitehouse.gov/blog/2009/11/05/white-house-tribal-nations-conference).
See also Keel's February 2010 statement to the U.S. Senate Committee on Indian
Affairs, oversight hearing on "Tribal Programs and Initiative Proposed in the
President's Fiscal Year 2011 Budget," which emphasizes discrepancies between
stated policy and historical and contemporary realities (http://indian.senate.gov
/public/_files/58128.pdf).

14. As David E. Wilkins and K. Tsianina Lomawaima point out, the U.S. federal government's vision of its "trust relationship" with native nations embodies
such a discrepancy: "If we think about the internal logic of the term 'trust relationship,'" they observe, "the inadequate representation or omission of the indigenous
vision of the trust doctrine is really quite remarkable" (*Uneven Ground: American Indian Sovereignty and Federal Law* [Norman: University of Oklahoma Press,
2001], 78).

15. See Den Ouden, *Beyond Conquest*, 144.

16. Richard M. Nixon, "Special Message on Indian Affairs," July 8, 1970, in *Documents of United States Indian Policy*, ed. Francis Paul Prucha (Lincoln: University of
Nebraska Press, 1975), 256–58.

17. Ibid., 257.

18. George Pierre Castile notes that "whether for personal or political reasons,
Richard M. Nixon is probably the only president in modern times to take a strong
interest in Indian affairs." Nixon's position on indigenous self-determination
reflected his intent to decentralize government so that "'power, funds and responsibility [would] flow from Washington to the states and to the people.' In this case,
the Indian people" (*Taking Charge: Native American Self-Determination and Federal
Indian Policy, 1975–1993* [Tucson: University of Arizona Press, 2006], 15).

19. For a seminal analysis of the articulation of indigenous rights in the global
context and its impact on international law, see S. James Anaya, *Indigenous Peoples
in International Law*, 2nd ed. (Oxford: Oxford University Press, 2004). For an
overview of the formation of the global indigenous rights movement, see Ronald
Niezen, *The Origins of Indigenism: Human Rights and the Politics of Identity* (Berkeley: University of California Press, 2003).

20. Matthew L. M. Fletcher, "Retiring the 'Deadliest Enemies' Model of Tribal-
State Relations," *Tulsa Law Review* 43 (2007): 73–87.

21. As Fletcher explains, the "deadliest enemies" phrase was articulated in
U.S. v. Kagama (118 U.S. 375, 1886) "as a means to offer a policy justification for
the extension of federal criminal jurisdiction over Indians in Indian Country. . . .

[B]ecause Indians were so weakened and dependent on the federal government—and because the local non-Indians and the states were so overwhelmingly hostile to tribal interests—federal legislation to extend federal criminal jurisdiction into Indian Country was necessary to protect tribal communities" (ibid., 74).

22. Ibid., 80.

23. Ibid., 82–83.

24. "Towns Rally against Tribes Seeking Recognition," Associated Press, July 14, 2000.

25. See "Reconsidered Final Determination to Decline to Acknowledge the Eastern Pequot Indians of Connecticut and the Paucatuck Eastern Pequot Indians of Connecticut," *Federal Register*, October 14, 2005, 60099–60101; "Reconsidered Final Determination to Decline to Acknowledge the Schaghticoke Tribal Nation," *Federal Register*, October 14, 2005, 60101–3.

26. Jane Gordon, "Recognition Rejected, Two Tribes Regroup," *New York Times*, October 23, 2005.

27. Connecticut Office of the Attorney General, "BIA Overturns Schaghticoke, Eastern Pequot Recognitions," May 13, 2005, www.ct.gov/AG/cwp/view.asp?a =1949&q=293554.

28. Rick Green, "Gaps in History Trip Up Tribes: Eastern Pequots, Schaghticokes Lose Status," *Hartford Courant*, May 14, 2005.

29. John Christoffersen, "Decision to Recognize Two Indian Tribes Reversed in Connecticut," Associated Press, May 13, 2005.

30. Virginia Groark, "Pequot Recognition Is Only the First Step," *New York Times*, June 30, 2002.

31. Connecticut, Office of the Attorney General, "Attorney General, Towns Appeal BIA's Recognition of the Eastern Pequot Tribe," September 26, 2002, www .ct.gov/ag/cwp/view.asp?A=1777&Q=283740.ge.

32. Ann Laura Stoler, "Colonial Archives and the Arts of Governance," *Archival Science* 2 (2002): 87–109.

33. Connecticut, Office of the Attorney General, "Indian Issues" press releases, www.ct.gov/ag/cwp/view.asp?a=1780&q=294038.

34. On the public debate about Mashantucket Pequot identity that was incited by a book intended to disparage Mashantuckets as well as their federal acknowledgment via an act of Congress as "fraudulent," see, e.g., "New Book Questions Ancestry of Foxwoods Casino Tribe," Associated Press, May 12, 2000; Lyn Bixby, "Questions Raised about Tribe's Authenticity," *Hartford Courant*, June 18, 2000; Eileen McNamara, "Mashantuckets say BIA Genealogical Log Refutes Critics' Claims," *New London Day*, July 14, 2000. See also Den Ouden, *Beyond Conquest*, chap. 6.

35. Kevin Bruyneel, *The Third Space of Sovereignty: The Postcolonial Politics of U.S.-Indigenous Relations* (Minneapolis: University of Minnesota Press, 2007), 256 n. 1.

36. See, e.g., Renée Ann Cramer, *Cash, Color, and Colonialism: The Politics of Tribal Acknowledgment* (Norman: University of Oklahoma Press, 2005), 137–67. The notion that petitioning tribal nations in Connecticut are merely impostors seeking casino profits is neatly summed up one newspaper headline: "Banking on Indian Identity. Gambling: In Connecticut, a Little Heritage Is Parlayed into a Multimillion-Dollar Casino. Or Two" (*Baltimore Sun Journal*, April 18, 2004). I have argued elsewhere that the genealogy of racialized attacks on Indian identity and the idea of the Indian impostor can be traced to disputes over reservation land in the eighteenth century. See Den Ouden, *Beyond Conquest*.

37. Coalitions of Connecticut towns opposing federal acknowledgment formed in 2000. In July 2000, the *New London Day* reported that Preston, Ledyard, and North Stonington, which had launched a coalition against federal acknowledgment of the Eastern Pequot tribal nation, were joined by Shelton, Colchester, Kent, Orange, Monroe, Trumbull, and New Milford, which opposed the federal acknowledgment of the Golden Hill Paugussetts. The mayor of Shelton commented that "being part of a multi-town coalition . . . will give all of the towns greater political strength. 'You're always stronger in numbers,' he said" (Eileen McNamara, "Towns' Coalition against Tribal Land Claims Growing," *New London Day*, July 21, 2000). First selectman Nicholas Mullane of North Stonington (the location of the Eastern Pequot tribal nation's reservation, established in 1683) was a much-quoted coalition leader between 2000 and 2005. In July 2000, Mullane returned from meetings with Connecticut's congressional delegation in Washington, D.C., and told reporters that "the most striking feature of all the meetings was the high level of interest in, and the growing knowledge of, the problems associated with federal Indian policy in Connecticut" (Jennifer Zeis, "Officials Return from Washington with Hope, No Promises," *New London Day*, July 1, 2001). These commentaries mark another important theme that emerged in the state's Indian policy at the turn of the century: the conflict between federal authority and that claimed by the state and towns in the realm of Indian affairs.

38. Beth Dufresne, "Expert on Indian Law May Soon Have Her Hands Full," *New London Day*, June 30, 2000.

39. Kate Spilde, "American Indian Identity Is Not a Gaming Issue," March 2001, www.indiangaming.org/library/articles/american-indian-identity.shtml.

40. Ibid.

41. Nicholas Mullane quoted in T. Colleen Morgan, "Town Wary Despite Pledge Schaghticokes Don't Build a Casino," *Litchfield Country Times*, June 29, 2000.

42. Lyn Bixby, "Questions Raised about Tribe's Authenticity," *Hartford Courant*, June 18, 2000.

43. The official transcript of the hearing includes spoken testimony and prepared written statements. See *Betting on Transparency: Toward Fairness and Integrity in the Interior Department's Tribal Recognition Process*, Hearing before the Committee on Government Reform, U.S. House of Representatives, 108th Cong., 2nd sess., May 5, 2004 (Washington, D.C.: U.S. Government Printing Office, 2004). Available online at http://www.gpo.gov/congress/house.

44. Ibid., 93, 75.

45. Ibid., 7–8.

46. For a thorough analysis of the BIA's mismanagement of allotted Indian lands, its impact on native people's lives, and native activists' struggles to preserve their allotments, see, Kristen T. Ruppel, *Unearthing Indian Land: Living with the Legacies of Allotment* (Tucson: University of Arizona Press, 2008). The *Cobell* case, or *Cobell v. Salazar*, 573 F. 3d (D.C. Cir. 2009), is a class-action federal law suit filed in 1996 (as *Cobell v. Norton et al.*, Case No. 1: 96CV01285) by Elouise Cobell (Blackfeet) charging the U.S. federal government with breach of its trust responsibility concerning billions of dollars from Indian trust accounts created after the General Allotment Act of (24 Stat. 388, 1887) that were not paid to the individual account holders. The *Cobell* case, argued on behalf of hundreds of thousands of Native people, reached a settlement agreement in 2009 and has undergone modifications since then. Information and updates on the $3.4 billion settlement can be found at http://www.indiantrust.com/index. See also Ty Shawn Twibell, "Rethinking *Johnson v. M'Intosh* (1823): The Root of the Continued Forced Displacement of American Indians despite *Cobell v. Norton* (2001)," *Georgetown Immigration Law Journal* 23, 1 (2008): 129–200.

47. *Betting on Transparency*, 65–66.

48. Ibid., 64.

49. Ibid., 28–29.

50. Ibid., 55.

51. Ibid., 158.

52. Ibid.

53. Jonathan D. Hill, "Introduction: Ethnogenesis in the Americas, 1492–1992," in *History, Power, and Identity: Ethnogenesis in the Americas, 1492–1992*, ed. Jonathan D. Hill (Iowa City: University of Iowa Press, 1996), 16.

54. Nicholas A. Robinson, "'Minimum Standards': The UN Declaration on the Rights of Indigenous Peoples," *Pace Environmental Law Review* 28 (2010): 348.

How You See Us, Why You Don't

Connecticut's Public Policy to Terminate the Schaghticoke Indians

RUTH GARBY TORRES

The reversal of the Schaghticokes' federal recognition was the pinnacle of Connecticut's effort to terminate its relationship with this tribe as well as the two remaining state-recognized tribes, the Eastern Pequots and the Golden Hill Paugussetts. With this critical victory in its pocket, Connecticut refuses to acknowledge its obligations to the Schaghticoke people and their reservation lands. During the campaign to reverse the Schaghticokes' federal acknowledgment, Connecticut took the position that the tribe was not self-governing and relied heavily on outside governments, in particular the state, to resolve internal disputes. By refusing to acknowledge the Schaghticokes, or to "see" them, Connecticut has taken the giant, albeit passive-aggressive, step toward terminating its own government-to-government relationship with the tribe.

Schaghticoke Road provides the only way to drive on or off the Schaghticoke reservation. One turns onto Schaghticoke Road from the state road where the private, expensive, and expansive Kent School is located. The school's website refers to the institution simply as "Kent," as if it were the reason for the rural but affluent Connecticut town known by the same name since 1739. The town is home to luminaries of various disciplines, and it is not unusual for Kent resident and former U.S. secretary of state Henry Kissinger to speak at the local Lions Club meeting or for fashion designer Oscar de la Renta to open his home and gardens for a *Vogue* feature.[1]

Schaghticoke Road runs just four miles, from the Kent School property at its northern end to the southern exit near quaint Bull's Bridge, one of Connecticut's few fully functioning covered bridges, built in 1842 at one of the narrowest expanses above the Housatonic River. The great river meets the smaller Ten Mile River, which flows from New York just south of Bull's

Bridge. For this confluence of waterways, Schaghticoke, like the state in which it lies, was named with an Algonkian word. The European mission workers referred to this place and the people there as "Pishgachtigok." Hikers often walk through this area, since the Appalachian Trail runs more or less parallel to Schaghticoke Road through the reservation and along the ridges of the Taconic and Berkshire foothills. The lushly forested reservation is home to timber rattlesnakes, ruffed grouse, white-tailed deer, wild turkeys, and of course the Schaghticoke people.

Schaghticoke Road winds alongside the great Housatonic, which the tribe's people once used to navigate to summer camps south of the present reservation and where Schaghticokes may still fish, though they can no longer consume their catch because upriver the General Electric Company poisoned the water with polychlorinated biphenyls (PCBs) and other hazardous substances.[2] On the eastern banks of the river, opposite the reservation, are the farmlands, open spaces, small businesses and homes of the Kent community. Like Schaghticoke Road, Connecticut Route 7 also runs north and south, but it is located along the eastern side of the Housatonic. It is a paved, lighted, and painted contrast to bumpy Schaghticoke Road.

The image of the road, with its one way in and out of the reservation, its twists and turns and its proximity to precipice, provides a context for the Schaghticoke people's journey through the federal acknowledgment process. It is not unlike the train tracks on which a locomotive enters and exits a tunnel. There is only one entrance and exit, and while we cannot see the train while it travels through the tunnel, we do see it go in as a train and come out the same. It does not shift shapes inside. The Schaghticokes' federal acknowledgment petition ultimately failed. The U.S. government accepted evidence that the tribe entered the tunnel as a "distinct community" with "political influence" on its citizens and exited fully intact. But others convinced the Office of Federal Acknowledgment that something must have happened when they could not see us. Inexplicably, they claim that we were not Indians when we were outside of their view—inside the tunnel—and therefore, do not merit a formal government-to-government relationship with the United States of America. This is the story of how the Schaghticoke tribal nation (STN) was essentially but not completely federally acknowledged for ninety-six days. It is a story that ends with the tribe holding dear to what others have been trying to take since first contact—the land itself.

A Brief History

I tell this story from my perspective not only as a citizen of the STN but also as a student of public policy. My knowledge of the story comes in part from having lived it in real time. A statement of my firsthand account serving as tribal councillor, advocating for state legislation to empower Connecticut's tribes, and my recollection of oral histories were included as evidence in the STN petition for federal acknowledgment. I read, shared, and collected hundreds of news reports published as the Schaghticoke petition proceeded through its many stages. After poring over testimony from congressional hearings held as the STN petition underwent the scrutiny of outside governments, I saved copies, which I analyzed for undergraduate research assignments. In a moment of serendipity and surrealism, my job as a state trooper took an unexpected turn. Just days before the Connecticut governor was about to give her uninformed testimony about the state's tribes before Congress, I was assigned to her security detail.

According to researchers for the STN, the first written account of a Schaghticoke presence in Connecticut dates from 1699. There is some disagreement among written records and historians, but the Schaghticokes assert in their petition for federal acknowledgment that the community originally consisted of Mahicans, Pequots, Pootatucks, and other Indians from what is now eastern New York and western Connecticut. Less than forty years later, in 1736, the English colony of Connecticut set aside an expanse of land exclusively for Schaghticoke use, effectively establishing one of the first Indian reservations. In 1739, the Town of Kent incorporated, and in 1788, Connecticut became the fifth state to join the new United States. Thus, the formalization and acknowledgment of the four polities—tribal, local, state, and federal, each with its own governing body—occurred in just over half a century.

A condensed version of the historical relationship between the Schaghticokes and the communities bordering the reservation does not differ significantly from that of the four other acknowledged Connecticut tribes. The Pequots and Mohegans of the southeastern part of the state and the Paugussetts of south-central Connecticut shared similar experiences with their non-Indian neighbors. Seen as valuable trade partners initially and potential combatants against the English settlers, the colonists concluded treaties with the tribes, recognizing the Indians' sovereign status. Many colonial documents settling land disputes bear the marks of native leaders of the time.

Keeping with the former colony's use of non-Indian overseers, the nascent state appointed Euro-American men as intermediaries between the tribes and the Connecticut government. These liaisons were low-level decision and policy makers for Connecticut government and may have been an early version of what would now be a called a state commissioner. During the late eighteenth century, overseers were charged with carrying out the state's trust responsibility to the tribes. [3] These Indian overseers, as they came to be known, kept meticulous records of Connecticut General Assembly appropriations and expenditures for reservation residents as well as of the revenue from Indian lands sold to supplement the state's Indian affairs budget. These land sales would come under scrutiny in the twentieth century, when some tribes sued for their return, arguing that the sales violated the federal Nonintercourse Act of 1790, which prohibited and invalidated sales of Indian land that were not "duly executed at some public treaty, held under the authority of the United States."[4]

Connecticut in Sync with Federal Indian Policies

In the mid-1920s, Connecticut transferred responsibility from individuals appointed as overseers to the state Parks and Forests Department (PFD). Through 1941, the PFD commissioner acted on behalf of the state tribes "as Indian agent, which was the title the U.S. government bestowed on the federal appointees entrusted with carrying out federal trust responsibilities" to the tribes acknowledged by the United States during the same period of time. Perhaps in response to the difficulties his family endured during the Great Depression, Schaghticoke chief, Howard N. Harris (my grandfather), petitioned the PFD commissioner for permission to return to Schaghticoke from Bridgeport, where he had moved for economic opportunities in the wake of World War I.[5] Times were tough in the 1930s, and he likely knew the family could depend on the reservation land to sustain them. He was denied permission to return at least twice, and many more of his letters were ignored during the 1930s and 1940s.

Connecticut was not immune to the influences of federal Indian policy. In 1941, responsibility for Indian affairs was moved from under the PFD to the Welfare Department. Was Connecticut Indian policy mirroring the changes happening at the federal level, where some Indian lands were about to be annexed from federal trust? In 1944, sensing that the era of federal termination and assimilation policy was near, tribal leaders founded the National Congress of American Indians (NCAI) to advocate on behalf of Native Americans.[6] During this period, Schaghticoke people continued to be prohibited from meeting on the reservation or staying overnight with families living there without the express permission of the Welfare Department commissioner. In the early 1960s, however, the state permitted Kent volunteer firefighters to burn reservation homes left vacant when the Connecticut government refused Schaghticoke people permission to take up residence. Present-day Schaghticokes remember their former meeting and socializing places as well as burial grounds falling victim to brambles and brush left unchecked without appropriate PFD oversight of the reservation. By denying tribal members residence on the reservation, creating unlivable conditions, and preventing Schaghticokes from moving into vacant homes, the state policy of termination contributed to the Schaghticokes' disappearance from view, like the train in the tunnel. Thus, it is no wonder that the proposed finding on the STN petition reported that the tribe did not provide sufficient evidence of a community from 1940 to 1967.

Chief Harris's death in 1967 coincided with the birth of the American Indian Movement the following year, a development that marked a transformation in both Connecticut and federal Indian policies. With his dying breath, the chief implored his son, Irving A. Harris (my uncle), never to give up the land and to protect Schaghticoke with all he could muster. Over the next six years, the new Chief Harris mustered legislative support, mobilized the five Connecticut tribes, and secured the political backing of the local United Auto Workers Union, actions that eventually resulted in the state's decision to remove Indian affairs from the Welfare Department. A new law established the Connecticut Indian Affairs Council with tribally appointed representatives and policies of Indian self-governance and self-determination. Robert L. Bee, an Indian policy expert and former chair of the University of Connecticut's anthropology department, credits the shift in the landscape to Chief Harris's leadership and to the civil rights movement of the same era.[7]

Federal Acknowledgment Pursuits and Land Claims in Connecticut

What happened to the Connecticut Indian Affairs Council after its conception in 1975 is a subject worthy of examination and further analysis beyond the scope of this chapter. For the next thirty-five years, Indians and

Indian policy would go through tumultuous times and experience sweeping changes. The Schaghticokes sued the Kent School in 1975 to reclaim tribal lands under the provisions of the 1790 Nonintercourse Act. New and significant federal legislation opened up opportunities for Connecticut's tribes. The federal regulations, 25 C.F.R. 83, *Procedures for Establishing That an American Indian Group Exists as an Indian Tribe*, were published in 1978, creating the Branch of Acknowledgment and Research (BAR) within the federal bureaucracy. As of July 2003, BAR became the Office of Federal Acknowledgment (OFA). According to the U.S. Bureau of Indian Affairs (BIA) website, "The acknowledgment regulations are the result of a rule-making process that included notice and extensive public comment."[8] This statement seems to serve as a reminder to those who would later challenge OFA's integrity.

Preceding the new regulations, the Eastern Pequot and Mohegan tribes had formally expressed their interest in seeking federal acknowledgment, so when 25 C.F.R. 83 was published and the BAR created, the two tribes were considered as having their letters of intent on record.[9] The Mashantucket Pequots sent their letter of intent to petition for acknowledgment in January 1979, with the Schaghticokes' following in 1981 and the Golden Hill Paugussetts' a year later. A land claim lawsuit similar to the Schaghticokes' filed by the Mashantuckets rocked southeastern Connecticut beginning in May 1976 and ended years later with Congress passing the Connecticut Indian Claims Settlement Act of 1983, which federally acknowledged the Mashantucket Pequot tribal nation.

In 1986, the Mashantucket Pequots opened their profitable and very popular high-stakes bingo hall. After the U.S. Supreme Court affirmed federally acknowledged tribes' rights to be free from state and county gambling laws, Congress responded by passing the Indian Gaming Regulatory Act in 1988.[10] Five years later, the Mashantuckets negotiated a government-to-government compact with the State of Connecticut; a few years later, they would open the Foxwoods Resort Casino.

Also in 1988, Congress officially repealed the policy of Indian termination. Long after the federal government granted Indians U.S. citizenship in 1924, the Connecticut General Statutes finally made Connecticut Indians "full citizens of the state" in October 1989 when Chapter 824, Section 47-59 was amended:

> The state of Connecticut further recognizes that the indigenous tribes, the Schaghticoke, the Paucatuck Eastern Pequot, the Mashantucket

Pequot, the Mohegan and the Golden Hill Paugussett are self-governing entities possessing powers and duties over tribal members and reservations. Such powers and duties include the power to: (1) determine tribal membership and residency on reservation land; (2) determine the tribal form of government; (3) regulate trade and commerce on the reservation; (4) make contracts, and (5) determine tribal leadership in accordance with tribal practice and usage.

When this amendment was enacted, the Mashantucket Pequots had been operating their bingo establishment for three years, and the BAR was poised to deliver a negative proposed determination on the Mohegan federal acknowledgment petition. Connecticut news outlets frequently reported on the effects of the bingo hall and editorialized about how life in southeastern Connecticut would never return to its pre–Indian gaming condition. The invasion of bingo players, the ensuing traffic, and the demands on municipal services were all increasing each year. Residents of the towns surrounding the Mashantucket reservation were ambivalent about gaming. Sure, it represented local employment opportunities and potential for economic development—two things that had grown less dependable with cutbacks at the nearby submarine base and shipyard—but it strained their lives, too. They pressed their elected officials for relief and solutions.

For the last time, the Connecticut Indian Affairs Council was able to produce a quorum in 1992. What followed was a flurry of legal action and intratribal political activity between 1992 and 1994. The Golden Hill Paugussetts filed their first land claim in federal court. It was first dismissed but then overturned on appeal. Affluent Fairfield County, where the suit threatened title on billions of dollars in real estate, became frenzied. In a challenge to the state's authority to tax cigarettes sold on the Paugussetts' Colchester reservation, Kenneth Piper, known as Moonface Bear, had an armed standoff with state troopers. Perhaps sensing a second Indian casino in southeastern Connecticut on the horizon, the legislature passed a bill during a special session that created a task force to study land-into-trust issues and the effects of Indian trust lands on local municipalities. The task force also proposed recommendations for how the state attorney general could best represent Connecticut in all matters related to Indian affairs. The task force's final report was noticeably silent about recommendations for representing the tribes' interests. The state's trust responsibility to Indians, like other state trustees, arguably should be executed through the office of the attorney general.

Schaghticokes and Eastern Pequots
Affected by State's New Policy

Somewhat without fanfare, the Schaghticokes submitted their petition for federal acknowledgment and the initial supporting evidence to BAR in 1994, the same year that the Mohegan tribe was federally acknowledged. By autumn, the Mashantuckets, the Mohegans, and Connecticut negotiated the Pequots' gaming compact and new compacts for each tribe. The Mohegan Sun casino opened for business just two years later, on Columbus Day. To this day, the compacts grant the two tribes exclusive rights to certain kinds of gambling and assure the state a steady stream of revenue from the casinos' slot machine operations.

The STN petition passed the BAR's scrutiny and was ready for active consideration in 1997. The assistant secretary for Indian affairs was required to issue a preliminary finding about whether the tribe was likely to be federally acknowledged within one year. If a petitioner receives a negative proposed determination, the secretary must specify which of the seven criteria the petitioner failed to satisfy. This information would later be used against the STN petition by opponents who believed that the Schaghticokes, like the train, entered and exited some time periods as Indians but because tribal activity went unseen, unnoticed, or undocumented, they had somehow lost that identity.

In light of legal theories that had developed since the 1975 lawsuit, the Schaghticokes filed a new land claim action supported by additional evidence uncovered by tribe's researchers. Meanwhile both Eastern Pequot petitions (a political rift within the Eastern Pequot tribe resulted in one faction filing a separate letter of intent in 1989) were advancing through the administrative process. On the first day of 1998, the Eastern Pequot petition No. 35 was placed on the BAR's list for active consideration. In the first of several controversial decisions, assistant secretary of Indian affairs Kevin Gover waived provisions in the department's regulations that allowed the Paucatuck Eastern Pequot petition No. 113 to jump the line, so to speak. Gover used his authority under federal guidelines to consider both petitions together while signaling the possibility that the two petitioners could be determined a singular tribe. In keeping with the law and precedent, Gover determined that "such waiver or exception is in the best interest of the Indians."[11]

In 2000, key events mobilized state officials to call for action against the three Connecticut tribes with active petitions before the BAR. Also that year, evidence of a collective strategy executed through the office of the Connecticut attorney general first surfaced. In July, Connecticut attorney general Richard Blumenthal wrote to Gover requesting that he recuse himself from the Eastern Pequot and Schaghticoke recognition decisions. Gover apparently failed to reply, and subsequently Blumenthal wrote to the solicitor of the U.S. Department of Interior to urge the withdrawal of the Pequot proposed findings that he claimed bore the "incurable taint" of Gover's participation.[12] Gover did not recuse himself, and his authority was not reduced by any action of the solicitor.

Likely frustrated by his ineffectiveness and with little more than a month before the state's deadline to submit comments in opposition to the Eastern Pequots' proposed findings, Blumenthal went to the BIA, accompanied by his legal team and attorneys representing several Connecticut municipalities, "to make a record that may well be before a court some day."[13] According to one BAR researcher and anthropologist who attended that meeting, "Blumenthal was there briefly (for your basic photo op) as were [representatives] of the Eastern Pequots."[14] At this meeting, BAR researcher Virginia DeMarce submitted a statement for the day in court that Blumenthal had foreshadowed. Her pronouncement surely added to the urgency felt by Connecticut officials and resulted in the next steps of their strategy. The *New York Times* quoted DeMarce as saying, "You may not like hearing this," but the best evidence supporting the Eastern Pequots' federal recognition comes from the state's own record, comes from the fact that the state has maintained and documented a continuous government to government relationship."[15] The article continues, "Attorney General Blumenthal said he was fighting the federal recognition of all petitioning Connecticut Indian tribes because of the added burdens of traffic and law enforcement that Indian casinos put on neighboring towns."[16] From this point on, the issues of federal acknowledgment and Indian gaming were married in Connecticut.

By late 2002, when the STN received notice that the BAR would issue a negative proposed determination on its petition, Connecticut seemed to be well along on its campaign to extinguish a tribe it claimed did not exist. In the fifteen months since the attorney general understood the value of state recognition and the government-to-government relationship it connotes, a rare congressional field hearing on federal recognition was held in Connecticut, the state legislature hosted an informational forum on the history and significance of tribal sovereignty, two revealing legal analyses on state recognition were produced by the state's Office of Legislative Research, the Eastern Pequots were federally recognized, U.S. Senator Christopher

Dodd's attempt to legislate a moratorium on all pending petitions failed (and was blasted by the NCAI), National Public Radio falsely reported that one or two tribes were being recognized each year, and anti-casino-expansion Governor John Rowland had been reelected.

STN Response and Final Determination

One news outlet reported that the proposed finding not to acknowledge the STN, "one of the oldest historically recognized tribes in the United States," was based on BAR's determination that "the tribe did not demonstrate continuous existence as a distinct community and failed to show political authority over its members for "certain periods of time."[17] In fact, a letter from the Interior Department's inspector general gives the simplest, most accurate report of what happened: the STN "failed to submit adequate documentation to BIA by the court-imposed deadline, and on December 5, 2002, BIA issued its Proposed Finding denying Federal acknowledgment."[18] This preliminary administrative pronouncement was heralded in a press release from the state attorney general as a "victory for the public interest, upholding the law and facts."[19]

Federal regulations give petitioners reasonable time to address deficiencies in an incomplete petition after a proposed finding is issued and to submit additional evidence in support. In the STN case, the two criteria needing support were what tribal members casually call "community" and "political," referring to the second and third of the seven criteria for federal acknowledgment. The process also includes opportunities for the submission of third-party comments and opposing evidence to a petition. The OFA then considers the additional evidence from all parties in the last phase of the administrative process, the petition's final determination.

A special January 12, 2003, meeting of the STN introduced those in attendance to Steven L. Austin, an anthropologist and former BIA employee, whom the Mohegan tribe retained after its petition received a negative proposed finding. Austin analyzed Schaghticoke marriage patterns during the nineteenth century to provide supplemental evidence addressing those periods of time when written accounts of what Schaghticokes were doing to maintain their distinct community were unavailable. The federal regulations allow evidence of endogamous marriage rates of at least 50 percent to support the second of the seven acknowledgment criteria. Very much like the train in the tunnel, opponents of the STN's federal acknowledgment (and potential additional casino) believed that when internal tribal activities were undocumented in an obvious format, the tribe must have disappeared. Using well-established methodologies, Austin concluded that our marriage rates exceeded 50 percent for the 1800s. He also submitted an analysis of "evidence for community and political leadership based on the majority of members living on the Reservation . . . and upon the perpetuation of traditional culture" during the same period.[20]

Around the same time Schaghticokes were meeting Austin, two Connecticut legislators proposed a bill that would have effectively terminated the state's relationship with the Eastern Pequots, Golden Hill Paugussetts, and Schaghticokes and would have created an administrative process for state acknowledgment.[21] The proposed legislation provided for seven criteria by which tribal applicants would be judged, and some of the language was taken verbatim from the federal acknowledgment regulations, which many state officials and tribes had excoriated as "fundamentally flawed," "a scandal," and in need of reform. The bill was referred to committee and assigned a date for public hearing but never moved further along in the legislative process.

Principal deputy assistant secretary for Indian affairs Aurene M. Martin's acknowledgment decision was preceded by a meticulous examination of the possible outcomes for the STN petition and careful consultation with the tribal recognition experts at the BIA. This change in procedure occurred under the George W. Bush administration: The OFA staff most familiar with a tribe's petition would offer options to the decision maker, provide a brief discussion of each option, and make a recommendation. In addition to consulting with the agency professionals, Martin met with Department of the Interior secretary Gale A. Norton. The STN decision was apparently an exception to her previous noninvolvement in the acknowledgment process.[22] OFA staff prepared a briefing memo outlining four options for Martin:

(1) acknowledge the Schaghticoke under the regulations despite the two historical periods with little or no direct political evidence, based on the continual state relationship with a reservation and the continuity of a well-defined community throughout its existence;

(2) decline to acknowledge the Schaghticoke based on the regulations and precedent;

(3) acknowledge the STN outside the regulations;

(4) decline to acknowledge the STN but support or not object to legislative recognition.[23]

The OFA staff recommended the second option, but the strength of the supplemental evidence submitted by STN and the state's inability to effectively counter it led Martin to decide that the STN petition contained sufficient proof to support a positive final determination. The tribe's long-standing government-to-government relationship with the state played a significant role in the final outcome. Specifically, Martin said,

> The Department's reevaluated position is that the historically contin-uous existence of a community recognized throughout its history as a political community by the State and occupying a distinct territory set aside by the State (the reservation), provides sufficient evidence for continuity of political influence within the community, even though direct evidence of political influence is almost absent for two historical time periods. This conclusion applies only because it has been demonstrated that the Schaghticoke have existed continuously as a community, within the meaning of criterion 83.7(b), and because of the specific nature of their continuous relationship with the State. Further, political influence was demonstrated by direct evidence for very substantial historical periods before and after the two historical periods. Finally, there is no evidence to indicate that the tribe ceased to exist as a political entity during these periods.[24]

In other words, the train did not cease being a train when it was in the tun-nel. Schaghticokes were acknowledged as an Indian tribe on January 29, 2004.

The state announced that it would appeal the decision to the Interior Board of Indian Appeals and ramped up its strategy to fight the Schagh-ticokes. Elected officials who opposed the STN final determination made good use of taxpayer-funded resources and easy access to media outlets to pressure the BIA and generate public outrage, all the while criticizing tribes for utilizing funds we were essentially borrowing from financial backers to respond to their attacks. In a local newspaper and later in a congressional hearing, the attorney general mischaracterized the OFA briefing memo to Martin as "shocking proof that the Schaghticoke recognition is a sham, without a shred of credibility or integrity." He termed the BIA "a rogue agency, out of control, lawless and ready to twist and distort logic and law in reaching a decision driven by money and politics."[25] Some members of Connecticut's congressional delegation met with Norton and pressured her to overturn the STN decision. Norton stood by what she characterized as "a reasonable decision, a reasonable interpretation" and said that she had made what she "thought was a reasonable judgment that state recognition should be considered in the specific facts of the Schaghticoke matter."[26]

Four members of the Connecticut delegation demanded that first Norton and then the inspector general of the Department of Interior investigate what was alternately labeled corruption, a bending of the regulations, inappropriate STN influence on the process, and personal bias against the state's attorney general. In March 2004, Representative Nancy L. Johnson introduced legislation seeking to circumvent the administrative process to repeal the federal acknowledgment of the STN.[27] As co-chair of the House Resources Committee, she scheduled an oversight hearing on the federal acknowledgment process that targeted the STN decision. A second hearing on the process was held by the House Committee on Government Reform two months later, and by the end of August 2004, the inspector general, Earl E. Devaney, delivered what was certainly disappointing news to Connecticut' senator Christopher Dodd and other STN opponents. After the thorough investigation requested by the Connecticut delegation, Devaney wrote to Dodd, "Although the STN recognition decision was highly controversial, we found that OFA and the Principal Deputy Assistant Secretary—Indian Affairs conducted themselves in keeping with the requirements of the administrative process, their decision-making process was made transparent by the administrative record, and those parties aggrieved by the decision have sought relief in the appropriate administrative forum—each, as it should be. Therefore, we are closing this matter."[28]

Lobbying and Private Dollars Make the Difference

I cannot pinpoint a credible source for how and exactly when a group of Kent residents organized themselves as Town Action to Save Kent (TASK) as there is scarce public record of their activities. The STN brief to the U.S. Court of Appeals Second Circuit says it was 2004, the same year TASK's cofounders hired an influential Washington lobbying firm, Barbour, Griffith, and Rogers. A Hartford newspaper reported that by April 2005, TASK was executing a "costly 'beneath the radar' assault" and "spending about $23,000 a month, with lobbyists in Hartford and Washington connected to the highest decision-makers, in a sophisticated effort to take down" the Schaghticokes.[29] An exhibit filed with an STN motion for summary judgment documents repeated communications among Connecticut elected officials, TASK founders, and their lobbying firm and sheds light on how their joint strategy was implemented.[30] Challenges to the motion's portrayal of the concerted strategy are neatly dismissed by TASK cofounder Kenneth Cooper's remark that "TASK is not leading the effort. It's being led by the Selectmen in town and the Attorney General. And they've been very well supported by the Congressional delegation. And others like us are there to make sure every avenue is looked at and every stone overturned."[31]

However, it was apparent that TASK's money was hitting its mark in Washington. During the 2005 winter session of the NCAI, tribal leaders were invited to the Bush White House. Schaghticoke Richard Velky's name initially appeared among those on the invitation list. But shortly before the visit was to take place, NCAI staff informed Velky that as a representative of a non–federally recognized tribe, he would not be welcome to participate in the meeting. One website reported that "a select group" of tribal leaders attended.[32] According to one journalist who regularly covered the STN at the time, a TASK cofounder "crowed about blocking" Velky from the White House. The next day, Johnson introduced her bill to terminate the STN.

A third congressional hearing, this time before the U.S. Senate's Committee on Indian Affairs, was held on May 11 after many emails and likely phone conversations among the TASK members, their lobbyists, and elected officials, including Connecticut governor M. Jodi Rell and her legal staff. Rell's February 25 letter to Arizona senator and SCIA chair John McCain contains glimpses of bias and misinformation that foreshadow her testimony later. The "guidance" offered by a representative from TASK's lobbying firm to Rell's counsel for policy may have focused on "tone" and "approach" rather than communicating a clear understanding of the federal acknowledgment process.[33] At the hearing Rell would testify incorrectly that "historical reservation lands no longer exist."[34] The hearing represented the culmination of STN opponents' efforts to meet their objective, and just one day later, the Interior Board of Indian Appeals issued an order vacating the STN and Eastern Pequot final determinations and remanding them to the assistant secretary for Indian affairs for reconsideration.

Martin resigned her post as deputy assistant secretary effective September 10, with a BIA spokesperson saying that Martin had resigned for personal reasons. In October 2005, the Schaghticokes were notified of associate deputy secretary James Cason's decision to deny STN federal acknowledgment in his reconsidered final determination. Cason rejected the methodology of the STN's endogamous marriage rates and Martin's reliance on the STN's "continuous relationship with the state" to fill in for direct evidence of "community" and "political" during limited and specific periods of time.

Back to Court

The STN's petition received expedited attention from the BIA because of a land claim case before the U.S. District Court in New Haven. Legal maneuvering caused District Judge Peter C. Dorsey to order that STN's status be determined before the lawsuit for illegal Indian land transfers could go forward. If the BIA extended federal acknowledgment to STN, the case would continue. As a result, the federal acknowledgment process for the STN was closely monitored by the Dorsey court.

Dorsey ultimately decided against the STN in August 2008. STN unsuccessfully argued that the revised final determination "was the product of undue political interference, arbitrary and capricious or outside the limits of the Appointments Clause or the Vacancy Reform Act."[35] Dorsey began his decision by noting, "This case concerns the politically loaded question of whether the Schaghticoke Tribal Nation . . . constitutes an Indian tribe within the meaning of federal law as provided in the federal acknowledgment regulations."[36] So how is a "politically loaded question" answered if politics are not in the mix?

STN met a similar fate in the U.S. Court of Appeals on October 19, 2009. The tribe was hopeful that a court outside of Connecticut would come to a different conclusion, but the Second Circuit was not persuaded by STN's evidence of political interference. In a risky move that may affect the rest of Indian Country, STN appealed to the U.S. Supreme Court in May 2010. This maneuver, arguably the STN's last chance, failed when the appeal was denied on October 4 of that year.

I believe that the Schaghticokes threatened the Kent status quo and became political adversaries in an atmosphere much different than that of the 1970s, when Chief Irving Harris found support for Indian self-determination within state government. Marrying the federal acknowledgment process to casinos proved a successful strategy employed in concert by elected officials and Kent residents, who funded influential Washington lobbyists. Connecticut politicians and residents who claimed to be concerned about the fairness of the process stopped advocating for reform of the federal recognition regulations once the STN and Eastern Pequot petitions were overturned. But to blame outsiders entirely for the outcome of the STN petition would be to relieve the Schaghticokes of our share of responsibility. Internal political piracy, disregard for tribal law, and the inability to mobilize Schaghticokes against the tribal administration inadvertently assisted the efforts of the outsiders. As Schaghticoke history continues to unfold, readers must bring informed analysis to this and other facets of the STN struggle for federal acknowledgment.

Notes

1. "The Room with a View," *Vogue*, December 2008.

2. "Housatonic River—Rest of River RCA Facility Investigation Report," prepared by Blasland, Bouck, and Lee, Inc. for General Electric Company, Pittsfield, Massachusetts, September 2003 (http://www.epa.gov/region1/ge/thesite /restofriver/reports/rcra_fir/200656.pdf).

3. Charles J. Hoadly, *Public Records of the State of Connecticut from October 1776 to February 1778 Inclusive* (Hartford: Case, Lockwood, and Brainard, 1894).

4. Act of July 22, 1790, P.L. 1-33, Section 4, 1 Stat. 137, 138.

5. Ruth G. Torres, "Explaining Variance in State Public Policy towards Connecticut's Indians," unpublished paper, Charter Oak State College, 2007, 3.

6. David E. Wilkins and Heidi Kiiwetinepinesiik Stark, *American Indian Politics and the American Political System*, 3rd ed. (Lanham, Md.: Rowman and Littlefield, 2011), 130.

7. Robert L. Bee, "Connecticut's Indian Policy: From Testy Arrogance to Benign Bemusement," in *The Pequots in Southern New England: The Rise and Fall of an American Indian Nation*, ed. Laurence M. Hauptman and James D. Wherry (Norman: University of Oklahoma Press, 1990), 196.

8. U.S. Department of the Interior, Bureau of Indian Affairs, Office of Federal Acknowledgment, "Who We Are," www.bia.gov/WhoWeAre/AS-IA/OFA /index.htm.

9. After an internal dispute could not be immediately resolved, several Eastern Pequots filed a second letter of intent in 1989 under the name Paucatuck Eastern Pequot Indians of Connecticut.

10. *California v. Cabazon Band of Indians*, 480 U.S. 202 (1987).

11. 25 C.F.R. 1.2, *Applicability of Regulations and Reserved Authority of the Secretary of the Interior*.

12. "Letter to John Leshy, Solicitor, Department of Interior," Connecticut Attorney General's Office, Press Release, July 27, 2000 (http://www.ct.gov/ag/cwp /view.asp?a=1775&q=283064). See also Jim Adams, "Gover Blasts Back at Critic, Defends Mashantucket Identity," *Indian Country Today Media Network*, August 16, 2000 (http://indiancountrytodaymedianetwork.com/ictarchives/2000/08/16 /gover-blasts-back-at-critic-defends-mashantucket-identity-85333); and "Request for Recusal in Eastern Pequot/Paucatuck and Schaghticoke Petitions," Connecticut

Attorney General's Office, Press Release, July 14, 2000 (http://www.ct.gov/ag/cwp/view.asp?a=1775&q=283060&pp=3).

13. Sam Libby, "U.S. Officials Questioned over Tribal Recognition," *New York Times*, August 20, 2000.

14. Steven L. Austin to author, January 9, 2011.

15. Libby, "U.S. Officials Questioned."

16. Ibid.

17. "McCaleb, 'Throwing Away a History of People,'" www.indianz.com, December 6, 2002.

18. *Schaghticoke Tribal Nation v. Dirk Kempthorne, Sec. Department of the Interior, et al.*, Case No. 08-4735 (C.A. 2, Nov. 4, 2009), petitioner's brief by Richard Emanuel, counsel for petitioner, court exhibit 25, Letter from Earl E. Devaney to Christopher Dodd, August 27, 2004. See also Rick Green, "Probe Upholds Ruling on Tribal Recognition," *Hartford Courant*, September 1, 2004 (http://articles.courant.com/2004-09-01/news/0409010621_1_indian-tribes-tribal-recognition-bia).

19. "Attorney General's Statement On The BIA's Proposed Denial Of Recognition For Schaghticokes," Connecticut Attorney General's Office, Press Release, December 5, 2002 (http://www.ct.gov/AG/cwp/view.asp?a=1777&q=283730).

20. Steven L. Austin, "Evidence of Community and Political Authority: Schaghticoke Marriage Patterns in the Nineteenth Century," August 8, 2003, submitted to the BIA on behalf of the Schaghticoke Tribal Nation as a supplement to the tribe's petition for federal acknowledgment. Copy available from OFA, BIA, 1849 C Street, NW, Washington, D.C.

21. House Bill 5336, An Act Concerning the Recognition of Indigenous Tribes and Establishing a Commission on Tribal Recognition, January Session, Connecticut General Assembly, 2003.

22. *Schaghticoke Tribal Nation v. Kempthorne*, Brief by STN, Appellant, U.S. Court of Appeals for the Second Circuit, March 6, 2009.

23. Office of Federal Acknowledgment, U.S. Department of Interior, Schaghticoke Briefing Paper, January 12, 2004, "Schaghticoke Tribal Nation: Final Determination Issues" (http://www.ct.gov/ag/lib/ag/press_releases/2004/indian/schaghticoke%20final%20determination%20issues.pdf).

24. "Final Determination to Acknowledge the Schaghticoke Tribal Nation," January 29, 2004, *Federal Register*, February 5, 2004, 5570–74.

25. Kathryn Boughton, "Is Schaghticoke Memo State's 'Smoking Gun'?," *Kent Dispatch*, March 19, 2004.

26. *Schaghticoke Tribal Nation v. Kempthorne.*

27. Schaghticoke Acknowledgement Repeal Act of 2005, 109th Cong., H.R. 1104, March 3, 2005.

28. *Schaghticoke Tribal Nation v. Kempthorne*, court exhibit 25, Letter from Earl E. Devaney to Christopher Dodd, August 27, 2004.

29. Rick Green, "Battle of Kent: A Savvy Strategist Defends His New Home," *Hartford Courant*, June 28, 2005.

30. Thomas J. Murphy et al., Attorneys for Petitioner, the Schaghticoke Tribal Nation, *Schaghticoke Tribal Nation v. Kempthorne*, Memorandum in Support of the STN's Motion for Summary Judgment, September 24, 2007, Exhibit A.

31. Sharon Hartwick, "TASK Gets Down to Business: Private Citizens Group Takes on the Schaghticoke Issue," *Kent Tribune*, January 28, 2005.

32. "NCAI Winter Session 2005 Wrap Up: Day 3, White House Briefing," March 4, 2005, http://64.38.12.138/News/2005/006838.asp.

33. Loren Monroe to Phillip Dukes, February 28, 2005 (email correspondence obtained by STN under the Freedom of Information Act).

34. Transcript, Oversight Hearing on Federal Recognition of Indian Tribes before the Committee on Indian Affairs, U.S. Senate, 109th Cong., 1st sess., May 11, 2005, Washington, D.C.

35. Ruling on Cross-Motions for Summary Judgment, *Schaghticoke Tribal Nation v. Kempthorne*, August 22, 2008.

36. Ibid.

The Nipmuc Nation, Federal Acknowledgment, and a Case of Mistaken Identity

RAE GOULD

The decision to rely on an erroneous designation of a Nipmuc ancestor from a nineteenth-century document provides an opportunity to deny the ancestry—and thus the authenticity—of a large percentage of the Nipmuc nation in its federal acknowledgment case. Several issues and questions are highlighted in this case: Why do historical documents written by outsiders in the past and interpreted by outsiders in the present continue to influence the rewriting of tribal history? What courses of redress do indigenous groups have following processes that clearly lack integrity and seek to deny their authenticity? And most important, the inaccurate perceptions created by flawed processes (such as the U.S. federal acknowledgment process) must be corrected by indigenous people reappropriating and redefining our past.

On a warm June day in 2004, tribal members and leaders anxiously gathered in the Nipmuc nation tribal office in Sutton, Massachusetts. Surrounded by our legal and political advisers and news reporters, we optimistically awaited the phone call that would decide so much about our future. Would our children have educational opportunities many older tribal members never had? Would health care no longer be something unemployed Nipmucs needed to worry about? Would we have the funds to maintain a tribal office and offer services to our members in the future? These and so many other unknowns would be answered once the phone rang and Aurene Martin, a deputy assistant secretary of the Bureau of Indian Affairs (BIA) confirmed our status as a tribal entity in the eyes of the federal government.

The group anticipated the words that would be so critical to our future as we listened to our chief and BIA officials wade through the formalities of introducing everyone in the room. The deputy assistant secretary then addressed the purpose of her call: the Nipmuc nation (petitioner 69A on the bureau's long list) did not meet the seven mandatory criteria out-lined in 25 C.F.R. 83 for being considered a tribe and establishing a gov-ernment-to-government relationship with the federal government. Looks of dismay, disappointment, and shock on the faces of those assembled were followed by a number of responses: tears, despondent head shak-ing by elders involved with this struggle for decades, nausea among those who had combed through thousands of documents searching for the right pieces of evidence, and an overall sense of sadness. How could it be that all the evidence we provided about our family genealogies, tribal interrela-tions and activities, and tribal history could be so easily dismissed in one phone call, in a "final determination" that the Nipmuc people were not a "tribe" in the twenty-first century despite our obvious continued existence in New England (and beyond)? Didn't the presence in the room of several Nipmuc family lines demonstrate our solidarity and continued existence? The words of our tribal chair, who had to provide a statement to television and newspaper reporters only minutes after the call came, summarized how many of us would have responded that day: We know who we are, and this decision does not change that.

Yet still the doubts lingered. How would this affect relationships with other tribes and with outsiders who now might view us as inauthentic, phonies who tried to convince the BIA to recognize yet another wannabe tribe? For those unfamiliar with the federal acknowledgment process and our twenty-eight-year case in particular, a small tribe from an obscure area in southern New England would not seem a likely candidate for recognition for a number of reasons. Historians had dictated for centuries that "real" Indians in this area had long ago vanished, and the acknowledgment criteria reinforce these perceptions, as they demand evidence from outside sources that have recognized a tribal group through time.

To be acknowledged by the BIA, the tribal group must demonstrate that it has been identified as an American Indian entity on a continuous basis since 1900;[1] most of a petitioning group is a community that has existed from historical times until the present;[2] and the tribe has had political influ-ence or authority over its members since historical times.[3] In addition to these historically focused criteria, a tribe must provide to the BIA a state-ment describing its membership criteria and governing procedures and evidence that its membership is composed of descendants from a docu-mented "historical Indian tribe." A petitioner must also demonstrate that its membership does not include a significant number of individuals who are members of an already acknowledged tribe and that no congressional legislation terminated or forbids a federal relationship with the tribe or its members.

In trying to make sense of the BIA's decision, members of the Nipmuc nation returned to these criteria during our review of the final determination issued by the bureau. We found that the document contained contradictions, misinformation, inaccuracies, and a critical case of mistaken identity. One of the important factors in our case was a decision by government officials about the identity and ancestry of Mary Curliss Vickers, a central ancestor to a large percentage of the tribe's membership. This mistaken identity is closely connected to a history of erasure and denial of the continued existence of native people in New England.

Contributing to the myth of erasure (which can be traced back to the early 1600s) is the fact that even though native people were clearly on the landscape during European colonization, their voices are a small part of the historical record and are often audible only through the writings of others. Indigenous accounts of events that occurred in the past or native perceptions of history (whether from the past or present) have for the most part been considered irrelevant.[4] The only history perceived as real was that documented by Euro-Americans in public records and other sources, which focused on settlement by English ancestors, taming the wilderness, and subduing "the savage Indian."[5] This is just one example of how historical documents written by nonnatives attempted to erase Indians from the landscape through specific language and the creation of a particular history.[6]

Nonnative officials, historians, and academics have for centuries perpetuated a discourse of erasure concerning native people in New England, but this discourse is not solely an element from the past. This practice continues today through the federal acknowledgment process, which either confirms or denies a tribe's status as a bona fide entity in the eyes of the government (and often the public). In this chapter, I discuss the government's use of a specific document from 1861, the Earle Report, that has become the foundation for interpreting much of the region's Indian history—and Nipmuc genealogy, in particular—and played a key role in the denial of federal acknowledgment to the Nipmuc nation of Massachusetts. Central to this discussion is how the federal acknowledgment process participates in the use and misuse of historical documentation to redefine and rewrite tribal history in the twenty-first century. Beyond the obvious mistakes made in

the interpretation of specific documents, the Nipmuc federal acknowledgment case demonstrates that the process tribes must undergo is fundamentally flawed and relies on racially based stereotypes and Western
epistemologies of both history and how Indians should appear and behave;
it is also highly politicized because of economics.

The Legacy of the Earle Report

Some current historians writing about Indians in the southern New England region have created their works separately from the native people
who continue to live and work here while relying on nineteenth-century
stereotypes that have defined—and for some people, still define—both
our past and present. Historical interpretations produced today are just as
much about contemporary values and perspectives as they are about the
past. How we understand the past as contemporary scholars working with
historical materials is influenced by which sources we believe are data and
which are interpretations. Even primary sources must be considered within
the context of their creation and according to the biases and personal histories of their recorders; no "data" are neutral, and all must be considered as
interpretations rather than facts.[7] Most contemporary scholars realize this
and use historical documents critically. The 1861 Earle Report provides an
opportunity for an important discussion on the legacy this primary source
has left and on government officials', historians', and anthropologists' practice of denying the continued presence of native people in New England
based on the information presented by the report's author. I seek to correct
the erroneous belief that Indians cannot adequately define themselves, both
in the 1800s and today, as well as provide a critique of the federal acknowledgment process in general.

In the late 1850s, the Massachusetts government commissioned John
Milton Earle to collect information about the tribes as it moved closer to
enfranchisement (making legal citizens) of its Indian population.[8] He was
charged with examining "the condition of all Indians and the descendants
of Indians domiciled in [the] Commonwealth, and . . . report[ing] . . . on . . .
the number . . . place of abode . . . distribution . . . age and sex . . . married and single; and also the number of persons reputed Indians, who are
of mixed or other race."[9] Earle's instructions clearly indicate that he would
be an authority for determining who was a "real" Indian and who was only
a "reputed" Indian "of mixed or other race." Earle also assessed the social,
political, religious, educational, and economic conditions of the state's

Indian population, including specifics about individual and communal land holdings. His ultimate goal was to help the state decide the best course of action for extending full citizenship to Indians and dividing any tribal lands held in common.[10]

Many researchers and government officials still rely on the 1861 Earle Report as an important source of information about nineteenth-century Massachusetts Indians, and it remains a useful document in many ways. Yet as Earle admitted, his knowledge of Indians in the region was incomplete. For example, Earle noted that soon after accepting the assignment to report on the state's Indian population, he found he "had entered on a wide field of research, with much ground to traverse and little to gather . . . as to make the pursuit a matter of much labor, with comparatively insignificant returns."[11] In other words, Earle sought to enumerate and define the Indian tribes of Massachusetts though he had few connections and little understanding of those on whom he was reporting. Despite these deficiencies and the document's mistakes, the Earle Report is often considered more accurate than tribal knowledge and greatly affects Indian people in southern New England today. How did the Earle Report become such a significant document, used by generations of scholars as a basis for reconstructing Indian history and creating an "official" narrative? Or we might ask, as Michel-Rolph Trouillot does, "What makes some narratives rather than others powerful enough to pass as accepted history if not historicity itself? If history is merely the story told by those who won, how did they win in the first place? And why don't all winners tell the same story?"[12] The Earle Report is one example of an accepted history used repeatedly by "winners" in the battle to define native history and identity.

Earle created what has become a controversial piece of history. The Massachusetts guardianship records, combined with research conducted by Earle, provided the basis of his report.[13] It was compiled for the state and intended to be a comprehensive account of Indian people in Massachusetts, thus demonstrating how states could exercise considerable control over their native populations—and their land—during the nineteenth century.[14] With the creation of this document began the practice of categorizing Indians into collective groups defined by outside officials that continues to affect both the interpretations and lives of their descendants. This is perhaps the most significant legacy of this document because it is one of the most widely used texts for those who study Massachusetts Indian history and culture, and it provides a conceptual model for how to understand Indian relations—past and present—from an outsider's perspective.

Since its publication, Earle's report has been considered an official record of the names, locations, activities, conditions, and identities of Massachusetts Indians. However, the Earle Report perpetuates nineteenth-century Euro-American stereotypes of Indians, and its use by scholars and government officials today provides an example of how information by a nonnative can be considered a more official history than tribal sources.

One of the stereotypes Earle perpetuated was that Indian people in southern New England were roaming and unproductive. He was frustrated by native mobility, claiming that Indians were "a race naturally inclined to a roving and unsettled life."[15] Earle also noted that if they had been confined to the reservations, his "labor would have been comparatively trifling," a statement that suggests that he resented having to track down those who did not conveniently live on reservation lands or had not adopted more sedentary Euro-American practices.[16] This statement is disconcerting because Earle was considered to be an authority on the Indian population of that time, yet he clearly evaluated native people from a lens of Euro-American notions of fixity rather than providing clear explanations of why Indians may have been more mobile than nonnative people and often did not (or could not) live on the small reservation lands that remained.[17]

Despite the apparent bias in this document and the acknowledgment of this bias today, the Earle Report is still considered an expert source of information and has left a lasting impression on some scholars and government officials. Critical has been Earle's categorizing all Indians according to their association with a tribal reservation or as "Miscellaneous" if he could not establish an obvious affiliation or decipher complicated family histories. One of the "roving" Indians who made his task of categorizing native people difficult was Mary Curliss Vickers, a granddaughter of Dudley Nipmuc Molly Pegan who also had Narragansett ancestry (as many Nipmuc people do). Earle wrote to several sources for information about the Indians he researched for his report.[18] One of his sources (who received information directly from Vickers) reported that her "grandmother on her mother's side was Indian, Dudley tribe"; a complete accounting of Vickers's maternal family history followed.[19] Yet Earle still described Vickers as a "Miscellaneous" Indian, aged "about 60," and a widow living in Uxbridge (though she had moved to Oxford by the time his report was published).[20] His source, the "H. Capron letter," has become one of the contested pieces of history between the modern-day Nipmuc nation and the government officials who continue the practice of determining our history and identity for us. The BIA uses this document to determine ancestry and tribal affiliations of Nipmuc people and other Indians in Massachusetts.

Earle's final assessment of Vickers has had long-lasting effects for her descendants; with his definition of her as a "Miscellaneous" Indian, her documented Nipmuc ancestry instantly became tangential rather than central to her identity. In its review of the Nipmuc nation petition for federal acknowledgment, the BIA relied on Earle's interpretation of Nipmuc tribal members as of 1860 rather than the petitioners' documentation and knowledge of their family lineages and identities, or Vickers's identification as a Pegan in the H. Capron letter. In its final negative determination, the BIA returned to Earle's classification of Vickers, a central ancestor of the tribe, as "Miscellaneous" to claim that descendants from this person were not Nipmuc, merely "Indian." Earle defined "Miscellaneous Indians" as those "whose classification may be doubtful, some of them having the blood of two or three tribes in them, who possibly may have descended from some tribe out of the State."[21] The BIA's assessment was made even though the bureau had previously acknowledged that the H. Capron letter stated that Vickers's grandmother was Nipmuc and that Vickers clearly knew her family history, as do modern-day tribal members.[22] This is an example of the production of legal identities and government naming practices discussed by James C. Scott.[23] Furthermore, both Earle in 1860 and the BIA in the twenty-first century disregarded the local, personal knowledge so critical for a real understanding of history, place, genealogy, and Indian identity in interpretations of the Nipmuc people.[24]

Details from the federal acknowledgment documents of this case further demonstrate how the recognition process used (and misused) historical documentation to redefine Nipmuc people and history and to deny the identity of this ancestor in particular. According to the final determination, "The current Vickers enrollees in 69A primarily descend from four children of Mary (Curliss) Vickers, who was listed as a 'Miscellaneous Indian': Sarah Ann, Chandler, Mary Ann, and Rufus Vickers. Of the total 290 descendants of Mary (Curliss) Vickers in the current 69A membership, 113 have descent from one of the Dudley/Webster Sprague lines as well. The other 177 Curliss/Vickers descendants in petitioner 69A do not have either Hassanamisco or Dudley/Webster ancestry." But the document also states that Vickers's descendants "do not have . . . Dudley/Webster ancestry" and that "the petitioner has not submitted any new evidence to demonstrate that the [sic] Mary (Curliss) Vickers was a descendant of either the Dudley Nipmuc

Indians or the Hassanamisco Nipmuc Indians. There is some evidence in the Earle papers that attributed Dudley Nipmuc ancestry to Mary (Curliss) Vickers's grandmother, Molly Pegan (1751–aft. 1841)." The document concludes, "The evidence . . . demonstrates that 34 percent (178 of 526) of 69A's membership descend from a woman listed under 'Miscellaneous Indians' in 1861 on the *Earle Report*. The evidence does not show that Mary (Curliss) Vickers was living in tribal relations or that she or her children were considered part of either the Hassanamisco or Dudley/Webster tribes as they were identified by the State of Massachusetts in 1861."[25]

In addition to ignoring the primary documentary evidence demonstrating Vickers's Nipmuc ancestry, these statements contradict the bureau's definition of this ancestor in its 2001 proposed finding for the Nipmuc nation, which specifically addressed the "Ancestry and Descendants of Mary (Curliss) Vickers," citing the H. Capron letter and stating: "According to the 1859 statement of Mary (Curliss) Vickers, her grandmother was a Dudley Indian (Capron to Earle 10/28/1859; Earle Papers). The statement could, to some extent, be confirmed from independently created contemporary documents."[26] The BIA's seeming acceptance of Vickers's ancestry could explain why the Nipmucs did not provide any new evidence about her lineage.

The proposed finding further confirmed that "the descendancy of Mary (Curliss) Vickers from Mary (Pegan) Pollock Woodland has been documented, although the family lived in Connecticut during the first half of the nineteenth century and was never on the Dudley/Webster guardians' documents. During the nineteenth century, there were also marriages and other documented social contacts between this family line and other Nipmuc families living in Worcester County, Massachusetts (Hemenway, Sprague)." The proposed finding also stated that Vickers and her descendants have "documented off-reservation Nipmuc descent."[27] The turning point took place when the final determination reclassified this family from "off-reservation Nipmuc" to "off-reservation Indian," stripping them of their identity as Nipmuc Indians. With this tactic, the bureau clearly ignored its own documentation.

This type of capricious—perhaps predictable—redefining confirms that contemporary interpretations of southern New England Indians can conform to the same ideology that prevailed in the mid-nineteenth century: classifying Indians according to a single tribal affiliation defined by Euro-American state borders and external interpretations of Indian identity that perpetuate a discourse of disappearance. The Vickers family, like many Indian families in southern New England, claims a multitribal heritage and has long acknowledged both Nipmuc and Narragansett ancestry; this does not negate connections to Nipmuc homelands and other Nipmuc families. Many of Mary Curliss Vickers's descendants remained in Massachusetts— even though Nipmuc homelands extend into northeastern Connecticut and northwestern Rhode Island and many tribal members today trace family roots to these locations—and maintained their Indian identity while intermarrying with other Nipmucs (as bureau officials acknowledged in the proposed finding). One descendant, Walter Vickers, assumed leadership of the tribe in the 1980s following a long apprentice-like relationship with the previous leader, Zara CiscoeBrough, clearly an indication (by most interpretations) that this family thought of itself as Nipmuc. Like his predecessor, Walter Vickers is proud of both his Nipmuc and Narragansett ancestry, has seen no conflict inherent in his dual ancestry, and has had no confusion about his role as a Nipmuc leader. The BIA's decision to use Earle's categorization of Mary Curliss Vickers as "Miscellaneous" rather than to rely on the evidence and tribal knowledge confirming her Nipmuc ancestry, demonstrates how nineteenth-century interpretations are used in the contemporary period to deny valid Indian histories, culture, and identity and to redefine southern New England Indians according to outside perspectives and political objectives.

Although Earle likely understood that his report would be an important and definitive statement on Massachusetts Indians during its time period, affecting both impending legislation and native people in the state for generations, he might not have foreseen that it would remain such a critical document for Massachusetts tribes into the next century and beyond. Nor could he appreciate how his definitions of tribal identity would be reread hundreds (perhaps thousands) of times as later scholars and government officials sought to understand who is Indian and what their "tribal affiliation" is.

Another issue with the Earle Report as a source of Indian history is that Earle, as a product of his times, carried nineteenth-century racial categories (in addition to stereotypes) about the Indians on whom he reported. His remark that some groups, such as the Hassanamiscos, had intermarried with whites to the point of losing "their identity as a distinct class" is followed by the lamentation that this "would have been a fortunate thing for all the tribes, if it had been so with them all."[28] Such statements confirm that this seminal document was written with a preconceived notion of how Indians should act and look and that they were perceived as a disappearing people. Despite his difficulties, Earle acknowledged that a considerable

number of Indians still existed, continuing to carry "the prominent characteristics of the Indians—the lank, glossy, black hair, the high cheek bones,
the bright, dark eye, and other features peculiar to the race."[29] In a period
when scientific racism and craniometry prevailed—and genocidal Indian
wars raged further west—Earle's assessment of Massachusetts Indians fit
well with the perceptions of the time and reaffirm how restrictive racial
classifications of Indians furthered the prevailing logic of elimination.[30] Not
clearly noted—either by Earle in 1861 or by the BIA in the twenty-first century—is that when asked, Indians such as Mary Curliss Vickers did know
their family history and native identity. Their outward appearances, though,
did not always provide the tell-tale signs that Euro-Americans needed to
identify them as Indians or that today convince the BIA of their authenticity. A complicated relationship still exists between federal recognition
policy and Indian identity, as does racism within the agencies carrying out
these policies.[31]

Other Foundations of Modern-Day Perceptions about New England Indians

Other scholars have also grappled with the legacy of the Earle Report and
the issue of racism within the BIA. Christopher Thee notes that by relying
on the Earle Report and other documents from this time period, the BIA
"invoked 19th-century, Euro-American, racially determined definitions of
Indianness."[32] Both Thomas Doughton[33] and Thee discuss at length how the
Earle and earlier 1849 Bird (or Briggs)[34] Reports advanced the beliefs that
the last of the Nipmuc were heading toward extinction and that those who
still lived in the region ceased to be "real" Indians because of their biological
impurity. This desire to believe that Indians were a disappearing race was
confirmed with the state's passing of the 1869 Enfranchisement Act, which
removed Massachusetts Indians from their special status as wards of the
state and privatized their lands. Just as important, the stereotypes created
from this period have continued to influence perceptions about New England Indians in the present by perpetuating beliefs about inauthenticity.

While a number of New England tribes have held onto (or rebuilt) some
reservation lands, the land loss that occurred between the seventeenth
and nineteenth centuries throughout the area permanently redefined how
native people would position themselves in relation to their Euro-American neighbors, both on the physical landscape and socially. The dispossession of identity, however, has continued into the twenty-first century.

Although land and identity are often intertwined for many native people, the Vickers case demonstrates that Indians throughout the area, even while seeming to be "roving" aimlessly because they were not tied to reservations, maintained their identity both within their social and familial circles and to outsiders. But a continued reliance on documents such as the Earle Report, especially by the BIA, has influenced modern-day perceptions about tribal people in general and the Nipmuc specifically. Most people relying on the final determination's assessment of Vickers as "Miscellaneous" Indian and not Nipmuc would not have access to the additional documentation that confirms her ancestry.

Modern-day perceptions have also been influenced by other sources produced in the century and a half since the Earle Report, as inaccuracies in public documents continued well beyond the nineteenth century. Much like the 1861 Earle Report, local histories and newspaper accounts from the late 1800s and into the 1900s demonstrated that many nonnative residents from the area believed Indians were indeed vanishing, in some cases offering a lamenting romanticism that the "last of" these tribes were passing away. Many of these accounts, however, are contradictory and conflicting. For example, at the same time that Julia Jaha was documented as the "Last of the Nipmucks" in the Oxford, Massachusetts, town history, her sister, Mary, was labeled "the last survivor of the once powerful tribe of Nipmuck Indians" in a nearby town.[35]

Another example from the early twentieth century notes the passing of the "last of" the Grafton Indians, Althea Hazzard. The fact that Hazzard was closely connected to Vickers and her family (noted in Hazzard's obituary) provided further evidence that the Vickers family maintained ties with other Nipmuc families. Hazzard lived with her neighbor, Monroe Vickers (Mary's son), for nearly two decades at the end of her life and was an "intimate friend" of Mary Vickers. This information, like the documentation of Vickers's Nipmuc ancestry, was discounted by the BIA in its final review of the Nipmuc nation case as government researchers instead focused on Earle's "Miscellaneous" designation of the Vickers family and preferred to claim that the Vickers family was not "living in tribal relations" with other Nipmuc people.[36]

While working on the federal acknowledgment case for the Nipmuc nation, tribal members and researchers (including me) saw such erroneous accounts of our "vanishing tribe" as amusing, especially since we were—several generations later—collecting such memorabilia to demonstrate our continued existence. Only later, at the end of the petitioning process, did we understand that others would turn to such documents (as they had with the Earle Report) to create conclusive definitions of Nipmuc identity and authenticity and that most people have long believed these public claims of our "vanished race."

In addition to the fact that these nineteenth- and twentieth-century sources were obviously inaccurate in their portrayal of disappearing Nipmuc Indians, a more critical issue relates to how "Indian" was and is defined by these and future historical documents and "experts." Were people interpreting the deaths of Hazzard (in 1903) and James Lemuel Cisco (in 1931) (as reported in the *Worcester Gazette*) as those of the last "real" (versus "mixed") Indians in Grafton? This question arose decades earlier with Earle and with historians Frederick Pierce and Harriette Forbes, who penned histories of central Massachusetts towns in the late 1800s.[37] Yet none of these "official" accounts agreed on the definition of what an Indian really was. Despite the confusion and inaccuracies apparent in these sources, they formed the basis of twentieth-century understandings of southern New England native culture and continue to influence how some contemporary historians and anthropologists—as well as the public—perceive Indians of this region.

Forbes's history of Westborough, Massachusetts, included numerous anecdotes about the vanishing Indian population of the region through her descriptions of universally drinking, roving, violent Indians who filled out local history as colorful figures from the past and provided the antithesis to the respectable white settlers of these proper New England towns. She maintained that although "the Indian, unmolested, roamed through the wilderness" at one time, "nearly every trace of him has disappeared."[38] In Grafton, however, one family of Nipmuc Indians survived, preserving a small land parcel and homestead over time.[39] Forbes also believed that the purity of this "race" had been tainted, noting that "there is probably no one living to-day of unmixed Hassanamisco blood."[40] Furthermore, she provided a stereotype of Nipmucs as the universally drunken Indian by noting that the family of Andrew Brown from Westborough, "like all the Indians . . . spent their time making baskets, and drinking up the profits from the sale of them."[41] These concerns may have been related to the emerging early twentieth-century eugenics movement, which represented white people's concern with loss of their own race's purity as America became home to increasing numbers of immigrants.[42] A sense of nostalgia may have also influenced how these non-Indian historians created their images of the past and present. Nostalgia emerges when people feel alienated from their present-day world and seek a sense of comfort and familiarity from the past.[43] In the changing world of late nineteenth-century New England, historians would have looked to the past to create a vision of how they wished their world had been, revising the past to serve the Victorian goals of propriety, morality, and respectability. Non-Indian people had to be defined as possessing all of these qualities and juxtaposed against something (or someone) else: Indians and blacks.

Such racially defined ideals of New England Indians continued into the twentieth century and are visible in the works of academics who have based their careers on studying the region's tribal people. Frank G. Speck (1881–1950) was a well-known anthropologist who recorded his interactions with New England Indians and was regarded by the BIA as an expert on the region. In this capacity, Speck also left a legacy that continues to define Nipmuc Indians by an outsider. Like those before him, he relied on ethnic identifiers and stereotypes of native people in his assessment of their authenticity. Although he did not subscribe to the biological concept of race, acknowledging that this was an anthropologically "obsolete term,"[44] Speck noted that "the characteristic of curly hair . . . has caused most recent writers . . . to reproduce the lop-sided rubric of 'race classification' and call [Indians] 'colored'; whence 'negro.' This will not pass challenge in all cases," perhaps because "in some Indian families, as well as individuals of no more than one-eighth negroid ancestry, the hair is less curly than in others of three-quarters white origin."[45] In attempting to clarify his understandings of racial identity, Speck's focus on hair curl provides a brief yet satisfying discussion for him. And while he theoretically did not believe in the "obsolete term" of race, he still distinguished those with "negroid" ancestry. Although Speck's discussion of ethnic identifiers is brief, it demonstrates that the issue of Indians mixing with other races was still an important consideration for nonnative people (including Speck) in the early twentieth century as they struggled to define Indians, just as Earle did through terms such as "Miscellaneous" decades earlier.

Speck, like others, also could not adequately define the tribal nature of the Nipmuc people that he studied in the 1940s. Although his opinion was that "the Nipmuc lack the character of a well defined nation"—a statement based primarily on loss of land and of "the political unity of the villages designated as Nipmuc" that existed before English settlement of the area— Speck also noted that "they teach their children to call themselves Nipmuc, and to a few . . . they are still Hassanamisco Nipmuc Indians."[46] Sarah Cisco Sullivan (who continued to reside on the reservation in Grafton and was Speck's only informant) told him that around two hundred Nipmuc descendants existed at that time, but for this anthropologist, the issue of identity revolved around the "intricate problems of acculturation"[47] that made tribal groups of the twentieth century so difficult to define. In his mind, the Nipmuc had acculturated and could no longer be defined as a tribe, although there is no evidence that he talked with any other Nipmuc people besides the Cisco family. Speck's confusion and struggle to clearly define this group is also evident in his statement that "one must admit that the *group*, though interfused and obscured, is one consciously apart in name [i.e., Nipmuc] identity."[48]

The BIA used Speck, as they did with Earle, as an authoritative outside source who documented the status of the Nipmuc despite inconsistencies and inaccuracies in his account. This example also demonstrates how existing "histories" are not detached from important social and political processes but still significantly influence modern-day interpretations of authenticity. The perceptions about the Nipmuc past—created from a "Western perspectival gaze in which the observer is always outside and above the action"—have perhaps been even more influential in how people understand Nipmuc history, culture, and identity than the information provided by tribal sources such as Mary Curliss Vickers or Sarah Cisco Sullivan.[49] Most important, these dominant outside perceptions have been used by the government to deny the authenticity of the Nipmuc people as a tribal entity.

Correcting Mistaken Identities and Addressing a Faulty Process

The histories, perceptions, and inaccuracies about Nipmuc Indians discussed in this chapter are rooted in colonial and neocolonial mind-sets that have perpetuated a discourse of disappearance about native people and influenced important decisions made by government officials (and others) today. The case of Mary Curliss Vickers's mistaken identity is just one example of how "established histories" create a power that is integral to and constitutive of the stories told by these histories, whether factual or not, and of how that power can be used in the deeply flawed federal recognition process.[50] More critical is whether that story is accepted. The presence of an accepted history, in effect, creates an opposing silenced history, as Trouillot has noted. The creation of these silences now must be addressed. The fact that this chapter focuses on correcting misconceptions, such as those that apparently still exist about Vickers's ancestry and identity, is a testament to the fact that the anthropological and historical narratives that have dominated both academia and public perceptions have been constructed to erase or rewrite native history and make claims about Indian identity.

Perhaps the most obvious issue related to histories such as these—and what is apparent in the BIA decision regarding the Nipmuc nation—is the inability to make connections between the history of the Indians being discussed and the living people today. Over the past few decades, a number of scholars exploring southern New England native history and culture have offered more accurate interpretations because they worked with living communities rather than based their scholarship solely on historical documents. Anthropologist William S. Simmons documented the continued existence of Indian spirituality.[51] In *Mashpee Indians: Tribe on Trial*, Jack Campisi incorporated indigenous knowledge of Wampanoag people in his important discussion of the implications of scholarship and "expert" definitions of New England tribal groups and their effects on the recognition process.[52] Donna K. Baron, J. Edward Hood, and Holly V. Izard have also contributed to correcting the myth of erasure so pervasive in this region, stating that although the Indians "were here all along," historians just did not know where to look for them.[53] Such works demonstrate that the tide has been turning toward a more complete understanding of the area's history.

Several other scholars have also addressed the misconceptions that form the basis of contemporary understandings about New England Indians. Jean M. O'Brien discusses "vanishing" Indians of the 1800s and local historians' practice of erasing native people who were clearly still present on the landscape.[54] And Colin G. Calloway has noted that this practice was related to the established idea that Eastern Indians were gone by the early nineteenth century.[55] Other New England scholars are combining archaeological evidence with historical documentation to create a more complete picture of the past. In their work on the Sarah Boston site in Grafton, Stephen Mrozowski, Heather Law, and Guido Pezzarossi discuss Nipmuc persistence and innovation well into the nineteenth century.[56] A larger goal of this project is re-creating what some observers have called the lost century of New England native history (1820–1920), which allegedly ended with the pan-Indian movement of the 1920s.[57] More important, these scholars have worked closely with tribal people to develop interpretations of our past and can attest to the fact not only that tribes still exist in this area but also that they take an interest in their past and how it is represented by others.

Perhaps the most important issue regarding misconceptions about Indi-ans in New England—one directly connected to the issue of authenticity so interwoven with recognition—focuses on what makes Indians so different when "they" live in raised ranch houses and send their children to public schools like their neighbors. As with the Mashpee case, native people are often defined according to how much Indian food they eat, whether they have Indian names and wear regalia, and whether they participate in "tradi-tional" activities such as dancing.[58] In the twenty-first century, control over resources (such as land) influences how the public recognizes tribes and why outsiders gauge authenticity through indicators such as these. These are the same issues—land, identity, and authenticity—that Earle addressed in 1861. For native people of New England, though, land has always been much more than a wilderness to be conquered or a commodity to barter with. It has been an anchor for kinship relations, tribal identity, and more recently definitions of sovereignty; Indians often define its meaning differ-ently than non-Indians do.

The BIA's failure to recognize the continued presence of a Nipmuc tribal entity should also mean that the land associated with the tribe would not be a recognized reservation (as the 2004 final determination claimed). As with its mistaken identification of Vickers, however, the BIA is confused about the status of the Hassanamisco Reservation, the Nipmuc nation's land base in Grafton, Massachusetts. This place has become symbolic of the contradiction about our status and is what I refer to as a "contested place."[59] While the BIA refuses to acknowledge our rights as a tribe, the agency has for decades acknowledged the presence of our Indian reservation through its inclusion on a government-produced map indicating the locations of "Indian reservations in the Continental United States."[60]

What is at stake today that such places and their associated tribal identi-ties could represent so much and be so contested in their meaning? The struggle for power and to define authenticity that still exists between native and nonnative people of southern New England is being played out in the battles for land, capital, and political authority that have defined America for the past five hundred years and continue to do so today. The struggle for identity in which both native and nonnative people engage on a daily basis is directly related to who gains (and maintains) control over the future by manipulating perceptions of the past and present. In southern New Eng-land, this battle is often related to economic success and related sovereignty issues. As Jessica Cattelino has noted, while economic success is often a key to the maintenance of tribal sovereignty, it can also be precisely the condition used to challenge sovereignty.[61] This challenge comes in the form of inaccurate retellings of the past, the denial of Indian identity, and the erasure of native people from the landscape. Appetites for money, land, and power have really not changed since colonial times.

The federal recognition process has become central to this centuries-old battle. Despite the incontestable presence of the Nipmuc land base and the descendants of Mary Curliss Vickers and others, the belief that native people of southern New England today are not authentic continues to be perpetuated and is visible not only in the minds and reactions of the public but also in the works on which the BIA relies for its decisions about acknowledgment. This flawed and very public process results in cases of mistaken identity that in essence seek to erase us from the past and of course the present. My work as a native scholar extends beyond struggling to maintain an identity and is part of a broader effort to reappropriate and redefine our past that started decades ago.[62] By sharing this case study, I am contributing to a better understanding of the native places and people on the landscape of southern New England. I have become part of a new legacy: Nipmuc people consciously refashioning, reshaping, and redefining our own history despite the misconceptions that persist about us.

Notes

1. Evidence for this criterion includes identification by the federal government as an Indian entity; treatment by a state government as an Indian tribe; or identification of the tribe by anthropologists, historians, or other scholars.

2. Requiring such evidence as significant social relationships between members, a significant degree of shared labor among the members, or the presence of shared rituals.

3. "Political influence or authority" can be by demonstrating that the tribe can or did mobilize its members or resources for group purposes; most members consider or considered actions taken by the group leaders important; or there is or was widespread knowledge, communication, and involvement in political processes.

4. Amy E. Den Ouden, *Beyond Conquest: Native Peoples and the Struggle for History in New England* (Lincoln: University of Nebraska Press, 2005), 15.

5. One example is the 1638 Treaty of Hartford ending the Pequot War. Following the 1637 massacre of several hundred Pequots, the colony of Connecticut "extinguished" the Pequots by proclaiming that the survivors "shall no more be called Pequots" and could no longer "live in the country that was formerly theirs, but now is the English by Conquest" (Den Ouden, *Beyond Conquest*, 12). See also the

Connecticut Indian Papers, RG001 Connecticut Archives: Indians Series I, 1647–1789, 2:120b. Yet the reservations established by that same colony just a few decades later (including the 1666 Mashantucket Pequot reservation) were a direct contradiction of the belief that Pequots or other Indians "shall no more be."

6. See Jill Lepore, *The Name of War: King Philip's War and the Origins of American Identity* (New York: Knopf, 1998).

7. Jocelyn Linnekin, *Sacred Queens and Women of Consequence: Rank, Gender, and Colonialism in the Hawaiian Islands* (Ann Arbor: University of Michigan Press, 1990), viii.

8. For a more detailed discussion of Indian enfranchisement in Massachusetts, see Ann Marie Plane and Gregory Button, "The Massachusetts Indian Enfranchisement Act: Ethnic Context in Historical Context, 1849–1869," in *After King Philip's War: Presence and Persistence in Indian New England*, ed. Colin G. Calloway (Hanover: University Press of New England, 1997), 178–206.

9. John Milton Earle, *Report to the Governor and Council, Concerning the Indians of the Commonwealth, under the Act of April 6, 1859* (Boston: White, 1861), 5.

10. Ibid., 5–6, 140–42.

11. Ibid., 6.

12. Michel-Rolph Trouillot, *Silencing the Past: Power and the Production of History* (Boston: Beacon, 1995), 6.

13. The Massachusetts Indian guardianship (or trustee) system dates back to Daniel Gookin, the first superintendent of Indians in Massachusetts. Gookin was appointed superintendent in 1656 to assist John Eliot in his mission to Christianize Indians in the area (Jean O'Brien, *Dispossession by Degrees: Indian Land and Identity in Natick, Massachusetts, 1650–1790* [New York: Cambridge University Press 1997], 50). Following King Philip's War (1675–76) and the return of surviving Indians to their settlements in the late 1600s and early 1700s, guardians were appointed to manage the affairs of tribal groups with land bases. Much of their work centered on selling Indian lands and allocating interest payments from these sales.

14. Deborah A. Rosen, *American Indians and State Law: Sovereignty, Race, and Citizenship, 1790–1880* (Lincoln: University of Nebraska Press, 2009).

15. O'Brien, *Dispossession by Degrees*, 210; Earle, *Report*, 6.

16. Earle, *Report*, 6.

17. By 1861, the Grafton (or Hassanamisco) Indian reservation had dwindled down to a mere 3 acres (Earle documented this as 2½ acres) and was occupied by Sarah Arnold Cisco and her family. The loss associated with this land base is discussed in D. Rae Gould, "Contested Places: The History and Meaning of Hassanamisco" (Ph.D. diss., University of Connecticut, Storrs, 2010). Earle's report

does discuss (to a degree) land loss and mismanagement of Indian funds by the Grafton guardians.

18. The John Milton Earle Papers, 1652–1863, American Antiquarian Society, Worcester, Massachusetts, include correspondence from various town clerks and others from whom Earle gained knowledge about Massachusetts Indians.

19. H. Capron to John Milton Earle, Earle Papers, Box 2, Folder 5.

20. Earle, *Report*, lxxv.

21. Ibid., 118.

22. This acknowledgment occurred at several points in time during this case, including at the 2002 technical assistance meeting held at the BIA offices with the Nipmuc nation. A full transcript of that meeting is available in the Nipmuc Nation Tribal Archive, Hassanamisco Indian Museum, Grafton, Mass.

23. James C. Scott, "The Production of Legal Identities Proper to States: The Case of the Permanent Family Surname," *Comparative Studies in Society and History* 44 (2002): 4–44.

24. James C. Scott, *Seeing Like a State: How Certain Schemes to Improve the Human Condition Have Failed* (New Haven: Yale University Press, 1999).

25. U.S. Department of the Interior, Bureau of Indian Affairs, Office of Federal Acknowledgment, *Summary under the Criteria and Final Determination against Federal Acknowledgment of the Nipmuc Nation* (2004), 46, 173, 177.

26. U.S. Department of Interior, Bureau of Indian Affairs, Office of Federal Acknowledgment, *Summary under the Criteria and Evidence for Proposed Finding: The Nipmuc Nation* (2001), 205–8.

27. Ibid., 208, 217.

28. Earle, *Report*, 10.

29. Ibid., 10.

30. Patrick Wolfe, "Settler Colonialism and the Elimination of the Native," *Journal of Genocide Research* 8 (2006): 383.

31. Brian Klopotek, *Recognition Odysseys: Indigeneity, Race, and Federal Tribal Recognition Policy in Three Louisiana Indian Communities* (Durham: Duke University Press, 2011).

32. Christopher J. Thee, "Massachusetts Nipmucs and the Long Shadow of John Milton Earle," *New England Quarterly* 79 (2006): 637.

33. Thomas L. Doughton, "Unseen Neighbors: Native Americans of Central Massachusetts, a People Who Had 'Vanished,'" in *After King Philip's War*, ed. Calloway, 207–30; and Thomas Doughton, "Like the Shadows in the Stream: Local Historians, the Discourse of Disappearance, and Nipmuc Indians of Central Massachusetts" (paper presented at the American Antiquarian Society, Worcester, Massachusetts, 1999).

34. F. W. Bird, Whiting Griswold, and Cyrus Weekes, *Report of the Commissioners Relating to the Condition of the Indians in Massachusetts* (Boston: Wright and Potter, 1849).

35. Doughton, "Unseen Neighbors," 209.

36. Anon., "Last of Her Tribe Dead," obituary notice of Althea Johns Hazzard, *Worcester Telegram*, Oct. 14, 1903.

37. Frederick Clifton Pierce, *History of Grafton, Worcester County, Massachusetts* (Worcester: Hamilton, 1879); Harriette Forbes, *The Hundredth Town: Glimpses of Life in Westborough, 1717–1817* (Boston: Rockwell and Church, 1889).

38. Forbes, *Hundredth Town*, 9.

39. The Hassanamisco Reservation and Cisco Homestead are maintained by the Nipmuc nation today. See Gould, "Contested Places" for a detailed discussion of the history and meaning of this place.

40. Forbes, *Hundredth Town*, 181.

41. Ibid., 171.

42. More detailed discussions of this movement include Daniel Kelves, *In the Name of Eugenics: Genetics and the Uses of Human Heredity* (New York: Knopf, 1985); Elof Axel Carlson, *The Unfit: A History of a Bad Idea* (Cold Spring Harbor, N.Y.: Cold Spring Harbor Press, 2001); Ruth C. Engs, *The Eugenics Movement: An Encyclopedia* (Westport, Conn.: Greenwood, 2005).

43. David Lowenthal, "Past Time, Present Place: Landscape and Memory," *Geographical Review* 65 (1975): 1–37.

44. Frank G. Speck, "A Note on the Hassanamisco Band of Nipmuc," *Massachusetts Archaeological Society Bulletin* 4 (1943): 51.

45. Ibid., 52.

46. Ibid., 49, 50.

47. Ibid., 50.

48. Ibid., 51; emphasis added.

49. Barbara Bender, ed., *Landscape: Politics and Perspectives* (Oxford: Berg, 1993), 10.

50. Trouillot, *Silencing the Past*, 28.

51. See William S. Simmons, *Cautantowwit's House: An Indian Burial Ground on the Island of Conanicut in Narragansett Bay* (Providence, R.I.: Brown University Press, 1970); William S. Simmons, *Spirit of the New England Tribes: Indian History and Folklore, 1620–1984* (Hanover, N.H.: University Press of New England, 1986). These works are also cited in O'Brien, *Dispossession by Degrees*, 4.

52. Jack Campisi, *Mashpee Indians: Tribe on Trial* (Syracuse, N.Y.: Syracuse University Press, 1991).

53. Donna K. Baron, J. Edward Hood, and Holly V. Izard, "They Were Here All Along: The Native American Presence in Lower-Central New England in the Eighteenth and Nineteenth Centuries," *William and Mary Quarterly*, 3rd ser., 53 (1996): 561–86.

54. Jean M. O'Brien, "'Vanishing' Indians in Nineteenth-Century New England: Local Historians' Erasure of Still-Present Peoples," in *New Perspectives on Native North America: Cultures, Histories, and Representations*, ed. Sergei A. Kan and Pauline Turner Strong (Lincoln: University of Nebraska Press, 2006), 414–32.

55. Colin G. Calloway, *First Peoples: A Documentary Survey of American Indian History* (Boston: Bedford/St. Martin's, 1999).

56. Stephen A. Mrozowski, Heather Law, and Guido Pezzarossi, *Archaeological Intensive Excavation, Hassanamesit Woods Property, The Sarah Boston Farmstead, Grafton, MA* (Boston: Fiske Center for Archaeological Research at the University of Massachusetts, Boston, 2006); Heather Law, "Daily Negotiations and the Creations of an Alternative Discourse: The Legacy of a Colonial Nipmuc Farmstead" (Master's thesis, University of Massachusetts, Boston, 2008); Guido Pezzarossi, "Consumption as Social Camouflage: 'Mimicry' and Nipmuc Survival Strategies in the Colonial World" (Master's thesis, University of Massachusetts, Boston, 2008).

57. Law, "Daily Negotiations."

58. James Clifford, *The Predicament of Culture: Twentieth-Century Ethnography, Literature, and Art* (Cambridge: Harvard University Press, 1988).

59. Gould, "Contested Places."

60. U.S. Department of the Interior, National Park Service, "Indian Reservations in the Continental United States," http://www.nps.gov/history/nagpra/documents/resmap.htm.

61. Jessica Cattelino, "The Double Bind of American Indian Need-Based Sovereignty," *Cultural Anthropology* 25 (2010): 235–62.

62. See, e.g., Vine Deloria Jr., *Custer Died for Your Sins: An Indian Manifesto* (Norman: University of Oklahoma Press, 1969).

Part III
Contemporary Recognition Controversies

A Right Delayed

The Brothertown Indian Nation's Story
of Surviving the Federal Acknowledgment Process

KATHLEEN A. BROWN-PEREZ

> Violence rarely, if ever, exists in a pure form. It always has a
> narrative dimension.... We play with our stories in ways we cannot
> with the *violence* itself.
>
> —VINCENT CRAPANZANO, "What Is Settler Colonialism?" (2003)

One of the many critical issues facing indigenous people worldwide is recognition from the colonizing government under which they now live. Despite an understanding that true sovereignty is inherent—it comes from within rather than from an external body—many indigenous governments seek some level of recognition from their country's dominant governing body. It is almost as if those who survived colonization want an acknowledgment of their continued existence. This matter is complicated, however, when the dominant governing body is seeking to decrease the number of indigenous people within its borders. In the United States, many of the tribes the federal government does not yet acknowledge now have the "opportunity" to petition for such acknowledgment. As Jessica R. Cattelino has noted in her article "The Double Bind of American Indian Need-Based Sovereignty," "Anthropologists and other scholars have analyzed the ways that indigenous peoples must fit themselves into preconceived expectations by settlers to achieve recognition, including but not only federal recognition as tribal governments. One of those expectations is a level of distinctiveness and political continuity that would elude many other polities."[1]

The Brothertown Indian Nation has spent three decades mired in the Federal Acknowledgment Process (FAP). It has been a long journey, despite the tribe's highly documented written history. The Brothertown Nation was formed in 1785 from the Christian members of the Montauk, Mohegan,

Pequot, Tunxis, Nehantic, and Narragansett tribes. By 1839, the tribe had left New York for Wisconsin and been granted U.S. citizenship.[2] With (or despite) this history, the Office of Federal Acknowledgment (OFA) has denied the tribe's petition. How does a tribe—whether it exists within the United States or elsewhere—proceed in the twenty-first century without acknowledgment of that existence from the dominant government? When a tribal government believes it gets its legitimacy from the U.S. government, for example, is it complacent in supporting continuing colonization? What happens when a government decides it will acknowledge no tribes? If hundreds of those tribes have hung their hats on the importance of federal acknowledgment, how do they switch camps and object to this externally granted sovereignty or lack thereof?

The Negative Proposed Finding

> Whilst our forefathers were blind, and ignorant yea drowned in Spiritous Liquors; the English striped them, yea as it were cut off their Right Hands;—and now we their Children just opening our eyes, and having knowledge grafted, and growing in our hearts, and just reviving, or coming to our senses, like one that has been drunk—I say that now we begin to look around and Consider and we perceive that we are striped indeed, having nothing to help ourselves, and thus our English Brethren leaves us, and laugh. So now Brethren, we leave the English those who have acted unjustly towards us in New England, I say we leave them all in the hands of that God who knoweth all things, and will reward every one according to their deeds whether good or evil.

> —JOSEPH JOHNSON (Mohegan/Brothertown), "Speech to the Oneidas on Behalf of the New England Indians" (1774)

On August 17, 2009, the acting principal deputy assistant secretary for Indian affairs, George T. Skibine, issued a proposed finding against federal acknowledgment of the Brothertown Indian Nation.[3] This decision denied to the Brothertown sovereign nation status and a government-to-government relationship with the United States. It made the tribe ineligible for most government benefits, including Indian health services and education assistance. The Indian Child Welfare Act, which Congress enacted to "protect the best interests of Indian children and to promote the stability and security of Indian tribes and families," does not protect Brothertown children from being adopted outside the community.[4] The Brothertown Nation cannot receive human remains, funerary objects, sacred objects, or objects of cultural patrimony under the Native American Graves Protection and Repatriation Act.[5] In a nutshell, any and all laws that pertain to federally acknowledged tribes do not apply to the more than three hundred unrecognized tribes.[6] How did the Brothertown Indian Nation get to this point?

Samson Occom, Mohegan

The Brothertown Indian Nation's unique history tends to captivate those who hear it. One intriguing characteristic is that the Brothertown Nation can point to an exact date of formation. On November 7, 1785, Samson Occom (1723–92) wrote in his journal, "We proceeded to form into a Body Politick—We Named our Town by the Name of Brothertown, in Indian Eeyamquittoowauconnuck."[7] Occom, a Mohegan and Presbyterian minister, feared for the survival of his people, seeing their numbers, land, and sovereignty dwindle more with each passing year. He brought together survivors of the Pequot Massacre, King Philip's War, and other genocidal events in an inspired attempt to survive colonization. His plan would require an understanding of the issues inherent in the close coexistence of American Indians and colonists, particularly as colonists sought more land on which to build their towns, expand their families, and welcome new immigrants.[8]

By the time Occom was born in 1723 to a Pequot mother and Mohegan father, the once-powerful tribes of New England, including the Mohegans, Pequots, and Narragansetts, had survived various attempts at genocide, including colonization, disease, and warfare.[9] In 1715, for example, the Connecticut General Assembly began gathering the Mohegans into villages "where they might have distinct properties . . . secured to the use of their respective families."[10] These northeastern tribes had also experienced less subtle forms of genocide that would hack away at the core of tribal structure by way of assimilation. Assimilation differs in theory and policy from disease and warfare, but it nonetheless eliminates Indians and diminishes tribes. One such assimilation tactic was conversion to Christianity. At a young age, Occom was influenced by the colonizer's religion, as the Great Awakening was taking place during most of his early years.[11]

In August 1759, Occom was ordained by the Suffolk Presbytery in Easthampton, Long Island.[12] Despite this accomplishment, he encountered daily reminders that the colonists were not interested in peaceful coexistence with American Indians. Occom had done many of the things the colonists enumerated as indicative of so-called civilized people, including converting to Christianity and living in a two-story clapboard house.

Occom was also an innovative educator and a multilingual entrepreneur. After finishing his formal education with the Reverend Eleazar Wheelock in the summer of 1749, he spent twelve years as a schoolteacher and minister to the Montauk Indians, marrying into the tribe and starting his family.[13]

Although Occom had many of the same experiences as civilized Europeans, he also embraced his Indian ways, not really knowing how to function entirely without them. However, the colonists would be satisfied only when Occom and his fellow Indians assimilated to the point that their own cultures were eradicated, erasing tribal identity and, in a perfect domino effect, causing tribal structure to disappear as well. The landscape would thus be cleared for expansion and perceived progress, since no one would be left to fight them. It also allowed for the introduction of Manifest Destiny into the nineteenth-century vernacular.[14] This concept has stubbornly wedged itself into the minds of many Americans, remaining there well into the twenty-first century and justifying the disparate treatment of American Indians.

Occom was keenly aware of the numerous obstacles to an undisturbed existence for Indian people in the Northeast. That existence was threatened daily, to the point that survival was not a passive pursuit but required planning, forethought, and vision. Occom was a visionary. His views seemed to disprove the claim of his mentor, Wheelock, who once wrote that "the Indian Natives of this Continent . . . have been perishing in vast numbers from Age to Age for lack of vision."[15]

Brothertown Genesis

Occom's vision eventually led to creation of the Brothertown Indian Nation.[16] The tribes that formed the Brothertown Nation were located in relatively close proximity to one other in Connecticut, Rhode Island, and Long Island. Occom, with the assistance of Montauk David Fowler (Occom's brother-in-law) and Mohegan Joseph Johnson (Occom's son-in-law), had originally envisioned Brothertown some years earlier, but the American Revolution interrupted their plans. Just prior to the war, Occom's followers moved to Oneida Country, in Upstate New York, where the Oneidas had agreed to provide the newcomers with a home. During the revolution, the location was not completely safe, despite the Indians' attempts at neutrality. Occom encouraged his brethren "not to intermeddle in these Quarrils among the White People."[17] Those who were already at their new settlement in New York moved east to Stockbridge, Massachusetts, where they waited out the war years with the Christian Stockbridge (Mohican) Indians.[18]

After the war, most of the Stockbridge Indians moved to New York with the Brothertown. Johnson, one of the originators of the plan for Brothertown, lost his life in 1776, just after receiving a letter of commendation from George Washington. As a result of Johnson's death and Fowler's quiet existence, Occom is generally credited with having single-handedly brought together the "Christian Indians of New England."[19]

Not surprising in retrospect, Oneida Country did not remain the haven for indigenous people Occom sought. The Brothertown, along with the Stockbridge and Oneida, began to seek land in the West. In April 1827, the General Assembly of New York gave the Brothertown Indians permission to sell their New York land.[20] The first Brothertowns arrived in Wisconsin in 1831, eventually making their new home on the east side of Lake Winnebago.[21]

Federal Indian Policy

Between the time the Brothertowns sold their land in New York and when they relocated to Wisconsin, Congress passed the Indian Removal Act.[22] The Brothertowns began thinking of ways to prevent themselves, too, from being removed farther west. In 1838, they asked Congress for U.S. citizenship and allotment of their reservation land, believing that as landowners, they could not be removed.[23]

On March 3, 1839, the Brothertown Indians became the first American Indian tribe in which all tribal members became U.S. citizens by the same congressional act. Their reservation land was allotted to individual tribal members. In August 2009, OFA would interpret the 1839 act as an act of termination that ended the tribe's sovereign nation status.[24]

The Administrative Federal Acknowledgment Process

This determination came after the Brothertown had spent three decades mired in the administrative FAP, which is unavailable to those tribes that Congress terminated. The Brothertown Indian Nation entered the process in April 1980, when it submitted its letter of intent to petition for acknowledgment to OFA (known at the time as the Branch of Acknowledgment and Research). In 1996, after years of compiling historical, anthropological, and genealogical research, the Brothertown Nation submitted its petition. OFA deemed the petition complete, and the wait began. In June 2008, the OFA staff (a historian, a genealogist, and an anthropologist) began reviewing the petition and the accompanying documentation.[25] The outdated but still circulated official guidelines prepared by OFA suggest that (1) petitioners can easily document a petition through members' volunteer efforts and (2) professional help is not necessary.[26] However, no petitioner has ever succeeded without extensive (and expensive) professional help and, in fact, OFA employs a staff of Ph.D.s to evaluate petitions. Over the years, the Brothertowns employed numerous anthropologists, historians, and genealogists to assist in the documentation of the petition.

The proposed finding issued by OFA in August 2009 details the ways in which the Brothertown petition failed on five of the seven mandatory criteria.[27] The first of the seven criteria requires evidence that "the petitioning group has been identified as an American Indian entity on a substantially continuous basis since 1900," and the Brothertown Nation was determined not to have met this requirement.[28] This criterion, along with the second and third criteria, have been modified by another section of the regulations if OFA determines that the tribe has "unambiguous previous federal acknowledgment."[29] In its review of the Brothertown petition, OFA made just such a determination, thereby changing the relevant dates of required evidence.[30]

Criterion (a)

Criterion (a) was modified to require that the tribe provide evidence between 1855, the date that OFA determined that the U.S. government had last acknowledged the tribe, and 1981. Unaware that OFA was going to find that the Brothertowns had unambiguous previous federal acknowledgment, the tribe failed to provide sufficient evidence for the additional forty-five years.[31] Ironically, while OFA claimed that the Brothertown petition failed to provide evidence for 1855–1981, the agency nonetheless determined that external observers had recognized the tribe as an American Indian entity since 1981. The proposed finding does not explain how the tribe disappeared for 125 years, only to reappear in 1981. This omission is consistent with OFA's policy that "the petitioner has the burden to present evidence that it meets the seven mandatory criteria in section 83.7."[32] Such a policy acts as official justification for the illogical conclusion that the Brothertowns had unambiguous previous federal acknowledgment until 1855 and again in 1981, but not in the intervening years. The tribe bears responsibility for providing evidence to support its existence in these years.[33]

Criterion (b)

The second criterion requires that the tribe prove that "a predominant portion of the petitioning group comprises a distinct community and has existed as a community from historical times until the present."[34] The Brothertown Nation failed to prove this criterion.[35] Like the first criterion, criterion (b) is also modified by previous federal acknowledgment. The tribe had to provide evidence to show that it comprises a distinct community "at present" rather than historically.[36] OFA determined that the Brothertown Nation "formally organized in 1980, and this event establishes a meaningful starting date for a contemporary period for evaluation." On the surface, this finding appears to help the tribe. However, the years it spent gathering evidence supporting a distinct community since "historical times" could have better been used focusing on the present. The OFA staff also spent significant time analyzing the historic period, as the proposed finding includes thirty-three pages of analysis covering the years 1831, 1839–1904, 1907–29, and 1930–60. This extended analysis is followed by only eight pages of analysis for 1980–2009.[37]

OFA's focus on 1980–2009 requires evidence for an additional thirteen years beyond the petition's 1996 submission. The regulations do not formally require a tribe to continue to submit evidence for each of the seven criteria as it waits decades in the notoriously long and drawn-out FAP. However, if a tribe fails to do so, it risks failing on at least one mandatory criterion.

Criterion (c)

The third criterion requires evidence that the tribe "has maintained political influence or authority over its members as an autonomous entity from historical times until the present."[38] OFA determined that the Brothertowns failed to prove criterion (c).[39] This criterion too is modified by previous federal acknowledgment, requiring the tribe to provide evidence from the point of last federal acknowledgment (1855) to the present. The proposed finding notes that "the evaluation of this petitioner considers whether the petitioning group was able after its loss of Federal status to maintain political influence over its members through control of local civil government, especially whether it was able to use public office to govern a population mostly of Brothertown Indians in the township created from the former Brothertown Indian Reservation."[40] The OFA staff determined that "after 1839 the Brothertown descendants organized almost exclusively to pursue various claims against the Federal Government."[41]

Criterion (e)

The fifth criterion requires the tribe to prove that its "membership consists of individuals who descend from a historical Indian tribe or from historical Indian tribes which combined and functioned as a single autonomous political entity."[42] The Brothertown Indians failed to meet criterion (e).[43] This failure stems from OFA's determination that the Brothertown Nation descends from the historical Brothertown Indian tribe of Wisconsin. This tribe evolved from the Brothertown Indian tribe of New York "as a large portion of the tribe that moved from New York to Wisconsin."[44] But a proper historical analysis of the tribe would have revealed that there is but one Brothertown Indian Nation, the tribe founded by Occom on November 7, 1785.

As a result, OFA took issue with the fact that the Brothertown constitution allows enrollment for direct descendants of tribal members from any one of three tribal rolls: (1) the 1839 allotment list, (2) the 1901 tribal roll, or (3) the 1967 tribal roll. The Department of the Interior considers only the 1839 document to be a membership list of the historical Brothertown Indian tribe of Wisconsin. That list identifies individuals who received land allotments as members of the Wisconsin Brothertown Indian tribe. OFA considered the 1901 and 1967 rolls descendancy lists rather than a list of tribal members.[45] This distinction is important to support OFA's conclusion that the Brothertown Nation failed to provide evidence of existence or culture or governance between 1855 and 1981. A tribe would have had tribal rolls, but the Brothertown documents from 1901 and 1967 were not tribal rolls but rather lists of descendants of the historic Brothertown Indian Nation. For purposes of federal acknowledgment, "American Indian" is a political classification rather than a racial classification. A tribal roll would support the claim of Brothertown governance as a political entity, whereas a descendancy list would support OFA's claim that the Brothertown Indian Nation in Wisconsin is but a group of Indian descendants rather than a tribe worthy of a government-to-government relationship with the United States.[46]

Regardless of the roll from which a tribal member claims descendancy, the Brothertown constitution requires that each member also descend from one of the families mentioned in the appendix of an 1899 book by W. DeLoss Love, *Samson Occom and the Christian Indians of New England*. OFA staff took issue with the fact that some of the people on this list were of the Brothertown Indian tribe of New York rather than the Brothertown Indian tribe of Wisconsin.[47] Again, the belief that there are two separate Brothertown tribes is a misinterpretation of Brothertown history.

OFA determined that many of the current tribal members should not appear on the tribal roll because they descend from a separate Brothertown tribe of New York.[48] In addition to this flawed analysis, the proposed finding pointed out that "there is no criterion excluding members who marry outside the group." It is unclear why OFA considered this an important point, except that the 1839 allotment list excluded women who had married outside the tribe. Such criteria, like blood-quantum requirements, diminish tribes by decreasing the number of people who qualify for enrollment. Like assimilation, this practice supports federal Indian policies that have as their end goal eliminating Indians and tribes, and OFA is but an arm of the federal government and thus doing its bidding.[49]

The proposed finding's analysis of criterion (e) refers to interviews conducted by Dr. Wendi-Starr Brown, OFA anthropologist, during a 2008 visit to Wisconsin. According to the document, "What little information was obtained about ancestors was primarily anecdotal 'family tradition.' If information on the relatives discussed in the oral histories is not provided elsewhere in the record, the petitioner needs to provide photocopies of birth, marriage, and death records, or other reliable evidence to substantiate claims made in the oral histories."[50] Yet six years earlier, in Brown's dissertation about her tribe, the Narragansetts, she wrote, "One of the core issues of Narragansett identity has to do with the maintenance of tradition. From First Contact until the present day, so says the oral tradition I grew up with, the Narragansetts preserved the traditions of the pre-Contact Narragansetts through song, story and dance. Non-Indian historians or researchers who said otherwise were either conspiring to deny Narragansetts their true history or wanted to prove that the Narragansetts were not really Indians at all, but were at best Black people with a trace of Native ancestry."[51] To support the conclusion that the Brothertowns failed on this criterion, Brown reconciled her willingness to accept her own oral tradition at face value with no need for documentation with her insistence that the Brothertown Indians be forced to document their oral traditions with "reliable evidence."[52] Such evidence is frequently not present in American Indian families. For example, in my mother's family (the Indian side of my family), I am in the first generation to have birth certificates issued at birth. My mother did not have one until it was issued in the 1970s, many years after her birth.

Criterion (g)

The seventh criterion, which the Brothertown Nation failed to prove, requires that neither the petitioner nor its members are the subject of congressional legislation that has expressly terminated or forbidden the federal relationship.[53] The regulations do not provide guidance on what types of evidence satisfy this criterion. The Brothertown petition provided little supporting evidence because as far as the tribe was concerned, there was no issue with this criterion. Instead, the OFA staff found that "Congress in the Act of 1839 brought Federal recognition of the relationship with the Brothertown Indian tribe of Wisconsin to an end."[54]

The OFA analysis of this issue is straightforward, relying on the language in the act to find "termination" despite the fact that the word is absent from the congressional record. The OFA staff found that "Congress did not compel the Brothertown Indians to become citizens rather than tribal members, but allowed them a way to achieve citizenship."[55] Citizenship supposedly led to the tribe's "rights as a tribe"—specifically, its power to act as a political and governmental entity—to "cease and determine."[56] This statement contrasts with the 1830 Treaty of Dancing Rabbit Creek, which ceded the last of the Choctaws' tribal land in Mississippi and allowed for their removal nine years prior to the Brothertown act.[57] Rather than requiring that all Choctaw remove west, the treaty allowed individual families to stay in Mississippi. Those who stayed, however, would receive state citizenship and lose their trust status in five years.[58]

In an 1855 report to Congress, Commissioner George Washington Manypenny said that the "Brothertown Indians 'became citizens' by the Act of 1839 and that 'the department has not exercised any supervision over them' since the allotment of their lands. Commissioner Manypenny concluded that by the terms of the Act of 1839 the Brothertown Indians 'lost . . . their relations to the government as an Indian tribe.'"[59] The OFA staff noted that an 1878 congressional act authorizing the General Land Office to give "full title to the Brothertown Indians" of land previously reserved to them by treaty was not a restoration of the federal relationship with the

Brothertowns as an Indian tribe. Rather, its purpose was to "correct a problem that had arisen in the implementation of the Act of 1839."[60]

Muddled Analysis

The OFA staff determined that the 1878 act's reference to Brothertown Indians as individuals rather than as a tribal entity is contrary to its conclusion for criterion (e), which requires evidence that the "membership consists of individuals who descend from a historical Indian tribe or from historical Indian tribes which combined and functioned as a single autonomous political entity." The Brothertown Nation failed on this criterion because OFA concluded that many of the current tribal members trace their ancestry to the Brothertown tribe of New York rather than Wisconsin. The contradiction exists in the assertion that for one purpose, individual Indians who remained behind in New York after the tribe's migration to Wisconsin could be a tribe (thus creating two tribes when there is only one), while for another purpose individual Indians are not a tribe. Such contradictions exist throughout the administrative FAP because OFA has been empowered not only to grant sovereign nation status to tribes but also to define the terminology and assign weight and relevance to evidence that will lead to either a positive or negative determination. The lack of objectivity in the administrative process is frequently overshadowed by the evidentiary burden and length of time the process takes. The OFA conclusions are based on that which helps support a negative proposed finding rather than a consistent, logical, fair, and objective analysis. In the case of the Brothertown Nation, OFA reinterpreted conclusions previously issued by the Solicitor's Office.

The scant evidence the Brothertowns submitted to OFA in support of criterion (g) consisted of a copy of a 1993 memorandum written by the acting associate solicitor, Division of Indian Affairs, of the Department of the Interior.[61] The 1993 memorandum was a follow-up to a 1990 letter issued by the Office of the Solicitor, Department of the Interior that detailed the solicitor's determination that citizenship did not result in termination.[62] To the contrary, the Brothertown Indians were federally acknowledged for 140 years after receiving citizenship. According to the 1990 letter,

> A judicial standard for determining termination of tribal existence does not exist, but clearly the standard for such a change in status should be as exacting as the standard for a finding that a reservation has been disestablished. The judicial standard for disestablishment

requires a clear expression of congressional intent. . . . Applying that standard to the Act of 1839, it falls short of a clear expression of congressional intent to terminate or to forbid the federal relationship. . . . Such a lack of clear intent to terminate should not be viewed as indicating that the Brothertowns were wrongfully terminated by the government. . . . The political status of the Brothertowns changed after the Act of 1839. However, that change should not be termed termination when examined in light of the 1978 regulations dealing with acknowledgment.[63]

The 1990 letter referenced a 1979 letter from the Office of Indian Services that listed the Brothertowns as one of the "unacknowledged Indian groups" in the Minneapolis area and that "may be interpreted to support the efforts of the Brothertown group by noting that in 1979, the BIA did not think of them as terminated so as to preclude them from using the process."[64] The relevant distinction here is between an "unacknowledged Indian group" and a "terminated tribe." Unacknowledged groups are eligible for the administrative process; terminated tribes are not because OFA may not reverse an act of Congress.

In the 1993 memorandum, the Solicitor's Office stated that it found "no reason to disagree with the [1990 letter] on this matter." Officials reasoned that "since we believe that the Brothertown tribe was not terminated by the Act of March 3, 1839, the group calling themselves the Brothertown Indians is eligible to petition the Department for federal acknowledgment as an Indian tribe pursuant to 25 C.F.R. 83. The process is open to all non–federally recognized Indian groups whose tribal existence has not been terminated by Congress and who wish to establish government-to-government relations with the United States."[65]

As a result of the 1990 and 1993 documents, the Brothertown Indians entered the administrative process, where they remained for nearly twenty years. In 2009, however, the OFA devised a new interpretation of the opinions from the Solicitor's Office. OFA conceded that the letter and the memorandum "considered the question of whether or not the group of Brothertown Indians could petition for Federal acknowledgment as an Indian tribe."[66] However, OFA claimed that the Solicitor's Office had misunderstood the regulations and that terminated tribes are not forbidden from entering the FAP.[67] Under criterion (g), however, a tribe cannot succeed in the administrative process if it was terminated. Therefore, the OFA position eludes logic. Why would a terminated tribe enter the long and expensive administrative process if it could not possibly succeed? Such a tribe has before it only one option: to ask Congress for an act restoring the tribe's status.[68] As William W. Quinn Jr. noted in 1992, "One must be careful to distinguish at the outset between 'acknowledgment' and 'restoration' of Indian groups. With regard to the latter, during the 'termination' phase of American Indian policy in the 1950s, Congress terminated the government-to-government relationship of several Indian tribes. . . . The termination policy subsequently failed. The tribes once terminated have gradually been 'restored' to their former legal statuses as federally acknowledged via congressional legislation, since the executive is precluded from acknowledging a congressionally terminated tribe."[69]

Congressional (Re)Recognition

It remains to be seen how congressional restoration will apply to the Brothertown Indians and other tribes that were victims not of the 1950s termination policies but rather of a much earlier, less explicit termination. The congressional termination of the Brothertowns was in fact cloaked in 1830s assimilation rhetoric of citizenship and land allotment.[70]

The issue of congressional termination of the Brothertown Indians' tribal status was addressed on January 4, 2010, at a formal, on-the-record technical assistance meeting held at the Department of the Interior. Meeting attendees included several Brothertown Indian Nation members, the OFA staff who had worked on the proposed finding, and a representative from the Solicitor's Office.[71] Upon being questioned about the significance of the 1990 letter and the 1993 memorandum, OFA staff historian John Dibbern explained OFA's position: The solicitor's memo addressed only the issue of whether the Brothertowns were deserving of immediate acknowledgment because of prior federal acknowledgment.[72]

The Solicitor's Office Response

Solicitor's Office representative Jane Smith confirmed this interpretation, disagreeing with the tribe's assertion that the process is not open to tribes that have been terminated by Congress. According to Smith, "The process is open to tribes that have been terminated, but acknowledgment of tribes that have been terminated is not possible."[73] Smith was then asked, "Why would a tribe go through the process—this very long expensive process—knowing that it was going to fail on 25 C.F.R. 83.7(g), which is the termination question. If they knew they were going to fail on it, why would they go through the process? It seems like any tribe that could determine that it had been terminated by Congress would simply not approach OFA." When Smith failed to immediately answer the question, Brothertown chair Richard Schadewald asked her whether she agreed with that statement. Smith replied, "Tribes that believe they had been terminated by Congress would look at (g) and figure that they wouldn't be able to make it—yeah."[74] Of course, if a tribe is in receipt of Solicitor's Office opinions that state the contrary, it might spend decades in the administrative process.

OFA insists on an interpretation of the Solicitor's Office letter and memorandum that runs contrary to the documents' explicit language. A full analysis of what may have led to this interpretation requires a consideration of several pieces of correspondence. A March 1979 letter from the Great Lakes Agency of the BIA to an individual researching the Brothertowns stated that "the Brotherton's [sic] are Federally recognized."[75] Just over a year later, the acting director of the Office of Indian Services wrote a memorandum to the Minneapolis area director stating that "the Brotherton [sic] is not a federally-acknowledged tribe."[76] What happened between March 1979 and March 1980?

The Administrative Federal (De)Acknowledgment Process

What clearly did not happen was the passage of a congressional act terminating the Brothertown Nation. What did happen, according to proposed finding, began in the prior century, when Congress passed the 1839 act that caused the Brothertowns' "rights as a tribe" and their "power of making or executing their own laws [to] cease."[77] Tribe members were made U.S. citizens, and their reservation land was allotted to individual tribal members. But federal government services to the tribe did not cease until 1980. The relationship continued, and the BIA's Great Lakes Agency, located in Ashland, Wisconsin, oversaw the tribe's affairs, frequently dealing with members seeking education assistance.[78] Felix Cohen's criteria in support of federal acknowledgment, which include "relations with the federal government," would seem to support the Brothertowns' claim that it is a tribe deserving of a government-to-government relationship with the United States.[79] Instead, OFA expressly discounts such evidence of tribal status.[80] So, while the Department of the Interior recognized the Brothertowns in 1979 and stopped recognizing the tribe in 1980, OFA insists on tracing the Brothertowns' terminated status to the 1839 act.

Congress has plenary power over Indian tribes.[81] It has delegated certain aspects of this authority to the Department of the Interior. For example, the department administers the FAP.[82] At no point, however, has Congress delegated to the department or the BIA the authority to terminate a tribe's status, yet that is exactly what happened to the Brothertown Nation. Mindful of the fact that only Congress may terminate a tribe, OFA did not want to point to illegal administrative action in 1979 or 1980 that resulted in the Brothertowns' terminated status. It had to point to an act of Congress. Conveniently, the 1839 act could be interpreted as an act of termination. The problem is that the 1839 act did not explicitly terminate the Brothertowns' tribal status. Termination is too significant an act to be found between the lines.[83]

Brothertowns' Response

Having failed on criterion (g), the Brothertown Indian Nation now faces an uncertain future as it continues in the administrative FAP. Having received a six-month extension to submit a response to the proposed finding, the tribe had an August 23, 2010, deadline to reply. OFA probably expected a detailed response to each of the criticisms, which the Brothertowns would have submitted if there were any chance for a final determination that differed substantively from the proposed finding. But that was not possible. OFA could not issue a positive final determination because it does not have the delegated authority to reverse an act of Congress, and the OFA had already taken the position that Congress had terminated the Brothertowns in 1839.

Instead, the tribe's response to the proposed finding argued that OFA's determination that the Brothertowns failed on criterion (g) was the equivalent of OFA stating that the Brothertowns were ineligible for the administrative process. Therefore, the tribe should be formally released from the process so that it could pursue the congressional route to federal acknowledgment. Without such a release, the Brothertowns would be forced to exhaust the administrative remedies before approaching Congress. The Brothertowns' abbreviated response to the proposed finding is also recognition of the fact that the submission of evidence following a proposed finding is not an appeals process. The same historian, genealogist, and anthropologist who wrote the proposed finding will review any additional evidence submitted by the tribe, and for all practical purposes, they have already made up their minds.

Federal Acknowledgment and
Twenty-First-Century Indian Policy

According to the BIA's website, the United States had 566 federally acknowledged tribes as of September 2011. Between 1978 and September 2008, 332 tribes had filed letters of intent to petition for acknowledgment through the administrative process. Fewer than twenty tribes have succeeded.[84] Since 1978, OFA has established new precedents for analysis and evaluation, increasing the evidentiary burden. Recent petitions dwarf those submitted in the earlier years of the acknowledgment regulations. OFA's first summary of evidence and recommendations for a proposed finding (Grand Traverse Band of Ottawa and Chippewa, 1979) totaled 67 pages. In 2001, its negative proposed finding for the Nipmuc exceeded 450 pages. In response, the Nipmuc submitted narrative reports that totaled 900 pages and a digital database containing in excess of 15,000 documents. OFA issued a negative final determination for the Nipmuc.

In 1890, the Census Bureau declared the West settled and the frontier closed.[85] More than a century later, the frontier still exists. It is the line that divides Indians and non-Indians. It is seen in the laws, regulations, and processes that give the federal government authority to determine who is an Indian and who is not as well as which tribes are granted a government-to-government relationship with the United States. OFA keeps the frontier in check by controlling the number of tribes the federal government recognizes. These are the "federally acknowledged" tribes, and this is just the latest federal Indian policy crafted to deal with the "Indian problem."[86]

While policies such as the General Allotment Act targeted the extermination of individual Indians via assimilation, others targeted entire tribes. During the termination policy era (1953–68), Congress ended the government-to-government relationship with 109 tribes. Indians whose tribes were terminated were encouraged to relocate to cities and assimilate into mainstream culture.[87] The current policy period is frequently called "tribal self-determination."[88] This is actually an outdated notion that never came to fruition. Instead, there are hundreds of tribes vying for official status as domestic dependent nations under the FAP. Those that already have that status do not know when that status will be terminated by the federal government. They live from day to day as the most disadvantaged group in the country. American Indians have the lowest life expectancy, the highest unemployment, and the lowest-quality housing and education of any group in the United States.[89]

When the Brothertown Indian Nation was formed in 1785, the plan was to overcome many of the hurdles placed before Indians. This remained the plan as the tribe migrated to Wisconsin in 1830, asking for citizenship and land allotment less than a decade later in an attempt to control their own destiny. The unique way in which the Brothertowns chose to embrace sovereignty created a history that does not translate well into the seven mandatory criteria espoused by Congress as proof of continuing tribal status. In this era of tribal self-determination, all tribes must choose between continuing as domestic dependent nations, beholden to congressional whim, or questioning the wisdom of federal acknowledgment. This status does, after all, give the federal government the final word on who is an Indian and what is an Indian tribe. That idea somehow seems misplaced, yet it provides the narrative dimension of the structural violence of not just the FAP but the concept of acknowledgment. The individual stories that have come out of the concept and the process need to be told, because those who cannot remember the past are condemned to repeat it.[90] As an American Indian woman, daughter, sister, wife, and legal scholar, I share in the responsibility to take control of our histories and our futures. That includes regaining control over the process of defining who we are.

Postscript

On September 4, 2012, Donald E. Laverdure, acting assistant secretary—Indian Affairs, issued the Department of Interior's Final Determination of the Brothertown Indian Nation's petition for acknowledgment under 25 C.F.R. Part 83.[91] Over three years had passed since the negative Preliminary Finding. What was expected was a mere confirmation of that Finding, failure on five of the seven mandatory criteria. What the department delivered, however, was something unexpected: failure based *solely* on criterion (g). The department confirmed only part of its original finding, that the Brothertown Indian Nation "was the subject of congressional legislation that expressly terminated or forbade the Federal relationship."[92]

It is the position of the department that the Brothertown Indian Nation was previously acknowledged by the federal government. However, when the tribe received U.S. citizenship and land allotment under a congressional act in 1839, this act was also an act of termination, despite the lack of wording to that effect in the act. The department's Final Determination further noted that, despite its Preliminary Finding, "neither the Department nor any other party should rely upon the factual findings, analysis, and conclusions in the Proposed Findings that do not directly pertain to 25 C.F.R. section 83.7(g)."[93]

Because the Brothertown Indian Nation failed on criterion (g), the Department of the Interior may not acknowledge the tribe through the administrative process. The department concluded the Final Determination by noting, "the Brothertown may wish to seek restoration through Congress."[94] The Brothertown spent thirty years in the administrative federal acknowledgment process. Over half of that *followed* the determination by the Solicitor's Office that the 1839 act was not an act of termination. Obviously, this is time that would have been better spent working toward congressional restoration, another long and complicated process. Instead, we spent it waiting, certain that, if nothing else, we would not fail on criterion (g).

Notes

1. Jessica R. Cattelino, "The Double Bind of American Indian Need-Based Sovereignty," *Cultural Anthropology* 25, no. 2 (2010): 235–62, 237.

2. Kathleen A. Brown-Perez, "'A Reflection of Our National Character': Structurally and Culturally Violent Federal Policies and the Elusive Quest for Federal Acknowledgment," *Landscapes of Violence* 2, no. 1 (2012): 5. Available at: http://scholarworks.umass.edu/lov/vol2/iss1/5.

3. U.S. Department of the Interior, Bureau of Indian Affairs, Office of Federal Acknowledgment, *Proposed Finding, Brothertown Indian Nation* (2009). See also Gale Courey Toensing, "BIA Denies Brothertown Federal Acknowledgment," *Indian Country Today*, September 11, 2009 ("The Brothertown Indian Nation is determined to continue its quest for federal acknowledgment despite a BIA preliminary ruling to deny them federal status.").

4. Indian Child Welfare Act, 25 U.S.C. 1902. Ironically, the Indian Child Welfare Act also declared "that Congress, through statutes, treaties, and the general course of dealing with Indian tribes, has assumed the responsibility for the protection and *preservation of Indian tribes* and their resources" (emphasis added).

5. Native American Graves Protection and Repatriation Act, 25 U.S.C. 3001 et seq. "Indian tribe" means any tribe, band, nation, or other organized group or community of Indians . . . which is recognized as eligible for the special programs and services provided by the United States to Indians because of their status as Indians (25 U.S.C. 3001, Section 2[7]).

6. According to the U.S. Department of the Interior, Bureau of Indian Affairs website, as of September 22, 2008 (the last time the list was updated), there were

332 tribes petitioning for federal acknowledgment. Five petitions have been at least partially processed, bringing the total waiting to have their petitions reviewed to 327 as of October 2010 (http://www.bia.gov/WhoWeAre/AS-IA /OFA/index.htm). (There are also unrecognized tribes that have this status either as a result of deciding to not petition for acknowledgment at all or because they have been denied acknowledgment in the FAP.) Considering OFA's history of inconsistently interpreting the criteria and the submitted evidence as well as OFA's failure to take into account contemporary tribal society, most of the tribes now awaiting "active consideration" will fail in their quest for federal acknowledgment. See Rachael Paschal, "The Imprimatur of Recognition: American Indian Tribes and the Federal Acknowledgment Process," *Washington Law Review* 66 (1991): 209.

7. Samson Occom Journal, November 7, 1785, Rauner Special Collections Library, Dartmouth College, Hanover, New Hampshire.

8. Brad D. E. Jarvis, *The Brothertown Nation of Indians: Land Ownership and Nationalism in Early America, 1740–1840* (Lincoln: University of Nebraska Press, 2010), 7.

9. Ibid., 22.

10. Ibid., 27.

11. Ibid., 34.

12. Harold Blodgett, *Samson Occom: The Biography of an Indian Preacher* (Hanover, N.H.: Dartmouth College Publications, 1935), 51. See also W. DeLoss Love, *Samson Occom and the Christian Indians of New England* (Boston: Pilgrim, 1899), 50–52.

13. Love, *Samson Occom*, 42–55. The Reverend Eleazar Wheelock was the founder of Dartmouth College. From 1765 to 1768, Occom visited England and Scotland on a fund-raising tour Wheelock suggested as a means of founding a school for Indian youth. He raised £12,000, a record sum for a colonial charity (equivalent to $1.9 million in 2012). In 1769, Wheelock redirected the funds to found Dartmouth. In a letter of disgust, Occom told Wheelock, "I verily thought once that your Institution was Intended Purely for the poor Indians—with this thought I Cheerfully Ventured my Body & Soul, left my Country my poor young Family all my Friends and Relations, to sail over the Boisterous Seas to England, to help forward your School" (Samson Occom to Eleazar Wheelock, July 24, 1771, Samson Occom Letters, Rauner Special Collections Library, Dartmouth College, Hanover, New Hampshire).

14. John L. O'Sullivan, "The Great Nation of Futurity," *United States Democratic Review* 6 (1839): 426–30.

15. Eleazar Wheelock to George Whitefield, March 1, 1756, Occom Letters.

16. Colin G. Calloway, *The American Revolution in Indian Country: Crisis and Diversity in Native American Communities* (Cambridge: Cambridge University Press, 1995), 91–92.

17. Love, *Samson Occom*, 228–29.

18. Calloway, *American Revolution in Indian Country*, 92.

19. Love, *Samson Occom*.

20. Ibid., 324.

21. Ibid. See also Jean M. O'Brien, *Firsting and Lasting: Writing Indians Out of Existence in New England* (Minneapolis: University of Minnesota Press, 2010), 142.

22. Russell Thornton, "Cherokee Population Losses during the Trail of Tears: A New Perspective and a New Estimate," *Ethnohistory* 31 (1984): 289–300.

23. Jarvis, *Brothertown Nation of Indians*, 222.

24. U.S. Department of the Interior, Bureau of Indian Affairs, Office of Federal Acknowledgment, *Proposed Finding*, 133–49.

25. Ibid., 2–3.

26. U.S. Department of the Interior, Bureau of Indian Affairs, Branch of Acknowledgment and Research, *Official Guidelines to the Federal Acknowledgment Regulations*, 25 C.F.R. 83, September 1997, 18.

27. The Brothertown petition proved the fourth and sixth criteria. The fourth criterion requires the tribe to provide a copy of its governing document, including its membership criteria. The sixth criterion requires that the tribe's membership be composed principally of persons who are not members of any acknowledged tribe. OFA determined that no one on the Brothertown roll was also on the Oneida tribal roll (Wisconsin), the Stockbridge Munsee roll (Wisconsin), or the Lower Sioux roll (Minnesota). See U.S. Department of the Interior, Bureau of Indian Affairs, Office of Federal Acknowledgment, *Proposed Finding*, 107–8, 132.

28. 25 C.F.R. 83.7(a); U.S. Department of the Interior, Bureau of Indian Affairs, Office of Federal Acknowledgment, *Proposed Finding*, 11–23.

29. 25 C.F.R. 83.8.

30. U.S. Department of the Interior, Bureau of Indian Affairs, Office of Federal Acknowledgment, *Proposed Finding*, 5–7.

31. 25 C.F.R. 83.7(a). Proving the first criterion requires evidence such as (1) identification as an Indian entity by federal authorities; (2) relationships with state governments based on identification of the group as Indian; (3) identification as an Indian entity by anthropologists, historians, and/or other scholars. Evidence supporting this criterion may also include (1) dealings with a county, parish, or other local government in a relationship based on the group's Indian identity; (2) identification as an Indian entity in newspapers and books; and

(3) identification as an Indian entity in relationships with Indian tribes or with national, regional, or state Indian organizations.

32. U.S. Department of the Interior, Bureau of Indian Affairs, Office of Federal Acknowledgment, *Notice of Proposed Finding* 4310-G1-P), 4.

33. Paschal, "Imprimatur of Recognition," 216.

34. 25 C.F.R. 83.7(b).

35. U.S. Department of the Interior, Bureau of Indian Affairs, Office of Federal Acknowledgment, *Notice of Proposed Finding*, 24–67.

36. 25 C.F.R. 83.7(b)(1). Relevant evidence for this criterion includes (1) significant rates of marriage within the group and/or patterned out-marriages with other Indian populations; (2) significant social relationships connecting individual members; (3) significant rates of informal social interaction that exist broadly among the members of a group; (4) a significant degree of shared or cooperative labor or other economic activity; (5) evidence of strong patterns of discrimination; (6) shared sacred or secular ritual activity encompassing most of the group; (7) cultural patterns shared among a significant portion of the group that differ from those of the non-Indian populations with whom it interacts; (8) the persistence of a named, collective identity continuously over a period of more than fifty years, notwithstanding changes in name; and (9) a demonstration of historical political influence. The second criterion can also be proven with evidence that (1) more than 50 percent of the members reside in a geographical area exclusively or almost exclusively composed of members of the group, and the balance of the group maintains consistent interaction with some members of the community; (2) at least 50 percent of the marriages in the group are between members of the group; (3) at least 50 percent of the group members maintain distinct cultural patterns; and (4) there are distinct community social institutions encompassing most of the members. See 25 C.F.R. 83.7(b)(2).

37. U.S. Department of the Interior, Bureau of Indian Affairs, Office of Federal Acknowledgment, *Notice of Proposed Finding*, 26–67.

38. 25 C.F.R. 83.7(c).

39. U.S. Department of the Interior, Bureau of Indian Affairs, Office of Federal Acknowledgment, *Notice of Proposed Finding*, 68–106.

40. 25 C.F.R. 83.8(d)(3); 25 C.F.R. 83.7(c). This criterion is proven by showing authoritative, knowledgeable external sources' substantially continuous historical identification of leaders and/or a governing body that exercise political influence or authority, together with one of the following: (1) the group can mobilize significant numbers of members and significant resources from members for group purposes; (2) most of the membership considers issues acted on or actions taken by

leaders to be important; (3) there is widespread knowledge, communication, and involvement in political processes by most of the group's members; (4) the group meets the second criterion at more than a minimal level; and (5) internal conflicts show controversy over valued group goals, decisions, etc.

41. U.S. Department of the Interior, Bureau of Indian Affairs, Office of Federal Acknowledgment, *Notice of Proposed Finding*, 69.

42. 25 C.F.R. 83.7(e). Acceptable evidence includes (1) rolls prepared by the secretary of the interior for the purposes of distributing claims money, providing allotments, or other purposes; or (2) government records identifying present members or their ancestors as being descendants of a historical tribe. See 25 C.F.R. 83.7(e)(1).

43. U.S. Department of the Interior, Bureau of Indian Affairs, Office of Federal Acknowledgment, *Notice of Proposed Finding*, 109–31.

44. Ibid., 109.

45. Ibid., 109–10.

46. See Sara-Larus Tolley, *Quest for Federal Acknowledgment: California's Honey Lake Maidus* (Norman: University of Oklahoma Press, 2006), 40 (quoting the BAR): "Generally, the following [types of petitioners] cannot be acknowledged [as tribes] under the 25 C.F.R. 83 regulations because they would not meet all seven mandatory criteria: Individual Indian descendants; The descendants of one Indian ancestor (a "lineage") who became separated from his or her tribe and now has many descendants; Groups of "Indian descendants" of one historic tribe who are no longer in tribal relations."

47. Ibid., 125.

48. Ibid., 110. ("1,593 of the petitioner's 3,137 members [51 percent] have documented descent, generation by generation, from a member of the historical Brothertown Indian tribe of Wisconsin as identified on the 1839 Allotment List.")

49. Compare this to the one-drop rule, which expanded the number of people who would be considered African American, lest they fool the general public into believing they were deserving of the privileges of whiteness.

50. U.S. Department of the Interior, Bureau of Indian Affairs, Office of Federal Acknowledgment, *Notice of Proposed Finding*, 122.

51. Wendi-Starr Brown, "The Church Is the People: The Role of a Christian Church in a Native American Community" (Ph.D. diss., Temple University, 2002), 10.

52. U.S. Department of the Interior, Bureau of Indian Affairs, Office of Federal Acknowledgment, *Notice of Proposed Finding*, 122.

53. 25 C.F.R. 83.7(g); U.S. Department of the Interior, Bureau of Indian Affairs, Office of Federal Acknowledgment, *Notice of Proposed Finding*, 133–49.

54. U.S. Department of the Interior, Bureau of Indian Affairs, Office of Federal Acknowledgment, *Notice of Proposed Finding*, 133.

55. Ibid., 135.

56. Ibid., 133.

57. Philip Lujan and L. Brooks Hill, "The Mississippi Choctaw: A Case Study of Tribal Identity Problems," *American Indian Culture and Research Journal* 4 (1980): 37–53.

58. Ibid., 39.

59. U.S. Department of the Interior, Bureau of Indian Affairs, Office of Federal Acknowledgment, *Notice of Proposed Finding*, 143. The OFA staff determined that 1855 was also the last year that external observers acknowledged the Brothertown Indians as a tribe.

60. Ibid., 144.

61. Ibid., 133; David C. Etheridge to Assistant Secretary—Indian Affairs, August 19, 1993 (in author's possession).

62. Marcia M. Kimball to Earl J. Barlow, August 28, 1990 (in author's possession). Similarly, the Indian Citizenship Act of 1924 did not result in the termination or deacknowledgment of any tribes.

63. Ibid.

64. Edmund Manydeeds to John Turcheneske, March 5, 1979 (in author's possession).

65. David C. Etheridge to Assistant Secretary—Indian Affairs, August 19, 1993 (in author's possession).

66. U.S. Department of the Interior, Bureau of Indian Affairs, Office of Federal Acknowledgment, *Proposed Finding*, 147.

67. Ibid. ("The regulations do not prevent groups that were terminated or forbidden a Federal relationship from petitioning for Federal acknowledgment, but from being acknowledged through the administrative process.")

68. Elizabeth S. Grobsmith and Beth R. Ritter, "The Ponca Tribe of Nebraska: The Process of Restoration of a Federally Terminated Tribe," *Human Organization* 51 (1992): 13, quoting Walter Mills. ("Since termination is no longer Federal policy and Congress has restored to Federal status most of the previously terminated tribes . . . in terms of equity there is little basis for leaving those terminated tribes without a Federal relationship [if they desire it restored] while the large majority of tribes still enjoy their special status as Indians. No discernable distinctions appear between those tribes which were terminated and those which were not.")

69. William W. Quinn Jr., "Federal Acknowledgment of American Indian Tribes: Authority, Judicial Interposition, and 25 C.F.R. §83," *American Indian Law Review* 17 (1991): 42 n. 21.

70. Act of Congress, March 3, 1839, c. 83, 7 (5 Stat. 351), concerning the Brothertown Indians.

71. Brothertown representatives included chair Richard Schadewald and the tribe's Federal Acknowledgment Committee chair (Kathleen A. Brown-Perez) and members (Phyllis Tousey, Jessica Ryan, and Edward L. Welsh Jr.), all of whom are attorneys. Arlinda Locklear (Lumbee), attorney, was also in attendance at the Brothertown table as an "interested observer." OFA staff in attendance included the team that worked on the Brothertown petition and wrote the proposed finding: Jan Earle, genealogist; John Dibbern, historian; and Wendi-Starr Brown, anthropologist. Also in attendance was Lee Fleming, director of OFA, and George Roth, moderator. Jane Smith represented the Office of the Solicitor.

72. U.S. Department of the Interior, Bureau of Indian Affairs, Office of Federal Acknowledgment, "Formal Meeting Transcript," January 4, 2010, 104.

73. Ibid., 105–6.

74. Ibid., 106

75. U.S. Department of the Interior, Bureau of Indian Affairs, to John Turcheneske, March 5, 1979 (in author's possession).

76. Acting Director, Office of Indian Services, to Minneapolis Area Director, March 24, 1980 (in author's possession).

77. U.S. Department of the Interior, Bureau of Indian Affairs, Office of Federal Acknowledgment, *Proposed Finding*, 133.

78. Edmund Manydeeds to John Turcheneske, March 5, 1979 (in author's possession). See also Joe Mooney to Martha Brown, May 12, 1980 (in Martha Brown's possession).

79. Felix S. Cohen, *Handbook of Federal Indian Law* (Washington, D.C.: U.S. Government Printing Office, 1945).

80. Paschal, "Imprimatur of Recognition," 210–11, 220.

81. "Plenary authority over the tribal relations of the Indians has been exercised by Congress from the beginning, and the power has always been deemed to be a political one, not subject to be controlled by the judicial department of the government" (*Worcester v. Georgia*, 31 U.S. 515 [1832]).

82. *United Tribe of Shawnee Indians v. U.S.*, 253 F. 3d 543 (10th Cir. 2001).

83. Felix S. Cohen, *Handbook of Federal Indian Law* (Washington, D.C.: U.S. Government Printing Office, 1945), 272. ("Generally speaking, the termination of tribal existence is shown positively by act of Congress, treaty provision, or tribal action or negatively by the cessation of collective action and collective recognition.")

84. U.S. Department of the Interior, Bureau of Indian Affairs, Office of Federal Acknowledgment, "Who We Are," www.bia.gov/WhoWeAre/AS-IA/OFA/index.htm.

85. Frederick Jackson Turner, *The Significance of the Frontier in American History* (Chicago: American Historical Association, 1893).

86. Lyman Abbott, "Our Indian Problem," *North American Review* 167 (1898): 719–28.

87. See Arthur V. Watkins, "Termination of Federal Supervision: The Removal of Restrictions over Indian Property and Person," *Annals of the American Academy of Political and Social Science* 311 (1957): 47–55. ("Thinking constructively of the Indian as a fellow American we are now seeking to assure him of equality in the enjoyment and responsibilities of our national citizenship. Congress has called for termination of federal supervision over him as soon as possible. The proposed solutions vary in method.")

88. Stephen L. Pevar, *The Rights of Indians and Tribes*, 4th ed. (New York: New York University Press, 2012), 12. ("In 1968, President Lyndon Johnson declared: 'We must affirm the rights of the first Americans to remain Indians while exercising their rights as Americans. We must affirm their rights to freedom of choice and self-determination.")

89. Ibid., 3.

90. George Santayana, *Reason in Common Sense* (New York: Dover Publications, 1980). Available at: http://www.gutenberg.org/files/15000/15000-h/vol1.html.

91. Donald E. Laverdure, Acting Assistant Secretary – Indian Affairs, to Richard Schadewald, September 4, 2012, 1.

92. Ibid.

93. Ibid., 3.

94. Ibid., 4.

From "Boston Men" to the BIA

The Unacknowledged Chinook Nation

JOHN R. ROBINSON

The Americans are our friends and allies.

—COMCOMLY TO DUNCAN MCDOUGAL (1813)

The modern Chinook nation is descended from the Chinookan peoples of the Lower Columbia River. In 1851, the Chinooks signed a treaty with the U.S. government, though the Senate never ratified the agreement. Today, descendants of the signatories to the treaty continue to fight for the recognition of their nation. In 2002, the federal government denied their petition for acknowledgment under the 1978 Branch of Acknowledgment and Research (BAR) regulations. The Chinooks continue to explore avenues to federal acknowledgment, including the possibility of gaining legislative recognition. The federal acknowledgment process judges the Chinooks through the lens of the U.S. political and legal history. In the face of cultural and historical difference, can such a process be legitimate? Can a bureaucracy ever be entrusted to reach accurate conclusions about identity and authenticity? How can the state provide legal protections to legitimate groups seeking acknowledgment while denying acknowledgment to those without valid claims? What does the federal acknowledgment process illustrate about the nature of tribal sovereignty today?

In July 1979, the Chinook nation filed a letter of intent to petition the U.S. government for federal recognition as an Indian tribe. In July 2002, the Department of the Interior's Bureau of Indian Affairs (BIA) denied that petition. What occurred during those twenty-three years illustrates the continuing controversy over Indian existence and identity in the United States. Further, the decision to deny Chinooks tribal recognition is anomalous in the face of historical evidence that appears to show a substantial, though not completely continuous, relationship between those Indians identifying themselves as Chinooks and the U.S. government.

Contact

During November 1813, the small Pacific Fur Company fort at Astoria, truly on the edge of the western world, found itself embroiled in an international conflict. John Jacob Astor's barely two-year-old venture became the center of British attention for control of the China fur trade as the War of 1812 raged. Over the previous two decades, British and American traders had coexisted on the Lower Columbia River as they participated in a lively business with the Chinooks, "the most powerful nation on the Pacific coast."[1] British Captain John Meares initiated this trade in 1788, when he became the first documented white sailor to make contact with Chinookan peoples at Shoalwater Bay (now called Willapa Bay). Four years later, the "Boston Men" came as Captain Robert Gray, sailing the *Columbia Rediviva*, crossed the treacherous bar of the great river of the West, naming it "Columbia" after his ship.[2]

Between 1792 and 1811, trade continued on a ship-by-ship basis, with neither the British nor Americans establishing a permanent post on the Lower Columbia. According to James P. Ronda, "more than 100 American ships had been engaged in fur operations on the Northwest coast between 1788 and 1803," and this count did not include the British.[3] During this time, the Chinooks essentially controlled commerce in the region, serving as middlemen of sorts and connecting the traders from across the sea with other tribes in the area. Using intimidation, sometimes coercion, and above all negotiation, the Chinooks cemented their position in the world market. In fact, in the early years of the trade, the "Boston Men" and the "King George" men had no option but acquiescence in the face of Chinook business demands, even if those demands required procuring ermine furs from the great market at Leipzig in Saxony.[4]

Astor's Pacific Fur Company changed the game in 1811 when it built Fort Astoria approximately ten miles from the sea on the south bank of the Columbia. This fort became the first permanently occupied American settlement on the Northwest Coast. Before the Americans solidified their control of regional trade, the War of 1812 intervened. British authorities believed Astor's presence on the river indicated the U.S. designs to lay sovereign claim to the region. Therefore, Pacific Fur negotiated a sale (perhaps under duress) to transfer control of Fort Astoria to the North West Company of Canada, thus placing it into the fold of imperial Britain, where it was renamed Fort George.[5]

Late in the fall of 1813, as the transfer neared completion, Chinook chief Comcomly gained knowledge of approaching British forces. They came aboard the ship *Raccoon* to occupy the newly acquired British territory. Comcomly rushed across the river to warn the Astoria men. He told Pacific Fur Company trader Duncan McDougal that the King George men came to enslave the Astorians, and rather than sitting idly by, he promised to lead eight hundred warriors in defense of the fort. "We are not afraid of King George's people," he said, "and we will not allow them to enslave you. The Americans are our friends and allies."[6] This friendship did not last, at least in the eyes of the Chinooks.

Consequences

Events of the next three decades devastated the Chinooks, both commercially and biologically.[7] In June 1825, after a merger between the North West Company and the Hudson's Bay Company, George Simpson, Hudson's Bay superintendent, removed fur-trade operations from Fort George upriver to the newly constructed Fort Vancouver. This action toppled the Chinooks from their position of hegemony in the Lower Columbia trade. The Hudson's Bay Company maintained Fort George as an outpost, and after reverting back to U.S. control, Astoria became an official port of entry, complete with a U.S. customshouse, though the Chinooks never again reclaimed their dominant position.[8] Added to the commercial pain of their declining trade dominance, the Chinooks faced a series of disease outbreaks in the 1830s, which took the lives of many tribe members, including Comcomly in 1835.[9] In the following decade, thousands of people streamed into the territory along the Oregon Trail. These settlers first gravitated toward the fertile Willamette Valley, drawn to the Northwest not by furs but by farming. The white population along the Lower Columbia grew slowly until the California gold rush began in 1848. Astoria became an entrepôt for men and supplies headed to the gold fields.[10] As the population grew along the Lower Columbia, whites, as in so many other places, pressured the Indians to give up their land.

Settlement

In Oregon's infancy as a territory, official U.S. policy required that citizens adhere to a very specific set of laws and regulations in their interactions with

Indian tribes. American settlers could not occupy Indian lands without first acquiring title to them. Neither individuals nor local governments had the right to acquire Indian land via any means, including purchase. Only the federal government could gain title; the land could then be distributed or sold to individual citizens or state or local governments.[11] Between 1815 and 1871, the federal government acquired title to Indian lands by negotiating treaties with tribes, often individually, sometimes in groups, as it did with the Chinooks. However, neither settlers nor state or territorial governments always conformed to the requirements of federal Indian policy.

By the end of the 1840s, as more settlers crowded into Astoria and the surrounding area, it became clear that the United States needed to negotiate a treaty with the Chinooks and other area tribes. Joseph Lane and Samuel Thurston, Oregon's first territorial governor and representative to Congress, respectively, wished to remove Lower Columbia tribes, including the Chinooks, east of the Cascade Mountains, far out of the way of white settlers in the agriculturally and commercially desirable western third of the territory. Prior to 1850, Lane acted as de facto superintendent of Indian affairs for Oregon Territory. Though not inconsistent with practices in other organized territories to this time, he certainly faced a conflict of interest in that he held the wishes of white settlers in higher regard than Indian rights and needs. Congress remedied this situation in June 1850 by passing an act creating the Office of Superintendent of Indian Affairs for Oregon Territory, appointing three commissioners, and charging them with the task of negotiating treaties with Oregon Indian tribes for the express purpose of removing them to the eastern side of the territory.[12] For the Chinooks, the remedy proved no more beneficial than the affliction.

Congress appointed Anson Dart as commissioner charged with negotiating treaties with the tribes of the Lower Columbia. Robert Shortess, married to a Clatsop woman, served under Dart as acting subagent of Indian affairs. In August 1851, Dart concluded treaties with the Chinook, Clatsop, Wahkiakum, Wheelapa, and Konnack bands of Chinookan peoples.[13] Likely as a consequence of resistance from the tribes and possibly influenced by the fact that Shortess, married to an Indian woman, may have held the tribes in higher esteem than many other white settlers, Dart abandoned the plan of removing the Indians eastward. Instead, he negotiated agreements with each tribe that called for a variety of annuities and reservation lands in exchange for transferring title to a 3-million-acre section of land that ran one hundred miles south along the coast from the north end of Shoalwater Bay to Tillamook Bay and extended inland approximately sixty miles.[14] The total offer to all tribes amounted to $91,300 in cash and annuities.[15]

Specifically, the treaty Dart signed with the Chinooks promised them "an annuity of $2000 for ten years," including $400 per year in cash and the rest to be paid in goods. The treaty also reserved for the Chinooks the right to occupy their traditional homeland, "for the purpose of building, fishing, and grazing their stock, with the right to cut timber for their own building purposes and for fuel." Further, it reserved their right "to pick Cranberries on the marshes, and the right to cultivate as much land as they wish for their own purposes."[16] These appear to be very favorable terms in light of the fact that Dart had originally been charged with removing the Chinooks from their ancestral lands.

Perhaps that is why the treaty never gained ratification. Perhaps ratification failed as a result of the lobbying efforts of Thurston and Lane. Regardless, the U.S. Senate never ratified the agreement. Dart speculated on the failure, assuming that the Chinook treaty, along with the others he negotiated, failed because of a provision calling for the removal of Washington Hall, a notorious whiskey dealer living on Chinook lands, or because some of the land promised to Indians had already been staked (legally or not) by white settlers. The treaty might have failed because when he reached an agreement with the Clackamas, a Chinookan people farther upriver, he acted alone rather than with an assistant. Historian C. F. Coan writing in the 1920s, claimed that the treaties never gained ratification because Dart had reached agreements with "insignificant" bands.[17] Whatever the reasons for the treaty's failure, the Chinooks signed in good faith and waited for the fulfillment of a promise that never came.

The Aftermath of a Failed Treaty

In 1863, Congress created Washington Territory out of that portion of Oregon Territory not destined to become part of the state of Oregon. Indian agent William H. Tappan, working under the authority of Washington Territorial governor and superintendent of Indian affairs Isaac I. Stevens, attempted to treat with the Chinooks. Reticent to do so as a result of the unfulfilled promises of 1851, the Chinooks gave no credence to Tappan's overtures.

In February 1855, Stevens took matters into his own hands, meeting with representatives of the Chinooks, Upper and Lower Chehalis, Quinaults, Satsops, Satchaps, and Cowlitz ten miles up the Chehalis River from Grays

Harbor. In these negotiations, he proposed removing these tribes to one big reservation on the central Washington coast, promising four thousand dollars to pay for improvements to the land so that the Indians might succeed at taking up an agricultural existence. During these talks, Narchotta of the Chinooks expressed his people's willingness to sell their land, but they refused to be removed. He asked for residence rights on their old lands so the Chinooks could avoid leaving their ancestors' graves. Furthermore, he claimed that the Chinooks would not move north among the Quinaults as a consequence of long-standing animosity between the tribes and the shortage of food resources in and around the proposed reservation.[18] Essentially, he asked for treaty terms similar to those to which the Chinooks had agreed in 1851. Stevens did not accept these terms, and the Chinooks discontinued negotiations without signing a new treaty. Thus began the Chinooks diaspora.

As the Tansey Point Treaty of 1851 failed to gain ratification and the Chinooks did not agree to any further treaties during the 1855 negotiations, they never actually surrendered title to their lands. Nevertheless (and contrary to official U.S. Indian policy), white settlers continued to arrive along the north bank of the Columbia in what is now southwest Washington state, slowly at first but with increasing frequency as the decades passed. Over the latter half of the nineteenth century, some Chinooks congregated in and around Bay Center, on the northeast corner of Willapa Bay, where they mixed, socially and culturally, with Chehalis Indians, who intentionally or not, encroached on traditional Chinook lands as the Chinooks maintained a tenuous grip on existence. Other Chinooks remained close to the river at Chinookville, Dahlia, and Ilwaco and as far east as Skamokawa and Cathlamet. Perhaps by choice but likely by necessity, individual Chinooks began to assimilate into white society.[19] This development is ironic in light of the fact that late-nineteenth-century U.S. Indian policy pressed reservation Indians to assimilate. The Chinooks did so as a direct response to failed treaty negotiations, a failure over which they had no semblance of control, and this failure to secure a treaty remains one of the reasons they have been unsuccessful in gaining federal recognition in the modern era.

Identity and Existence

Indians of the Pacific Northwest have long contended with the fact that white settlers placed definitions on them that had little connection to indigenous reality. At the most basic level, the terms "Indian" and "tribe" are constructions of the Europeans who first settled along the rivers and bays of Chinookan territory. Further, most Indian groups throughout the coastal Northwest identified themselves by village or family. In addition, they established trade and kinship networks among themselves that make hard and fast historical relationships difficult to discern. In other words, "tribes" often serve to delineate different groups only from the mid-nineteenth century to the present. Shared language and cultural patterns certainly meant that some groups related easily with one another, whereas language barriers and cultural differences caused other groups to remain distant or aloof. However, historical Northwest Indian societies are marked more by cultural bridges than cultural barriers.[20] The Chinooks fit solidly into this pattern.

The treaty-making era of the 1850s, initiated by Joseph Lane and continued by Isaac Stevens, contributed to a shift in identity among Northwest Indian groups. In many ways, treaty negotiations and their consequences changed the way whites viewed Indians and, perhaps even more important, how Indians viewed themselves. During the century between the end of the treaty-making era and the beginning of the self-determination era, as the political ground constantly shifted beneath them, Northwest Indians pointed to the treaties they had signed with the federal government as unalienable proof of their rights and their continuing existence.[21] Of course, to the United States, only ratified treaties mattered.

Throughout the twentieth century and especially beginning in the 1950s, Northwest tribes that had signed treaties that never gained ratification as well as tribes that never had the opportunity to sign treaties began making claims to the government for redress of their financial and political grievances.[22] Perhaps unexpectedly, the Indian Claims Commission eased this process. Since treaties became the foundation on which Northwest Indian identity and even existence rested, the Chinooks and others intended to press the government for the fulfillment of promises made to them. These attempts were not confined to the tribes of the Pacific Northwest, and by the 1970s, it again became necessary for the federal government to change the trajectory of official Indian policy.

Policy in Brief

The history of federal Indian policy and the interactions between tribal nations and the U.S. government have been tumultuous. While an in-depth discussion is beyond the scope of this chapter, some key points are germane to the question of federal acknowledgment. Chief Justice John Marshall's decision in *Cherokee Nation v. Georgia* set in motion a series of events that have long affected Indian policy in the United States (to say the least).[23] In brief, the idea that tribal nations are "domestic dependent nations" has not only proved foundational for tribal sovereignty but also allowed Congress to assail that sovereignty with regularity.

Throughout the nineteenth century, Indian policy moved inexorably toward the idea of assimilation, a trajectory most clearly evidenced by the General Allotment Act of 1887. Under this act, tribal nations lost title to much of their land, while individual Native Americans gained allotments of varying sizes so that they might take up the sedentary agricultural lifestyle of the (mostly mythical) American yeomanry. From 1887 until 1934, being a member of an acknowledged or recognized tribe held little advantage for Native Americans.

The situation changed with the advent of the Indian Reorganization Act and John Collier's administration of the Office of Indian Affairs from 1934 until 1945. To be sure, the act and Collier's administration of it left much to be desired in regard to tribal sovereignty and the end of federal paternalism. On the flip side, however, the legislation did help restart the drive for self-determination among tribal nations. Ironically, it also helped lead to termination, whereby the federal government pushed to end its trust relationship with tribal nations. The furnace of termination and the subsequent resistance to it among Native Americans and U.S. society as a whole forged the renewal of self-determination marked by the Johnson and Nixon administrations of the 1960s and 1970s. In the 1970s, being acknowledged as a tribal nation again provided substantial benefits for Native Americans. Thus, unacknowledged groups began agitating for a change in policy, while heretofore recognized tribal nations exercised their newfound political muscle to influence the process by which this change would occur.[24]

The Acknowledgment Process

In 1978, the BIA responded to pressure from unrecognized Indian tribes by publishing a list of criteria that an unrecognized tribe would have to meet to gain official federal acknowledgment.[25] This action occurred against the backdrop of a change in Indian policy as the termination era of the 1950s to the early 1970s waned and the era of self-determination began. The 1978 regulations outlined seven criteria that Indian groups must meet before the BIA will extend official recognition. These criteria require that an unrecognized group prove it has been identified from historical times until the present "on a substantially continuous basis, as 'American Indian' or 'aboriginal.'" It must provide "Evidence that a substantial portion of the petitioning group inhabits a specific area or lives in a community viewed as American Indian and distinct from other populations in the area." A petitioning group is required to prove political authority over its members "throughout history until the present." The group must also provide a copy of its current "governing document," such as a tribal constitution, as well as a list of members based on the tribe's own criteria. Finally, it must prove that membership in the group "is composed principally of persons who are not members of any other North American Indian tribe" and that the group is not "the subject of congressional legislation which has expressly terminated or forbidden the Federal relationship."[26] According to the 1978 regulations, "Failure to be acknowledged pursuant to these regulations does not deny that a group is Indian," and perhaps even more critically, "A petitioner shall not fail to satisfy any criteria herein merely because of fluctuations of tribal activity during various years."[27]

The BIA accepted petitions under the 1978 regulations until 1994, at which point it revised the regulations, streamlining some requirements and making slight changes to the seven mandatory criteria. On the whole, the burden of proof required of petitioning groups remained substantially the same. However, two changes were of utmost importance in regard to the 1979 Chinook petition for recognition. The revised regulations changed the first criterion. Instead of calling for identification as an American Indian entity from "historical times" on a "substantially continuous basis," it required groups to meet that criterion from 1900 onward. Further, the same section of the 1994 regulations stated that "evidence that the group's character as an Indian entity has from time to time been denied shall not be considered to be conclusive evidence that this criterion has not been met." Second, the BIA added a section to the regulations that allowed Indian groups to prove "unambiguous previous federal acknowledgment." Any tribe that could do so only had to provide evidence that it met the seven mandatory criteria for recognition from the point of last federal acknowledgment to the present.[28]

The Modern Chinooks and the Federal Government

Given the change in the revised regulations of 1994 that has called for tribes to demonstrate their continuous existence since 1900, examining interactions between the Chinooks and the federal government during the twentieth century is vital to the story of the Chinook recognition petition.

The works of historians Robert H. Ruby and John A. Brown as well as of Clifford Trafzer, in addition to the BIA's 1997 proposed finding, 2001 final determination, and 2002 reconsidered final determination, include numerous examples of the interaction between the Chinooks and the federal government beginning in 1899. Four major examples well illustrate the volatile relationship between the Chinooks and the United States between that time and the denial of the Chinook petition for recognition in 2002.

In 1899, Chinook descendants of the signatories to the Tansey Point Treaty of 1851 began the process of preparing a claim against the federal government in hopes of earning a Court of Claims settlement for the financial accommodations promised them by the treaty.[29] Before the Court of Claims can hear such cases, however, Congress first must approve jurisdiction.[30] In 1900, Congress consented, allowing the Chinooks to proceed with their case. As is often the case when dealing with government, things moved slowly for the Chinooks. In 1907, the Office of Indian Affairs recommended against a finding in favor of the Chinooks. The Court of Claims disagreed, and in 1912 it awarded twenty thousand dollars to the Chinooks.[31] Once the Court of Claims finds in favor of a plaintiff, Congress must appropriate the funds to pay the settlement. Session 2 of the Sixty-Second Congress did just that on August 24, 1912.[32] In deed, if not in word, Congress and the Court of Claims retroactively ratified the Tansey Point Treaty.

In March 1911, the Chinooks gained another favorable decision from the U.S. government when Congress "authorized and directed" the secretary of the interior "to make allotments on the Quinealt Reservation, Washington, under the provisions of the allotment laws of the United States, to all members of the Hoh, Quileute, Ozette, or *other tribes of Indians in Washington who are affiliated with the Quinealt and Quileute tribes* in the treaty of July first, eighteen hundred and fifty-five, and January twenty-third, eighteen hundred and fifty-six, and who may elect to take allotments on the Quinealt Reservation rather than on the reservations set aside for these tribes."[33] Though not specifically mentioned in the enactment, the Chinooks were affiliated with the Quinaults by virtue of their participation in the 1855 treaty negotiations with Stevens, even though they did not sign any treaty at this time. The U.S. Supreme Court, while not speaking to Chinook recognition per se, upheld this interpretation as part of the 1931 *Halbert v. United States* decision.[34] And, some Chinooks did choose allotments on the Quinault reservation in the early decades of the twentieth century.

Neither of these two examples refers to the Chinooks as a tribe. Rather, they allowed individual people of Chinook descent to gain redress of grievances against the U.S. government. As such, examined narrowly, without context, they do not necessarily provide evidence of "unambiguous prior federal acknowledgment." However, in 1925, Congress expressly referred to the Chinooks as a tribe. Once again, this congressional recognition came in regard to the Court of Claims. On February 12, 1925, Congress passed a measure requiring

> that all claims of whatsoever nature, both legal and equitable, of all the tribes and bands of Indians, or any of them . . . with whom were made any of the treaties of . . . December 26, 1854 . . . January 22, 1855 . . . January 26, 1855 . . . May 8, 1859, growing out of said treaties, or any of them, and that all claims of whatever nature, both legal and equitable, which the Muckleshoot, San Juan Islands Indians; NookSack, Suattle, Chinooks, Upper Chehalis, Lower Chehalis, and Humptulip Tribes or Bands of Indians, or any of them (with whom no treaty has been made), may have against the United States shall be submitted to the Court of Claims, with right of appeal by either party to the Supreme Court of the United States for determination and adjudication.[35]

Though the Court of Claims apparently never decided a case in favor of the Chinooks based on this act, Congress nevertheless seemingly recognized the Chinooks as a tribe. Regardless of BIA actions, Congress reserves the right to recognize—or, conversely, to terminate—the federal acknowledgment of Indian tribes.[36]

After World War II, "the difficulty encountered by Indian tribes seeking suits against the United States in the Court of Claims led . . . to the formation of the Indian Claims Commission."[37] The Chinooks submitted a claim to the commission in 1951. This claim, registered as Docket 234, asked for further compensation regarding the unratified Tansey Point Treaty. The Chinooks believed that the money they received in 1912 did not adequately compensate them for the lands they had lost and asked instead for 30 million dollars.[38]

This claim spent the next twenty years winding its way through the system. In 1970, the Indian Claims Commission decided in favor of the Chinooks, finding the 1912 settlement "unconscionable" but awarding the Chinooks only $75,000 (minus the $26,307.95 they had previously received), far less than the amount for which the tribe had asked.[39] After appeals, and findings concerning attorney fees, the Indian Claims Commission finally closed Docket 234 in September 1975.[40] Although an award decision that amounts to around one dollar per acre (including the original 1912 settlement) may seem unconscionable in itself, the actual amount is not important here; rather, the significance of the action lies in the fact that the U.S. government (1) dealt with the Chinooks and (2) found in their favor.

The Chinook Acknowledgment Petition

The Chinooks' next major interaction with the federal government did not end as well for them. Less than one year after the BIA published its "Procedures for Establishing That an American Indian Group Exists as an Indian Tribe," the Chinooks filed their letter of intent "to petition Secretary of Interior for Recognition as a Federally Acknowledged Indian Tribe," received by the BIA on July 25, 1979.[41] Gathering evidence to prove a petitioner meets all seven mandatory criteria for administrative recognition is a daunting task, and the Chinook story consequently moved rather slowly through the 1980s. Nearly two years passed between the submission of the Chinooks' letter of intent and the filing of the petition on June 12, 1981. After review, the BAR responded with a technical assistance letter outlining evidentiary deficiencies in the petition. After addressing the concerns raised in the letter, Chinook legal counsel resubmitted the petition in July 1987. The BAR conducted an obvious deficiency review and sent another letter outlining alleged evidentiary problems to the Chinooks in November 1988. As before, the Chinooks and their legal counsel responded to these concerns. Finally, on January 28, 1994, the BIA placed the Chinook petition on "active consideration."[42]

All tribes and groups whose petitions came under review prior to the revised regulations of 1994 were permitted to choose whether the petitions were considered under the 1978 or 1994 regulations. The Chinooks originally requested that their petition be considered under the 1978 rules but later asked for a change to the 1994 regulations. The time period for requesting a change had expired, and the BIA initially denied the request. Kevin Gover, assistant secretary of Indian affairs from 1997 until 2001, subsequently determined that he had "erred" in denying the change and considered the petition under both sets of regulations.[43] Gover's successor, Neal McCaleb, agreed that Gover acted within his rights in doing so.[44]

On August 11, 1997, Ada Deer, Gover's predecessor as assistant secretary, issued a "proposed finding against Federal acknowledgment of the Chinook Indian Tribe, Inc." In it, she concluded the Chinooks met four of the seven mandatory criteria under the 1978 regulations. They had provided a current governing document for the tribe, the list of current tribal members, and a membership roll that consisted primarily of individuals not enrolled in other tribes, and they had proved that they were not subject to congressional termination.[45] Neither the final determination of 2001 nor the reconsidered final determination of 2002 disputed these points.[46] Conversely, Deer alleged the Chinooks had not satisfied the criteria regarding identification as an Indian tribe on a "substantially continuous" basis since "historical" times, the requirement that a "substantial portion" of the group inhabited a "community viewed as American Indian and distinct from other populations in the area," or the maintenance of "tribal political influence . . . over its members . . . throughout history until the present."[47]

Under the regulations, the Chinooks responded to the proposed finding with further evidence to bolster their case, and Gover, who had replaced Deer, called for an "independent audit" of the petition, enlisting the services of an anthropologist heretofore uninvolved in the case.[48] The information uncovered in the subsequent investigation, along with the supplementary evidence provided by the Chinooks, led Gover to find that the Chinooks met all seven criteria.

Specifically, he found that Congress had statutorily recognized the Chinooks in the 1911 allotment decision, the 1912 Court of Claims settlement appropriation, and the 1925 Court of Claims jurisdiction enactment. He placed significant weight on the 1925 enactment as "unambiguous prior Federal acknowledgment" of the Chinooks as a tribe. Further, his decision to consider the petition under both the 1978 regulations and the 1994 regulations meant the Chinooks now only had to prove the identification, community, and political authority criteria from 1925 until the present.[49] Gover found evidence of social interactions between Chinooks living at Bay Center and those living at Ilwaco and Dahlia and considered those interactions sufficient to prove that the Chinooks not only inhabited a specific area but constituted a community "distinct from other populations in the area." Moreover, given the "unambiguous prior federal acknowledgment" of 1925, the Chinooks merely had to provide evidence of community in the present.[50] Finally, Gover asserted, "The congressional actions directed at the Chinooks in 1911, 1912, and 1925 indicate the influence of a political entity that pursued tribal political and legal objectives from the turn of the 20th century until 1925." He considered "the claims organizations [of the late 1920s and early 1930s to be] transitional tribal governing bodies, and the evidence shows an evolving political structure."[51] Gover found that this evidence, coupled with the political nature of the group pressing the Indian

Claims Commission case of 1951–70, satisfied the criterion demonstrating political authority within the tribe.[52]

Victory seemed at hand for the Chinooks. The BIA issued a final determination granting recognition to the Chinook nation on January 3, 2001. Nearly 22 years after filing the petition and 150 years after the failed Tansey Point Treaty negotiations, the Chinooks gained official validation of their existence. Then, as had so often previously been the case, events beyond Chinook control changed the game.

Petition Denied

Under the 1994 regulations, the BIA had to provide a ninety-day comment period so that the tribe in question and all "interested parties" might request reconsideration of the acknowledgment decisions. The regulations defined an interested party as "any person, organization or other entity who can establish a legal, factual or property interest in an acknowledgment determination and who requests an opportunity to submit comments or evidence or to be kept informed of general actions regarding a specific petitioner."[53] Examples of interested parties include the governor or attorney general of the state where the petitioning tribe is located, local government, or other recognized and unrecognized Indian tribes.[54]

The Quinault Indian Tribe, the Columbia River Crab Fisherman's Association, and Michels Development Company, a casino management firm located in Lakewood, Washington, all petitioned for "interested party" status to dispute the final determination. The Chinooks disputed the claim that Michels Development and the Columbia River Crab Fisherman's Association met the criteria to be recognized as "interested parties." The Internal Board of Indian Appeals (IBIA) essentially sidestepped the issue when it decided that since all three parties based their appeal on similar points, hearing the Quinaults' appeal would effectively address the concerns of the other two petitioners as well.[55]

It is possible that the Quinaults felt threatened by pending Chinook recognition because some Chinook petitioners hold allotments on the Quinault reservation. Chinooks may control as much as 52 percent of the land base on the Quinault reservation, although apparently not all Chinooks with allotments on the Quinault reservation took part in the petition or consider themselves a part of the Chinook nation.[56] Whatever the reasons, the Quinaults alleged that Gover's decision was "not supported by reliable or probative evidence," that his research was "materially incomplete," and that he failed to explain his "departures from past departmental interpretations." These are the only allegations over which the IBIA accepted jurisdiction, and the agency found them to be without merit.[57] In addition, the Quinaults alleged nine other issues that the IBIA forwarded to the secretary of interior since they did not fall under IBIA jurisdiction. In sum, the Quinaults believed that Gover lacked authority to review the petition under the 1994 regulations; if he did have that authority, he had abused his discretion; his interpretation of the 1911, 1912, and 1925 congressional acts ran "contrary to longstanding departmental interpretations"; he "improperly departed from departmental regulations" by considering claims acts proof of prior acknowledgment; he improperly interpreted evidence of Chinook community; he accorded the Chinooks a "presumption of continued existence"; his use of an outside consultant ran afoul of the "regular departmental decision making process"; and his decision "reflected bias" and a "personal political agenda."[58]

Between the publication of the final determination and the end of the comment period, Neal McCaleb succeeded Gover, and Gale Norton became the new secretary of interior. Norton referred eight of the nine issues raised by the Quinaults back to the BIA for McCaleb's reconsideration.[59] He found that Gover did have authority to consider the petition under both the 1978 and 1994 regulations and to enlist the services of an outside consultant and that the evidence did not suggest Gover improperly gave the Chinooks a "presumption of continued existence."[60] However, McCaleb asserted that Gover had improperly interpreted the events of 1911, 1912, and 1925; that the 1925 matter did not constitute "unambiguous" previous acknowledgment; that Gover's interpretation of community "departed from the . . . regulations and prior Departmental interpretations"; and that he erred in his interpretations of Chinook claims activities.[61]

McCaleb considered 1855 to be the last date of "unambiguous prior federal acknowledgment" and determined that the Chinooks did not meet all seven mandatory criteria for recognition from that time until the present. Thus, on July 5, 2002, he reversed Gover's final determination. Once the appeal process has been exhausted and the assistant secretary for Indian affairs issues any reconsidered final determination, a tribe or group may not again petition the BIA for recognition.[62] Therefore, McCaleb's decision is final. Twenty-three years of Chinooks' efforts disappeared with one stroke of the pen.

What It Means

Fundamental differences appear to exist between how Gover and McCaleb construed their authority under the 1994 acknowledgment regulations. McCaleb analyzed the Chinook petition in a very narrow, legalistic fashion, basing his decision on precedent and prior governmental action. Furthermore, he heavily weighted the words of past government officials involved with the Chinooks over those officials' deeds. His proclivities in this regard are undoubtedly legitimate from a narrowly drawn and strict-constructionist perspective. And in fact, given the nature of the administration under which he worked, his decision is not even terribly surprising. A conservative-leaning executive is almost sure to reach conservatively bounded conclusions.

Conversely, McCaleb's assertion that Gover somehow "erred" in his interpretation of the criteria under the 1994 regulations does not hold up under close scrutiny. The regulations state, "A criterion shall be considered met if the available evidence establishes a reasonable likelihood of the validity of the facts relating to that criterion." Further, "*Conclusive Proof* of the facts relating to a criterion *shall not be required* in order for the criterion to be considered met."[63] In addition,

> Evaluation of petitions shall take into account historical situations and time periods for which evidence is demonstrably limited or not available. The limitations inherent in demonstrating the historical existence of community and political influence or authority shall also be taken into account. Existence of community and political influence or authority shall be demonstrated on a substantially continuous basis, but this demonstration does not require meeting these criteria at every point in time. Fluctuations in tribal activity during various years shall not in themselves be a cause for denial of acknowledgment under these criteria.[64]

Finally, the regulations call for "political influence" and "community" to be "understood in the context of the history, culture, and social organization of the group."[65] The regulations appear to give the assistant secretary of Indian affairs broad powers to interpret the facts of each petition on a case-by-case basis. A historian might say that in doing so, Gover did not "err." Rather, he cast his net wide to gather and interpret evidence to give the Chinooks the best possible chance to gain recognition. Considering the nature of the administration under which he worked, Gover's initial findings are no more surprising than McCaleb's reversal. And under the requirements of the 1994 regulations, they do not appear to be improper. It is hard to believe that had Gover remained in his position as assistant secretary throughout the entire appeal process, he would have reversed his own decision. In that regard, the Chinooks are victims of bad political timing, if nothing else.

Since the Chinooks failed to gain recognition in 2002, historians, political scientists, and legal scholars have continued the work of analyzing and interpreting the federal policy of acknowledgment. This body of work clearly shows that no single reason exists for the denial of an Indian nation's official existence and the de facto denial of sovereignty that such decisions represent. The seven mandatory criteria allow for myriad reasons to deny acknowledgment. They also allow for the real reasons behind denial to remain shrouded in mystery.

Renée Ann Cramer and Jessica R. Cattelino make strong cases for the fact that the rise of tribal gaming has made it more difficult for unacknowledged tribes to gain recognition and has led to legal and cultural assaults on the sovereignty of Indian nations already acknowledged by the United States. To put it simply and inelegantly, "rich Indians" cannot be "real Indians," and once Indians are wealthy, they no longer need or deserve "special" rights. Furthermore, acknowledging more Indian nations will lead to the expansion of tribal gaming and the subsequent expansion of all the supposed evils that go along with it, or so state governments and certain business interests contend.[66]

Brian Klopotek and Mark Edwin Miller have examined federal acknowledgment proceedings through the lens of race and population. In *Recognition Odysseys: Indigeneity, Race, and Federal Tribal Recognition Policy in Three Louisiana Indian Communities*, Klopotek illustrates how racial conceptions of Indian identity in society at large have made it difficult for petitioning nations to gain federal acknowledgment. In short, Indians with African ancestry face a great deal of opposition when they exert their Indian identity. Even when such nations are granted acknowledgment, they must constantly defend themselves against accusations that they are not authentically indigenous and that they are merely opportunists looking for government handouts. This assault on identity comes not only from the federal government and the dominant white society but also from other Indian nations attempting to preserve their hard-fought political, social, and economic gains.[67]

In *Forgotten Tribes: Unrecognized Indians and the Federal Acknowledgment Process*, Miller considers the racial aspects of recognition policy, especially regarding the case of the Houma of Louisiana, while raising the possibility that an Indian nation's population plays a significant role in the determination of petitions. The more than fifteen thousand members of the unacknowledged United Houma nation have Indian and African ancestry. Other residents of southern Louisiana are threatened by such a large population, especially in regard to economics and resource use. Miller is convincing in his assertion that Houma population plays a significant role in their continuing inability to gain federal acknowledgment.[68]

But what does this mean for the Chinooks? Questions of race and indigeneity play less of a role for unacknowledged tribes in the Pacific Northwest, at least insofar as African heritage is concerned, because of the region's demographic and racial realities. And while the Chinooks are not small in number, they do not enroll nearly as many members as the Houma nation or the Lumbee tribe of North Carolina. The Quinault Indian Tribe, the Columbia River Crab Fisherman's Association, and Michels Development Company clearly sought to avert Chinook acknowledgment. One can assume their reasoning came at least in part from economic self-interest and their desires to preserve access to resources. However, their concerns are not the official reason for the denial of Chinook acknowledgment.

Prior to the George W. Bush administration, Indian nations petitioning for acknowledgment could expect about a 50 percent chance of success. Between 2001 and 2009, however, the process ended favorably for only two of fifteen petitioners.[69] Federal acknowledgment policy has become an entrenched bureaucratic tool for denying legitimate Indian nations sovereignty that is rightfully theirs, as Klopotek illustrates by tracing the evolution of the process through its official title. It began as the Federal Acknowledgment Project in 1978. "Project" implies a beginning and an end. It subsequently became the Branch of Acknowledgment and Research, implying more permanence yet also subordinate status. Finally, it is now the Office of Federal Acknowledgment, a name that indicates a position of primacy within the BIA.[70]

It is hard to say what should occur in regard to reforming the process of federal acknowledgment. Indeed, any historian who attempted to do so would be remiss. It is easy to see, however, that the current system is ineffective at best and oppressive at worst. Perhaps the federal bureaucracy can be entrusted to shepherd the process of determining indigenous sovereignty and identity, but the Office of Federal Acknowledgment is largely failing in that duty under current regulations.

Going Forward

Today, the federally unrecognized Chinook nation includes more than two thousand members.[71] They are recognized as a tribe by the State of Washington, and from 2002 until 2005 they collaborated with Portland State University to construct a plankhouse on the grounds of the Ridgefield National Wildlife refuge.[72] They live throughout the Lower Columbia region, from their traditional homelands of Chinook and Bay Center to the Portland/Vancouver area and beyond. They continue to celebrate ancient traditions, such as the first salmon ceremony, and their tribal council is active in pursuing social and political goals.[73] Furthermore, whether or not they can prove "unambiguous" federal acknowledgment, they unambiguously exist, and they have not given up on gaining official recognition.

In September 2011, descendants of William Clark presented a thirty-seven-foot-long canoe to the Chinook nation to right a wrong that occurred two centuries earlier. In what has become a famous tale in Pacific Northwest lore, the Corps of Discovery stole a canoe from the Chinooks in 1806.[74] Justice is ageless. People are not. One hopes the Chinook nation will not have to wait two more centuries for justice to be done by the U.S. government.

Notes

1. Anson Dart, 1851, quoted in Clifford E. Trafzer, *The Chinook* (New York: Chelsea House, 1990), 87.

2. For Fort Astoria and the international conflict, see Robert Ruby and John A. Brown, *The Chinook Indians: Traders of the Lower Columbia* (Norman: University of Oklahoma Press, 1976), 148; for Meares and Gray, see 38 and 40, respectively. The Chinooks referred to Americans as "Boston Men" because so many of them came from that particular U.S. port; similarly, they called British sailors "King George Men" (Trafzer, *Chinook*, 30).

3. James P. Ronda, *Lewis and Clark among the Indians* (Lincoln: University of Nebraska Press, 1984), 201.

4. For Chinook trade dominance, see Ruby and Brown, *Chinook Indians*, chs. 4, 5; for the ermine furs specifically, see 84.

5. Ibid., chs. 8, 9; approximate distance from river mouth to Fort Astoria calculated with Google Earth.

6. Ibid., 148. Ruby and Brown quote from Alexander Ross, *Adventures of the First Settlers on the Oregon or Columbia River* (London: Smith, Elder, 1849), 148. At this time, the Chinook consisted of numerous autonomous villages. As such, Comcomly did not occupy a position of absolute authority, the Americans and British referred to him as chief in part because he appeared to exercise the most power in the trade. See Ruby and Brown, *Chinook Indians*, chs. 6–8; U.S. Department of the Interior, Bureau of Indian Affairs, Office of Federal Acknowledgment, "Historical Technical Report," in *Summary under the Criteria and Evidence for Proposed Finding against Federal Acknowledgment of the Chinook Indian Tribe, Inc.* (1997), 10.

7. Chinookan peoples inhabited the banks of the Columbia all the way to the Dalles. The terms "Chinook proper" and "Lower Chinook" are often used to refer to the Lower Columbia tribe that occupied the north bank of the river at its mouth. In addition, Clatsops, Wahkiakums, and Cathlamets are also Chinookan peoples. See Trafzer, *Chinook*; U.S. Department of the Interior, Bureau of Indian Affairs, Office of Federal Acknowledgment, "Historical Technical Report," 1, 6. Throughout the essay, I use "Chinook" to denote the historical "Chinook proper," "Lower Chinook," and the modern iterations of the Chinook nation and Chinook Indian Tribe, Inc.

8. Ruby and Brown, *Chinook Indians*, 175; for the decline of Chinook trade prominence in general, see ch. 10.

9. For the effects of disease in the 1830s, see ibid., ch. 11; Trafzer, *Chinook*, 76–79. In addition to smallpox, the Chinooks faced some sort of fever that they called the "Cold-Sick." Others referred to it as the "intermittent fever." Through the years, scholars have asserted that it may have been malaria or ague, though no one is entirely sure.

10. Ruby and Brown, *Chinook Indians*, 213–14.

11. Francis Paul Prucha, "United States Indian Policies, 1815–1860," in *Handbook of North American Indians*, ed. Wilcomb E. Washburn (Washington, D.C.: Smithsonian Institution Scholarly Press, 1988), 4:40.

12. C. F. Coan, "The First Stage of the Federal Indian Policy in the Pacific Northwest, 1849–1852," *Quarterly of the Oregon Historical Society* 21 (1921): 48–54. See also Ruby and Brown, *Chinook Indians*, 221–22.

13. Coan, "First Stage," 75–86.

14. Ibid., 58–59.

15. Ruby and Brown, *Chinook Indians*, 225. In fact, 6,000 square miles (100 miles × 60 miles) equals approximately 3.8 million acres. Curiously, the distance from the north end of Willapa Bay to the south end of Tillamook Bay is approximately 80 miles. Dart appears to have misstated or miscalculated the distance,

and that error has been perpetuated both by Coan, "First Stage," and Ruby and Brown, *Chinook Indians*. Regardless, 80 × 60 is 4,800 square miles—more than 3 million acres.

16. Treaty reproduced in Coan, "First Stage," 75–78.

17. Ibid., 62–63.

18. Ruby and Brown, *Chinook Indians*, 235–36.

19. Ibid., chs. 13, 14. See also U.S. Department of the Interior, Bureau of Indian Affairs, Office of Federal Acknowledgment, "Historical Technical Report," 1–2.

20. See Alexandra Harmon, *Indians in the Making: Ethnic Relations and Indian Identities around Puget Sound* (Berkeley: University of California Press, 1998).

21. Ibid., esp. introduction, ch. 6.

22. Ibid.; for the importance of treaties in regard to Indian identity, see ch. 6.

23. *Cherokee Nation v. Georgia*, 30 U.S. 1 (1831).

24. For a concise summary of the trajectory of federal acknowledgment processes, see William W. Quinn Jr., "Federal Acknowledgment of American Indian Tribes: The Historical Development of a Legal Concept," *American Journal of Legal History* 34 (1990): 331–64. For very good brief accounts of the 1978 acknowledgment regulations and case studies of acknowledgment petitions from the East, Deep South, and Southwest, see Mark Edwin Miller, *Forgotten Tribes: Unrecognized Indians and the Federal Acknowledgment Process* (Lincoln: University of Nebraska Press, 2004); Renée Ann Cramer, *Cash, Color, and Colonialism: The Politics of Tribal Acknowledgment* (Norman: University of Oklahoma Press, 2005).

25. Regarding the confusing lexicon of federal Indian policy, the 1978 regulations concern the process by which tribes outside the federal pale may become "acknowledged." It is quite common, in the study of this subject, to encounter the word "acknowledgment" and the word "recognition" used interchangeably. I have adopted that model here. The official term "acknowledgment" and the colloquial term "recognition" mean essentially the same thing.

26. *Federal Register*, September 5, 1978, 39,363. See also Francis Paul Prucha, ed., *Documents of United States Indian Policy*, 3rd ed. (Lincoln: University of Nebraska Press, 2000), 290–91.

27. *Federal Register*, September 5, 1978, 39,361, 39,363.

28. 25 C.F.R., ch. 1, 272–75. The two assistant secretaries of Indian affairs responsible for determining the disposition of the Chinook petition agree that the burden of proof under both the 1978 regulations and the 1994 regulations is substantially the same.

29. Ruby and Brown, *Chinook Indians*, 246.

30. Harmon, *Indians in the Making*, 183. In ch. 6, Harmon provides an excellent study of Indian/government relations in the Northwest in the early decades of the twentieth century, though her study area does not include the Chinook.

31. Ruby and Brown, *Chinook Indians*, 246–47. See also U.S. Department of the Interior, Bureau of Indian Affairs, Office of Federal Acknowledgment, "Historical Technical Report," 32–38.

32. U.S. Statutes at Large, 62nd Cong., 2nd sess., ch. 388, 1912, 535.

33. U.S. Statutes at Large, 61st Cong., 3rd sess., ch. 246, 1345–46; emphasis added.

34. U.S. Department of the Interior, Bureau of Indian Affairs, Office of Federal Acknowledgment, *Summary under the Criteria and Evidence for Final Determination for Federal Acknowledgment of the Chinook Indian Tribe/Chinook Nation (Formerly: Chinook Indian Tribe, Inc.)* (2001), 8; *Halbert v. United States*, 283 U.S. 753, 51 S.Ct. 615, 75 L.Ed. 1389 (1931).

35. U.S. Statutes at Large, 68th Cong., 2nd sess., ch. 214, 886–87.

36. "Federally Recognized Indian Tribe List Act of 1994, November 2, 1994," in *Documents of United States Indian Policy*, ed. Prucha, 356.

37. Ibid., 231.

38. Docket 234 before the Indian Claims Commission, *The Chinook Tribe and Bands of Indians, Petitioner, v. the United States of America, Defendant*, Opinion of the Commission, April 16, 1958.

39. Ibid., Opinion of the Commission, November 4, 1970. The discrepancy concerning the 1912 amount, $20,000 versus $26,307.95 appears to arise from the fact that the 1951 petition included descendants of Chinook bands that were treated separately in the 1912 case, such as the Wahkiakum. By 1951, descendants of these separate bands joined together for the purposes of petitioning the Government.

40. Ibid., Findings of Fact on Attorneys' Fees and Expenses, September 18, 1975.

41. Copy of letter of intent, in possession of the author.

42. U.S. Department of the Interior, Bureau of Indian Affairs, Office of Federal Acknowledgment, *Summary under the Criteria and Evidence for Proposed Finding*, 2. The proposed finding of 1997, the final determination of 2001, and U.S. Department of the Interior, Bureau of Indian Affairs, Office of Federal Acknowledgment, *Reconsidered on Referral by the Secretary and Summary under the Criteria and Evidence for the Reconsidered Final Determination against Federal Acknowledgment of the Chinook Indian Tribe/Chinook Nation (formerly: Chinook Indian Tribe, Inc.)* (2002) all contain essentially the same administrative history regarding the chronology of the Chinook petition.

43. U.S. Department of the Interior, Bureau of Indian Affairs, Office of Federal Acknowledgment, *Summary under the Criteria and Evidence for Final Determination*, 2.

44. U.S. Department of the Interior, Bureau of Indian Affairs, Office of Federal Acknowledgment, *Reconsidered on Referral*, 3.

45. U.S. Department of the Interior, Bureau of Indian Affairs, Office of Federal Acknowledgment, *Summary under the Criteria and Evidence for Proposed Finding*, 37–39.

46. U.S. Department of the Interior, Bureau of Indian Affairs, Office of Federal Acknowledgment, *Reconsidered on Referral*, 106–9; U.S. Department of the Interior, Bureau of Indian Affairs, Office of Federal Acknowledgment, *Summary under the Criteria and Evidence for Final Determination*, 76–78.

47. U.S. Department of the Interior, Bureau of Indian Affairs, Office of Federal Acknowledgment, *Summary under the Criteria and Evidence for Proposed Finding*, 4–36.

48. Stephen Dow Beckham to author, April 7, 2008.

49. U.S. Department of the Interior, Bureau of Indian Affairs, Office of Federal Acknowledgment, *Summary under the Criteria and Evidence for Final Determination*, 7–10.

50. Ibid., 53–71.

51. Ibid., 75.

52. Ibid.

53. 25 C.F.R., ch. 1, 269.

54. Ibid.

55. Internal Board of Indian Appeals, *In Re Federal Acknowledgment of the Chinook Indian Tribe/Chinook Nation: Order Affirming Final Determination and Referring Nine Issues to the Secretary of the Interior*, 246.

56. Peggy Disney, interview by author, March 25, 2008; Stephen Dow Beckham to author, April 7, 2008.

57. Internal Board of Indian Appeals, *In Re Federal Acknowledgment*, 247–49.

58. Ibid., 250–51.

59. U.S. Department of the Interior, Bureau of Indian Affairs, Office of Federal Acknowledgment, *Reconsidered on Referral*, 1.

60. Ibid., 3–5.

61. Ibid.

62. 25 C.F.R., ch. 1, 270.

63. Ibid., 272; emphasis added.

64. Ibid.

65. Ibid., 268–69.

66. See Cramer, *Cash, Color, and Colonialism*; Jessica R. Cattelino, "The Double Bind of American Indian Need-Based Sovereignty," *Cultural Anthropology* 25 (2010): 235–62.

67. Brian Klopotek, *Recognition Odysseys: Indigeneity, Race, and Federal Tribal Recognition Policy in Three Louisiana Indian Communities* (Durham: Duke University Press, 2011).

68. Miller, *Forgotten Tribes.*

69. Klopotek, *Recognition Odysseys,* 264

70. Ibid., esp. introduction, ch. 10.

71. Disney, interview.

72. For Washington state recognition, see Trafzer, *Chinook,* 100, 105. For the longhouse project, see Angela Sanders, "Chinook Nation," *Portland Magazine,* Winter 2005.

73. Disney, interview; www.chinooknation.org.

74. Edward Stratton, "Clarks Make Good on Stolen Canoe," *Daily Astorian,* September 26, 2011.

Mapping Erasure

The Power of Nominative Cartography in
the Past and Present of the Muwekma Ohlones
of the San Francisco Bay Area

LES W. FIELD *with Alan Leventhal and Rosemary Cambra*

In the twentieth century, the erasure of the Ohlones, the indigenous people of the San Francisco Bay area, was constructed around the unilateral and arbitrary termination of their relationship with the federal government in 1927, on the one hand, and an "extinction sentence" inscribed by Alfred Kroeber in his authoritative tome, *Handbook of the Indians of California* (1925), on the other.[1] But the processes by which the presence of Ohlone peoples in their aboriginal territories was decisively obscured and disestablished had been ongoing since the initiation of the Spanish colonial regime in the late eighteenth century. These processes involved transformation of geography and place-names that not only erased the Ohlones and their long history but filled that absence with colonial presence. This chapter closely interrogates "nominative cartography," the power to erase and also implant, to disappear but also to substantiate, and to displace and replace in the service of colonial projects, tracing the changing map of Ohlone home territories in Central California as they were transformed by and during Spanish, Mexican, and U.S. colonial regimes. The Ohlones did not disappear, and their persistence is reflected in contemporary strategies to gain federal recognition and reestablish their presence in the landscape.

In June 2002, the Branch of Acknowledgment and Research (BAR, now renamed the Office of Federal Acknowledgment) of the Bureau of Indian Affairs (BIA) notified the Muwekma Ohlone tribe of its intention to find negatively on their federal recognition petition. The Muwekma Ohlone tribe is the contemporary tribal organization of the indigenous Ohlone peoples of the San Francisco Bay area (predominantly East and South Bay lineages) that has struggled to obtain federal recognition since the mid-1980s.[2] In 1996, the BAR conceded that the federal government had previously unambiguously recognized the Muwekmas' ancestors as the Verona Band of Alameda County as late as 1927. This finding meant that the Muwekmas had only to prove a continuous historical relationship between themselves and the Verona band since 1927. The Ohlones rejoiced, since they had already assembled materials that demonstrated that all of their members were direct descendants of the Verona band and could therefore demonstrate they had maintained a kin-structured social organization over the years. "Kin-structured social organization" refers to the quotidian relationships of mutual aid between intermarried Ohlone families, reflected in ongoing participation in the rituals of baptism, marriage, and funerals and reaffirmed by the informal leadership of specific individuals who organized the families to continuously enroll with the BIA in 1933, 1955, and 1970 and to participate in the California Claims Act of 1955. The Ohlones were asking for a reaffirmation of their previously recognized status, which seemed to them far less fraught than having to prove who they were from scratch. Nevertheless, the BAR had ruled negatively in their case.

Unrecognized or unacknowledged status can be thought of as a lack or absence of recognition. Such status is not merely a denial or repression of recognition, nor are the barriers to achieving recognition constructed of incomplete or distorted information. Nonrecognition and the maintenance of nonrecognized status are therefore not the consequence of an oversight or a lapse in administrative efficiency that can be straightforwardly rectified via sustained effort. Following Foucault's by-now well-trod path, we identify nonrecognition itself as a powerful discourse that produces knowledge and is sustained by entrenched discursive practices built into the cultural, ideological, political, ecological, and spatial/geographical environments.[3] Consequently, gaining recognition is not and has never been simply a matter of providing the BAR with the appropriate materials and information. The power of the discourse of nonrecognition discards and discounts such information and the material documentation of it as part of its regularized procedures.[4] The spatial/geographical character of colonialism as it shaped the unrecognized status of contemporary Ohlone people is intrinsic, but this chapter focuses on what we will call "nominative cartography"—that is, the power to erase and also implant, to disappear but also to substantiate, and to displace and replace in the service of colonial projects. Our focus on place-names stems from recent experiences watching and listening to the ways that a people's presence can be obscured and eliminated through the renaming of places in Palestine.[5]

Our emphasis on space and cartography is inspired by Neil Smith's theoretical work on the geography of uneven development in capitalist societies. Smith's summation that "uneven development is social inequality blazoned into the geographical landscape, and it is simultaneously the exploitation of that geographical unevenness for certain socially determined ends" provokes me to wonder how to apply such a profound insight to colonial projects that remake, restructure, and rename landscapes.[6] Rashid Khalidi offers one suggestion for how to apply a spatial, cartographic perspective to colonialism: "This process of naming [places] is an attempt to privilege one dimension of a complex reality at the expense of others, with the ultimate aim of blotting out or decisively subordinating them."[7] This chapter, then, hinges on the quite literal transformation of the map of the San Francisco Bay area under successive colonial regimes as a central underpinning of the unacknowledged status of the Ohlone people.

The Ohlone case has been especially illuminated by a "comparable" case: what Meron Benvenisti has called "the Israelification of Palestinian geography."[8] Benvenisti's work draws attention to particular colonial practices and outcomes that substantively erase and replace constitutive features of social and cultural landscapes when indigenous peoples lose control not only over their homelands but also over documenting historical memory of how their homelands looked and functioned before the onset of a colonial regime.[9] This chapter begins with a discussion of the Hispanification of Ohlone geography during the Spanish colonial era (1770–1821). After a somewhat speculative discussion of changes transforming the Ohlone map during the period of the Mexican republic in California (1821–48), we argue that the Spanish colonial project made possible the categorical erasure of the Ohlone presence that occurred after U.S. statehood (1850). In coastal California, then, the sequence of two distinct colonial regimes shaped a particular fate for peoples such as the Ohlones. Better said, the ways in which the former shaped the possibilities of the latter, rather than the singular impact of either of these regimes, gave rise to the form geographical erasure took in Ohlone country. In these historical discussions, it is clear that in the California case, the erasure of the Ohlones from the map is the consequence not just of the conjugation of Spanish and American colonialisms but also of the specific forms of Spanish and American colonialism in their distinct time periods. That is, Spanish colonialism's transformation of coastal California came very late in the history of that empire and was marked by the primary impact of the use of Franciscan missions, while the subsequent U.S. colonial regime was distinct in the role played by resource extraction and massive sudden waves of immigration that gave California immense national importance since its admission to the United States. These specificities further complicate and embroider the conjugation of two colonialisms that shaped the nonrecognized status of the Ohlone peoples in the San Francisco Bay area.

In conclusion, we will describe the Muwekma Ohlone tribe's efforts to directly confront their erasure from the map of the Bay Area through deliberate, self-reflexive efforts to reimplant their history and contemporary presence into the landscape of places using the power of nominative cartography. These efforts have proceeded notwithstanding the BAR's negative ruling in 2002, as the Muwekmas continue their struggle for recognition by other means.[10]

The Hispanification of Native Geography: The Ohlone Case

At first blush, the question of the Hispanification of native geography in California seems self-evident. Looking at any map of the state, one can immediately see that there are a preponderance of Hispanic place-names, particularly (and unsurprisingly) in the zone where missionization took place between the current Mexico-California boundary in the south to the northernmost extent of mission activity in what is now Sonoma County. By contrast, there are very few native place-names in this region, and the few that exist—Malibu, Lompoc, and Port Hueneme in the south, Petaluma in the north, for example—are not understood by the vast majority of people in California as native in origin or linked to the contemporary presence and activities of native peoples.[11] But if the results are self-evident to any map reader, how did this process of Hispanification take place? And what happened to indigenous place-names and to the indigenous places themselves?

One way to begin a discussion of the transformation of place would entail discussing precontact social structure and how native places were made and named before the arrival of the Spaniards. The anthropological literature about precontact California Indian society and social structure has developed contradictory approaches to those issues. On the one hand, the iconic work of Alfred Kroeber, embodied in his still-authoritative tome, *The Handbook of the Indians of California*, employed the term "tribelet" to describe what were supposed to be small, autochthonous sociopolitical units that he considered the dominant structure in precontact California.[12] On the other hand, in Lowell Bean and Thomas Blackburn's pathbreaking edited volume, *Native Californians: A Theoretical Retrospective*, numerous authors write about large-scale social, political, and ritual integration of native societies across relatively great distances via relations of trade, kinship, and ceremonial interaction.[13] It is indeed quite difficult to describe precisely the nature of precontact place and social structure, given what Randall Milliken has called "a vast discrepancy between the two cultures [native and Spanish]; there was a disparity in technology and an incongruity in world views." Thus, because the Spaniards were the first to report on precontact societies[14] in coastal California, the picture that emerges is necessarily distorted and contentious. Steven W. Hackel argues that the Franciscans and other Spaniards were utterly uninterested in California Indian culture and believed that the native peoples in the missionized areas were primitives who had attained only the most rudimentary social, cultural, and religious levels.[15]

Milliken, however, provides a rigorous framework for discussing the transformation of place and social structure in the Ohlone region.[16] While he does not theoretically commit himself to the older Kroeberian framework, his analysis takes for granted that villages and village social structure comprised the basis for precontact native society, a view that is also accepted by the later theorists from Bean and Blackburn onward. According to Milliken, Mission Santa Clara, one of the five missions in the aboriginal territory of Ohlone peoples, "lay at the northeastern edge of the Tamien tribal district. . . . Three large villages of over 120 inhabitants each lay within a four mile radius of the Santa Clara Mission site; the native names of those villages are not now known," but their Spanish designations—San Francisco Solano, Santa Ysabel, and San Joseph Cupertino—have survived.[17] Santa Clara was established in 1777, whereas Mission Dolores in what is now urban San Francisco was built in 1776. Santa Cruz, site of the current city of the same name, was established in 1791. Mission San Jose, in what is now the East Bay city of Fremont was founded in 1797. Earliest of all, Mission San Carlos, in what is now Monterey, south of the Bay Area but still within the aboriginal territory of Ohlone peoples, was established in 1770.

Robert H. Jackson and Edward Castillo argue that the Spaniards' use of Franciscan missions to colonize California in the last quarter of the eighteenth century was "a warmed over version of the 16th century policy of congregación and reducción, modified by two hundred years of practical experience in missions" all over Spanish America and designed "to transform native society into sedentary populations that could provide labor and pay taxes according to the model [the Spaniards had] developed in central Mexico."[18] Writing about Mission San Jose, Jackson also concludes that the mission project, at least with regard to its organization of agricultural production and ranching and the architectural design of the mission itself, specifically aimed to resettle "dispersed [native] populations into large communities modeled on the corporate indigenous communities of central Mexico," and in this way the colonization of California hinged upon the success of the missions.[19] Thus, we should understand Spanish mission colonialism in the late eighteenth century, accompanied by the establishment of military presidios designed to protect the missions and act as their enforcers, as itself the product of almost three hundred years of Spanish colonialism in the Americas. As Kent Lightfoot has noted, Spain sought geopolitically to compete with Britain and Russia in laying claim to the Pacific littoral of North America, which for Europeans at the time was one of the planet's most remote regions.[20] Spain's efforts in this regard also accelerated following U.S. independence as Americans began encroaching on Spanish territories and claims in Florida, and in the immense territories interior to the St. Louis/middle Mississippi River Valley region. The expeditions of Lewis and Clark, who reached the Pacific coast on November 7, 1805, underscored the ever-expanding reach of Anglo-American territorial ambitions in North America.[21]

The collapse of native places and geographies in the face of missionization was a complex and never quite complete process. Lightfoot comments that in California, "the founding of new European colonies often involved the removal of native peoples from their ancestral lands and their resettlement in newly created colonial places, including missions, plantations, mines and barrios"; in the Ohlone region specifically, "the ultimate consequence of placing missionary colonies in the coastal zone was the structural collapse of local native societies."[22] Milliken explains that collapse as a complex historical process that lasted decades. He explains that "in contrast with the Spanish missionaries, many local people initially respected the new forms of worship practiced by the foreigners" but that Ohlone people soon made calculated alliances with what seemed to them powerful newcomers as increasingly damaging changes began taking their toll on native society.[23] Their emotional ambivalence, Milliken argues, was transformed by the Spaniards' "stunning technology and complex social organization," which challenged native social and economic values as epidemiological and ecological catastrophes ensued.[24]

This process snowballed, and the Franciscans and other Spaniards may not have realized exactly how their actions would unfold. Hackel and Milliken agree that local native peoples were lured to the missions through Franciscans' gifts of food.[25] Very soon after the arrival of the Spaniards, epidemic diseases began decimating native populations, a process that accelerated, Hackel argues, as natives came to the missions hoping that the power of the priests could protect them from the wave of death. David Weber writes that the "Franciscans did not succeed unless Indians cooperated and Indians cooperated only when they believed they had something to gain from the new religion and the material benefits that accompanied it, or had too much to lose from resisting it."[26] The Franciscans interned neophytes (recently baptized Indians) in sex-segregated, filthy barracks-type quarters that contributed to the spread of diseases. Neophytes who attempted to escape were forcibly recaptured by soldiers from nearby presidios and flogged by the priests, enduring an almost complete loss of personal autonomy. Lightfoot contends that the missions resembled a penal system.[27] The livestock that the Spaniards brought with them almost immediately began damaging the native vegetation on which the Ohlones and other coastal native peoples had depended. The Franciscans suppressed controlled burns, an especially important technique of native food resource management.[28] Environmental degradation, demographic implosion, and the deterioration of the psychological and cultural environment caused by the systematic mistreatment of neophytes ultimately led the native social structure to erode. Ritual practices and respect for elders and cultural experts deteriorated as natives realized that their old ways provided no protection against disease and mistreatment and had apparently become irrelevant. All of these effects irrevocably transformed both interior landscapes (the intellectual and behavioral bases for indigenous cultural systems) and exterior landscapes (the reconfirmation of cultural understandings through a named geography with which individuals and groups interacted on a daily and highly practical basis).

If the Spaniards did not initially understand all the effects of their activities, they certainly came to that understanding over time and, according to Milliken, mounted an increasingly aggressive campaign against native ways of life. He strongly implies that as Christianity and its worldview spread among the neophytes and more widely, it fed a sense of powerlessness, unworthiness, and apathy in the Ohlone region. Christianity also seemed to access new realms of power. The old villages were abandoned, their place-names forgotten and replaced by Hispanic designations, as were the personal names of individual natives who underwent baptism.[29] Hackel contends that "native identity often was obscured not just by given Spanish names but by the terms Spanish officials and missionaries used to classify people and establish their place within the colonial order."[30] As the old place, polity, and personal names fragmented and then evaporated, Lightfoot describes the development of a new kind of Indian identity, constructed in the missions around the intermarriage between individuals from many different villages who spoke different Ohlone languages or languages from other adjacent regions.[31] As Hackel argues, the missions became the central, essential places around which native identity recongealed.[32] But the fate of those identities and the places associated with them was not a foregone conclusion. Before the Americans came to occupy and define what is now the state of California, this geography and particularly the coastal missionized region was part of the Mexican Republic. Had Mexico prevailed, the future might have turned out somewhat differently for the indigenous peoples and places of California.

Ohlone Places and Identities in Mexican California (1821–1848)

By 1822, the successful conclusion of the Mexican independence struggle against Spain brought a new administration to the region that would later become the state of California.[33] The chaotic struggles within the Mexican state no doubt affected the political structure in the territories of Alta California. But Mexican independence's main effect on the native peoples of the coast, including the San Francisco Bay area, was the Mexican Republic's secularization of the Franciscan missions, which occurred in 1832.

Soon after the arrival of the new Mexican bureaucracy, officials convened with both the Franciscans and the secular-military authorities in the Spanish presidios; among the key topics discussed was the fate of the missions' neophytes. According to James A. Sandos, Mexican authorities initially concluded that the neophytes could not function on their own and "should remain subject to missionaries."[34] Some Indians, judged useful to the local economy, were permitted to move out of the mission compounds. The status quo was unstable, and in 1827, growing anti-Spanish sentiment in the Mexican government led to demands that the Franciscans swear allegiance to the new republic. The resulting conflict with the Spanish Franciscans was matched by Mexican officials' worries that were the missions to simply close, they would cease producing the food that supported the entire Hispanic population (both those born in California, the Californios, and more recent immigrants from Mexico) in Alta California.[35] Therefore, Sandos explains, the Mexican authorities turned control over the missions from Sonoma to Carmel—the aboriginal homeland of Ohlone peoples—to a Mexican Franciscan order from Zacatecas.[36] This change later led to the complete secularization of the missions, their transformation into regular church parishes, and the emancipation of the neophytes, who were recognized as adult citizens of the republic. Whereas in 1800 the mission population stood at more than eighteen thousand, by 1839, the neophyte population had dwindled to less than one thousand.[37]

But given that the missions had become the central—indeed, essential—places, for native peoples such as the Ohlones, what did emancipation mean for the neophytes and associated missionized populations in coastal areas like the Ohlone homelands? According to Milliken, writing in collaboration with the Muwekma Ohlones,

> Under Spanish law, Mission lands were to be held in trust for the Indians until the government felt that they had become enough like Europeans to be considered "people of reason." The Mexican government came under strong pressure during the 1820s to ignore Indian land rights and open up mission lands to settlement by the families of ex-soldiers and by new settlers from Mexico. The government of Mexico finally gave in to these new pressures. . . . [O]n paper these acts protected Indian land rights. Administrators were to divide mission properties among the Indians, with the left over lands to be allocated to Mexican immigrants through petition. A veritable landrush began among local Mexican families from San Jose. . . . Within a two year period an instant feudal aristocracy was formed complete with a population of Indian serfs. These new land owners continued to live in [the town] of San Jose, while former Mission San Jose Indians did all the labor on various ranchos.[38]

The Mexican land grants in the southern end of the Bay Area, around Mission Santa Clara, included at least four grants to neophytes, two of which are important in light of this discussion. Rancho Ulistac, granted by the Mexican governor in 1845 to several Ohlone men, is a place-name that may mean "place of the basket" in several Ohlone languages and that has remained associated with the same location.[39] Although the ranch went through a complete depopulation of its indigenous inhabitants and many significant ecological changes from orchard to golf course to neglect, it remained the last forty acres of open space in the city of Santa Clara and was officially designated the Ulistac Natural Area in 1997. How closely the current residents of Santa Clara associate the name "Ulistac" with Ohlone history and, more importantly, with contemporary Ohlone people is an open question. In a second case, an Ohlone village name was given to another land grant, the Rancho Posolmi, also awarded in 1844 to an Ohlone connected to Mission Santa Clara. The indigenous name and history were subsequently buried (literally and metaphorically) by the historical events that transformed the original ranch lands into a military area by the early 1930s, and by 1953 into Moffett Field, the site of major aerospace industries. The example of these two ranchos underscores the incomplete nature of cartographic transformations.

Sandos elaborates that following secularization, many Indians groups that had for up to two generations lived in or around the missions returned to old village sites.[40] This was true in the case of Ohlones who had been associated particularly with Mission San Jose and to a lesser extent with Mission Santa Clara. By the early 1840s, Ohlones began returning to an old village site in the Livermore Valley located on the Rancho El Valle de San Jose (later known as the Bernal Ranch), granted to three Hispanic Californian families in 1839, where they reestablished a small settlement that came to be known by the Spanish name "Alisal" (the alder grove).[41] Alisal was the home of the Verona band, the most significant early twentieth-century Ohlone community in the Bay Area. Alisal and a number of other smaller post mission communities were not antiquarian revivals of pristine precontact culture, society, and place. Sandos points out that postmission native communities in the Ohlone region were composed of multilingual postneophytes who spoke Spanish as their common language as well as one among many mutually unintelligible Ohlone languages or languages from the Yokutsan, Miwokan, or other families.[42] Lightfoot refers to "pan-mission identities" formed out of the intermarriages that took place in the missions.[43] Jackson and Castillo describe the emerging economy of Mexican California as based on cattle ranching, dominated by a small landed elite in which Indians—from Alisal in the case of the Ohlone territories—performed the multiple and essential menial labor as vaqueros.[44] In this situation, cattle and horse rustling was linked to outright rebellion against the authorities, and the history of one such rebel, Estanislao, a Yokuts-speaker from Mission San Jose who led a band of Miwok and Ohlone speakers, saw his defeat by the Mexican Army's Lieutenant Mariano Guadalupe Vallejo.[45]

Under Mexican rule, California was headed for a regime of labor, social stratification, and cultural diversity that is familiar to scholars of Latin American history and society. In such societies, there is no question about the need for a large pool of subaltern laborers who are marked ethnically as indigenous and whose non-Hispanic practices are tolerated even though to a great extent indigenous religious, sociopolitical, and kinship practices are in Latin America already always transformed by long-term impacts from and interactions with Catholicism and Hispanic notions of gender, social status, and hierarchy. The social order thereby constructed featured patron-client relationships between Hispanic landowners and Indian laborers structured by ritual godparenthood, or *compadrazgo*.[46] The postmission Ohlones and other natives of the coastal region were certainly still recognizable as Indians to the Hispanic Californios and immigrant Mexicans, and as in the rest of Latin America, indigenous settlements in California such as Alisal were part of a Hispanified cartography in which Spanish names were not incompatible with indigenous places.[47] Following this line of thinking, had the Mexican regime in California endured, the question would not be whether indigenous identities and places existed—as became the case under the U.S. regime—but rather what rights such identities and places could claim under a highly stratified and unequal political, social, and economic system.

The "Disappearance" of Ohlone Places and Identities in American California

According to Jackson and Castillo, "The discovery of gold in 1848 following the American conquest of California led to the rapid populating of California and statehood in 1850, and conflicts between Mexican and Anglo-American settlers over land. Indians in the coastal area where missions previously operated were increasingly marginalized and identified by Anglo-Americans as part of an unwanted and despised Mexican underclass."[48] These authors describe an Anglo-American vision of California built out of frontierism, the individual ethic of self-reliance and a racially profiled egalitarianism in which only Anglo-American farmers, prospectors, and merchants would have the right to belong and be treated as equals. In such a society, the coastal, formerly missionized Indians evaporated because they did not fit the Anglo-American expectation of how Indians should look and act, while their looks and behaviors characterized them as Mexicans, the racially and linguistically marked underclass under the new regime. In these circumstances, an indigenous map of places and indigenous identities was subsumed and ultimately erased by their Hispanification.

For all native peoples in California, two main thrusts determined the unfolding of the American colonial project: on the one hand, the overwhelmingly unstoppable drive toward resource extraction, epitomized by the Gold Rush that accompanied—indeed, propelled—statehood; and on the other hand, what Tomás Almaguer has described as the institutionalization of white supremacy as "the central organizing principle" during and since the formation of the state of California.[49] On January 7, 1851, in Governor Peter Burnett's first address to the new state's legislature, he declared that "a war of extermination will continue to be waged between the races, until the Indian race becomes extinct."[50] The native peoples of the Sierra Nevada and North Coast, whose aboriginal territories lay exactly within the Gold Rush zone (and later the most important zones of timber extraction) experienced the drive toward resource extraction as genocide, which has been well documented for peoples such as the Sierra Miwok, the Maidu, and the Hupa.[51] The resource extraction bonanzas had less direct effects on the coastal native peoples in the missionized zone. For the Ohlone peoples, the accelerating urbanization of what became the San Francisco Bay Area meant sudden and decisive demographic changes that made native peoples even smaller minorities in a population of Euro-American migrants eager to shape an unfamiliar environment into a comfortable one and in this way to fulfill utopian desires.[52] Thus, the effects of demographic changes converged with the project of establishing white supremacy, leading to a horizon of erasure for native peoples in the coastal region.

We can underscore the nature of geographical-cartographic erasure for the Ohlones by contrasting their experience with native groups in California that did not undergo missionization, were officially recognized by the United States on a continuous basis since California statehood, and did receive a land base on which to maintain their cultural identity. That contrast is provided by a recent book about the Central Valley Yokuts and their struggles for cultural identity and tribal sovereignty on the Tule River reservation.[53] Before statehood, Yokuts peoples had emerged relatively unscathed by the Spanish and Mexican regimes. Under the U.S. regime, these Yokuts peoples coalesced as the Tule River Tribe, composed of multiple "closely related but politically and dialectically distinct Southern Valley and Foothill Yokuts tribes" that had "occupied villages of varying sizes along the rivers, creeks, springs and lakes throughout California's vast Central Valley and foothill regions." Their federally recognized status includes a reservation land base of 55,396 acres—very large by California standards.[54] The reservation was established by executive order of Ulysses S. Grant in 1873 and was one of only four reservations in California that the federal government created in that era. One might expect that under such conditions and with such an outcome, the Central Valley Yokuts should have maintained a certain degree of cartographic integrity—in other words, some of the native places of the past would still exist with their native names intact.

But nothing of the sort occurred. Under the American regime, the Yokuts peoples were moved from the Tejon Reservation in the 1850s to the first Tule River Reservation, created in 1864, and then forcibly removed to the second (current) Tule River Reservation by 1873. All along, old village sites were abandoned and destroyed; new ones were only temporarily occupied before being destroyed; and subsistence enterprises, including both foraging for wild foods and agriculture, were continuously and repeatedly disrupted and rendered unproductive.[55] During the late nineteenth century, the federal government was disentangling itself from the older policies and views that had mandated the designation of greatly reduced portions of aboriginal lands as Indian Territory, where native peoples could nevertheless live apart from the larger Euro-American society. In its place came a new conception of reservations as much smaller and divorced from aboriginal territorial rights and where Indians were to be "civilized."[56] Indeed, by the 1850s, the state and federal governments had decided that the Land Commission Act of 1851 had effectively abolished aboriginal claims to land in the state of California. As Gelya Frank and Carole Goldberg show, the Tule River reservation was established through other means, and its sovereign status was only maintained through continuous struggle.[57] Cartographic integrity has consequently not been a feature of Yokuts identity and sovereignty in the lands controlled by this tribe.

With this case—perhaps the best-case scenario in California—in mind, how did Ohlone relationships with place and place-names fare, given that they bore an additional burden of Spanish colonialism that led Anglo-Americans to discredit or simply not see Ohlones and other formerly missionized native peoples as Indians? The highly ambivalent case of Ulistac in Santa Clara notwithstanding, the connections between Ohlone identity and place, between indigenous existence and a piece of land, were most clearly maintained after statehood and into the twentieth century among the largest group of Ohlones located at Alisal and several other smaller nearby settlements in the East Bay. These connections occurred, in contrast with the Yokuts case, in the absence of any kind of official recognition or sanction.

In the late nineteenth century, the rancho estates of the Californios, like the Bernal Ranch where Alisal was located, passed out of the hands of the old Hispanic elite because new American laws made it very difficult to validate Californios' titles. An extreme drought destroyed agricultural production and obliged the old owners to sell to the wealthy Anglo-Americans settling in the San Francisco Bay area. No better example of this transition could be found than the acquisition of the Bernal Ranch by U.S. Senator George Hearst and his wife, Phoebe Apperson Hearst, parents of publishing magnate William Randolph Hearst. The Hearsts permitted the native community at Alisal, which had by then become known as the Verona band because the Verona railroad station had been built adjacent to their homes, to continue to occupy this terrain. This informal relationship sustained a revitalized cultural syncretism in which multiple Ohlone, Miwok, and Yokuts languages were spoken and ceremonial life was reinvigorated. Ohlones from Alisal participated in the Ghost Dance revitalization movement that in California fused with much older traditions such as the Kuksu ceremonial dance and religious complex. Numerous anthropologists documented these linguistic, ritual, and sociocultural phenomena at Alisal during the late nineteenth and early twentieth centuries.[58]

The informal relationship between the Verona band and the land where Alisal was located could not withstand the continued wave of demographic and economic change engulfing the Bay Area. The increasingly large number of Anglo-American immigrants and the tendency of new Anglo landowners to discontinue the use of Indian labor in favor of the droves of young men of European descent who seldom had families to support dried up the slender economic base on which the Verona band had depended. Assimilationist pressures were even stronger because the Ohlones, like other formerly missionized coastal peoples, were invisible as Indians under the American regime. As individuals from the Verona band drifted away from Alisal to live in other parts of the Bay Area, their invisibility became formalized when the federal government disassociated itself from the Verona band in 1927. Les W. Field and the Muwekma tribe elaborated the Verona band's listing on the California Indian census conducted in 1905–6, and the appearance of the Verona band on the "Indian Map of California" produced by Indian Service Bureau special agent C. E. Kelsey. He identified the Verona band as among twenty-four Indian bands for which land should be purchased, as reported to the Indian Service Bureau (of the BIA) by special agent C. H. Asbury from the Reno agency in 1914.[59] The Verona band appeared again as a landless tribe in the BIA's Reno agency 1923 annual report. But this historic relationship, which formed the basis for the BAR's 1996 admission that the Verona band had previously been unambiguously recognized, was in effect unilaterally terminated in 1927 when the BIA's Sacramento superintendent, L. A. Dorrington, wrote in a report to Congress, "It does not appear at the present time that there is need for the purchase of land for the establishment of their [the Verona band's] homes."[60] The end of the Ohlones' relationship with the federal government, through the idiosyncratic decisions of one Indian agent, was matched by the declaration by the one of anthropology's patriarchs, Kroeber, who wrote that the "Costanoans" were "for all practical purposes" extinct.[61]

The Verona band ceased to exist as a residential group at Alisal because as a landless band, the community could not economically sustain itself, particularly after it was denied the formal land base federal recognition would have afforded. As Muwekma tribal scholarship has shown, without land—a place of their own—the family lineages of the Verona band continued to function as a cohesive social and cultural group; continued to enroll as individuals in BIA censuses from 1929 to 1932, from 1950 to 1957, and from 1968 to 1970; and even remained within a relatively small geographical area.[62] The name "Alisal," not an indigenous one even if it was an indigenous place, was covered over by time and Bay Area real estate development. In the end, the coercive economic and political forces of American statehood, with which anthropology perhaps unwittingly cooperated, coming on the heels of Spanish missionization, denied the Ohlones their cultural existence and erased their cartographic presence. But although the places where they had lived as a community went into a decisive occultation behind Hispanic and Anglo place-names, neither the places nor the people went extinct, refusing to disappear.

Concluding Thoughts: Reinserting Ohlone Places and People in the Twenty-First Century

The descendants of the Verona band reorganized in 1965–71 to save their historic cemetery at Mission San Jose from destruction. In 1984 they solidified their reorganization as the Muwekma Ohlone Tribe, pursuing federal recognition and utilizing multiple professional, intellectual, political, and cultural tools to reassert their identity and reinsert their presence in their old homelands. From archaeological excavation to language revitalization, from leadership training workshops to abalone feasts, and from overnight camping and hiking trips in the Alisal area to participating in Bay Area political alliances, the Muwekmas have emerged from erasure as an increasingly visible tribal organization of the indigenous people of the Bay Area. Notwithstanding BAR's negative finding in 2002, the tribe continues to struggle toward federal recognition.

Reinserting their presence in their aboriginal territory implies the redefinition of places and the renaming of those places. Muwekma leaders have made no secret of their desire, once they receive federal recognition, to secure property in and around the old Alisal community site. The successful reestablishment of an Ohlone presence at Alisal may result in multiple renamings, but so far, naming has emerged as a practice primarily in association with archaeological excavation and interpretation undertaken by the Muwekma Ohlone tribe's cultural resources management firm, Ohlone Families Consulting Services. These practices were recently detailed in a report for the City of San Jose's Department of Public Works, written in collaboration with San Jose State archaeologist Alan Leventhal and other professional archaeologists. Their report included a highly elaborated ethnohistory chapter that interpreted the findings at the CA-SCL-869 excavation site:

> Towards the completion in August 2008 of the archaeological and burial recovery program at [CA-SCL-869], it became apparent that the most significant aspect of this site was the recovery of four elderly ancestral Ohlone Indian women. A decision was made by the Muwekma Ohlone Tribal leadership and the Tribe's Language Committee . . . to honor their deceased ancestors by renaming the site with a new name in the Tribe's aboriginal Ohlone Chocheño language.
>
> This practice follows Tribal tradition which has over the past decades renamed some of their ancestral village and cemetery sites. . . . As mentioned above, because of the discovery of four elderly women who were buried near each other and had died very close in time to each other, the Muwekma Tribal Language Committee decided upon the name Katwás˘ Ketneyma Waréeptak, which literally means "The Four Elderly Women" or the "Four Matriarchs" as the alternative native name for this site.[63]

The significance of these renaming practices may primarily benefit the tribal members who appreciate the meaning of these names. But the effects may not always be so limited. In another resonant case, the construction of a railroad station in San Jose in the late 1980s and early 1990s on the site where an enormous fruit cannery had once stood uncovered a major archaeological site with eighty-one burials. The California Department of Transportation constructed "a permanent exhibit structure within the heavy rail station which describes the story of the archaeological recovery." The rail station was named Tamien Station, after the local Ohlone village, and included "artifacts not associated with the burials" in the exhibit display.[64] The department intended that "the large number of commuters using this station [would be exposed] to the prehistory and rich cultural heritage of the Santa Clara Valley."[65] A brass plaque at the Tamien Station states, "Tamien Caltrain Station Grand Opening, June 27, 1992, 'Dedicated to the Muwekma Tribe of the Ohlone Indian Community who lived on this site for centuries.'"[66] This marker, placed with the collaboration of the Ohlone Families Consulting Services and the Muwekma tribe, seeks to inform a broad public about the contemporary existence of Ohlone people by reemplacing them in the world of daily life and work.

All such efforts to reemplace the Muwekmas within their aboriginal homelands through nominative cartography offer illuminating ethnographic perspectives on Patrick Wolfe's recent efforts to tease apart the relationships between settler colonialism and the elimination of native peoples through genocide.[67] In the United States, as Wolfe notes, settler colonialism was not necessarily isomorphic with genocide; in California, in specific instances, the war against native people was indeed tied up with genocidal campaigns.[68] In the Muwekma Ohlone case, erasure—a synonym for elimination—played out in the anthropology of California Indians as well. Resisting their erasure, the Muwekma Ohlones seek to literally put themselves back on the map in the highly urbanized San Francisco Bay Area, just one nodal point of an increasingly urbanized planet. Perhaps the urban battlegrounds, rather than the remote, rural locations where indigenous peoples were supposed by anthropologists to always have the best chances of survival, are the places where the power of renaming as well as the defense of indigenous places will matter most in this century, even as the technologies of settler colonialism develop ever more rapidly.

Notes

1. Alfred Kroeber, *Handbook of the Indians of California* (New York: Dover, 1925).

2. Throughout most of the twentieth century, anthropologists referred to Ohlone peoples as "Costanoan," derivative of the Spanish for "coastal people," *costeños*. Apparently misheard and mispronounced by early English-speaking

settlers as "costanos," anthropologists transformed a misnomer into the even more absurd "Costanoan," perhaps believing it sounded more "scientific." The ethnonym "Ohlone" is a self-identifying term with a reasonably long history. The ancestors of these peoples spoke related, although mutually unintelligible languages, but were affiliated with one another through intermarriage, trade, and annual ceremonial cycles. In the East and South Bay, the term "Ohlone" has been used among the descendant families for at least a century. See Alan Leventhal, Les W. Field, Hank Alvarez, and Rosemary Cambra, "Back from Extinction: A Brief Overview of the Historic Disenfranchisement of the Ohlone Indian Peoples," in *The Ohlone Past and Present: Native Americans of the San Francisco Bay Region*, ed. Lowell John Bean (Menlo Park, Calif.: Ballena, 1994), 297–337; Alan Leventhal, Diana Di Giuseppe, Melynda Atwood, David Grant, Rosemary Cambra, Charlene Nijmeh, Monica V. Arellano, Susanne Rodriguez, Sheila Guzman Schmidt, Gloria E. Gomez, Norma Sanchez, and Stella D'Oro, "Final Report on the Burial and Archaeological Data Recovery Program Conducted on a Portion of a Middle Period Ohlone Indian Cemetery, Katwás˙ Ketneyma Waréeptak (Four Matriarchs) CA-SCL-869, Located at 5912 Cahalan Avenue, Fire Station #12 San Jose, Santa Clara County, California" (Prepared for the City of San Jose Department of Public Works by the Muwekma Ohlone Tribe and Ohlone Families Consulting Services, 2009). The term "Muwekma" ("the People" in Chocheño and Tamien, the East and South Bay Ohlone language) was also used into the 1930s (Leventhal et al., "Back from Extinction").

3. Michel Foucault, *The History of Sexuality* (New York: Vintage, 1990).

4. See Les W. Field and the Muwekma Tribe, "Unacknowledged Tribes, Dangerous Knowledge: The Muwekma Ohlone and How Indian Identities Are 'Known,'" *Wicazo Sa Review* 18 (2003): 79–94. As with our other collaboratively produced work, the tribe has edited, revised, and critiqued this article in an extensive fashion. Other scholars have described aspects of the historical construction of unacknowledged status for the Muwekma Ohlones and other coastal California indigenous peoples. See especially Randall Milliken, *A Time of Little Choice: The Disintegration of Tribal Culture in the San Francisco Bay Area, 1769–1810* (Menlo Park, Calif.: Ballena, 1995); Randall Milliken, *Native Americans of Mission San Jose* (Banning, Calif.: Malki-Ballena, 2008); Steven W. Hackel, *Children of Coyote, Missionaries of Saint Francis: Indian-Spanish Relations in Colonial California, 1769–1850* (Chapel Hill: University of North Carolina Press, 2003); Robert H. Jackson, "The Development of San Jose Mission," in *Ohlone Past and Present*, ed. Bean, 229–49; Robert H. Jackson and Edward Castillo, *Indians, Franciscans, and Spanish Colonization: The Impact of the Mission System on California Indians* (Albuquerque: University of New Mexico Press, 1995); James A. Sandos, *Converting California: Indians*

and Franciscans in the Missions (New Haven: Yale University Press, 2008); Kent Lightfoot, *Indians, Missionaries, and Merchants: The Legacy of Colonial Encounters on the California Frontiers* (Berkeley: University of California Press, 2003).

5. In May 2011, I co-organized and led an ethnographic field school in Palestine with Alex Lubin, the chair of the American Studies Department at the University of New Mexico. With seventeen undergraduate and graduate students, we visited and witnessed areas of the West Bank and East Jerusalem currently undergoing ethnic cleansing and colonial transformation; the effects of the 420-mile-long "separation barrier" on West Bank villages, some of which are enclosed on four sides by the wall; Arab villages within the pre-1967 boundaries that had been destroyed and erased; Israeli national parks built atop massacre sites; and many other locations, all in an effort to decolonize the study of Palestine.

6. Neil Smith, *Uneven Development: Nature, Capital, and the Production of Space* (Athens: University of Georgia Press, 2008), 206.

7. Rashid Khalidi, *Palestinian Identity: The Construction of Modern National Consciousness* (New York: Columbia University Press, 2010), 15.

8. Meron Benvenisti, *Sacred Landscape: The Buried History of the Holy Land since 1948* (Berkeley: University of California Press, 2002), 70.

9. For the Palestine case, see also Chiara De Cesari, "Creative Heritage: Palestinian Heritage NGOs and Defiant Arts of Government," *American Anthropologist* 112 (2010): 625–37; Rochelle Davis, *Palestinian Village Histories: Geographies of the Displaced* (Stanford: Stanford University Press, 2011). I do not consider the case of Israel's domination of Palestinian geography through, on the one hand, the power of nominative cartography, and, on the other, a distinct form of the discourse of nonrecognition with respect to the Palestinian people living within Israel's 1948 "Green Line" boundaries, more brutal, onerous, or terrible than colonial practices utilized in other settler-colonial projects, including in the United States, Canada, Australia, or elsewhere. The Israel/Palestine case is simply much more recent and, thanks to excellent scholarship by both Palestinian and Israeli academics, quite well documented and dissected.

10. Since 2002, the Muwekma Ohlone tribe has pursued federal recognition largely through a court-based judicial strategy that entails obliging the Department of the Interior (where the BIA and the BAR are housed) to act in good faith, according to its own rules and regulations. This strategy is slowly bearing fruit (for news about their ongoing recognition struggle, see www.muwekma.org).

11. The missionized zone of coastal California has a number of important place-names of indigenous origin, although because of the general invisibility of native peoples in the state, I am not sure that the majority of denizens in those towns and cities are aware of this fact. Malibu, Lompoc, and Port Hueneme are place-names

from Chumash languages; Petaluma was the Coast Miwok name for a precontact village. In the case of one indigenous place-name outside of the missionized zone, Ukiah (from a Pomoan language), I found that many nonnative people were in fact aware of the indigenous origin of their city's name. Knowledge about and relations to place-names thus varies considerably around the state.

12. Kroeber, *Handbook*.

13. Lowell John Bean and Thomas C. Blackburn, *Native Californians: A Theoretical Retrospective* (Menlo Park, Calif.: Ballena, 1976).

14. Milliken, *Time of Little Choice*, 58.

15. Hackel, *Children of Coyote*.

16. Milliken, *Time of Little Choice*; Milliken, *Native Americans*.

17. Milliken, *Time of Little Choice*, 66. "Tamien" was the name of a village or perhaps (as Milliken argues) of an entire district of multiple villages in the area surrounding where the mission was established and in the middle of the contemporary city of Santa Clara. "Tamien" has also been used to refer to the South Bay Ohlone language. See Richard Levy, "Costanoan," in *Handbook of North American Indians*, ed. Robert F. Heizer (Washington, D.C.: Smithsonian Institution, 1978), 8:485–95.

18. Jackson and Castillo, *Indians, Franciscans, and Spanish Colonization*, 6.

19. Jackson, "Development of San Jose Mission," 230.

20. Lightfoot, *Indians, Missionaries, and Merchants*.

21. See, for example, Colin G. Calloway, *The American Revolution in Indian Country: Crisis and Diversity in Native American Communities* (New York: Cambridge University Press, 1995).

22. Lightfoot, *Indians, Missionaries, and Merchants*, 88.

23. Milliken, *Time of Little Choice*, 59.

24. Ibid., 221.

25. Hackel, *Children of Coyote*; Milliken, *Time of Little Choice*.

26. David Weber, *The Spanish Frontier in North America* (New Haven: Yale University Press, 1992), 115.

27. Lightfoot, *Indians, Missionaries, and Merchants*, 62.

28. Lowell John Bean and Harry Lawton, "Some Explanations for the Rise of Cultural Complexity in Native California with Comments on Proto-Agriculture and Agriculture," in Bean and Blackburn, *Native Californians*, 29–35. See also Kat M. Anderson, *Tending the Wild: Native American Knowledge and the Management of California's Natural Resources* (Berkeley: University of California Press, 2006); Kent Lightfoot and Otis Parrish, *California Indians and their Environment: An Introduction* (Berkeley: University of California Press, 2009).

29. Milliken, *Time of Little Choice*, 223–24.

30. Hackel, *Children of Coyote*, 12.

31. Lightfoot, *Indians, Missionaries, and Merchants,* 198–202.

32. Hackel, *Children of Coyote,* 422.

33. Mexican independence and state formation was an extended historical process. Whereas independence was first declared in 1810, Spanish forces did not leave the country until 1821. A monarchy ruled Mexico until 1824, and internecine struggles between those favoring federalism versus those favoring strongly centralized models of government raged during most of the mid-nineteenth century.

34. Sandos, *Converting California,* 106.

35. Jackson, "Development of San Jose Mission."

36. Sandos, *Converting California,* 108.

37. Ibid., 110.

38. Randall Milliken, Alan Leventhal, and Rosemary Cambra, "Interpretive Recommendations and Background Report for the Coyote Hills Museum" (Submitted to the East Bay Regional Park District, Oakland, Calif., 1987), 11.

39. The information in this paragraph derives from personal communication with Alan Leventhal, February 2011.

40. Sandos, *Converting California,* 110.

41. Edward W. Gifford, *California Shell Artifacts* (Berkeley: University of California Press, 1947); Les W. Field, Alan Leventhal, Dolores Sanchez, and Rosemary Cambra, "A Contemporary Ohlone Tribal Revitalization Movement: A Perspective from the Muwekma Ohlone Indians of the San Francisco Bay Area," *California History* 71 (1992): 412–31; Leventhal et al., "Back from Extinction."

42. Sandos, *Converting California* 21; Randall Milliken, "Ethnohistory of the Lower Napa Valley," in *Final Report of Archaeological Investigations in the River Glen Site (CA-NAP-261)* (Mill Valley, Calif.: Archaeological Consulting and Research Service, 1978); Randall Milliken, "The Spatial Organization of Human Population in Central California's San Francisco Peninsula at the Time of Spanish Arrival" (Master's thesis, Sonoma State University, 1983); Randall Milliken "An Ethnohistory of the Indian People of the San Francisco Bay Area from 1770–1810" (Ph.D. diss., University of California, Berkeley, 1991).

43. Lightfoot, *Indians, Missionaries, and Merchants,* 199.

44. Jackson and Castillo, *Indians, Franciscans, and Spanish Colonization,* 110–11.

45. See Jack Holterman, "The Revolt of Estanislao," *Indian Historian* 3 (1970): 43–54; Stephen J. Pitti, *The Devil in Silicon Valley: Northern California, Race, and Mexican Americans* (Princeton: Princeton University Press, 2003); James J. Rawls, *Indians of California: The Changing Image* (Norman: University of Oklahoma Press, 1986).

46. See Sidney J. Mintz and Eric Wolf, "An Analysis of Ritual Co-Parenthood (Compadrazgo)," *Southwestern Journal of Anthropology* 6 (1950): 341–68.

47. Les W. Field, "Blood and Traits: Preliminary Observations on the Analysis of Mestizo and Indigenous Identities in Latin vs. North America," *Journal of Latin American Anthropology* 7 (2002): 2–33.

48. Jackson and Castillo, *Indians, Franciscans, and Spanish Colonization*, 111.

49. Tomás Almaguer, *Racial Fault Lines: The Historical Origins of White Supremacy in California* (Berkeley: University of California Press, 1994), 7.

50. Albert L. Hurtado, *Indian Survival on the California Frontier* (New Haven: Yale University Press, 1988), 135.

51. For the Sierra Miwok, see Jack Burrows, *Black Sun of the Miwok* (Albuquerque: University of New Mexico Press, 2000). For the Maidu, see Sara-Larus Tolley, *Quest for Tribal Acknowledgment: California's Honey Lake Maidu* (Norman: University of Oklahoma Press, 2003). For the Hupa, see Byron Nelson Jr., *Our Home Forever: The Hupa Indians of Northern California* (Salt Lake City: Howe, 1978); Jack Norton, *When Our Worlds Cried: Genocide in Northern California* (San Francisco: Indian Historian Press, 1979).

52. See Kevin Starr, *Americans and the California Dream, 1850–1915* (Oxford: Oxford University Press, 1986).

53. Gelya Frank and Carole Goldberg, *Defying the Odds: The Tule River Tribe's Struggle for Sovereignty in Three Centuries* (New Haven: Yale University Press, 2010).

54. Ibid., 4–5.

55. Ibid., 151.

56. Ibid., 30.

57. Ibid., 22–62.

58. See Madison S. Beeler, "Northern Costanoan," *International Journal of American Linguistics* 27 (1961): 191–97; Edward W. Gifford, "Handwritten Linguistic Notes on San Lorenzo Costanoan," Ethnographic Document, unpublished manuscript 194, Bancroft Library, University of California, Berkeley, 1914; John P. Harrington, *Costanoan Field Notes: Chochenyo Linguistics* (New York: Krause International, 1921–39); Alfred Kroeber, "The Languages of the Coast of California South of San Francisco," *University of California Publications in American Archaeology and Ethnology* 2 (1904): 29–80; Alfred Kroeber, "The Chumash and Costanoan Languages," *University of California Publications in American Archaeology and Ethnology* 9 (1910): 237–71; J. Alden Mason, "The Mutsun Dialect of Costanoan, Based on the Vocabulary of de la Cuesta," *University of California Publications in American Archaeology and Ethnology* 11 (1916): 399–472; C. Hart Merriam, *Ethnographic Notes on California Indian Tribes III: Central California Indian Tribes*, ed. Robert F. Heizer (University of California Archaeological Surveys Reports 68, no. 3, 1967).

59. Field and Muwekma Tribe, "Unacknowledged Tribes."

60. Ibid., 87.

61. Kroeber, *Handbook*, 464.

62. See Field et al., "Contemporary Ohlone Tribal Revitalization Movement"; Leventhal et al., "Back from Extinction."

63. Leventhal et al., "Final Report," XX.

64. Mark Hylkema, "Tamien Station Archaeological Report," in *Ohlone Past and Present*, ed. Bean, 249–71.

65. Ibid., 268.

66. Alan Leventhal to author, February 2011.

67. Patrick Wolfe, "Settler Colonialism and the Elimination of the Native," *Journal of Genocide Research* 8 (2006): 387–409.

68. See, e.g., Hurtado, *Indian Survival*; Norton, *When Our Worlds Cried*.

Precarious Positions

Native Hawaiians and U.S. Federal Recognition

J. KĒHAULANI KAUANUI

In 1903, following the U.S.-backed illegal overthrow of the Hawaiian Kingdom and the unilateral annexation of the islands in 1898, the U.S. federal government passed legislation acknowledging the indigenous people of Hawaiʻi. More than a century later, over 160 federal statutes address the conditions of Native Hawaiians in the areas of health, education, labor, and housing. Some observers have argued, therefore, that the U.S. Congress has already recognized that a "special relationship" exists between the United States and the Native Hawaiian people and that it should be formalized through the process of federal recognition of a Native Hawaiian governing entity. This chapter examines the impetus for the proposal for federal recognition of Native Hawaiians and explores a range of historical and legal issues that shed light on the multiple claims constituting the complex terrain of Hawaiian sovereignty politics. The proposal for federal recognition is extremely controversial for several reasons, including because it was initiated by a U.S. federal representative and because many Hawaiian political organizations oppose it in favor of Hawaiʻi's independence claim under international law. What is the legal basis for U.S. federal recognition of a Native Hawaiian nation within federal Indian law? How has the contemporary context of legal challenges to Native Hawaiian programs and funding by the U.S. government served as a catalyst for broad-based Hawaiian support despite a thriving independence movement? Looking comparatively at assertions of federal plenary power, how do the cases of Indian Country, Native Alaska, and the unincorporated territories in the Pacific Islands shed light on the limits of federal recognition as a model for self-determination?

The conspirators, having actually gained possession of the machinery of government, and the recognition of foreign ministers, refused to surrender their conquest. So it happens that, overawed by the power of the United States to the extent that they can neither themselves throw off the usurpers, nor obtain assistance from other friendly states, the people of the Islands have no voice in determining their future, but are virtually relegated to the condition of the aborigines of the American continent.

—HRH LILI'UOKALANI, *Hawaii's Story by Hawaii's Queen* (1898)

Queen Lili'uokalani's words of anger and frustration at the raw power used by the United States in relation to Native Hawaiian people during the late nineteenth century resonate strongly with twenty-first-century indigenous opposition to attempts by U.S. government officials to limit Native Hawaiians' political status to that of a federally recognized Indian tribe. A controversial proposal repeatedly introduced in the U.S. Congress for more than a decade would recognize a "Native Hawaiian governing entity" within the confines of U.S. federal policy. Beginning in the 106th U.S. Congress in 2000 and continuing through the present, Senator Daniel Akaka, a Democrat from Hawai'i, has sponsored this legislation—the Akaka Bill—that proposes to recognize Native Hawaiians as an indigenous people who have a "special relationship" with the United States and thus a right to limited self-determination. Proponents claim that passage of the bill would lay the foundation for a nation-within-a-nation model of self-governance that federally recognized tribes have, yet the proposal does not even offer that. U.S. federal Indian policy has defined tribal sovereigns as "domestic dependent nations" that have a limited right to self-government. Federally recognized tribes have the right to assert jurisdiction over their people and their land bases legally classified as "Indian Country" and held in trust by the U.S. government; define their own tribal membership criteria; create tribal legislation, a measure of law enforcement and court systems; and tax their own citizens.

This chapter examines the impetus for the proposal of federal recognition of Native Hawaiians. It also explores a range of historical and legal issues that shed light on the multiple claims constituting the complex terrain of Hawaiian sovereignty politics. The proposal for federal recognition is extremely controversial for several reasons. For one, it was initiated by a U.S. federal representative, not the Native Hawaiian people, supposedly as a remedy against a battery of lawsuits that sought to threaten U.S. federal funding and programs for Native Hawaiians.[1] Second, numerous Hawaiian political organizations oppose what they see as an effort to contain Hawai'i's independence claim under international law. I first provide a historical overview of the events that affect the current situation and provide a legal basis for U.S. federal recognition. Then I briefly discuss a particular set of contemporary conditions that catalyzed widespread support for federal recognition—that is, the implications of the U.S. Supreme Court's ruling in *Rice v. Cayetano* (2000) and subsequent legal challenges to Native Hawaiian programs and funding by the U.S. government. I also discuss the broader context for recognizing Native Hawaiians as an indigenous people within the United States, which includes a broader legal history of incorporating Native Hawaiians within the definition of "Native American." I then highlight some of the difficulties with the promise of federal recognition as a solution to the "Hawaiian problem" by comparatively examining Indian Country, native Alaska, and the Pacific Islands, especially the U.S. unincorporated territories. Finally, I show how the proposed legislation not only does not provide for parity with tribal nations as a consequence of the role afforded by the state but undercuts efforts to restore Hawaiian independence.

A History of Illegality

The history of the Hawaiian Kingdom—recognized as a state by all major global powers throughout the nineteenth century—provides Kanaka Maoli (indigenous Hawaiians) and others with a rare legal claim that shows the current state-driven push for federal recognition to be problematic for outstanding sovereignty claims.[2] A series of critical historical events provide the backdrop for understanding the complex terrain of Hawaiian sovereignty politics. In 1893, U.S. minister of foreign affairs John L. Stevens, with the support of a dozen white settlers, organized a coup d'état and overthrew Queen Lili'uokalani, the monarch of the Hawaiian Kingdom.[3] The queen yielded her authority under protest, as she was confident that the U.S. government and President Benjamin Harrison would endeavor to undo the actions led by a U.S. official. Within months, however, Harrison was out of office and Grover Cleveland became the next U.S. president. After sending an investigator to look into the matter, Cleveland eventually declared the action under Stevens an "act of war" and acknowledged that the overthrow, backed by U.S. Marines, had been unlawful and should be undone. Specifically, he recommended that the provisional government (made up of those who had orchestrated the overthrow) should step down, but they refused. Cleveland did not compel them to do so and thus did not assist in restoring formal recognition to the queen. In the interim, the provisional government established the Republic of Hawai'i on July 4, 1894, with Sanford Ballard Dole as president. As the de jure government, asserting jurisdiction over the entire island archipelago, this group seized roughly 1.8 million acres—Hawaiian Kingdom Crown and Government lands.[4]

In 1898, when the United States illegally annexed Hawai‘i, the republic ceded these lands on the condition that they be held in trust for the inhabitants of the Hawaiian Islands.[5] In her pathbreaking research, Noenoe K. Silva has brought to light a powerful resistance history that reveals broadbased Hawaiian opposition to U.S. annexation—opposition so strong that it defeated a proposed treaty of annexation in 1897.[6] Hawaiians organized into two key nationalist groups, Hui Aloha ‘Āina (which had men's and women's wings) and Hui Kālai‘āina, each of which submitted petitions representing the vast majority of Hawaiian people alive in Hawai‘i at the time. In those petitions, called the Kū‘ē Petitions (*kū‘ē* translates as "to oppose, resist, protest"), Hawaiians clearly stated their opposition to becoming part of the United States "in any form or shape." The U.S. Senate accepted these petitions but found it impossible to secure the two-thirds majority vote required in the Senate for a treaty. Nevertheless, during U.S. president William McKinley's term, the Republic of Hawai‘i and other proannexationists proposed a joint resolution of Congress, which required only a simple majority in both houses, which passed in 1898.[7] Thus, the United States did not annex the Hawaiian Islands by treaty, as required under customary international law at the time.

To many outsiders today, the history of the illegal overthrow and annexation may seem irrelevant, given the fact that Hawai‘i is currently counted as one of the fifty U.S. states. But as many Hawaiian activists point out, statehood is also contestable. Like many other colonial territories, in 1946 Hawai‘i was inscribed on the United Nations list of non-self-governing territories.[8] Although Hawai‘i was on that list and therefore was entitled to a process of self-determination to decolonize, the U.S. government predetermined statehood for Hawai‘i by treating its political status as an internal domestic issue. The 1959 ballot in which the people of Hawai‘i voted to become a state included only two options, integration and remaining a U.S. colonial territory.[9] Among those allowed to take part in the vote, settlers as well as military personnel outnumbered Hawaiians.[10] By citing the internal territorial vote, the U.S. State Department then misinformed the UN, which in turn considered the people of Hawai‘i to have freely exercised their self-determination and chosen to incorporate within the United States.[11]

By UN criteria established in 1960 and certainly known to the United States at the time, the ballot should have included independence and free association as choices. On December 14 of that year, the UN General

Assembly issued the Declaration on the Granting of Independence to Colonial Countries and Peoples—Resolution 1514 (XV).[12] Also in 1960, the assembly approved resolution 1541 (XV) that defined free association with an independent state, integration into an independent state, and independence as the three legitimate options of full self-government.[13]

UN General Assembly Resolution 1541 refers to territories that are "geographically separate and distinct ethnically and/or culturally" without specifying what "geographically separate" must entail.[14] Nonetheless, this chapter of the resolution has been accepted as applicable mainly to overseas colonization, thereby relegating indigenous peoples to a condition of "internal colonization."[15] At stake is prohibiting the indigenous claim to the same self-determination granted to "blue water" colonies by Resolution 1514, "which can logically lead to independence."[16] Hence, the phrase "all peoples have the right of self-determination" has been mainly applied to inhabitants of territories destined for decolonization rather than to indigenous peoples.[17]

The situation changed to some degree with the UN General Assembly's 2007 passage of the Declaration on the Rights of Indigenous Peoples, but even that documents imposes conditions regarding what constitutes "self-determination" encompass them. On the one hand, Article 3 states, "Indigenous peoples have the right of self-determination. By virtue of that right they freely determine their political status and freely pursue their economic, social, and cultural development." But on the other hand, Article 46 states, "Nothing in this Declaration may be . . . construed as authorizing or encouraging any action which would dismember or impair, totally or in part, the territorial integrity or political unity of sovereign and independent States."[18]

Shifting Rationales for Federal Recognition

Proponents of the Akaka Bill have continuously advanced two key legal developments for their argument in support of federal recognition for Native Hawaiians: the "Apology Resolution" (Public Law 103-150) regarding the 1893 overthrow, passed by Congress in 1993, which calls for "reconciliation"; and the wave of legal assaults that occurred over the following decade. The Apology Resolution acknowledges U.S. complicity in the overthrow of Queen Lili'uokalani and the constitutional monarchy. In addition to accounting for the events that led to the U.S.-backed coup, the resolution acknowledges that "the indigenous Hawaiian people never directly relinquished their claims to their inherent sovereignty as a people or over their national lands to the United States, either through their monarchy or through a plebiscite or referendum." This resolution defines "native Hawaiian" inclusively as "any individual who is a descendant of the aboriginal people who, prior to 1778, occupied and exercised sovereignty in the area that now constitutes the State of Hawaii."[19] Although the apology includes a disclaimer stating that nothing contained in the resolution can be used to settle a case against the United States, it still constitutes a congressional finding of fact.

Supporters also cite the Hawaiian Homes Commission Act of 1920, approved by the U.S. Congress in 1921, which allotted approximately two hundred thousand acres of land, with ninety-nine-year lease provisions, to those who qualified as "native Hawaiians." In this case, "native Hawaiians" were defined as "descendants with at least one-half blood quantum of individuals inhabiting the Hawaiian Islands prior to 1778."[20] These allotted lands were formerly part of the Kingdom's Crown and Government lands. The Hawaiian Homes Commission Act was originally conceived as a rehabilitation project for the Native Hawaiian population, which had been experiencing dramatic declines linked to colonial urbanization. The act has been cited as evidence that the U.S. government has already acknowledged that one class of Hawaiians (those with 50 percent or more blood quantum) has entitlements that parallel those of American Indians.[21] Proponents of the bill argue that the act institutionalized a trust agreement and therefore constitutes a special legal relationship like that between the U.S. government and Indian tribes.

As early as 1903, the U.S. government passed legislation acknowledging the indigenous people of Hawai'i, and more than 160 federal statutes now address the conditions of Native Hawaiians.[22] Since the 1970s, in the midst of a thriving Hawaiian rights movement, the U.S. Congress has enacted numerous special provisions for the benefit of Native Hawaiians in the areas of health, education, labor, and housing. Thus it could be argued that the U.S. Congress has already recognized that a "special relationship"—that is, a political one, not a racial one—exists between the United States and the Native Hawaiian people. Congress extended to Native Hawaiians the same rights and privileges accorded to American Indian, Alaska Native, Inuit, and Aleut communities in the Native American Programs Act of 1974. This act also includes American Samoan natives and indigenous peoples of Guam, the Commonwealth of the Northern Mariana Islands, and the Republic of Palau—all designated as "Native American Pacific Islanders." And Native Hawaiians are included in the American Indian Religious Freedom Act,

National Museum of the American Indian Act, Native American Graves Protection and Repatriation Act, National Historic Preservation Act, and Native American Languages Act.[23] In addition, several federal acts specifically target Native Hawaiians, comparable to measures providing for American Indians and Alaska Natives, such as the Native Hawaiian Health Care Act and the Native Hawaiian Education Act.[24] Whether all this legislation qualified Native Hawaiians as politically analogous to American Indians was a key question brought before the U.S. Supreme Court in 1999 and in subsequent challenges to Hawaiian rights to state and federal funding and indigenous-specific institutions, such as the Office of Hawaiian Affairs (OHA) and the Department of Hawaiian Home Lands.

The U.S. Supreme Court ruling in the case of *Rice v. Cayetano* served as the central impetus for the proposal regarding federal recognition of Hawaiians.[25] At stake in *Rice* were not only restricted elections for OHA trustees but also the office's existence. Prior to the court ruling, participation in OHA elections was restricted to Native Hawaiians, of any Hawaiian ancestry, who resided in Hawai'i. Harold F. Rice, a fourth-generation white resident of Hawai'i, was denied the right to vote because he is not Hawaiian by any statutory definition (he is neither "native Hawaiian" nor "Native Hawaiian"). The OHA, established in 1978, is governed by a nine-member elected board of trustees and holds title to all real or personal property set aside or conveyed to it through the state admission act of 1959 as part of the "ceded" public lands trust. It is also meant to hold the income and proceeds derived from a portion of a trust for "native Hawaiians" as defined in the Hawaiian Homes Commission Act and granted to the State of Hawai'i at the time it was admitted to the United States.[26] As the plaintiff, Rice charged that both the trust managed by the office and the OHA voting provisions were racially discriminatory and violated the Fourteenth and Fifteenth Amendments to the U.S. Constitution, which are meant to provide equal protection and to guarantee that the right of citizens to vote shall not be denied or abridged on account of race, color, or previous condition of servitude. But even though the trust itself is for the benefit of "Native Hawaiians," the U.S. Supreme Court's majority opinion decreed that the state's electoral restriction enacted race-based voting qualifications and thereby violated the Fifteenth Amendment.

In *Rice v. Cayetano*, Hawaiians were in a fraught position, with no direct voice in the case, even though it was central to Hawaiian concerns.[27] Governor Benjamin Cayetano, notorious for his anti-Hawaiian veto power, was held accountable for the OHA voting practices because the office is a state agency. Still, the State of Hawai'i argued that the OHA limitation on the right to vote was based not on race but on the unique status of Hawaiian people in light of the state's trust obligations. Thus, the limitation on the right to vote for the OHA trustees was based on a legal classification defining those people who are the beneficiaries of the trust. But because neither the U.S. government nor the U.S. Supreme Court recognizes Hawaiians collectively as a sovereign entity, the State of Hawai'i maintained that the voting classification was rationally tied to its requirement to uphold a congressional requirement—in other words, because the United States has a "special relationship" with and obligation to "native Hawaiians" stemming from the Hawaiian Homes Commission Act of 1920.[28] Thus, the defense in the *Rice* case rested on the claim that Congress has the power to enter into special trust relationships with indigenous peoples—a power that is not confined to tribal Indians—and that the state stood in for the United States with regard to land claims and related entitlements.

Although the majority opinion in *Rice v. Cayetano* did not address the issue of the Fourteenth Amendment and thus did not affect the trust that the OHA manages, the ruling laid the essential groundwork for further assaults on Hawaiian lands and people through a rash of lawsuits throughout the 2000s. These new cases threatened the existence of all Hawaiian-specific funding sources and institutions, including the OHA; all federal funds for Hawaiian health, education, and housing; and the state Department of Hawaiian Home Lands and the lands it manages. Plaintiffs charged that these institutions are racially discriminatory because they violate the Fourteenth Amendment. Within the broader context of these legal assaults, where any indigenous-specific program is deemed racist, many Native Hawaiians and their allies support Senator Akaka's proposal for federal recognition, especially since he pitched the legislation as a protective measure against such lawsuits because federally recognized tribal nations are immune from Fourteenth Amendment legal challenges. However, even early on, it seemed clear that the bill itself is about something more insidious.

The Akaka Bill: What It Is, What It Is Not

The bill originated in March 2000, just one month after the ruling in *Rice*, when Hawai'i's congressional delegation formed the Task Force on Native Hawaiian Issues, chaired by Akaka. As its immediate goal, the task force sought to clarify the political relationship between Hawaiians and the United States through Congress. During the 106th U.S. Congress, the senator introduced federal legislation that proposes to recognize Hawaiians as indigenous people who have a "special relationship" with the United States and thus a right to self-determination under federal law. The Akaka Bill delineates a process for the formation of a governing entity to be approved by the U.S. government. The entity would be formed by a commission of nine members appointed by the secretary of the interior; their first and foremost duty would be to report to the secretary.[29] The legislation addresses only the recognition of a Native Hawaiian governing entity and not the rights of that entity, which would be subject to later negotiations among the U.S. federal government, the Native Hawaiian entity, and the Hawai'i state government. This is a prime example of what Jeff Corntassel and Richard C. Witmer II have identified as the era of "forced federalism" in U.S. indigenous policy beginning in 1988. They explain that the forced federalism era differs from the previous era of self-determination because while recognized tribes are locked into a federal relationship, the rapid devolution of federal power to states has undermined tribal sovereignty. This transfer of power means that indigenous nations have "been forced into dangerous political and legal relationships with state governments that challenge their cultures and nationhood status."[30]

Federal protection was now being sold to Native Hawaiians as a defense against average citizens who challenge the Hawaiian trusts that the United States never upheld in the first place—trusts that are based on the theft of a nation.[31] These political misdeeds continue to go unquestioned and have problematic implications for the future, as can be seen even in the process of drafting and putting forth the proposal. Not only has the proposal's development involved little Hawaiian participation, but it has also served as a political football, blocked by conservatives. For example, only for the earliest 2000 draft of the bill (S 2899) were hearings held in Hawai'i, and then only in Honolulu. Moreover, while the video record of that lone hearing shows overwhelming opposition to the bill, the delegation disingenuously reported the opposite to Congress.

Conservatives' refusal to support the measure became more pronounced when the Bush administration spent eight years opposing the legislation. Although throughout that period, the legislation gained committee approval in both the House and Senate, it remained stalled when it came to a floor debate. Despite multiple revisions and reintroductions of new drafts aimed at satisfying Department of Interior concerns and appeasing Republican critics who called the proposal a plan for "race-based government," the legislation never progressed to a Senate vote.[32] The ongoing opposition in the U.S. Senate throughout the 2000s has come from Republicans; however, their conservative antagonism has, at times, shifted to qualified support as the bill has been repeatedly revised and watered down to appease their concerns.

Under the new leadership of Barack Obama, the presidential administration shifted to firm support for the Akaka Bill.[33] In both of the most recent versions before committee, the negotiations that would follow concern land, governmental authority, the exercise of criminal and civil jurisdiction, and more. None of these powers is guaranteed in the bill. All versions of the bill reaffirm the delegation of U.S. government authority to the State of Hawai'i to address the condition of "native Hawaiians" under the Hawai'i state admissions act. The legislation specifies that after the Native Hawaiian governing entity is created, both the United States and the State of Hawai'i may enter into negotiations with the Native Hawaiian governing entity. This sets the bill apart from other forms of federal recognition of native nations, which do not typically give state governments any part in negotiations with the exception of matters related to Indian gaming. This bill allows the State of Hawai'i to sit at the table to negotiate regarding matters including the transfer of lands, natural resources, and other assets and the protection of existing rights related to such lands or resources; the exercise of governmental authority over any transferred lands, natural resources, and other assets, including land use; the exercise of civil and criminal jurisdiction; the delegation of governmental powers and authorities to the Native Hawaiian governing entity by the United States and the State of Hawai'i; any residual responsibilities of the United States and the State of Hawai'i; and grievances regarding assertions of historical wrongs committed against Native Hawaiians by the United States or by the State of Hawai'i. The three parties to the negotiation are not placed on equal footing here: All negotiations must take place within the framework of U.S. federal law and policy with regard to Indian tribes and under U.S. plenary power.

In the last version, section (e) of the bill stated, "Nothing in this Act alters the civil or criminal jurisdiction of the United States or the State of Hawai'i over lands and persons within the State of Hawai'i." It further states, "The status quo of Federal and State jurisdiction can change only as a result of further legislation, if any, enacted after the conclusion, in relevant part, of the negotiation process established in section 8(b)." In other words, when the representatives of the Native Hawaiian governing entity negotiate with the federal and state agents, they cannot negotiate for civil or criminal jurisdiction over any land. Doing so would require the passage of further legislation.[34]

The Limits of Domestic Sovereignty: Lessons from Other (Is)Lands

It is not at all clear that the passage of this bill would protect anything, given that it could be found to be unconstitutional if the courts determined that the U.S. Constitution did not consider Native Hawaiians to be an "Indian tribe." Hawaiians can look to cases from Indian Country and Native Alaska to shed light on the problems and pitfalls of federal recognition.[35] The proposal for Hawaiians is modeled on similar legal precedents for 566 federally recognized native governing entities. Yet it seems more likely that this limited proposal would pave the way for an arrangement resembling those for the more than 229 Alaska Native villages that have such entities. Those villages hold a somewhat different status than most tribal nations because they are corporate entities subject to state law and do not have land held in trust on which to assert sovereign jurisdiction in a way recognized by the federal government.

Alaskan Natives' federal recognition status shifted radically between the Clinton and Bush administrations. Under President Bill Clinton, Alaska Natives were listed on the register of federally recognized nations, a status that was challenged under George W. Bush.[36] Moreover, Alaska Natives' political status was disputed in *Alaska v. Native Village of Venetie Tribal Government* (1998), when the U.S. Supreme Court ruled that Venetie's land base did not count as Indian Country in the legal sense.[37] Indian Country is legally defined to include all dependent Indian communities in the United States, and Venetie did not qualify because its lands are not held in trust by the U.S. federal government. Thus, the village's tribal government cannot assess taxes, enforce its own laws, or assert jurisdiction over these lands as American Indian governments do on reservations. Moreover, the Alaska Native villages are subjected to Alaska state laws. Therefore, when Senator Akaka asserts that his bill "focuses solely on self-determination within the framework of federal law and seeks to establish equality in the federal policies extended towards American Indians, Alaska Natives and Native Hawaiians," one has to seriously question his understanding of the concept and measure of parity.[38] There are exceptions in Indian Country, including the tribal nations located in Maine, which are also subject to state interference as spelled out in the contested terms of the Maine Indian Claims Settlement Act of 1980.

At most, the Hawaiian self-governing model proposed through the federal recognition process would allow for a domestic dependent entity under the full and exclusive plenary power of Congress.[39] While U.S. policy on Native Americans states that the federal government must consult with tribal governments regarding decisions about tribal lands, resources, and people to honor the government-to-government relationship, Congress has a long history of abusing its plenary power to subordinate tribal governments. Even worse, the Congress most often delegates its power to agencies in the executive branch of the federal government, such as the Bureau of Indian Affairs within the Department of the Interior, which is directed by presidential appointees. To fully recognize Hawaiians as having a political trust relationship with the United States similar to that of American Indians and Alaska Natives undercuts Hawaiian claims, particularly those to independent statehood.

In addition to the cases of American Indians and Alaska Natives, lessons can be learned from other Pacific Islands, including Guam and American Samoa, both of which are unincorporated U.S. territories, organized and unorganized, respectively. Their histories shed light on the political limitations of domestic governing entities within the U.S. nation-state. These two island entities are also subject to U.S. congressional plenary power under the authority of the Territorial Clause of the U.S. Constitution as interpreted by the U.S. Supreme Court. Therefore, legal cases move beyond the federal district courts any time there is a question about their sovereign power. These matters are then adjudicated by the U.S. Supreme Court under territorial case law, which upholds the doctrine that Guam and American Samoa are, along with the U.S. Virgin Islands, "foreign in a domestic sense."[40] Even the Commonwealths of the Northern Mariana Islands and Puerto Rico are subject to exclusive congressional power by the United States.

Cases of successful disentanglement do exist. The only island nations that have managed to extract themselves from the grip of U.S. plenary power besides the Philippines are those of the former UN trust territory of the Pacific Islands: the Republic of the Marshall Islands (RMI), the Federated States of Micronesia (FSM), and the Republic of Belau. While the legacy of U.S. nuclear testing and military dominance bears on these cases, the process is instructive. For example, after the U.S. government entered into political status negotiations with representatives of the peoples of the FSM and the Marshall Islands, compacts of free association were signed on

October 1, 1982, and June 25, 1983, respectively. In accordance with the trusteeship agreement, the United Nations Charter, and the stated objectives of the trust territory system, the United States promoted the development of self-government and independence according to the freely expressed wishes of the islanders themselves.

The compact was approved by majorities of the peoples of the FSM and the RMI in UN-observed plebiscites conducted on June 21, 1983, and September 7, 1983, respectively. Furthermore, the FSM and RMI governments were formed on-island prior to any negotiation with the United States. The compact of free association was also approved by the FSM and RMI governments in accordance with their constitutional processes. Only after the FSM and RMI plebiscites was the compact approved as a joint resolution (Public Law 99-239) by the U.S. Congress on January 14, 1986.

The process of the compact agreement is instructive for Hawaiians in that the order in which the political process unfolded in the FSM and the RMI differs strikingly from the process in which the proposal for federal recognition of Hawaiians has taken place. The compacts were developed via a bilateral process guided by the United Nations. First meetings were held and the people approved the process. Next, prior to any negotiations with the United States, the people formed new governments, and these governing bodies approved the compact proposals in accordance with their own constitutional processes. Only then did the U.S. Congress pass the legislation.

The Marshall Islands compact also delineated a section to protect unadjudicated claims. For example, with regard to the lands on Ejit (a small island in Majuro Atoll), the compact stated that the president of the United States would negotiate an agreement with the government of the Marshall Islands, without prejudice, regarding any claims that have been or may be asserted by any party as to rightful title and ownership. If Hawaiians were to consider demanding a mutual-consent decree to ensure bilateral agreements, a section could also be included to preserve their title to the so-called ceded lands—1.8 million acres of former Crown and Government lands of the Hawaiian Kingdom. A request for a mutual-consent decree would certainly be telling for supporters of federal recognition, since when Chamorro activists in Guam worked for the inclusion of a mutual-consent decree in their draft proposal for commonwealth status, the United States, through the Department of the Interior, entirely rejected the idea. That rejection indicates that the U.S. government will continue to assert its plenary power.

Foreclosing Independence?

Those who support Hawai'i's independence from the United States have pointed out problems with the proposal because of the limitations on recognizing Hawaiian sovereignty within the domestic dependent nation model. These groups include those who are part of the Hawaiian Independence Action Alliance: the Pro–Kanaka Maoli Independence Working Group, Ka Pakaukau, Komike Tribunal, HONI (Hui o Na Ike), Ka Lei Maile Ali'i Hawaiian Civic Club, Koani Foundation, 'Ohana Koa, NFIP—Hawai'i, Spiritual Nation of Kū—Hui Ea Council of Sovereigns, Living Nation, Settlers for Hawaiian Independence, MANA (Movement for Aloha No Ka 'Aina), as well as the Hawai'i Institute for Human Rights. Also, the group Hui Pu, while not an independence group per se, has been at the center of resistance to the Akaka Bill since the organization's founding in 2004 with the primary goal of opposing the legislation.

Because of the proposed limits on independent national sovereignty under the federal recognition plan, dozens of Hawaiian sovereignty groups have persistently and consistently rejected the application of U.S. federal Indian law that would recognize a Hawaiian domestic dependent nation—as ward to guardian. Moreover, the exercise of federal plenary power comes not only from the Congress, the president, and the Department of the Interior but also from the U.S. Supreme Court, which has been ruling against tribal power for Indian nations and increasing states' power over them.[41] The U.S. Supreme Court abusively construes the powers granted by the U.S. Constitution to the Congress through its interpretation of the Constitution's Indian Commerce Clause. Through a series of precedents set by the rulings in Indian cases, the U.S. Supreme Court has ruled time and time again that the federal government has exclusive power over Indian affairs.[42]

The proposed legislation is a violation of both sovereignty and self-determination claims already acknowledged in the Apology Resolution. Given that Hawaiian Kingdom sovereignty was not lost via conquest, cession, or adjudication, those rights to self-rule remain in place under international law. Hawaiian people lost the ability to be self-determining through unilateral political processes—annexation and imposed statehood—but at no time did that amount to a legal termination of our inherent rights of sovereignty. Moreover, passage of the legislation could be used against Hawaiians and cited to show that claims that exceed the domestic sphere have been forfeited, especially since by then the Hawaiian governing entity would be subject to U.S. plenary power. This containment of our sovereignty draws attention away from demands for Hawai'i's independence and decolonization from the United States based on international law. While the history of the overthrow can justify Hawaiians' right to federal recognition, that same history complicates any mode of sovereignty that is exclusively aboriginal, especially since citizenship under the Hawaiian Kingdom was not limited to Hawaiians. Leaders of the various Hawaiian independence initiatives argue that those most in support of federal recognition do not represent the Hawaiian people. Instead, those who work for the OHA, the Department of Hawaiian Home Lands, the Native Hawaiian Health Project, and other agencies represent the state, federal, and nonprofit organizations for which they work, the same institutions that receive the funding being challenged in the courts. Therefore, supporting the proposal for federal recognition ensures their continued employment.

Those who support independence oppose federal recognition because at most, it would allow for no more than a domestic dependent entity under the full and exclusive plenary power of Congress. Alternatively, supporters of federal recognition insist that nothing in the Akaka Bill would compromise Hawai'i's national claims under international law. But supporters of this position do not attend to the ways in which the United States unilaterally asserts its plenary power to keep indigenous sovereigns subordinated. In 2001, Akaka articulated the line that he would hold for the following decade: "This measure does not preclude Native Hawaiians from seeking alternatives in the international arena" and "Let me be clear—It is not my intention, nor the intention of the delegation, to preclude efforts of Native Hawaiians at the international level. The scope of this bill is limited to federal law."[43] Akaka's assertions that passage of the bill would not preclude Kanaka Maoli from seeking "alternatives in the international arena" have been his standard response to challenges posed by the legislation's opponents who favor Hawaiian independence—that is, the restoration of a Hawaiian nation under international law. However, Akaka's response, which has been echoed repeatedly by Hawai'i's state and federal officials, speaks only to the rights of indigenous peoples under international law.[44] But because his mentions of "alternatives in the international arena" here and elsewhere are ill defined, he has led many to infer that Kanaka Maoli could pursue full independence in a post-federal-recognition political scenario. Proponents of the Akaka Bill refuse to acknowledge that this strategy differs from the prevalent Hawaiian independence position from the outset.

While many proponents of U.S. federal recognition presume that Kanaka Maoli independence activists merely want continued access to the United Nations as indigenous peoples, the vast majority of pro-independence Native Hawaiians support two entirely different legal strategies under international law, decolonization and deoccupation, neither of which is based on indigeneity. The former is specific to colonized peoples in non-self-governing territories, while the latter pertains to occupied states. Counter to Akaka's assurances, passage of the bill is likely to foreclose the sovereignty claim for Hawaiian independence under international law. The legislation appears to be a preemptive attempt to squash outstanding sovereignty claims unsuccessfully extinguished by Hawai'i's admission as the fiftieth state in the American Union. If the bill passes, the will of the people will seem to have been expressed—as a form of self-determination in support of federal recognition—in a way that would make international intervention much more far-fetched given the likelihood that the world community would see the Hawaiian question as even more of a U.S. domestic issue than is now the case. At any rate, passage of the Akaka Bill would certainly entrench the Hawaiian sovereignty claim further within the U.S. government since the Native Hawaiian governing entity would be subordinate to both the Hawai'i state government and the U.S. federal government.

Most immediately, federal recognition would set up a process for extinguishing most claims to land title—except for whatever the state of Hawai'i and the federal government may be willing to relinquish in exchange for that recognition—and even then, the U.S. federal government would hold the land in trust. At stake here is the 1.8 million acres of former kingdom Crown and Government lands and the obliteration of the Hawaiian nation's title to them. As the 2009 U.S. Supreme Court case regarding these lands shows, there is absolutely no guarantee that any future Native Hawaiian governing entity would hold any of these lands.[45]

Conclusion

The historical harm the United States first committed in Hawai'i in 1893 brought down not a Native Hawaiian government but the independent Hawaiian Kingdom composed of Kanaka Maoli as well as non–Kanaka Maoli subjects. The Hawaiian people and other Hawaiian Kingdom heirs have subsequently accumulated fundamental political and other claims under international law that the United States must recognize rather than hope to dispel via the enactment of the Akaka Bill. Moreover, a possible tension between Hawaiian self-determination and kingdom heirs' right to sovereignty needs further exploration. Nonetheless, in the eyes of many observers, passage of this bill would constitute nothing less than a second illegal denial of the Hawaiian people's right to self-determination and the kingdom heirs' right to sovereignty.

On April 13, 2009, a self-selected group of Kanaka Maoli, *kupuna* (elders), *kumu* (educators), and representatives wrote an "Urgent Open Letter to Barack Obama" on behalf of the Kanaka Maoli people as well as other Hawaiian Kingdom heirs. A number of our *kako'o* (supporters) also added their names to the letter.[46] The letter's primary purpose was to inform the president of the signatories' categorical opposition to the proposed legislation. It also proposed an alternative bilateral approach to addressing the complex legacy of Hawai'i's history with the United States in a way that promotes restorative justice. According to the letter,

> The Bill arrogantly attempts to unilaterally characterize the historical transgressions of the United States against our people and kingdom, and to unilaterally specify their remedy. We insist otherwise. U.S. crimes against our Kanaka Maoli people and other Kingdom heirs from 1893 on require, for their redress, that a mechanism composed of U.S. agents and wholly independent representatives of Kanaka Maoli and Kingdom heirs be bilaterally set up by your Administration and us to make findings of fact and conclusions of international law that could serve as a road-map for the resolution of the political and legal issues now outstanding between our two parties.[47]

The legislation limits Hawaiian self-determination as a consequence of the fundamental legal distinction between "Indian tribes" and "foreign nations" under the U.S. Constitution.

The legislation's name alone represents what is problematic for Hawaiian sovereignty and nationhood under international law. Embedded in its title, the Native Hawaiian Government Reorganization Act of 2009, is a fundamental historical lie: there can be no attempt to *re*organize a Native Hawaiian government, because the Hawaiian Kingdom was an internationally recognized state that in the nineteenth century afforded citizenship status to more than just the indigenous Hawaiian people. The Akaka Bill's formal name misconstrues the nature of the government-to-government relationship between the United States and the Hawaiian Kingdom. A more accurate name would be the Native Hawaiian Government Organization Act.

By July 2010, when the Akaka Bill seemed dead, the OHA trustees moved to work with Abercrombie to select state legislators to push for a law that would offer state recognition of a Native Hawaiian governing entity. On July 6, 2011, Abercrombie signed into law the First Nation Government Bill.[48] Although the state version is modeled after the Akaka Bill, it does not authorize a government-to-government relationship between the U.S. federal government and a Native Hawaiian governing entity. Instead, it authorizes a First Nation-to-fiftieth state relationship. But just like the Akaka Bill, this legislation is structurally problematic. The new law sets up a commission to produce a "Native Hawaiian roll," where Kanaka Maoli sign on to take part in the formation of the First Nation within the state process—the first time there would be documented evidence of acquiescence to the U.S. government or its subsidiaries. With the formation of a state-recognized Hawaiian First Nation, advocates of the Akaka Bill have vowed to press on and mobilize for federal recognition through that new governing entity. So, it seems, the federal legislation may ultimately be revived.

Now more than ever, Hawaiians and others wishing to protect Hawai'i's national claims under international law must voice a resounding statement of refusal to consent. Advocates of independence are divided between two central legal strategies: decolonization from the United States through UN protocols, and U.S. deoccupation through protocols mandated by the laws of occupation.[49] In the case of unifying for the purposes of stopping federal recognition, the legacy of the 1897 Kū'ē Petitions is instructive. As mentioned earlier, two different Hawaiian nationalist groups, Hui Aloha 'Āina and Hui Kālai'āina, opposed annexation. Hui Aloha 'Āina's petition unequivocally stated its resistance to U.S. incorporation. The petition by Hui Kālai'āina went a step further, not only articulating the group's refusal of incorporation but also demanding the restoration of the kingdom. Although the two groups' goals differed, together they defeated the 1897 Treaty of Annexation by demonstrating their lack of consent to becoming part of the United States.

Notes

An earlier version of this essay appeared in *The Contemporary Pacific* 17 (2005): 1–27.

1. In 1987, the Hawaiian people organized into a sovereignty group, Ka Lāhui Hawai'i, with a membership roll of more than twenty thousand citizens, and initiated a proposal for federal recognition. But the Hawai'i congressional delegation,

including Senators Akaka and Daniel Inouye, opposed the plan, which leads people to wonder why they are so forcefully supporting it now.

2. The United States and members of the international community also recognized the kingdom's independence through treaty relations with the major powers of the world, including not only with the United States (1849, 1870, 1875, 1883, and 1884), but also Austria-Hungary (1875), Belgium (1862), Denmark (1846), France (1846 and 1857), Germany (1879), Great Britain (1836, 1846, and 1851), Italy (1863), Japan (1871 and 1886), the Netherlands (1862), Portugal (1882), Russia (1869), Samoa (1887), Spain (1863), the Swiss Confederation (1864), and Sweden and Norway (1852).

3. Haunani-Kay Trask, *From a Native Daughter: Colonialism and Sovereignty in Hawai'i* (Monroe, Maine: Common Courage, 1993); Noel Kent, *Hawai'i: Islands under the Influence*, 2nd ed. (Honolulu: University of Hawai'i Press, 1993); Lawrence H. Fuchs, *Hawaii Pono: A Social History* (San Diego: Harcourt Brace Jovanovich, 1961).

4. Tom Coffman, *Nation Within: The Story of America's Annexation of the Nation of Hawaii* (Maui: Koa, 1998).

5. Ibid.; Noenoe K. Silva, "Kanaka Maoli Resistance to Annexation," *'Ōiwi: A Native Hawaiian Journal* 1 (1998): 40–80; Ulla Hasager and Jonathan Friedman, eds., *Hawai'i: Return to Nationhood* (Copenhagen: International Working Group for Indigenous Affairs, 1994).

6. Silva, "Kanaka Maoli Resistance"; Noenoe K. Silva, *Aloha Betrayed: Native Hawaiian Resistance to American Colonialism* (Durham: Duke University Press, 2004).

7. One hundred years later, the United Nations issued the findings of a nine-year treaty study and found the annexation of Hawai'i legally invalid. Pat Omandam, "UN Report: Annexation Could Be Declared Invalid," *Honolulu Star-Bulletin*, August 11, 1998.

8. Trask, *From a Native Daughter*.

9. Ibid., 68–87.

10. After a massive increase in American migration to Hawai'i, statehood emerged as a real prospect. As early as 1950, two special elections were held to choose sixty-three delegates who would draft a state constitution. In addition, among those who were allowed to take part in the vote were settlers as well as military personnel, who together outnumbered Hawaiians. See Mililani Trask, "The Politics of Oppression," in *Hawai'i Return to Nationhood*, IWGIA-Document 75, ed. Ulla Hasager and Jonathan Friedman (Copenhagen: IWGIA, 1994), 68–87.

11. Ibid., 80.

12. United Nations, Declaration on the Granting of Independence to Colonial Countries and Peoples, December 14, 1960, http://www.un.org/en/decoloniza tion/declaration.shtml.

13. In 1962, the assembly established a special committee, now known as the Special Committee of 24 on Decolonization, to examine the application of the declaration and to make recommendations on its implementation. See United Nations, Declaration on the Granting of Independence.

14. Russell Lawrence Barsh, "Indigenous Peoples: An Emerging Object of Inter-national Law," *American Journal of International Law* 80 (1986): 373.

15. Ibid.

16. Esther Ann Griswold, "State Hegemony Writ Large: International Law and Indigenous Rights," *PoLAR: Political and Legal Anthropology Review* 19 (1996): 101 n. 14.

17. Ibid., 93.

18. United Nations, Declaration on the Rights of Indigenous Peoples, March 2008, http://www.un.org/esa/socdev/unpfii/documents/DRIPS_en.pdf.

19. Captain Cook first arrived in the island archipelago in 1778; thus, that year marks a time prior to which it is assumed that no one other than Hawaiians was present there. The apology was not extended to non-Hawaiians who also endured the legacy of the overthrow—that is, those nonindigenous descendants of citizens of the Hawaiian Kingdom. Silva, *Aloha Betrayed*, 18, questions whether Cook was the first European to land in Hawai'i. United States Public Law 103-150, 1993 Joint Resolution of Congress, "To acknowledge the 100th anniversary of the January 17, 1893 overthrow of the Kingdom of Hawaii, and to offer an apology to Native Hawaiians on behalf of the United States for the overthrow of the Kingdom of Hawaii," 103rd Cong., 1st sess. (107 Stat. 1510).

20. For an analysis of what led to the 50 percent blood criterion, see J. Kēhaulani Kauanui, "'For Get' Hawaiian Entitlement: Configurations of Land, 'Blood,' and Americanization in the Hawaiian Homes Commission Act of 1921," *Social Text* 59 (1999): 123–44; J. Kēhaulani Kauanui, "The Politics of Blood and Sovereignty in *Rice v. Cayetano*," *PoLAR: Political and Legal Anthropology Review* 25 (2002): 100–128; J. Kēhaulani Kauanui, *Hawaiian Blood: Colonialism and the Politics of Sover-eignty and Indigeneity* (Durham: Duke University Press, 2008).

21. Kauanui, "'For Get' Hawaiian Entitlement."

22. Daniel Inouye, "Hawaii Congressional Delegation Introduces Native Hawaiian Federal Recognition Bill," February 11, 2003, http://inouye.senate.gov /~inouye/03pr/20030211pr03.html.

23. However, data for Native Hawaiians, Samoans, and other Pacific Island-ers have historically been subsumed within the panethnic racial rubrics of "Asian

and Pacific Islanders" and "Asian Pacific Islanders." This administrative practice has meant that all U.S. data for Native Pacific Islanders have been disaggregated and lumped with those of Asian Americans. It also obscures both the differences between the Asian and the Native Pacific Islander subpopulations and the similarities in outcomes for native Pacific Islanders, American Indians, and Alaska Natives. Hopefully, the "Hawaiian and Other Pacific Islander" classification option provided in the 2000 U.S. census will inspire the U.S. Office of Management and Budget to direct agencies to collect meaningful racial data accordingly.

24. In all of these acts, Hawaiians are defined by the most inclusive definition: "Any individual who is a descendant of the aboriginal people who, prior to 1778, occupied and exercised sovereignty in the area that now constitutes the State of Hawai'i."

25. *Rice v. Cayetano*, 528 U.S. 495 (2000).

26. Melody Kapilialoha MacKenzie, *Native Hawaiian Rights Handbook* (Honolulu: University of Hawai'i Press, 1991).

27. Some Hawaiian groups, including those pressing for federal recognition of a native governing entity, submitted amicus curiae (friend of the court) briefs on behalf of the respondent. The State Council of Hawaiian Homestead Associations, Hui Kāko'o 'Āina Ho'opulapula, Kalama'ula Homestead Association, and the Hawaiian Homes Commission collectively submitted a brief. Another was collectively submitted by the Office of Hawaiian Affairs, Ka Lāhui, the Association of Hawaiian Civic Clubs, the Council of Hawaiian Organizations, the Native Hawaiian Convention, the Native Hawaiian Bar Association, the Native Hawaiian Legal Corporation, the Native Hawaiian Advisory Council, Hā Hawai'i, Hui Kālai'āina, Alu Like Inc., and Papa Ola Lōkahi. The Kamehameha Schools Bishop Estate Trust also offered amici curiae, as did the Hawai'i congressional delegation and the National Congress of American Indians.

28. The court determined that it would subject the legislation in question to rational basis analysis rather than to strict scrutiny, dictating all other cases understood as race-based. In *Adarand Constructors Inc. v. Pena* (515 U.S. 200 [1995]), the Supreme Court ruled that "a group classification such as one based on race is ordinarily subjected to detailed judicial scrutiny to ensure that the personal right to equal protection of laws has not been infringed. Under this reasoning, even supposedly benign racial classifications must be subject to strict scrutiny."

29. This process of appointments already set the proposal apart from the Indian Reorganization Act of 1934.

30. Jeff Corntassel and Richard C. Witmer II, *Forced Federalism: Contemporary Challenges to Indigenous Nationhood* (Norman: University of Oklahoma Press, 2008), 5.

31. See Harold Morse, "Home Lands Lawsuit to Be Filed Today, Could Total $100 Million," *Honolulu Star-Bulletin*, December 29, 1999; Gordon Y. K. Pang, "Land You Bought May Actually Be Home Lands," *Honolulu Star-Bulletin*, February 17, 1995; Hawai'i Advisory Committee to the U.S. Commission on Civil Rights, *A Broken Trust: The Hawaiian Homelands Program: Seventy Years of Failure of the Federal and State Governments to Protect the Civil Rights of Native Hawaiians* (Honolulu: Hawai'i Advisory Committee to the U.S. Commission on Civil Rights, 1991); Susan Faludi, "Broken Promise: How Everyone Got Hawaiians' Homelands Except the Hawaiians," *Wall Street Journal*, September 9, 1991; Federal-State Task Force on the Hawaiian Homes Commission Act, *Report to the U.S. Secretary of the Interior and the Governor of the State of Hawai'i* (Honolulu: U.S. Department of the Interior, 1983); Mitsuo Uyehara, *The Ceded Land Trusts, Their Use and Misuse* (Honolulu: Hawaiiana Almanac, 1977).

32. For a critical analysis of the neoconservative forces on-island that organized against the legislation because they regarded it as a proposal for race-based government, see Kauanui, *Hawaiian Blood*. U.S. senator Daniel Inouye of Hawai'i (also a Democrat) explained the delay in passing the federal recognition legislation by pointing to the Senate being overwhelmed by appropriation bills, which are no doubt linked to the U.S. imperial presence in Iraq. Furthermore, Inouye said it was his intent to push the bill through before the end of session in 2004. He also noted that political unity in Hawai'i—which includes support from Governor Linda Lingle, all of the state's mayors, county and state lawmakers, and the entire U.S. congressional delegation—should go a long way in helping to secure Republican support in the Senate. Lingle declared before the U.S. Senate Committee on Indian Affairs that passage of the proposal was "vital to the continued character of our state, and it is vital to providing parity and consistency in federal policy for all native peoples in America." See Vicki Viotti, "Inouye: Maybe 2004 for Akaka Bill," *Honolulu Advertiser*, August 30, 2003; Richard Borreca, "Akaka Bill Gets Week of Lobbying," *Honolulu Star-Bulletin*, February 23, 2003; Richard Borreca, "Akaka Bill Gets Additional Support," *Honolulu Star-Bulletin*, December 10, 2003.

33. Since the start of the 111th Congress (January 3, 2009), three sets of proposals that made their way to the table, all titled the Native Hawaiian Government Reorganization Act of 2009: S 381 and HR 862 introduced on February 4, 2009; S 708 and HR 1711 introduced on March 25, 2009; and S 1011 and HR 2314 introduced on May 7, 2009. The third set of bills saw the most political activity. For information on these bills and their predecessors, see http://www.govtrack.us/congress/bills/111/hr1711/text.

S 1011 received a hearing before the U.S. Senate Committee on Indian Affairs on August 6, 2009, and HR 2314 received a hearing before the U.S. House Committee on Natural Resources on December 16, 2009. Little further activity took place on either measure until December 17, when the Senate committee passed a newly amended version with changes developed by the Department of Justice in conjunction with the OHA, the Council for Native Hawaiian Advancement, and the Native Hawaiian Bar Association. A day earlier, U.S. representative Neil Abercrombie had tried to pass the same heavily amended version of HR 2314 in the House Committee on Natural Resources, but last-minute letters of opposition from Lingle prompted him to set aside the proposed revisions and the committee passed the unamended version. This development was no surprise, since Abercrombie had already announced plans to resign his seat and run for governor. On February 23, 2010, Abercrombie succeeded in getting the House committee to pass the Senate version of the bill.

But in July 2010, Governor Lingle moved to pressure Hawai'i's congressional delegates to amend S 1011 to protect the state's regulatory power. They revised the bill in an attempt to overcome Republican opposition, making the new S 1011 look like the old HR 2314. Although other distinctions exist between the two bills, both allow the Hawai'i state government a seat at the negotiating table with the federal government and the Native Hawaiian governing entity, thereby setting this legislation apart from the dominant model of federal recognition legislation and processes. The Senate version potentially gives the Native Hawaiian governing entity more power than the House version. In HR 2314, Section 9, "Applicability of Certain Federal Laws," clarifies that certain laws pertaining to federally recognized Indian tribes would not apply to the Native Hawaiian governing entity, and those laws greatly benefit tribal nations. The Native Hawaiian governing entity would not be allowed to claim rights under Indian Gaming Regulatory Act or to have the secretary of the interior take land into trust on the entity's behalf. This provision is important because only land held in trust by the federal government on behalf of native nations is allowed to be used by Indian tribes as part of their sovereign land base where they can assert jurisdiction. The Native Hawaiian governing entity would not be allowed to rely on the Indian Trade and Intercourse Act to challenge how the state acquired the Hawaiian Kingdom Crown and Government lands. No other Native Hawaiian group would be eligible for recognition under the federal acknowledgment process. The Native Hawaiian governing entity would not be eligible for Indian programs and services.

Most notably, this section of the bill also states that "nothing in this Act alters the civil or criminal jurisdiction of the United States or the State of Hawaii over lands and persons within the State of Hawaii." The Senate version does not make the same stipulation. S 1011 states that the Native Hawaiian governing entity, the federal government, and the state "may enter into negotiations" that are "designed to lead to an agreement" addressing land, governmental authority, and the exercise of criminal and civil jurisdiction. This legislation did not pass, and by the end of this session, the Akaka Bill looked like it had finally died, but it has recently reemerged in a different form. See J. Kēhaulani Kauanui, "Understanding Both Versions of the Akaka Bill," *Indian Country Today*, January 15, 2010, http://www.indiancountrytoday.com/opinion/81699482.html.

34. This section of the bill also includes a disclaimer: Nothing in the act can create a cause of action against the United States or any other entity or person or alter "existing law, including existing case law, regarding obligations on the part of the United States or the State of Hawai'i with regard to Native Hawaiians or any Native Hawaiian entity." Moreover, nothing in the bill can create any new obligation to Native Hawaiians under federal law, and the measure specifically outlines and protects the federal government through sovereign immunity against lawsuits for breach of trust, land claims, resource-protection or resource-management claims, or similar types of claims brought by or on behalf of Native Hawaiians or the Native Hawaiian governing entity. The legislation also asserts that the state of Hawai'i "retains its sovereign immunity, unless waived in accord with State law, to any claim, established under any source of law, regarding Native Hawaiians, that existed prior to the enactment of this Act." This section, among others, especially raised concerns within the Native Hawaiian Bar Association. On June 11, 2009, the association sent in testimony to the House Committee on Natural Resources regarding the House version of the Akaka Bill (HR 2314). Although the bar association expressed its support for the bill, its testimony outlined some major concerns. The first is the role of the U.S. Department of Defense (as it relates to the Office for Native Hawaiian Relations and the Native Hawaiian Interagency). The second is the role of the U.S. Department of Justice, because unlike earlier versions of the bill, the current legislation does not include a provision authorizing the designation of a department representative to assist in the implementation and protection of the rights of Native Hawaiians and their political, legal, and trust relationship with the United States. The third concern was the section of the bill relating to "claims and sovereignty immunity." The Native Hawaiian Bar Association noted, "We believe it is unnecessary and premature to include provisions on claims and sovereign immunity prior to federal recognition of a Native Hawaiian Government and recommend that these provisions under section 8(c) be taken out of the bill." In response, Representative Abercrombie suggested that the legislation be revisited to assess whether another revision was needed. Some within the Native Hawaiian community have speculated that Abercrombie's responsiveness to the bar association's concerns may have been linked to his ultimately successful 2010 campaign for the Hawai'i governorship.

35. Vine Deloria Jr. and Clifford M. Lytle, *The Nations Within: The Past and Future of American Indian Sovereignty* (New York: Pantheon, 1984).

36. On October 15, 1993, the secretary of the interior published a list of federally recognized tribes that included Alaska Native villages as tribal entities. The pre-amble read, "The villages and regional tribes [are] listed as distinctly Native communities and have the same status as tribes in the contiguous 48 states." But there is currently a debate over Alaska Natives' legal status, as evinced in former Republican senator Ted Stevens's push to consolidate governmental funding for these entities into regional organizations, and in attorney and historian Don Mitchell's assertion that the Department of the Interior acted unlawfully when it put the villages on the federal list. See Native American Rights Fund, "A Move toward Sovereignty: Interior Publishes Alaska Tribe List," *NARF Legal Review* 19, 1 (1994): 1; "Alaska Natives Confront Debates over Legal Status," October 21, 2003, http:// www.indianz.com/News/archives /002107.asp.

37. *Alaska v. Native Village of Venetie Tribal Government*, 522 U.S. 520 (1998).

38. Daniel Akaka, "Native Hawaiian Federal Recognition Bill Introduced," January 22, 2001. http://www.akaka.senate.gov/press-releases.cfm?method=releases .view&id=57af6979-5d16-4929-8e33-1adc627c2e63.

39. David E. Wilkins, *American Indian Sovereignty and the U.S. Supreme Court: The Masking of Justice* (Austin: University of Texas Press, 1997).

40. Christina Duffy Burnett and Burke Marshall, *Foreign in a Domestic Sense: Puerto Rico, American Expansion, and the U.S. Constitution* (Durham: Duke University Press, 2001).

41. Wilkins, *American Indian Sovereignty*.

42. Ibid.

43. Akaka, "Native Hawaiian Federal Recognition Bill"; "Statement of Senator Daniel K. Akaka on Revisions to the Native Hawaiian Federal Recognition Bill," April 16, 2001, http://www.senate.gov/~akaka/speeches/2001427548.html.

44. Clyde Namuo, "Misinformation Abounds on Revisions to Akaka Bill," *Honolulu Advertiser*, May 2, 2004.

45. On March 31, 2009, the U.S. Supreme Court issued its ruling in the case of *State of Hawaii v. Office of Hawaiian Affairs et al.* (No. 07-1372, 117 Haw. 174, 177 P. 3d 884, reversed and remanded). The state of Hawai'i asked the high court whether the state has the authority to sell, exchange, or transfer 1.2 million acres of land formerly held by the Hawaiian monarchy as Crown and Government lands. Prior to the state's appeal to the Court, the Hawai'i Supreme Court unanimously ruled that the state should keep the land trust intact until Kanaka Maoli claims to these lands are settled, prohibiting the state from selling or otherwise disposing of the properties to private parties. The Hawaiian court issued its ruling based on the

1993 Apology Resolution. The U.S. Supreme Court reversed the judgment of the Hawai'i Supreme Court and remanded the case for further proceedings with the stipulation that the outcome not be inconsistent with the U.S. Supreme Court's opinion. The contested land base constitutes 29 percent of the state's total land area and almost all the territory Hawai'i claims as "public lands." These lands were unilaterally claimed by the U.S. federal government when it annexed the Hawaiian Islands. The Court insists that the apology does not change the legal landscape or restructure the state's rights and obligations. Once the case was remanded back to the state, the Hawai'i Supreme Court threw it out after some of the original plaintiffs brokered a deal with the governor and attorney general to have the case dismissed because of new state legislation to provide for the piecemeal sale of these lands through resolutions. Although one lone plaintiff refused to take part in the sellout, the Supreme Court dismissed the case by saying it was no longer "ripe for adjudication."

46. For a list of the signatories, see Kekuni Blaisdell, Lynette Hi'ilani Cruz, George Kahumoku Flores, et al., "An Urgent Open Letter to Barack Obama: Why the Native Hawaiian Reorganization Act Must Be Rejected," *Counterpunch*, April 15, 2009, http://www.counterpunch.org/2009/04/15/why-the-native-hawaiian -reorganization-act-must-be-rejected/.

47. Ibid.

48. The political term "First Nation" itself is curious in this context given that the term is typically used to refer to the indigenous peoples of the Americas located in what is now Canada, except for the Arctic-situated Inuit, and the Métis. For the text of the bill, see: Hawai'i State Senate, *S.B. 1520*, 26th Legislature, 2011, http://www.capitol.hawaii.gov/session2011/bills/SB1520_CD1_.htm. For a legislative history of the bill, see Hawai'i State Legislature, "SB1520 Archive Measure Status," http://capitol.hawaii.gov/Archives/measure_indiv_Archives.aspx?billtype=SB &billnumber=1520&year=2011.

49. J. Kēhaulani Kauanui, "Hawaiian Nationhood, Self-Determination, and International Law," in *Transforming the Tools of the Colonizer: Collaboration, Knowledge, and Language in Native Narratives*, ed. Florencia E. Mallon (Durham: Duke University Press, 2011), 27–53.

Afterword

DAVID E. WILKINS

The preceding chapters have more than ably described, analyzed, and evaluated a powerful and ever-shifting set of clashing, interconnecting, yet overlapping issues, including indigenous sovereignty and self-determination, federal and state recognition/acknowledgment or denial of the same for native peoples, congressional plenary power and the trust relationship, and the role that international accords should play in the recognition of human rights for native nations in the United States.

Since the broad subject of political recognition of one polity by another polity is a dynamic topic, as fluid and meandering as the great river systems in North America, it is safe to say that if the same subjects are discussed a generation from now, many of the actors, assumptions, and "facts" of today about individual groups in hot pursuit of recognition will no longer be considered valid because additional research and changing local, domestic, and international norms and policies will have provided new data that may require us to modify, clarify, or even overturn our current understandings. That said, the essays in this volume will likely stand the test of time because of the strength of the questions raised and the quality of the authors' scholarship.

In 1992, Vine Deloria Jr., that indigenous intellectual titan, wrote a short essay confronting the five hundredth anniversary of Columbus's arrival. Deloria commented on the first half a millennium of contact between indigenous peoples of North America and those who arrived from other parts of the world and who now wield the self-assumed power to decide who may or may not be "recognized" as an aboriginal people in the United States. He emphasized that the United States faced a profound task, a "gigantic task of redefinition," if it expected to survive as distinctive, influential, and stable state.[1]

Current events at the national and state levels—the dysfunctional situation in which many state governments find themselves, the political and economic gridlock at the national level over the debt ceiling and taxation matters, the dramatic and devastating ecological disasters, drought, tornadic activity, flooding, and so on that have plagued the country—confirm that the redefinition process is still under way and is nowhere near conclusion.

Deloria emphasized that a central element in the U.S. redefinition of itself would include how it dealt with the needs and status of native nations: "If the struggle for living space has ended, and it was always a quest for a secure national identity, then our present and future task is to create, once and for all, an adequate history of the human race, a history in which even the smallest and least significant people are understood *in the light of their own experiences*. For Americans that means coming to grips with the real meaning of the past five centuries and understanding what actually happened between the original inhabitants of this hemisphere and those who tried to erase and replace them."[2]

As the data in this book reveal, in the two decades since Deloria wrote those words, the United States has made little substantial improvement in its overall political, legal, and cultural relationships with native nations. The critical question, of course, is why. What factor or more accurately set of factors precludes the U.S. government and most state governments from forging honest and more amicable relations with both recognized and especially nonrecognized indigenous communities that would take into account their unique histories and their inherent rights of self-determination?

A close reading of the essays in this volume unearths a number of major questions and explanatory themes that profoundly complicate indigenous-state intergovernmental and intercultural relations. The questions and themes cover a wide swath of emotional, intellectual, racial/ethnic, territorial, political, and legal ground and are inherently variable, which makes them unpredictable. And since each native community is an original entity, not every question or theme will be relevant to every petitioning native group. That said, let us explore the broad ideas unleashed in this study.

THEME 1   Despite the relatively meager demographic size and political powerlessness of most indigenous groups, they are frequently viewed, as Amy E. Den Ouden and Jean M. O'Brien point out in their essay, as bona fide "threats" by both the federal and state governments. The basis of this paranoia varies from nation to nation, but it is a persistent notion that traces back to the precontact era and continues unabated today.

THEME 2   Since the historic political and economic alliance between each native nation and the federal government has long been touted as a nation-to-nation relationship—signifying a bilateral affair frequently rooted in diplomatic arrangements such as treaties—when and on what basis did the United States grant to itself the unilateral (plenary) authority to decide what the essential characteristics of an aspiring native nation were to be? How is such definitional power squared with the federal government's countervailing recognition of the inherent right of indigenous sovereignty?

THEME 3 The United States is a federal republic in which the national government shares power with subnational or state governments while simultaneously providing explicit recognition of a third set of sovereigns— "Indian tribes." Since the notion of federalism cannot be permanently settled by the opinions of any one generation, how do federal officials and state lawmakers conceptualize indigenous sovereignty? Treaty making is a federal constitutionally enumerated power; the constitutions of most western states include disclaimer clauses in which the states were required to agree never to interfere in internal indigenous affairs or the native-federal relationship; and the federal Supremacy Clause elevates national treaty and statutory law over state law. In light of these facts, why have some states, both eastern and western, insisted that they, too, may wield what amounts to plenary power over native peoples and their lands, population, and resources?

THEME 4 The United States is a leader in the international community, but it has frequently challenged United Nations policies and programs aimed at recognizing indigenous peoples' human rights. As several of the essays discuss, the United States was the last state to formally adopt the UN Declaration on the Rights of Indigenous Peoples. But even after the declaration's adoption, some native peoples and organizations remain concerned that the federal government's commitment to all the principles outlined in the document is not particularly sincere or robust.

THEME 5 Since the founding of the American republic, the federal government's policies, laws, and regulations have, in the words of U.S. Supreme Court associate justice Clarence Thomas, been "to say the least, schizophrenic. And this confusion continues to infuse federal Indian law and our cases."[3] This schizophrenia, as several of the essays show, also is in evidence at the state level. Neither federal nor state officials have ever consistently maintained a position vis-à-vis native nations that supports inherent aboriginal autonomy. Such inconstancy, rooted in conflicting attitudes about native peoples, produces conflicting policies and programs that continue to bedevil indigenous peoples.

THEME 6 Indigenous individual and collective identity, like that of all human communities, is fluid and evolving, not static. And native peoples, of necessity and choice, will both resist and sometimes appropriate definitional characteristics that suit their community's needs, depending on the circumstances they confront. But let us imagine the infinite possibilities of indigenous political, social, and cultural development if native communities were not required to expend so much capital pursuing federal or state recognition. When people or polities are constantly having to measure up to criteria that are external to their own understanding of who they are and how they came to be, a devastating psychic and emotional imprint must result, potentially causing profound cultural dissonance.

THEME 7 Precisely what does citizenship mean for native individuals who maintain a core political allegiance to their recognized or unrecognized community while exercising their legally and politically recognized state and federal citizenship rights and responsibilities?

THEME 8 When federal and state policies, regulations, and governing norms collide with indigenous communities, whether recognized or not, they do not bounce off one another like so many billiard balls. Native individuals and their national governments have historically played and increasingly today play some role in the kind of policies and laws that are enacted or stymied. Sometimes the active indigenous agent's role works to the direct disadvantage of other native communities, and sometimes strong alliances are formed in which particular groups express genuine solidarity with other vulnerable groups.

THEME 9 Finally, we saw the implications of what happens when other racial/ethnic groups and their members, especially African Americans or Latino Americans, are utilized or exploited by the larger society or other native groups to dilute the indigenous communities' status or to foil their attempts to secure recognition. That is, the larger society, especially state and federal lawmakers, will sometimes claim that as a consequence of intermarriage with African Americans or Latino Americans, native "blood" is so diluted as to undermine particular groups' rightful claims to recognition. Moreover, already-recognized tribes rely on similar tactics to argue against recognition of aspiring groups. This phenomenon has occurred throughout American history and continues to plague interracial and interethnic relations.

These themes and questions, then, militate against any smooth set of processes that might ultimately culminate in a fair, effective, and comprehensive set of recognition policies and procedures that could rectify the present-day byzantine recognition process. Here again, Deloria's words remind us of how beneficial and timely just such a shift would be for both native and nonnative polities:

> The native peoples of the American continents suffered total inundation, lost a substantial portion of their population, and in coming into the modern world surrendered much of the natural life which had given them comfort and dignity. But they have managed to survive. Now, at a time when the virtues they represented, and continue to represent, are badly needed by the biosphere struggling to remain alive, they must be given the participatory role which they might have had in the world if the past five centuries had been different. The attitudes and beliefs that have kept the natives of the Western Hemisphere hidden and neglected must be changed so that world history becomes the story of mankind on this planet and not the selected history of a few people and their apology for what has happened to our species.[4]

Deloria, of course, was a realist and was not prone to Pollyannaism. He knew all too well that lodged deep within the American character were powerful attitudinal, cultural, religious, economic, territorial, and political forces that would mightily resist such adjustments in policy and law, making it difficult if not impossible to achieve more amicable intercultural relations.

Enter David C. Williams. In a recent essay, Williams expounds on why the United States has been reluctant to grant reparations to native peoples. One particular statement rings equally true with regard to why the United States and many individual states are so fervently resistant to fully recognizing native peoples on their own terms. In fact, the substitution of just a few words makes Williams's statement directly on point:

> I propose a different explanation for the reluctance to grant reparations [recognition] to tribes: they are collective sovereigns asking for reparations [recognition] for the unjust taking [denial] of their

sovereignty. But the United States is extremely reluctant to acknowledge that the taking [denial] of sovereignty was [is] unjust, because America came into legal being only by that taking. America could have territory for its own legal system only by displacing the legal system of the sovereigns already here. To call that displacement a wrong is to call America's own legitimacy into question. And it should not come as a surprise that the courts and Congress of the United States would be reluctant to question the basis of their own sovereign power. Indeed, American sovereign actors could not logically take sovereign action that would deny the legitimacy of their own sovereignty—because then they would have no ability to take sovereign action in the first place.[5]

This disturbingly accurate assessment goes far, along with the previous questions and themes, toward explaining the federal and state governments' reluctance comprehensively to embrace the acknowledgment of previously unrecognized native peoples. The few native nations that have been officially recognized in the past thirty years or so tend to be groups that are fairly small and pose little if any economic, cultural, or political threat to the vested status and interests of the states, the federal government, the corporate world, or previously recognized and well-entrenched native nations. Larger groups, like the Lumbees of North Carolina, have long been confronted by a battery of specious arguments—with economic and demographic concerns being two dominant factors—wielded by other tribal nations, state officials, and those in the Bureau of Indian Affairs and Congress to stymie tribal efforts at securing full recognition.

The future is unscripted, and it is impossible to predict how these complicated interethnic affairs will turn. But these essays powerfully remind us that native communities are a focused and resilient set of peoples and that they will continue to do all they can to assert their distinctive collective identities even when they have been formally denied recognition.

Notes

1. Vine Deloria Jr., afterword to *America in 1492: The World and the Indian Peoples before the Arrival of Columbus*, ed. Alvin M. Josephy Jr. (New York: Knopf, 1992), 431.

2. Ibid.; emphasis added.

3. *United States v. Lara*, 541 U.S. 193, 219 (2004).

4. Deloria, afterword, 442–43.

5. David C. Williams, "In Praise of Guilt: How the Yearning for Moral Purity Blocks Reparations for Native Americans," in *Reparations for Indigenous Peoples: International and Comparative Perspectives*, ed. Federico Lenzerini (New York: Oxford University Press, 2009), 242.

Appendix

Useful Resources for Further Study

The main objective of this volume is to introduce the complexities of recognition, tribal nation sovereignty, and indigenous rights in the United States to a broad audience, particularly students interested in learning about these and related issues from the perspective of multiple academic disciplines. We also hope that this volume will deepen public knowledge of recognition cases and tribal nations' ongoing struggles to defend and assert their sovereignty and will encourage nonspecialists to learn the facts of these cases and struggles from Native American voices and sources and with attention to the laws and policies that continue to affect tribal nations. To that end, the following list of resources for further study includes citations and links to relevant tribal media and organizations, websites, key legislation, reports, and records of hearings that provide important information regarding recognition cases, the Bureau of Indian Affairs (BIA) recognition process, and debates about federal recognition policy and its effects.

Government Websites, Reports, and Hearings on Federal Recognition

U.S. Department of the Interior, Bureau of Indian Affairs. *Acknowledgment Decision Compilation List* (collection of acknowledgment decisions with proposed finding and final determination decision documents and *Federal Register* notices, press releases, technical assistance letters, and other associated documents). www.bia.gov/WhoWeAre/AS-IA/OFA/ADCList/index.htm

U.S. Department of the Interior, Bureau of Indian Affairs, Office of Federal Acknowledgment. Criteria, Procedures, Lists of Petitioners, Status Summary of Acknowledgment Cases. www.bia.gov/WhoWeAre/AS-IA/OFA/index.htm

U.S. Government Accountability Office. *Indian Issues: Improvements Needed in Tribal Recognition Process* (report), November 2001. www.gao.gov/new.items /d0249.pdf

―――. *Indian Issues: Federal Funding for Non–Federally Recognized Tribes* (report), April 12, 2012. www.gao.gov/assets/600/590102.pdf

U.S. House of Representatives, Committee on Government Reform. *Betting on Transparency: Toward Fairness and Integrity in the Interior Department's Tribal Recognition Process: Hearing before the Committee on Government Reform, U.S. House of Representatives*, 108th Congress, 2nd sess., May 5, 2004. www.gpo.gov /fdsys/pkg/CHRG-108hhrg95868/pdf/CHRG-108hhrg95868.pdf

U.S. House of Representatives, Committee on Resources. *Federal Recognition and Acknowledgement Process by the Bureau of Indian Affairs: Oversight Hearing before the Committee on Resources, U.S. House of Representatives*, 108th Cong., 2nd sess., March 31, 2004. www.gpo.gov/fdsys/pkg/CHRG-108hhrg92827 /pdf/CHRG-108hhrg92827.pdf

U.S. Senate, Committee on Indian Affairs. *Federal Recognition: Hearing before the Committee on Indian Affairs, U.S. Senate*, 109th Cong., 1st sess., May 11, 2005. www.indian.senate.gov/public/_files/May112005.pdf

————. *Fixing the Federal Acknowledgment Process: Hearing before the Committee on Indian Affairs, U.S. Senate*, 111th Cong., 1st sess., November 4, 2009. www .gpo.gov/fdsys/pkg/CHRG-111shrg56575/html/CHRG-111shrg56575.htm

————. *Oversight Hearing on Federal Recognition: Political and Legal Relationship between Governments*, July 12, 2012 (webcast). www.indian.senate.gov/hearings /hearing.cfm?hearingID=e732c9af25adb336b52074279297237e

————. *Process of Federal Recognition of Indian Tribes: Hearing before the Committee on Indian Affairs, U.S. Senate*, 110th Cong., 1st sess., September 19, 2007. www.indian.senate.gov/public/_files/September192007.pdf

————. *Reorganization of the Bureau of Indian Affairs: Hearing before the Committee on Indian Affairs, U.S. Senate*, 108th Cong., 1st sess., May 21, 2003. www.gpo .gov/fdsys/pkg/CHRG-108shrg87357/pdf/CHRG-108shrg87357.pdf

————. Website. http://www.indian.senate.gov/

Additional Pertinent Legislation

Indian Gaming Regulatory Act. Public Law 100-497, October 17, 1988. www.nigc .gov/Laws_Regulations/Indian_Gaming_Regulatory_Act.aspx

Indian Reorganization Act (Wheeler-Howard Act). Public Law 73-383, June 18, 1934. aghca.org/wp-content/uploads/2012/07/indianreorganizationact.pdf

Native American Graves Protection and Repatriation Act. Public Law 101-601, November 16, 1990. www.nps.gov/nagpra/mandates/25usc3001etseq.htm

Apology Resolutions

Native American Apology Resolution

S.J. Res. 14—To Acknowledge a Long History of Official Depredations and Ill-Conceived Policies by the Federal Government Regarding Indian Tribes and Offer an Apology to All Native Peoples on Behalf of the United States. 111th Cong., 1st sess. http://thomas.loc.gov/cgi-bin/query/z?c111:S.J.RES.14:.

Native Hawaiian Apology Resolution

S.J. Res. 19—A Joint Resolution to Acknowledge the 100th Anniversary of the January 17, 1893, Overthrow of the Kingdom of Hawai'i, and to Offer an Apology to Native Hawaiians on Behalf of the United States for the Overthrow of the Kingdom of Hawai'i. http://thomas.loc.gov/cgi-bin/bdquery/z?d103:SJ 00019:|TOM:/bss/d103query.html|.

Tribal Nation Organizations

National Congress of American Indians. http://www.ncai.org/.
Tribal Leaders Directory and List of Federally Recognized Tribes (aka the Indian Entities Recognized and Eligible to Receive Services from the U.S. Bureau of Indian Affairs. www.bia.gov/WhoWeAre/BIA/OIS/TribalGovernment Services/TribalDirectory/index.htm
United South and Eastern Tribes, Inc. www.usetinc.org/Home.aspx

United Nations Resources

UN Declaration on the Rights of Indigenous Peoples. www.un.org/esa/socdev /unpfii/documents/DRIPS_en.pdf
UN Permanent Forum on Indigenous Issues website. social.un.org/index /IndigenousPeoples.aspx
UN Special Rapporteur on the Rights of Indigenous Peoples (James Anaya) website. http://unsr.jamesanaya.org/.

Resources for Following Current Events

Indian Country Today Media Network. http://indiancountrytodaymedia network.com/.
Indian Law Resource Center. http://www.indianlaw.org/.
Native American Rights Fund. http://www.narf.org/.

Contributors

JOANNE BARKER (Lenape [Delaware Tribe of Indians]) holds a doctorate in the history of consciousness from the University of California, Santa Cruz. She has held the Ford Foundation Fellowship with an association at the Center for Race and Gender at the University of California, Berkeley (2005–6), received the San Francisco State University Presidential Sabbatical Award (Spring 2010), and served as a visiting scholar at the American Indian Studies Center at the University of California, Los Angeles (2010–11). She is an associate professor of American Indian studies at San Francisco State University. She currently serves on the Nominations Committee of the Native American and Indigenous Studies Association. She is the editor of *Sovereignty Matters: Locations of Contestation and Possibility in Indigenous Struggles for Self-Determination* (2005) and author of *Native Acts: Law, Recognition, and Cultural Authenticity* (2011).

KATHLEEN A. BROWN-PEREZ (Brothertown Indian Nation) holds a master's degree in business administration and a law degree from the University of Iowa and has practiced law in Phoenix and Boston. She currently teaches criminal law and federal Indian law and policy at the University of Massachusetts Amherst. She chairs the Five College Native American Indian Studies Program and the UMass Amherst Global Indigenous Studies Program development task force. She has worked extensively on her tribe's fight for federal acknowledgment, most recently as chair of the tribe's Federal Acknowledgment Committee. She is the tenth great-granddaughter of Samson Occom (Mohegan), founder of the Brothertown Indian Nation.

ROSEMARY CAMBRA (Muwekma Ohlone), the great-granddaughter of Avelina Cornates Marine, who was baptized at Mission San Jose in 1864, is the elected chair of the Muwekma Ohlone tribe of the San Francisco Bay area. For more than three decades, she has helped organize the Muwekma tribal government and has been involved in the reaffirmation of the Muwekmas as a federally recognized tribe. She has also worked with other unacknowledged tribal groups and along with the Muwekma Tribal Council has sponsored various educational workshops for tribal councils, governmental agencies, and the general public and has helped coordinate meetings of all of California's terminated and unrecognized tribes.

AMY E. DEN OUDEN is an associate professor in the Women's Studies Department at the University of Massachusetts Boston. She is the author of *Beyond Conquest: Native Peoples and the Struggle for History in New England* (2005). For more than a decade, she worked as an oral history interviewer, archival researcher, and writer for the Eastern Pequot and Golden Hill Paugussett tribal nations' federal acknowledgement projects. She helped to launch UMass Boston's first Native American student society and developed an ongoing series of native studies symposia featuring indigenous scholars, activists, and educators. She is currently collaborating with Trudie Lamb Richmond and Ruth Garby Torres to document the history of indigenous activism and Indian policy formation in twentieth-century Connecticut. Den Ouden serves on the advisory board for First Peoples: New Directions in Indigenous Studies and is volunteering as a consultant with the Connecticut Humanities Council, helping to develop an online resource on the history of the state's native peoples.

TIMOTHY Q. EVANS (Haliwa-Saponi Tribe of North Carolina) holds a law degree from Cornell Law School as well as a master's in public affairs from Princeton University's Woodrow Wilson School of Public and International Affairs. He is now an attorney with Holland and Knight LLP in Washington, D.C., with nearly a decade of experience in the firm's Indian Law Practice Group, representing tribes and their governmental subdivisions. He works closely with his tribe in matters of tribal governance and its rights as a state-recognized tribe under North Carolina law.

LES W. FIELD is a professor in the Department of Anthropology and director of the Peace Studies Program at the University of New Mexico. He has conducted research in South, Central, and North America, establishing relations of collaboration with communities concerning the goals, methods, agendas, and products of anthropological work. He has worked as ethnohistorian and ethnographer with the Muwekma Ohlones since 1991, primarily in support of the tribe's petition for federal acknowledgement.

ANGELA A. GONZALES (Hopi) is an associate professor in the Department of Development Sociology at Cornell University, where she is also affiliated with the American Indian Studies program. She holds masters' degrees in education and sociology and a doctorate in sociology from Harvard University. She served as a co-curator of *IndiVisible: African-Native American Lives in the Americas*, a collaborative exhibition between the National Museum of the American Indian (NMAI), the National Museum of African American History and Culture, and the Smithsonian Institution Traveling Services. The exhibit examines the dynamics of race, community, and culture, and the often hidden, but common histories and lived realities of people who share African American and Native American heritage. The exhibit opened at the NMAI in November 2009 and continues to travel to venues throughout the United States, Canada, and Latin America.

RAE GOULD (Nipmuc) holds a doctorate in anthropology from the University of Connecticut. She currently serves as repatriation coordinator in the Department of Anthropology at the University of Massachusetts Amherst. Her teaching and research interests focus on Northeast Native Americans in the postcontact centuries, material culture studies, and legal and sovereignty issues.

J. KĒHAULANI KAUANUI (Kanaka Maoli) is an associate professor of American studies and anthropology at Wesleyan University in Connecticut. She holds a doctorate in the history of consciousness from the University of California, Santa Cruz. She is the author of *Hawaiian Blood: Colonialism and the Politics of Sovereignty and Indigeneity* (2008) and is currently at work on *Thy Kingdom Come?: The Paradox of Hawaiian Sovereignty*, a critical study on gender and sexual politics and the question of indigeneity in relation to state-centered Hawaiian nationalism. Kauanui is the producer and host of a public affairs radio program, *Indigenous Politics: From Native New England and Beyond*, that airs in ten states on the Pacifica radio network. She is also a member of the Dream Committee, an anarchist radio collective that produces *Horizontal Power Hour*. From 2005 to 2008, she served on the steering committee that worked to cofound the Native American and Indigenous Studies Association, and she has subsequently served on the association's council.

K. ALEXA KOENIG holds a law degree from the University of San Francisco School of Law and a master of laws from the University of California, Berkeley, School of Law, where she is executive director of the Human Rights Center and currently a doctoral candidate in jurisprudence and social policy. She has served as a tribal consultant since 1998.

ALAN LEVENTHAL is an administrative staff member in the Office of the Dean, College of Social Sciences, at San Jose State University and is a lecturer in the school's anthropology department. For more than three decades, he has served as tribal ethnohistorian and archaeologist for the Muwekma Ohlones, documenting their legal history as a federally recognized tribe. He has also worked closely with other tribes throughout California as they seek restoration and reaffirmation of their federally recognized status. He has collaborated with representatives from several California tribes to author publications and reports.

MALINDA MAYNOR LOWERY (Lumbee) is an associate professor in the Department of History at the University of North Carolina, Chapel Hill. She is the author of *Lumbee Indians in the Jim Crow South: Race, Identity, and the Making of a Nation* (2010) and numerous articles.

JEAN M. O'BRIEN (White Earth Ojibwe) is a professor in the Department of History at the University of Minnesota, where she is also affiliated with the Department of American Studies and the Department of American Indian Studies. She is the author of *Dispossession by Degrees: Indian Land and Identity in Natick,*

Massachusetts, 1650–1790 (1997) and *Firsting and Lasting: Writing Indians Out of Existence in New England* (2010) as well as numerous articles. She is a cofounder and past president of the Native American and Indigenous Studies Association.

JOHN R. ROBINSON is a doctoral student at the University of Montana studying Native American, western American, and environmental history. His research focuses on modern Native American policy—specifically, how it relates to recognized and unrecognized tribes in the Pacific Northwest.

JONATHAN STEIN holds a law degree from the University of Pennsylvania and has been a practicing attorney for nearly three decades, concentrating in business litigation and entertainment and gaming law, including federal and state Indian law matters across the country. He chairs the Litigation Section of the Beverly Hills Bar Association.

RUTH GARBY TORRES (Schaghticoke) holds a master's degree in public administration from Harvard University's Kennedy School of Government and is a retired state trooper. She is the youngest person to be elected to the Schaghticoke Tribal Council. She is an active member of Connecticut's Native American community, serving on the advisory board of Yale University's Native American Cultural Center.

DAVID E. WILKINS (Lumbee) holds a doctorate in political science from the University of North Carolina at Chapel Hill. He holds the McKnight Presidential Professorship in American Indian Studies at the University of Minnesota, with adjunct appointments in political science, law, and American studies. He has written and edited numerous books, including *The Hank Adams Reader* (2011), *The Legal Universe* (with Vine Deloria Jr., 2011), *Documents of Native American Political Development: 1533 to 1933* (2009), and *On the Drafting of Tribal Constitutions* (2006), as well as articles that have appeared in social science, law, history, and ethnic studies journals.

Index

Acknowledgment. *See* Federal recognition; State recognition

Act Concerning the Indian of Commonwealth (1862), 156–57

African American ancestry: acknowledgment policy and, 75, 19; Indian identity and, 19, 28 (n. 10), 45, 46, 49–55, 67, 71–73, 74–75, 116, 129, 137, 159–60, 161, 225–26, 279–80, 340–41; Jim Crow and, 71–72; Lumbees and, 67, 71–72, 74; one-drop rule and, 54; Ramapoughs and, 45, 49–51, 52–54; triraciality and, 52, 55; white supremacist ideology and, 67, 71–72, 75, 116, 129

African Americans, 28 (n. 10), 46, 52, 71, 78, 156, 159, 340–41; Indian relationships with and comparisons to, 46, 71, 74, 78, 80, 159, 340–41

AIPRC (American Indian Policy Review Commission), 17, 38, 104

Akaka, Daniel, 312, 318–19, 321, 325–26

Akaka Bill, 26, 312, 315, 318–21, 324, 325, 326, 327–28, 334 (n. 34)

Alaska Natives, 26, 39, 60 (n. 16), 110 (n. 9), 111 (n. 17), 112 (nn. 37, 38), 312, 313, 316–17, 321–22, 331, 335 (n. 36)

Allotment, 65–66, 78–79, 155–57, 158, 193 (n. 46), 241, 244–45, 246–47, 249, 252–54, 270, 272, 275, 276–77

Almaguer, Tomás, 298

American Indian Chicago Conference (1961), 1, 17

American Indian Movement (AIM), 199

American Indian Policy Review Commission (AIPRC), 17, 38, 104

American Samoa natives, 316–17, 322

Anaya, S. James, 6, 7, 10–11

Anthropologists: and NAGPRA, 103; and scientific racism, 77–78

Antimiscegenation laws, 71

Apess, William, 155

Apology Resolutions, 315–16, 324, 336, 346

Aquinnah Wampanoag Tribe of Gay Head, 157, 161

Assimilation, 46, 65, 226, 268

Austin, Steven L., 204–5

Authenticity, 1, 2, 17, 19, 23, 37, 62 (n. 55), 106, 150; and African American ancestry, 28 (n. 10), 279; and colonialism, 8; and federal recognition, 2, 107, 229; and gaming, 2, 4; and "Indian phenotype," 17, 28 (n. 10), 65–66, 77–78, 221–22, 224–26; and Indian poverty, 4; and Nipmucs, 213–14; and race, 216–17; and sovereignty struggles, 9

Baker, Lee, 78

Barker, Joanne, 6–7

Beacham, Deanna, 136

Bean, Lowell, 291

Bee, Robert L., 199

Belau, Republic of, 322–23

Benvenisti, Meron, 289

Bernal Ranch, 296, 300

BIA. *See* Bureau of Indian Affairs

Blackburn, Thomas, 291

252–53, 279; Indian policy, 172–75, 269; and race, 81–83, 150; relationship with tribes, 12–15, 21, 39–42, 57–58, 66, 76, 79, 116, 119, 120–21, 193 (n. 46), 266, 269–70, 271–72, 287, 301, 319, 328, 338–39; and responsibilities to tribes, 11, 82, 250, 322; and sovereignty, 22, 40, 321, 326; and state recognition, 118–19, 132, 136, 138 (n. 1); and UN Declaration on the Rights of Indigenous Peoples, 12

Federal recognition, 16, 20–21; advantages of, 16; alternatives to, 324–26; and attempted moratorium on, 203–4; and authenticity, 2, 107, 229; backlash toward, 2, 170, 175, 192 (n. 37), 206–7, 277–79; and blood quantum, 150; Bureau of Indian Affairs and, 14, 104–5; colonialism and, 85–87, 118, 123–24, 288, 299, 336; cultural vitality and, 3–4; defined, 1, 15, 39, 40; definition of federally recognized tribes, 14; denial of, 5, 17, 20, 58, 115–18, 126, 161–62, 169–70, 195–210, 213–14, 263, 274, 300; denial of right to petition for, 106; description of procedures for, 18–19; and Eastern Pequots, 3; economic aspects of, 118; evidentiary issues of, 44–45, 51, 52, 106, 214–21, 242–48, 251, 256 (n. 27), 257 (n. 36), 275–77; by federal legislation, 56–57, 75; gaming and, 2, 15, 182; and Golden Hill Paugussetts, 3; history of, 40; inconsistencies in, 254; Indian identity and, 42, 51–54, 59, 62 (n. 55), 83, 219, 222, 252–53, 279; indigenous arguments against, 10, 16, 311–13, 319–21; and intermarriage, 17; and lobbying against, 207–8 (n. 6); Lumbees and, 56–57, 77; and Mashantucket

Pequots, 3; and Mohegans, 4; and Native Hawaiians, 26, 311, 318–20, 331 (n. 27), 332 (nn. 32, 33), 334 (n. 34); opposition to by other tribes, 22–23; overturning of, 20–21; process of, 18–19; public attitudes toward, 2; racism and, 2, 216, 279; and Ramapough Indians, 37; rescinded, 162; resistance to, 10, 15; and Schaghticokes, 3, 162; sovereignty and, 5, 10, 23; struggles for, 8, 10, 24–26, 162, 169, 186–88, 213, 215–16, 238–39, 241–47, 263, 271–72, 274–78, 280–81, 287–88, 301–3; termination of, 22, 176, 195; and treaties, 38; tribal identity and, 24; vs. state recognition, 115–16, 121–22, 129–30, 137. *See also* State recognition

Federal Register, 21, 44, 96, 105

Federal-tribal relationships, 2, 4, 7–8, 12–15, 21, 39–42, 57–58, 66, 76, 79, 116, 119, 120–21, 126, 193 (n. 46), 266, 269–70, 271–72, 287, 301, 319, 328, 338–39

Federal-tribal-state relationships, 5

Federated States of Micronesia (FSM), 322–23

Field, Les W., 300

Fletcher, Ernie, 125

Fletcher, Matthew L. M., 29 (n. 11), 175–76

Flowers, Marcia, 184

Forbes, Harriette, 224

Fowler, David, 240

FoxNews.com, 12

Frank, Gelya, 299

Gabrielino-Tongva Indians, 117, 133–34

Gaming, 1, 3, 20, 24; and anti-Indian discourse, 3; and authenticity, 2, 4;

backlash against, 2–3, 112 (n. 42), 182; bingo, 201; Bureau of Indian Affairs and, 185; colonialism and, 29 (n. 15); cultural appropriateness and, 4; cultural vitality and, 3–4; economic development and. 4, 201; federal recognition and, 15, 27 (n. 5), 182, 279, 320; federal-tribal relationships and, 15; Indian Gaming Regulatory Act (1988), 28 (n. 8), 200–201; Mashantucket Pequots and, 3–4; and national renewal, 3–4; regulation of, 120, 131, 333; sovereignty and, 4, 20, 279; state-tribal relationships and, 4, 29–30(n. 17), 175, 202–3; stereotypes and, 2, 4, 28 (n. 8). *See also* Casinos

Garroutte, Eva Marie, 81–82

Genealogy, 44, 52–53, 77, 80–82, 89 (n. 15), 97, 105–9, 128, 131, 137, 214, 215, 219, 242, 251

General Allotment Act (1887), 193 (n. 46), 252, 270

Genocide, 5, 7, 8, 16, 26 (n. 2), 97, 101–2, 239, 298, 303

Ghost Dance, 300

Goldberg, Carole, 299

Golden Hill Paugussett Indian Nation: and African American ancestry, 28 (n. 10); and backlash toward federal recognition efforts, 3, 22, 170, 192 (n. 36); and denial of federal recognition, 161–62; and federal recognition, 200–201; history of, 197–98; and legal action, 201; and state recognition, 195, 205

Gover, Kevin, 202–3, 274–78

Grand Traverse Band of Ottawa and Chippewa, 252

Grant, Ulysses S., administration of, 299

Gray, Robert, 264

Great Depression, 198

Guam, 316, 322, 323

Hackel, Steven W., 291, 293–94

Halbert v. United States, 272

Handbook of American Indian Law, 41, 115

Harmon, Alexandra, 70

Harris, Howard N., 198–99

Harris, Irving A., 199, 209

Harrison, Benjamin, administration of, 313

Hartford Courant, 28, 178

Hassanamisco Nipmucs, 161–62, 221, 224, 225–26; and federal recognition struggles, 213–16, 226–29; history of, 218–26

Hatcher, Harold, 137

Hawai'i, and U.S. colonialism, 21, 312–16

Hawaiian Homes Commission Act (1920), 316–18

Hawaiian Kingdom, 311, 313–14, 323, 324–25, 327, 330 (n. 19)

Hayward, Skip, 23

Hazzard, Althea, 223–24

Health care, 3

Hearst family, 300

Hill, Jonathan D., 187

Houma Nation, 280

Hrdlicka, Ales, 78–79

Identity. *See* Indian identity

Independence, 324–26

Indian Child Welfare Act, 238

Indian Citizenship Act (1924), 151, 156, 165 (n. 29), 200–201, 259 (n. 62)

Indian Claims Commission, 269, 273–76

Indian Country Today, 11

Indian Gaming Regulatory Act (1988), 200

Indian Health Service, 14, 238

Khalidi, Rashid, 289
King Philip's War, 238, 239
Klopotek, Brian, 15–16, 17, 19–20, 23,
   279
Kroeber, Alfred, 287, 290–91, 301

Land Commission Act (1851), 299
Lane, Joseph, 266, 269
Languages (Indian), 86, 296, 297,
   302–3, 305 (n. 11)
Laverdure, Donald E., 253
Law: antimiscegenation and, 71;
   authenticity and, 37; *Carcieri v. Salazar*, 57; *Cherokee Nation v. Georgia*,
   14, 40, 153, 270; *Cobell v. Salazar*, 185,
   193 (n. 46); and federal recognition,
   2, 6; and *Halbert v. United States*,
   272; *Handbook of American Indian
   Law*, 41, 115; and Indian identity,
   37, 58–59; Indian, 5–6, 12, 118–19,
   122–24; and Indian legal traditions,
   5–6; and Indian treaties, 14, 38, 39,
   40, 41, 43, 47, 76; *Johnson v. M'Intosh*,
   14, 40; *Loving v. Virginia*, 144 (n. 88);
   and Mohegan land claim case, 6;
   Passamaquoddy v. Morton, 17; plenary power and, 14, 40, 102, 118–20,
   123–25, 251, 260 (n. 81), 312, 320,
   322–25, 337, 339; *Rice v. Cayetano*, 313,
   317–18; and state recognized tribes,
   120; Supreme Court and, 14, 39, 40,
   57, 116, 124, 144 (n. 88), 189 (n. 10),
   200, 209, 272–73, 313, 317–18, 321–22,
   324, 326, 331 (n. 28), 336 (n. 45),
   339–40; and tribal sovereignty, 15;
   Worcester v. Georgia, 14, 40
Levanthal, Alan, 302
Lightfoot, Kent, 292, 294, 296
Lili'uokalani (queen of Hawai'i), 21,
   312, 313, 315
Locklear, Elisha, 82, 83, 84, 93 (n. 42)

"Logic of elimination," 8, 9
Lomawaima, K. Tsianina, 22, 190
   (n. 14)
Loving v. Virginia, 144 (n. 88)
Lumbee Recognition Act, 86
Lumbee Tribe of North Carolina: African American ancestry and, 71, 74,
   75, 80; Cherokee designation, 75–77;
   Croatan designation, 50, 73–75, 76;
   education and, 73, 74; and federal
   recognition, 56–57, 77; history of,
   70; Indian identity and, 46, 65–66,
   67–68, 70, 71, 77–86; intermarriage
   and, 71; and mixed-race ancestry,
   71–72, 76; recognition applications
   and, 75; Siouan designation, 65,
   76–77, 83

Maine Indian Claims Settlement Act
   (1980), 322
Manifest Destiny, 240
Mann, Otto, Sr., 48
Mann family, 45, 49
Manypenny, George Washington, 246
Marshall, John, 14, 40, 124, 153, 269–70
Marshall Islands, Republic of, 322–23
Marshall Trilogy, 14, 40, 124–25; and
   "domestic dependent nations," 14,
   20, 40, 124, 252–53, 270, 312, 322,
   324–25
Martin, Aurene M., 205–6, 213
Mashantucket Pequot Tribal Nation:
   and compact with Connecticut, 4;
   and federal recognition, 2–3, 4–5, 16,
   23, 161, 200–202; and gaming, 2, 3–4,
   24, 180–81; identity and, 191 (n. 34);
   and intermarriage, 17; massacre of in
   1637, 16; and sovereignty, 3; and state
   recognition, 3, 29 (n. 11)
Mashpee Wampanoag, 155, 158, 161,
   227–28

Mason, John, 171, 188 (n. 6)

Massachusetts Indian Enfranchisement Act (1869), 153, 155, 157, 222

Mattaponi Indian Nation, 117, 128

McCaleb, Neal, 274, 277–78

McDougal, Duncan, 265

McKinley, William, administration of, 314

Meares, John, 264

Meyer, Melissa, 79, 83

Miller, Mark Edwin, 3, 20, 279–80

Milliken, Randall, 291, 293, 295

"Mixed-race" people, 48–51, 54–55, 71–73, 74, 76, 78–79, 81–82, 216, 224–25

Modernity, 68–69, 171

Mohegan Tribe, 166 (n. 40), 169, 197; and citizenship, 153; and federal recognition, 4, 161, 200–202, 204; and gaming, 4, 24, 180–82; history of, 6, 158, 174, 237, 239, 158; land rights of, 6; sovereignty of, 6; and termination, 162

Monacan Indian Nation, 128

Mooney, James, 76

Morton, Rogers C. B., 172–74, 186

Mullane, Nicholas, 184, 187

Muwekma Ohlones, 26; and federal recognition struggles, 287–88, 301–3; history of, 289, 291–301, 303 (n. 2); and "nominative cartography," 287, 288–303

Nansemond Indian Tribal Association, 128, 143 (n. 78)

Narchotta, 268

Narragansett Indians, 152, 158–62, 162, 218, 221, 238, 239, 245

National Congress of American Indians (NCAI), 11, 22, 136, 173, 199

National Governor's Interstate Indian Council, 136

National Indian Gaming Association, 182

National Tribal Chairmen's Association, 22

Native American Graves Protection and Repatriation Act (NAGPRA; 1990), 24; and anthropologists, 103; colonialism and, 97–98, 103–4; and "cultural affiliation," 98–99, 102, 103–4, 107–8; defined, 96–97, 109 (n. 9); and federal plenary power, 100–103; federal recognition and, 99, 238–39; history of, 104, 109 (n. 7); as human rights legislation, 95–96, 97, 109; Indian identity and, 95, 104; and Kennewick Man, 104; problems with, 99–100; racism and, 98, 102–3; and self-determination, 100

Native American Programs Act (1974), 316

Native American Rights Foundation (NARF), 104

Native Hawaiian Government Reorganization Act (2009), 327

Native Hawaiians, 21; and blood quantum, 316; colonialism and, 21; and federal recognition, 26, 318–19, 331 (n. 27), 332 (nn. 32, 33), 335 (n. 45); history of, 313–15, 330 (n. 19); and inclusion in Native American Acts, 316–17; independence and, 324–26; NAGPRA and, 96, 98, 109 (n. 9); sovereignty and, 21, 26, 313, 315–16, 324–26; and United Nations, 314–15

Newcomb, Steven, 11–12

Newton, Nell Jessup, 4, 30 (n. 18), 181–83

New York Times, 176–77, 179, 203

Niantics, 153, 158

Nipmuc Nation: and authenticity, 213, 226; and externally imposed definitions of identity, 213–26; and family history, 217–24; and federal recognition struggles, 25, 161–62, 213, 215–16

Nixon, Richard M., administration of, 174, 190 (n. 18), 270

"Nominative cartography," 287, 288–303

Nonintercourse Act (1790), 123–24, 198, 200

North Carolina: and legal definitions of Indian, 73–74; and recognition, 75

Northern Cherokee Tribe, 134

Northern Mariana Islands, 322

Norton, Gale A., 205–7, 277

Nottoway of Virginia, 128

Obama, Barack, administration of, 12, 97, 189 (n. 13), 320, 327

O'Brien, Jean M., 171, 227

Occom, Samson, 239–40, 244, 245, 349

Office of Federal Acknowledgment (OFA), 17–19, 86, 105, 200; African American ancestry and, 19; criticism of, 19; and failure to recognize oral history, 19, 245–46; nonrecognition and, 238; and recognition procedures, 18–19, 242–47, 280–81; Schaghticokes and, 205–6. See also Branch of Acknowledgment

Office of Hawaiian Affairs, 317

Office of Indian Affairs (OIA). See Bureau of Indian Affairs

Ohlone. See Muwekma Ohlones

Oral history, 19, 245–46

Organick, Aliza Gail, 11

Pamunkey Nation, 117, 128

Passamaquoddy Tribe, 17

Passamaquoddy v. Morton, 17

Patawomeck Tribe, 128

Paucatuck Pequot. See Eastern Pequot Tribal Nation; Mashantucket Pequot Tribal Nation

Pegan, Molly, 218–20

Pierce, Frederick, 224

Piper, Kenneth, 201

Plane, Ann Marie, 155–56

Plenary power, 14, 40, 102, 118–20, 123–25, 251, 260 (n. 81), 312, 320, 322–25, 337, 339

Procedures for Establishing That an American Indian Group Exists as an Indian Tribe, 17–18, 41; and NAGPRA, 104; and Ramapough failure to meet criteria, 44, 47

Quinault Indian Tribe, 268, 272, 276–77

Quinn, William W., Jr., 249

Racial Integrity Act (1924), 116, 129

Racial minority status, 1–2, 17

Racial politics: African American ancestry and, 71–72, 75; and "race shifting," 21–22; white supremacy and, 68–69, 71, 75

Racism: anti-Indian, 2–3, 75; and authenticity, 1, 2, 17, 19, 23, 37, 62 (n. 55), 224–25; and bias toward Indians with African ancestry, 19, 28 (n. 10), 45, 46, 49–55, 67, 71–73, 74–75, 116, 129, 137, 159–60, 161, 225–26, 279–80, 340–41; and blood quantum, 157; and Indian identity, 74, 77–81, 192 (n. 36), 221–22; and "Indian phenotype," 17, 28 (n. 10), 65–66, 77–78, 221–22, 224–26; and "Jackson Whites," 49, 50–51, 53–54; Jim Crow and, 69, 73, 75; scientific, 24, 50–51, 62 (n. 55), 65–67, 69,

and, 5; and state recognized tribes, 119–20, 131, 134–35; and state-tribal relationships, 29 (n. 11), 118, 186; struggles for, 3, 5–10, 13, 17, 20–22, 24–26, 119, 121, 125–26, 127, 160, 177, 228–29, 298–99, 315–16; Supreme Court and, 39–40; white supremacist ideology and, 116

Speck, Frank G., 225–26
Spilde, Kate, 182–83
Spruhan, Paul, 85
Stark, Heidi Kiiwetinepinesiik, 13, 15, 17, 22
Starna, William, 5
State recognition, 3, 21, 24, 29 (n. 11), 41; and administrative recognition, 129–32; and Cherokee descent groups claims, 21–22; defined, 14, 115; and Eastern Pequots, 20, 153–54; and executive recognition, 134–35; and "fraudulent tribes," 121–22; history of, 122–26, 152–54; and legislative recognition, 132–34; and Mashantucket Pequots, 3; and Schaghticokes, 20; sovereignty and, 118; termination of, 24–25, 158
—criteria for: in South Carolina, 130–31; in Virginia, 128–29
—laws, 127–29; abolition of, 140 (n. 26)
—relationship to federal recognition: compared to, 115–16, 117, 121–22, 129–30, 137; as grounds for, 117, 129, 133; as unrelated to, 20, 178
State-tribal relationships, 29 (n. 11), 122–23, 126–27, 132, 133–34, 135–36, 176, 205–6; Connecticut's attacks on federal recognition and, 173–88, 195; and gaming, 3, 4; and Mashantucket Pequots, 3–4; and Mohegans, 4
Stereotypes, 2, 25; and Indian gaming, 4, 28 (n. 8); and myth of Indian

disappearance, 2, 149–50; of "casino Indian," 2, 28 (n. 8), 181; of "Indian phenotype," 17, 23, 28 (n. 10), 65–66, 77–78, 221–22, 224–26; of Indian poverty, 4, 279; of "Indianness," 17; and "Vanished race," 223, 227, 301

Stevens, Isaac I., 267–68, 269, 272
Stevens, John L., 313
Stoler, Ann Laura, 180
Strickland, Joey, 136–37
Strickland, Rennard, 10
Sturm, Circe, 21–23
Sullivan, Sarah Cisco, 225–26
Supreme Court, U.S., 14, 39, 40, 57, 116, 124, 144 (n. 88), 189 (n. 10), 200, 209, 272–73, 313, 317–18, 321–22, 324, 326, 331 (n. 28), 336 (n. 45), 339–40
Swanton, John, 76

Talcott, Joseph, 174
Tansey Point Treaty (1851), 268, 272–73, 276
Tappan, William H., 267
Termination, 1, 15, 22, 24–26, 86, 104, 151, 155–62, 199, 200, 241, 246, 247–51, 252, 253–54, 270, 275, 287; defined, 14–15, 17
Thee, Christopher, 222
Thomas, Cyrus, 171
Thurston, Samuel, 266
Trafzer, Clifford, 272
Trail of Tears, 124
Treaties, 14, 40, 43, 47, 76, 246; defined, 39; federal recognition and, 38; history of, 266–67; and unrecognized tribes, 41, 117. See also specific treaties
Treaty of Dancing Rabbit Creek (1830), 246
Treaty of Easton (1756), 43, 47
Trouillot, Michel-Rolph, 217, 226–27
Trust relationship, 14, 38, 149, 190 (n. 14); defined, 15